Women in Muslim Societies

Women in Muslim Societies

DIVERSITY WITHIN UNITY

edited by

Herbert L. Bodman
Nayereh Tohidi

LYNNE
RIENNER
PUBLISHERS

BOULDER
LONDON

Published in the United States of America in 1998 by
Lynne Rienner Publishers, Inc.
1800 30th Street, Boulder, Colorado 80301

and in the United Kingdom by
Lynne Rienner Publishers, Inc.
3 Henrietta Street, Covent Garden, London WC2E 8LU

Library of Congress Cataloging-in-Publication Data
Women in Muslim societies: diversity within unity /
   edited by Herbert L. Bodman, Nayereh Tohidi.
     p.   cm.
     Includes bibliographical references (p.   ) and index.
     ISBN 1-55587-558-0 (hc : alk. paper). — ISBN 1-55587-578-5
     (pbk. : alk. paper)
     1. Muslim women. 2. Women in Islam. 3. Women—Islamic countries—
Social conditions. I. Bodman, Herbert L. II. Tohidi, Nayereh
Esfahlani, 1951– .
HQ1170.D5   1998
305.48'6971—dc21   97-40395
                                                  CIP

British Cataloguing in Publication Data
A Cataloguing in Publication record for this book
is available from the British Library.

Printed and bound in the United States of America

The paper used in this publication meets the requirements
of the American National Standard for Permanence of
Paper for Printed Library Materials Z39.48-1984.

5 4 3 2 1

Contents

Preface

The production of this book has been both a challenge and a delightful intercultural experience for the editors. We can hardly conceive of accomplishing the task without the innovation of e-mail; through its technology we were able to communicate with authors as distant as Japan and Kazakstan. Not always easily, to be sure, but still a far cry from earlier generations' difficulties.

The authors of the chapters are as diverse a group as the subject with which they deal. They were educated in a variety of disciplines: anthropology, history, sociology, religious studies, and medicine, for example. Some are native to the countries they write about, others undertook their specializations through special interests. All draw on extensive fieldwork for their studies.

We the editors wish to express our appreciation for their efforts and their understanding as we badgered them for rewrites and source citations. We hope they will take pride in this end result.

It is also our pleasure to thank the staff of Lynne Rienner Publishers for their support and patience. Our special thanks go to Bridget Julian, acquisitions editor, and Shena Redmond, senior project editor. And a cordial note of gratitude to Lynne Rienner herself for her encouragement of academia throughout the world.

We appreciate as well the support of our colleagues and students for their intellectual inspiration and encouragement. We thank especially our families for their support over the years, notwithstanding our occasional outbursts of frustration. Finally, as coeditors, we must acknowledge that this book would not have been possible without a great measure of rapport between us. It has been a most enjoyable collaboration.

Herbert L. Bodman
Nayereh Tohidi

1

Introduction

Herbert L. Bodman

Some half a billion women in the world are Muslim. Concentrated in a broad belt from Senegal to the Philippines, with the largest number on the South Asian subcontinent, these women may also be found in such countries as Norway, Trinidad, and Japan, as well as throughout many communities in the United States and Canada. Thus they form a worldwide gender community.

Yet, surveying the literature in English, we find it quite unrepresentative and ideologically misleading. It focuses especially on women in Egypt, Iran, Turkey, and Palestine[1] and is otherwise uneven: an anthropological study of a village, a survey of the legal status of women in a particular country, perhaps the memoirs of an expatriate Western woman married into a Muslim family. Seldom for societies outside these countries is there enough textual information to develop a nuanced picture of gender relations or to grasp the myriad, complex issues affecting women throughout the Muslim world.

Why this distortion? Among Westerners a pervasive and historical correlation of Islam with the Middle East and especially with Arabs certainly contributes, despite the fact that less than a quarter of the Muslim population is to be found in that region. Since the Crusades, Western Europeans have tended to regard the Mediterranean Sea as a frontier to be defended against an alien religion. Later, such inherited preconceptions held by European colonial administrators and settlers were reinforced by Muslim resistance to their political and economic hegemony in South and Southeast Asia as well as Africa. To the British government in the 1880s, for example, the specter of a militant pan-Islamism aroused fears that endured until virtually the end of the empire, in much the manner that Islamic "fundamentalism" is viewed today throughout the Western world. In the United States the post–World War II emphasis, encouraged by government support, on area studies as opposed to academic disciplines served to isolate

1

the Middle East as the land of Muslims par excellence and to marginalize them elsewhere. Only in the last generation have Western scholars begun to broaden their outlook, recognizing to some degree the diversity among Muslims and occasionally understanding that considerations other than religion may be salient in their lives.

In addition, the burgeoning field of women's studies is beginning to focus on women in Muslim societies, although those in the Middle East still receive the most attention. That regional focus all too frequently tars all Muslim peoples with strident allegations of male oppression or of defensive apologetics, whatever may be the facts on the ground.

The relative difficulty of field research also contributes to this distorted image. The heavy concentration of works on women in Egypt may be due in part to the long European association with that country as well as the variety of materials available in Cairo and in European libraries and archives. Opinion surveys have occasionally supplemented personal observation. In contrast, field research on women is today virtually impossible in Afghanistan, Algeria, Iraq, Libya, Saudi Arabia, Somalia, and Sudan. Elsewhere, conditions may be daunting, officially discouraged, or obstructed by the effective censure of Muslims hostile to Western "influence" in any form.

Perhaps, too, the more dramatic, more sensational material relating to "Muslim women" has emanated from the Middle East in the form of newspaper accounts, television broadcasts, and film documentaries exploiting the widespread, pejorative image of Islam, especially its presumed dictates on women. Hence, conclusions about their status throughout the world are almost exclusively conditioned by outsider presentations questionably relevant to even a mere portion of the mass.

The aim of this book, therefore, is to offer a consideration of the many factors—including but not limited to Islam—that affect women who consider themselves Muslim. The coeditors have sought new as well as established authors, native to the country of study wherever feasible, to assess the issues facing women in various countries of the Muslim world—how they are coping with challenges such as modernity, inherited custom, and conservative reaction. We sought to paint a broader, more nuanced picture specific to time and place, for much diversity is to be found in such a large population from one society to another and even within each. Such diversity within the overall unity of the Muslim world must always be emphasized in any discussion, but especially of its women.

Yet unity, too, must receive attention, since in the view of those outsiders who look closely at the whole, the unity of the far-flung Muslim world, especially the bonds among its women, may be questioned. To the degree that unity exists among these women, it is their adherence to the religion of Islam that provides a core, albeit of varying importance. The sense that they are all Muslims does confer a common identity, a distinction from others, that may serve to bridge wide cultural, social, and economic differences among them. Common bonds among women in general may be gradually seeping into the consciousness of an educated Muslim elite, as the horizons of that small minority become global through broadening communications and the experiences of international conferences and travel. Yet even then an identity as women who happen to be Muslim would appear to modify the broader link of gender. Issues such as the persistence of patriarchal social structures, inequality of compensation, and lack of political and economic power should be viewed, therefore, against the background of those aspects of Islam relating to women. These issues are detailed in the chapters of this book.

An overview of the status of women in pre-Islamic cultures, followed by an analysis of the Islamic texts that relate to women and the manner in which those texts—or their presumed content—have been interpreted over the centuries, forms the initial topic of this Introduction. The long history of patriarchy as a social structure present from the earliest documents from Mesopotamia down to the seventh century of our era demonstrates the virtual inevitability of such a power structure being inherited by Islamic societies, especially once they had absorbed neighboring polities. The Qur'an undeniably reflects the patriarchal society of Mecca and Medina, the earliest milieu of Islam.

In contrast, the chapters provide an analysis of how women in Muslim societies have been and are interacting with the many diverse forces that impinge on their lives, not only those deriving from traditionalism and aspects of the Islamic resurgence but also those stemming from particular historical conditions and the many facets of modernity and social change.

THE LEGACY TO ISLAM

The religion of Islam emerged very late in history. The millennia prior to the seventh century had seen a very substantial change away from what is understood to have been a cooperative, undivided, hunting and foraging existence in the early Neolithic period. With the development of hoe agriculture, women may even have become the primary producers, their small plots close to home a more reliable source of food than the male hunter. Theorists of social evolution suggest that the early family may have been matrilineal and matrilocal, but no evidence supports an assumption of a pure matriarchy then or at any time since.[2]

The emergence of plow agriculture about 3000 B.C.E. is thought to have initiated a patriarchal social structure throughout Southwest Asia. The plow required the domestication of large animals and fields more distant from the home, presenting difficulties for breastfeeding women. Women assumed alternate tasks close to home such as processing and storing food, milking, and caring for children and small animals.³ Larger communities for protection and mutual support evolved into cities and specialization, culminating ultimately in the city-state ruled by a king.

Religiously, the Neolithic period is associated with the mother-goddess and fertility cults seeking agricultural prosperity, but in historical times a supreme god gradually assumed a central role, with the principal goddess as his consort. The mother-goddess, despite her relative demotion, remained a major spiritual force and the popular favorite, especially among women. Temples dedicated to her were often made wealthy from donations, and priestesses endured as influential figures in a patriarchal society.

Documents from Mesopotamia in the second millennium B.C.E. provide considerable detail relating to laws of personal status. The male was the virtual owner of his family. He could sell his wife and children or pawn them as security for debt. He could divorce his wife and was required only to repay her dowry. If she did not bear him descendants, he could take a concubine and have intercourse with his female slaves. For the latter to bear him children was to their advantage, since it was the route to freedom after his death. The punishments for contravention of these laws seem to grow stricter as time passed, yet it must be kept in mind that these were laws on the books. Practice may have been different; certain known cases would indicate that the severe punishments may have been designed primarily as deterrents.

Of particular relevance to the history of women in Islamic times are the provisions in Middle Assyrian law governing the use of a veil. They required women of the nobility, widows, and married women to cover their heads when in the streets. A concubine accompanying her mistress had to do likewise. Harlots and unmarried prostitutes of the temple as well as female slaves were *not* to wear veils, seemingly distinguishing them from those who were under a man's protection and thus commanding social respect.⁴ This regulation from the late second millennium B.C.E. reveals the antiquity of a practice associated with Islam in the popular stereotype yet not widely used today among the vast majority of women in Islamic lands.

Polygyny, too, was widely practiced in those days. In the Sasanian empire of Persia, 221 B.C.E.–651 C.E., royal harems, secluded and guarded by eunuchs, numbered in the thousands.⁵ Conquered by the Muslims, many of the Sasanian nobility were integrated into Islamic society but still emulated Persian royal customs.

The roots of the patriarchal structure of society thus are to be found deep in the social history of Southwest Asia. Its customs thrive in the pages of the Old Testament, not withstanding the pastoral origins of the Hebrews that contributed to the first monotheistic, confessional religion. Despite that momentous innovation, the social laws of Deuteronomy bear a close resemblance to those of Mesopotamia in their emphasis on the overlordship of the patriarch.

WOMEN IN THE QUR'AN

The last of the great monotheisms, Islam distinguishes itself from its pre-decessors, Judaism and Christianity, by declaring that the Holy Qur'an is the direct speech of God, communicated in inimitable Arabic through the angel Gabriel to Muhammad, the Messenger of God to the Arabs and to the world for all eternity. Muslims thus consider it obligatory to preserve forever the exact text of the Qur'an, first and foremost as an act of devotion but also as a means of averting the errors they contend befell the Jews and Christians. Thus a marvel of Islam is its dogmatic insistence over the centuries on maintaining the exactness of the scripture, even as the Arabic language itself has undergone profound changes. A corollary doctrine establishes that any translation of the Qur'an is not the original.

Over fourteen centuries, the Qur'an has served as a guide for Muslims in devotion and in life. God commands obedience, threatens punishment for transgressions, but has compassion for the wayward should they return to the straight path. The Qur'an exhorts, it warns, and it teaches and explains not only ritual duties and morals but even manners.

The Qur'an makes unmistakably clear that in the eyes of God women are the equal of men. Eve is not the temptress of Adam but just as disobedient of God's commands as he.[6] A famous passage defining the ideal traits of Muslims links both men and women in each case.[7] The righteous, both husbands and wives, will enjoy paradise.[8] The ritual duties of Islam—declaring the faith, prayer, fasting, almsgiving, and pilgrimage—apply equally to men and women with only certain practical exemptions for the latter, for example, when fasting would endanger pregnancy.

As to relations between human beings, however, in contrast to their relationship with God, the Qur'an varies between generalized declarations and specific decrees. These are addressed to the Prophet and to other males, only rarely directly to women. A substantial part of the fourth sura (chapter) deals with relations between men and women in which the latter are clearly subordinated to the former:

> Men are the protectors and maintainers of women, because God has given the one more [strength] than the other, and because they support them from their means. Therefore the righteous women are devoutly obedient, and guard in [the husband's] absence what God would have them guard.
> As to those women on whose part ye fear disloyalty and ill-conduct, admonish them [first], [next], refuse to share their beds, [and last] beat them [lightly]; but if they return to obedience, seek not against them means [of annoyance]: for God is Most High, Great [above you all].[9]

The Qur'an makes clear that marriage is the preferred relationship between a man and a woman and specifies the limits of kinship from which the man may secure a wife. A verse allows him to have four wives, provided he treat them equally, but a later passage casts divine doubt: "Ye are never able to be fair and just as between women even if it is your ardent desire."[10]

Divorce by the husband is permitted in the Qur'an, but it is carefully circumscribed to ensure the parentage of a child in the womb, declaring he must maintain as previously his former wife until she has completed suckling the infant. For the wife, her recourse in desiring divorce is limited, should her husband agree, to yielding the dowry given her at marriage and waiting for three monthly periods before remarriage. Moreover, the children of their marriage belong to the husband. Husbands are enjoined, however, not to treat their wives harshly in order to force them to surrender their dowry in this manner.[11]

As to inheritance, a woman's share is half that of the equivalent male heir, although what property she may receive is her own. In these regulations governing division of the property the Qur'an is overwhelmingly specific, providing Muslim legal scholars much to debate over the centuries.[12]

The half-share concept in inheritance is reflected in judicial matters as well: a woman's testimony is valued as only half that of a man.[13] If she is charged with adultery, however, and four eyewitnesses have not been brought forth against her, she may clear herself by swearing her innocence with the same number of oaths required of a man.[14]

Modesty is enjoined upon both men and women in identical wording, but for women it is followed by the more detailed declarations that

> they should not display their beauty and ornaments except what (must ordinarily) appear thereof; that they should draw their veils over their bosoms and not display their beauty except . . . [to those males of their nuclear family], and that they should not strike their feet in order to draw attention to their hidden ornaments.[15]

For the wives of the Prophet, however, the prescribed comportment and dress is stricter. The punishment for "unseemly conduct" is doubled, as is their reward for righteousness. They are declared to be not like other women, so they should mind their language, stay in their houses, and maintain a pious demeanor. They should speak to males only when screened from the latter's gaze and are not allowed to remarry when widowed. Together with other women, their public dress—an outer cloak—should be such as to designate them as "believing women" not to be "molested."[16]

Muslims recognize that many passages in the Qur'an, such as those related to his wives, were revealed to the Prophet as site- and time-specific. Some passages correct practices said to have been practiced in pre-Islamic Arabia, such as the levirate (marriage of a widow to the brother of her deceased husband) and female infanticide. These have readily been generalized for all time as reforms initiated by Islam. The rules on marriage, however, did not apply to Muhammad. That exemption was unique to him, but those passages relating solely to his wives, might they not contain principles applicable to others? This question and many others required further divine guidance.

THE SUNNA

From the first century of Islam, Muslims recognized the need for elaboration of the Qur'anic passages. At first, following the Prophet's death in 632 C.E., the community of Muslims enjoyed the wisdom of those close to him, the Companions, but as that generation died off, the Muslims found guidance in the speech and actions of the Prophet. These hadiths, or narratives believed to incorporate the Sunna (custom) of the Prophet, multiplied as the expanding realm encountered new situations demanding transmitters from the Prophet through succeeding generations. In time, six collections came to be accepted as valid sources of the Sunna. Together, the Qur'an and the Sunna form the basic sources of the religion.

Why six collections, not one? No single authority existed in the Muslim world to decree conformity. The realm became too vast, communications too slow, and the attachment of legal scholars and preachers to their favorite collection too fervent. The caliph, successor to Muhammad in the latter's mundane roles, never achieved spiritual authority and soon lost most temporal power as well. The Muslim community, the *umma,* came to be guided by consensus, the consensus of the ulema, the scholars of Islam.

The goal of the ulema has always been to discover God's will even in the most minute degree through exhaustive study of the sacred texts. Their conclusions, always tentative—for who truly knows God's will?—remain subject to the consensus of their peers. The process of achieving that consensus retains its relevance even today. Orthodoxy is not achieved through councils or synods but through debate among the ulema. Any proposition considered a departure from established doctrine necessitates debate, for silence may be construed as tacit agreement and thus become binding. Hence these scholars of Islam must declare their views, and they do so in polemics. Polemics, written or oral, have thus been a characteristic of classical Islamic jurisprudence. If an author is shouted down, he and his proposition disappear into oblivion; if, however, they receive support, generally meaning that the change is hardly innovative, the debate dies away and consensus is thereby attained.[17]

This process is invariably conservative, especially when applied to issues affecting women. Coupled with deep respect for teachers and forebears, strengthened by the chain of reliable transmitters associated with "sound" hadiths—the best of those allegedly from the Prophet—the desire to conserve the past while digging ever deeper into scholastic debates over precious details has been a hallmark of traditional Islam.

Research conducted by Barbara Freyer Stowasser over a number of years has explored the history of hadith literature with regard to women's issues. Her findings are significant: Through consensus a number of "ideal paradigms" have been derived by the ulema from the somewhat ambiguous language of the Qur'an and the extensive hadith literature. Moreover, "it is not surprising to find that the late medieval Islamic authorities and their modern, conservative successors lean heavily toward the restrictive *Hadiths* when they map out the blueprint of the ideal social order and the woman's place in it."[18] Stowasser's most recent work extends her conclusions to the women of the Qur'an, not only the Prophet's wives but also those of the pre-Islamic era. These women—only one of whom, Mary, the mother of Jesus, is mentioned by name—are exemplars of either righteous or perverse conduct for later generations of Muslims. Their treatment in the hadith, however, differs in important respects from the Qur'anic context.[19] The reasons are to be found in the interaction of Islam and the cultures it encountered as its realm expanded.

ISLAMIC CULTURE

Muhammad was born in the late sixth century C.E. into an urban milieu. The prevailing tribal customs in Mecca and Medina are known to us almost exclusively through an Islamic filter, the Muslim accounts written down at least a century after Muhammad's death. These reports tend implicitly to contrast conditions in pre-Islamic times with those instituted through the Qur'an and the Sunna. A tribal structure emphasizing blood kinship appears to have been widespread. Other than that, customs regarding women may have varied widely throughout the vast, predominantly arid peninsula.

Muhammad's conversion of Arab men and women to Islam undermined tribalism by creating a higher focus of loyalty, but the Islamic transformation of women's status did not reach the equality that the Qur'anic verses previously cited would indicate. The new society was the interaction of an ideal with the reality of customs apparently too deeply imbedded for the charisma of Muhammad to reform. Fatima Mernissi, Moroccan sociologist and avowed feminist, suggests that the Prophet's desire to see gender equality in Islam was compromised by the attacks of opponents on his wives' openness, which forced their seclusion and the covering of freeborn women in public to distinguish them from slaves,[20] her thesis being that this reversal initiated veiling for Muslim women.

Texts relating to sixth-century events in the Christian city of Najran, located to the south of Mecca, raise questions regarding such a thesis. These texts clearly demonstrate that high-born women of that city were accustomed to veiling and seclusion. Moreover, such women also held property in their own name a century before the Qur'an decrees it for the women in Muslim societies.[21] Was Najran so different from the first cities of Islam? The Qur'an is the only contemporary Muslim document. Yet it is not a history, and the history derived from it has passed through many Muslim hands. One can say with a degree of confidence only that the persistence of tribalism in Mecca and Medina was a constraining factor in the initial formation of an Islamic society.

In the first centuries after Muhammad's death, the expansion of Islamic territory brought the Muslim community into contact with societies having well-established customs of seclusion for elite women. The Muslims conquered the Sasanian imperial center and the Abbasid dynasty of caliphs soon made it their own, thus inheriting the latter's legacy of royal custom and prerogatives. Nabia Abbott's classic study, *Two Queens of Baghdad*, tacitly underlines the vast difference in status between the elite women of Medina and the Abbasid queens of Baghdad.[22] Guarded by eunuchs, confined to immense palaces, and surrounded by the caliph's innumerable concubines, these queens became models for the new Persianate practices of the Muslim empire. Their power behind the scenes and their fabulous wealth could hardly be emulated by others, but the negative attitudes toward women formed by their imposed lifestyles radiated throughout Abbasid society. Contrary to the Qur'an, women came to be characterized as the "weaker sex," an attribute supported by hadiths attesting that Eve was created from Adam's rib. The privilege heretofore enjoyed by noble Arab women to attach conditions to their marriage contract now required a protracted legal struggle to enforce.[23] The practice of seclusion, moreover, instilled caution in the male chroniclers who related events in the royal harem. To the dismay of modern researchers, chroniclers all but ignored familial relations.

The widespread practice of concubinage among Muslim males able to afford female slaves contributed enormously to this devaluation of women in Abbasid society. The Arab Muslim conquerors readily adopted this custom from their predecessors. The training of female slaves for the entertainment of the wealthy became a major business, for the prices accomplished singers, musicians, and dancers commanded were extraordinary. The Qur'anic commendation of marriage as most pleasing to God was applied less and less to concubines since their intimate role was sexual dalliance rather than reproduction. It was not in the owner's material interest for his concubines to bear his children (although it often happened), for then she could not be sold; upon his death, she became free and her child his legal heir together with his wives' children. In most circumstances, a wife was faced with the rivalry of a series of concubines for her wealthy husband's affections. Although her legal status was far superior, she could suffer in comparison to those with whom her husband sought new pleasures.[24]

The veil was associated with seclusion. As Mernissi aptly puts it, "Sexual segregation divides all social space into male and female spaces," the women's space being private and the men's public, the latter entered by elite women only on limited occasions. "The veil," she continues, "is an expression of the invisibility of women on the street, the male space *par excellence*."[25] Although its use by a concubine could be coquettish, as many tales from Abbasid and later times attest, those veiled in public reinforced the basic concept of seclusion, that women's lives and activities were a private sphere to be closely guarded in defense of male "honor."

THE SHARI'A

As Abbasid royalty established models to emulate for the new Arabo-Persian society and its successors, so Islamic jurists interacted with the practices of new peoples in the evolution of Islamic law, known as the Shari'a. In the various regions conquered by Muslim armies, the day-to-day administration of justice yielded a law merging Qur'anic precepts with local practice. Hence, Shari'a law in North Africa, for example, differed from that developed in Iraq. Ultimately, four schools of law emerged among Sunni Muslims, the mainstream of Islam, whereas dissenting communities such as the Shi'a had their own legal variations. Although Muslim jurists insist that the differences among the schools are minor, they have often been significant on gender issues. For example, in the Maliki school of Medina the only relatives considered in inheritance are those on the father's side, reflecting the tribal emphasis of the Arabian peninsula. However, the Iraqi school of Kufa, known as the Hanafi, admits daughters' and sisters' children to inheritance in the absence of father's sons, reflecting the more cosmopolitan view of women in that conquered territory. Moreover, the Hanafi school permits women to contract their own marriage but requires attention to equality of social class, whereas others require a male guardian to conclude the contract. A rigorous application of tribal custom that nullifies even the Shari'a has been the denial among some Berbers of North Africa of any inheritance rights whatsoever to women.[26]

The four schools of Islamic law spread with the expansion of the domain of Islam, the Hanafi passing into Central Asia and South Asia and the Maliki becoming primarily a system for African jurists. The coasts of East Africa, western India, the Malay peninsula, and the Indonesian archipelago are linked by the Shafi'i school along maritime routes. The Hanbali, however, acquired a geographical center only in the eighteenth century when it was adopted by the puritan Wahhabi movement of Arabia. Thus, inherent in the evolution of Islamic law, especially in provisions regarding women, has been a diversity inculcated from local customs.

The Shi'a, a branch of Islam numbering today some ten percent of the total, assert that Muslims abandoned the straight path by refusing to name as Muhammad's successor his cousin, Ali, also husband of his daughter, Fatima. The Muslim majority then compounded the "error" by persecuting and murdering the Prophet's progeny from that union, his only direct descendants, who thus possessed a divine right to lead the umma.

In view of Fatima's importance to the Shi'a, the law of succession in the large Twelver branch dominant in Iran today is somewhat favorable to women, since it is the immediate family—parents and children, female as well as male—that have priority in succession. The law of divorce among the Twelver Shi'a is more restrictive and formalized than among the Sunni Muslims.[27]

An unusual and controversial dimension of Shi'a law respecting women is the legitimacy of *mut'a* (temporary marriage), which Sunni law strictly forbids. Said to be of ancient origin in the region, the practice (popularly known in Iran as *sigheh*) was outlawed by the second caliph, Umar, as being the equivalent of fornication. Not recognizing the legitimacy of Umar's caliphate, the Shi'a defend mut'a by their reading of Sura 4:24, one of the more ambiguous Qur'anic passages. The custom may be defined as a contract between a man and an unmarried woman, be she a virgin, divorced, or widowed, in which both the period that the marriage shall last and the amount of money to be paid the woman must be specified.[28]

Since the Ayatollah Khomeini endorsed and encouraged mut'a, the mullahs of contemporary Iran have generally argued that it represents a recognition by Muhammad of two laws, the law of God and "natural law," legitimizing sexuality as a human necessity. They distinguish it from prostitution by pointing out that, following the expiration of the temporary marriage, the woman must undergo a period of sexual abstinence to identify the legitimate father if she is pregnant. Children born of temporary unions are legitimate and may inherit.[29] Nevertheless, Shahla Haeri's field research demonstrates that attitudes toward the practice are ambivalent and the women are often exploited without legal recourse since mut'a marriages are not registered. Legal though their status may be, they find themselves on the margin of society.[30] Mut'a is thus a legacy from pre-Islamic times that endures only within a particular branch of Islam because of its unique interpretation of one specific Qur'anic passage.

The Shari'a, whether Sunni or Shi'i, is quintessentially men's law, just as the Qur'an is addressed more to men than to women. Jurisprudence was the province of men with formal education in the Islamic sciences. If women received more than rudimentary education, it was provided only by the family in the home. Since A'isha, Muhammad's favorite wife, is said to have transmitted some 2,210 hadiths, her prestige allowed a few women in the classical age of Islamic culture to achieve status as hadith transmitters,

learned scholars, calligraphers, and the like. The effect of their achievements on the evolution of the Shari'a, however, has rarely been acknowledged in classical Islamic literature.[31] More commonly, Muslim males
have cited hadiths stigmatizing women as emotional and irrational, even
mentally deficient, to vindicate banning them from such responsible pursuits as judges of Shari'a courts.[32]

SUFISM AND THE SECOND EXPANSION
OF THE MUSLIM WORLD

The role of women in Sufism, the mystical dimension of Islam, has been
somewhat different from their role in the development of the Shari'a, although their stature as mystics has often been won grudgingly from male
authors, Muslim or Western. The first true saint of Islam was Rabi'a al-
Adawiyya of Basra, an eighth-century former slave, still revered for her
all-consuming love of God. Yet Fariduddin Attar's twelfth-century hagiog-
raphy says of her: "When a woman walks in the way of God like a man,
she cannot be called a woman."[33] Medieval narratives, moreover, describe
how the beauty of female Sufis distracted males in their mutual search for
gnosis, and others record debates on the merits of celibacy as well as expressions of outright misogyny.[34]

By the eleventh century the search for the Sufi path to God became institutionalized into orders of mystics, following the way of a master. Here
women were able to play a larger role. Convents wherein they might
jointly pursue the mystic path were led by one of their own. Especially in
the Indian subcontinent, some such women became saints, objects of a devotion manifested through pilgrimage, their shrines guarded by women.

Male Sufis played an important part in the second major expansion of
the Muslim world in the early centuries of the present millennium. The
Mongol incursions of the thirteenth century are regarded as having had a
role in this dispersal of Muslims. Yet commerce more than conquest was
the hallmark of this movement in South and Southeast Asia as well as in
sub-Saharan Africa. Merchants, many with Sufi connections, were agents
of conversion, blending their culture with existing popular beliefs in complex combinations. Thus Islamic culture came to blend in many different
ways with Indian, Sudanese, Turkish, Malay, and even Chinese civiliza-
tions. For example, Turkish shamans migrating with their peoples from
Central Asia into Anatolia brought into Islamic culture their own forms of
devotion that were repellant to the ulema but meaningful to their rude followers.[35] These peoples and their customs participated in the conquest of
the Balkans, but the subsequent dominance of Ottoman orthodoxy in the
latter region generally limited the blending effect.

In contrast, the Sufis who reached the islands of the East Indies
(present-day Indonesia) could marry into the royal families of port cities

but could only very slowly and incompletely integrate the island populations into a culture infused with Islam. The heritages of ancient Javanese religions overlaid by a deep Hindu layer were too established to be displaced. Instead, Islamic elements were easily absorbed into Javanese culture.[36] These are but a few illustrations of the role of Sufism in developing an interaction between expanding Muslim peoples and existing traditions in areas of what is now characterized as the Muslim world.

ISLAMIC SOCIETIES AND MODERNITY

Whereas early Islamic literature is often brimming with confidence and anticipation, in recent centuries it generally betrays an atmosphere of doubt and anguish concerning the rising power of European countries— and eventually the United States—over Muslim peoples. European occupation and colonization of Muslim societies tended to magnify the practice of women's seclusion; guarding them particularly from foreign eyes became a touchstone of the male concept of honor. In Chapter 2, Barbara Cooper details, for example, how the political and agricultural roles of women receded with the British occupation of Nigeria.

Yet as the tide of modernity flowing from the Western nation-states crept inexorably across the Muslim world, some aspects, such as improvements in health and transportation, were welcomed in the recipient societies. Others aroused fear that their moral values were being undermined. As the tide became a flood in the twentieth century, nationalist aspirations gathered ideological strength and soon caught many women in Muslim countries in a web of contradictions.

A key element of the nationalist agenda was the defense of Islamic culture. In the early stages of many nationalisms in Muslim societies, the social status of women, as more rigidly interpreted over the centuries, formed an integral part. The ideology demanded that women's bodies symbolize the rejection of an alien culture by maintaining traditional customs, such as veiling, deprecating female opinion, and subordinating them to all male members of the family.

In contrast, some women were seized with a need to join in the struggle against imperialism, supported by some progressive males as well as those male ideologues who sought to demonstrate to the occupier the gathering force of their movement. When women marched and spoke or merely encouraged their menfolk in the nationalist crusade, they acquired a new sense of their own inherent worth. They soon demanded opportunities for education, employment, legal rights, and greater social justice.

Such gains did not come easily or swiftly. Although by World War I a significant minority of men in most Muslim societies recognized the national liability of secluded, uninformed women and became dedicated to encouraging their advancement, a process that gained momentum in the period between the world wars, their efforts were stubbornly resisted by the male masses as well as by a great many women uncomprehending or fearful of change.

As Nadia Hijab has convincingly demonstrated in *Womanpower,* the employment of Arab women has been a key to their empowerment.[37] With growing urbanization and the decline of subsistence economies, necessity has been the propelling force in many Muslim societies—and elsewhere, too—in breaking down male resistance. Women's wages have become an essential part of family incomes. The appeal of higher wages for greater skills has forced even reluctant fathers to permit more than rudimentary education for their daughters; a better educated young woman, too, might attract a more prestigious son-in-law to the family. All such accretions of income enhance the appeal of modernity in the form of more comfortable lifestyles: refrigerators, telephones, automobiles, and air travel, for example. Growth in the economic position of women has been intimately linked with the spread of the trappings of modernity.

Thus during the twentieth century women in Islamic societies have been pulled in opposing directions, as Bouthaina Shaaban explains in her chapter in this book. To demonstrate their support for nationalism, they emerged from their households. To become more effective, they sought more education and larger roles in political life. Yet those very enhancements brought misgivings, resistance, and even retaliation from conservatives. In Chapter 8, on Azerbaijan, Nayereh Tohidi illustrates how women's greater public presence was ideologically important to the nationalist cause even as it contradicted the established customs of gender separation and subordination of women.

Most Muslim areas, with the exception of those in the Soviet Union, had witnessed the establishment of independent states by the end of the 1960s. The fervor of the nationalist effort had yielded to demands for modernized infrastructures, which entailed heavy expenditures for such needs as administrative services, education, housing, road networks, and utilities. More and more women pressed for opportunities to participate in all aspects of public life such as government bureaucracy, private enterprise, and media services. Still, in pursuit of those opportunities they remained generally hampered by ingrained social prejudice even when the countries desperately needed their contribution.

Moreover, as the pace of material modernity, intercontinental communications, and intercultural contacts of every sort outdistanced social change at the local level, a sense of frustration, of being torn from their roots, of fractured identity, of, in a word, anomie became increasingly expressed in Muslim societies. The many disappointments suffered by migrants to the cities—unemployment, slum living, and scenes jolting to their sense of morality—accumulated a potentially explosive dissatisfaction with a wide range of consequences. (See Dina Siddiqi's analysis in

Chapter 11 of the situation in Bangladesh). Political instability in many countries led to the suppression of any manifestation of unrest; or a rapid change of government, often inspired by the military, sought to assuage the masses with promises of reforms that were seldom achieved. A landed and wealthy, often traditional elite controlled the political process to their own advantage. Class differences in privilege, education, lifestyles, and above all in power grew immense.

ISLAMISM

As in the Western world, the building of nation-states accented the secular tendencies in Muslim societies to such a degree that a few outside observers even questioned the viability of Islam in the modern world. Although the constitutions of the newly independent countries usually enshrined Islam as the state religion, there were notable exceptions such as Turkey, Indonesia, and Bangladesh. Above all, the heads of state usually paid little more than lip service to the religious beliefs of the majority of their constituents. The mood of the nationalist era was indeed secular in outlook.

That mood was favorable to progress in the status of women, despite the underlying resistance of conservative elements. Laws enhancing the rights of women in divorce, promoting unveiling, or improving conditions of employment, for example, were passed in several states of the Muslim world. The ulema might grumble and speak out in Friday sermons, but the state usually controlled the religious establishment, paid the salaries, or maintained the mosques, thus curbing criticisms of government from that quarter. Less risky was to preach against the moral fiber of society and the source of the influences that led to its excesses, namely "Western civilization" or "Western cultural imperialism." Hollywood films featuring offensive story lines and women scantily clad by Muslim standards became targets of specific criticism not only from the pulpit but also in the conservative Muslim press.

Railing against Western imperialism and its sabotage of Muslim values, however, was not enough, nor were the usual exhortations of the ulema. New voices outside the religious establishment in closer contact with the people were required to provide a more positive, Islamic message to inspire prospects for moral rejuvenation and reverse the secular mood. From Muslim India came the voice of Abu'l Ala Maududi in the 1920s and 1930s, who through his writings formulated an "Islamic system of life" based on thorough scholarship.[38] His contemporary in Egypt, Hasan al-Banna, originally a teacher in the state schools, crafted a message that went far beyond the teaching of the ulema.[39] Both men created organizations of their followers to spread their ideology of Islamic renewal to other countries and peoples as well as to pressure governments and the public to adhere to their views. Another Egyptian, Sayyid Qutb, converted to the new Islamic attitude rather late in life, blended in his writings the still vibrant appeal of nationalism with a call for Islamic action against imperialism and any government that adopted ideologies of Western origin. The summons for Islamic militancy led to his imprisonment and execution by the Nasser government, augmenting his appeal by martyrdom.[40] These three pioneers of the Islamic resurgence laid the foundations for the Islamism of today.

Islamism, or Islamic fundamentalism, has many aspects. We the editors prefer the former term because the dictates of its adherents regarding women's behavior have a strong political, authoritarian, and ideological dimension, quite consistent with other "isms." Although no one summary can possibly include the many nuances of Islamism in its various contexts, its effects on women possess remarkably common patterns.[41] Society is sharply segregated into male and female, with male adherence emphasized by beards and feminine sexuality totally obscured. Roles, too, are clearly defined: the man is the family provider and the sole source of authority, the woman the homemaker and nurturer of traditional values in future generations. The "fundamentalist" tenor derives from a presumed revival of the aboriginal values of the Muhammadan era, unadulterated by all foreign importations, medieval and modern.

Among the Islamists women are to be found in significant numbers; many more are on the fringes, variously adopting degrees of "Islamic" dress, supporting the moral values, or voicing anti-imperialist themes. Most are young and well educated and blend their Islamism with aspects of modernity selected as consistent with their theology. Many of the men, too, reflect a similar profile, although they are more diverse. Iran, as seen in Hisae Nakanishi's account herein, provides an illustration of these aspects of Islamism.

Although the Iranian Revolution of 1979 brought Islamism to world attention in dramatic fashion and has continued to be regarded in the West as its epitome, its unique character is often ignored. As a nation predominantly Shi'i in adherence, its ulema have historically played a different, more independent role than Sunni clerics. In Sunni societies the leading Islamists have not had formal religious training but are laypeople who have no great respect for the average cleric. The overthrow of the Shah of Iran led by the Islamists and their followers had an immense impact throughout the Muslim world (which largely ignored the role in the revolution of many Iranian secularists). Yet only in Afghanistan has the model been replicated in the Sunni sphere. Indeed, the Iranian presidential election of May 1997 may have signaled a shift to moderation, especially regarding the position of women.

The chapters in this book may provide opportunities for reflection on the diversity among women in Islamic societies. Common threads do appear, some related to similarities in practices deemed locally to be Islamic and others to similarities in stages of economic and social development. The symbols of Islamism in the Muslim world are highly visible, its images dramatized and its extremists cast in the Western media as role models of religious fanaticism. Yet the many in the Muslim world who abhor the objectives and methods of the radical Islamists (those in Algeria and Afghanistan especially), who bewail the gender divisions of Islamist ideology, and who wish for progress toward modest feminist goals receive little considered attention beyond their own society. This book seeks a more informed understanding of the realities for women in Muslim societies.

NOTES

1. Michelle Kimball and Barbara R. von Schlegell, *Women in the Muslim World: A Bibliography with Selected Annotations* (Boulder: Lynne Rienner Publishers, 1997), index.

2. Margaret Ehrenberg, *Women in Prehistory* (Norman: University of Oklahoma Press, 1989), chs. 1 and 2.

3. Ibid., ch. 3.

4. Gerda Lerner, *The Creation of Patriarchy* (New York: Oxford University Press, 1986), 134–135.

5. Leila Ahmed, *Women and Gender in Islam: Historical Roots of a Modern Debate* (New Haven: Yale University Press, 1992), 17f.

6. *The Holy Qur'an: Text, Translation and Commentary*, trans. A. Yusuf Ali (Brentwood, MD: Amana, 1983), Sura 7, 19–25.

7. Ibid., 33:35.

8. Ibid., 40:8–9; 3:195; 4:124.

9. Ibid., 4:34. The words in brackets are the additions of the translator, A. Yusuf Ali. All citations are to this translation.

10. Ibid., 4:3, 22ff, 129.

11. Ibid., 2:228–233, 236–237, 241; 4:35, 19.

12. Ibid., 4:7, 11–13, 176; 2:240.

13. Ibid., 2:282.

14. Ibid., 4:9; 24:6–9, 13.

15. Ibid., 24:30–31.

16. Ibid., 33:28–34, 50–52, 53–55, 59–62. The command that the Prophet's wives should "stay in their houses" and that they wear cloaks when going out must mean they were not always confined to their dwellings.

17. George Makdisi, "The Hanbali School and Sufism," *Humaniora Islamica* 2 (1974):71.

18. Barbara Freyer Stowasser, "Religious Ideology, Women, and the Family: The Islamic Paradigm," in *The Islamic Impulse*, ed. Barbara Freyer Stowasser (Washington, DC: Center for Contemporary Arab Studies, Georgetown University, 1989), 264.

19. Barbara Freyer Stowasser, *Women in the Qur'an: Traditions and Interpretation* (New York: Oxford University Press, 1994).

20. Fatima Mernissi, *The Veil and the Male Elite: A Feminist Interpretation of Women's Rights in Islam*, trans. Mary Jo Lakeland (Reading, MA: Addison-Wesley, 1991), part 2. Leila Ahmed comes to a similar conclusion in *Women and Gender in Islam*, 67.

21. Eleanor A. Doumato, "Hearing Other Voices: Christian Women and the Coming of Islam," *International Journal of Middle East Studies* 23 (1991): 183–185.

22. Nabia Abbott, *Two Queens of Baghdad: Mother and Wife of Harun al-Rashid* (Chicago: University of Chicago Press, 1946).

23. Ibid., 15–16, 46. The "Adam's rib" hadiths are a clear example of the adaptation of Bible-related lore to Islamic exegesis: see Stowasser, *Women in the Qur'an*, 21.

24. Ahmed, *Women and Gender in Islam,* 92–93.

25. Fatima Mernissi, *Beyond the Veil: Male-Female Dynamics in Modern Muslim Society*, rev. ed. (Bloomington: Indiana University Press, 1987), 97.

26. Noel Coulson, *A History of Islamic Law* (Edinburgh: Edinburgh University Press, 1964), 48–49, 30, 136–137. Other examples may be found in Coulson's *Conflicts and Tensions in Islamic Jurisprudence* (Chicago: University of Chicago Press, 1969), ch. 2.

27. Coulson, *History,* 112–114.

28. Shahla Haeri, *The Law of Desire: Temporary Marriage in Shi'i Iran* (Syracuse: Syracuse University Press, 1989), 2.

29. Ibid.

30. Haeri, *Law of Desire,* 147–152, 186.

31. Wiebke Walther, *Women in Islam*, rev. ed. (Princeton, NJ: Marcus Weiner, 1993), ch. 5; Ahmed, *Women and Gender in Islam,* 73, 113.

32. Stowasser, *Women in the Qur'an*, 28.

33. Quoted in Annemarie Schimmel, *Mystical Dimensions of Islam* (Chapel Hill: University of North Carolina Press, 1975), 426.

34. Ibid., appendix 2. This appendix is an adroit survey of the role of women in Sufism, from which the following material is drawn.

35. See, for example, Halil Inalcik, *The Ottoman Empire: The Classical Age, 1300–1600* (New York: Praeger, 1973), 186. See also *The Book of Dede Korkut: A Turkish Epic*, trans. and ed. by Faruk Sümer, Ahmet E. Uysal, and Warren S. Walker (Austin: University of Texas Press, 1972) for the position of women in Turkish folklore.

36. See, for example, Ann Kumar, "Dipanagara and the Java War," *Indonesia* 1 (1974):69–118.

37. Nadia Hijab, *Womanpower* (New York: Cambridge University Press, 1988).

38. Mumtaz Ahmad, "Islamic Fundamentalism in South Asia: The Jamaat-i-Islami and the Tablighi Jamaat," in *Fundamentalisms Observed,* ed. Martin E. Marty and R. Scott Appleby (Chicago: University of Chicago Press, 1991), 457–530.

39. John O. Voll, "Fundamentalism in the Sunni Arab World: Egypt and the Sudan," in *Fundamentalisms Observed*, ed. Martin E. Marty and R. Scott Appleby (Chicago: University of Chicago Press, 1991), 345–402.

40. Ibid.

41. Helen Hardacre, "The Impact of Fundamentalisms on Women, the Family, and Interpersonal Relations," in *Fundamentalisms and Society: Reclaiming the Sciences, the Family, and Education,* ed. Martin E. Marty and R. Scott Appleby (Chicago: University of Chicago Press, 1993), 130.

PART ONE

Africa

2

Gender and Religion in Hausaland: Variations in Islamic Practice in Niger and Nigeria

Barbara M. Cooper

In this chapter I set out both temporal and geographical variations in how women in a region of the West African Sahel have experienced Islam. I embark on this task by exploring some of the implications of a nineteenth-century "holy war" (jihad) for subsequent understandings of religion and gender in the region. The uneven success of this war (alternatively known as the Fulani jihad, the Sokoto jihad, or the jihad of Usman 'dan Fodio) meant that some regions escaped the close ideological and political controls of the jihadists, leading to at least two quite distinct patterns of spiritual practice, dress, agricultural production, and administrative structure within the contiguous Hausa-speaking region of central Sudan. The implications of these initial differences were in some ways vitiated by the shared experience of colonial rule throughout Hausaland in the twentieth century. Certainly the Hausa/Fulani of northern Nigeria fell under British control, while the resistant Hausa of Niger fell under French domination. However, the enforced colonial peace, the generalized growth of peanut production to meet tax needs, and the development of communications and transport within Hausaland led to closer relations between the two formerly warring regions than had occurred in the closing decades of the nineteenth century. Nevertheless, the positioning of the Hausa-speaking regions within their respective colonial states was such that in the postcolonial period the implications of Islam for gender relations and regional nationalism in the independent nations of Niger and Nigeria have been quite different. I will explore these shifting differences in the colonial and postcolonial periods in order to insist that local understandings of Islam and gender can be quite specific historically and geographically.

The purpose of this chapter, then, is to illustrate the broad range of ways in which Islam has figured in the lives of women of one ethnic and linguistic group (the Hausa) and to suggest how that range emerges out of the complex history of this region. It is tempting for scholars, and for feminist scholars in the West in particular, to reduce all the constraints that women in Muslim regions of the world experience to "patriarchal Islam." As Marnia Lazreg characterizes works on Muslim women, "with few exceptions gender inequality is attributed to Islam's presumed influence upon the lives of women and men in North Africa and the Middle East. The unstated assumption is that religion is at once the cause of and the solution to gender inequality."[1] By attending more closely to the historical and cultural forces that give rise to the particularities of gender relations in given locales, it is possible to move beyond reductive accounts of women and Islam. Specific historical configurations of gender and religion simultaneously emerge from and facilitate political and economic competition, colonial and postcolonial intervention, and ethnic nationalism.

Such a subtle and complex understanding of Islam is all the more urgent today at a moment when, as John Esposito notes, there is a danger that the Islamic world will replace the communist world in the U.S. national imagination as the external threat against which the United States defines itself and its politics.[2] By understanding the complex history of gender and religion in a region that has counted itself part of the Muslim world since the fourteenth century, we can resist the Western impulse to caricature and demonize Islam in the name of uplifting the women purportedly subjugated by that religion.

THE CONTEXT OF THE JIHAD

Prior to the jihad in question, aristocrats of the Hausa ethnic group ruled over farmers, herders, traders, scholars, and artisans within their kingdoms. Some of the scholars and herders in the region were Fulani rather than Hausa and spoke Fulfulde as their mother tongue. One of these Fulani Muslim scholars, Usman 'dan Fodio, amassed a large following and in 1808 launched a holy war against the Hausa-speaking aristocracy of the kingdom of Gobir. He and his followers referred to their armed resistance to the Hausa overlords as a jihad, seeing their struggles as being akin to the holy wars the Prophet Muhammad waged against "unbelievers" in the early days of Islam. This conflict continued for roughly half a century, culminating in the consolidation of a broad empire broken into two caliphates based in the towns of Sokoto and Gwandu and headed largely by Fulani scholars and bureaucrats.

The outcome of this war contributed to temporal variations in how women experienced Islam in this region, for women's roles and positions within Hausa society were profoundly altered both by the course of the war itself and by the transformation of the bureaucratic structures through which the territories were governed. The war also laid the groundwork for some contemporary geographical variations in women's roles and in the practice of Islam in the Hausa-speaking region today, variations which result at least in part from the failure of the jihadists to conquer the entire Hausa-speaking region. Thus the Maradi region of Niger, outside the territory conquered by the forces of the scholar Usman 'dan Fodio and his followers, reveals quite different patterns of female activity and gender roles than those in much of northern Nigeria, the heartland of the territory conquered by the jihadists.

Few religious wars are fought solely on religious grounds, and it is worth sketching out briefly some of the relevant political and economic context for the jihad.[3] Prior to the eighteenth century, this region was marked by rivalry and warfare between a number of Hausa-speaking kingdoms—principally Kano, Zaria, Kebbi, Katsina, and Gobir—which were linked linguistically and culturally but did not join together to form a single political unit. These kingdoms relied upon revenue from the tribute of agriculturally based populations within their respective spheres of influence and from levies on the trans-Saharan and coastal trades. Competition for control of trade routes and tributary populations created long-standing rivalries between the aristocracies of the central Hausa-speaking kingdoms, despite a broadly shared culture and a myth of common origin.

All of the major Hausa kingdoms have traditions dating the advent of Islam and Muslim rulers to at least the fifteenth century, and in some cases well prior to that. The adoption of Islam facilitated trade by creating a network of individuals with a common religion, cultural idiom, and language through which commercial contacts, credit facilities, and living arrangements could be established within a diverse trading population. Three major trade routes dominated the trade of the region; the first route linked Hausaland with North Africa, the second ran from Bornu (to the east) through Hausaland and on into Gonja in the Ashanti hinterland, and the third axis ran south from Hausaland to the coast.

On the eve of the jihad, Gobir was an expanding and extremely mobile military state. The fall of the Songhai empire in the late sixteenth century had left a power vacuum in the central Sudanic region, engendering competition among the western Hausa states for regional hegemony. By the beginning of the nineteenth century, the constant warfare in the western regions had generated considerable discontent among the agricultural population, which bore the burden of taxation, conscription, food requisitions, and uncertainty. Furthermore, because revenues for continuing the warfare often came from trade in captives, the local populations were vulnerable to slave raiding even from their own rulers. Other segments of the population had cause to be unhappy, notably the pastoral Fulani, who resented a tax on cattle known as the *jangali*. Finally, the indigenous slave population may have rallied to the jihadists' cause because after converting to Islam they could argue that they had been enslaved illegally.

Hence the jihad became an idiom through which a broad range of discontents arising from a particular historical moment could be given voice, even among portions of the population that had not counted themselves as Muslim prior to the jihad. The critiques employed by the jihadists to justify their attack on Gobir and later upon the other Hausa kingdoms reflected some of these broader discontents, focusing heavily upon issues of "proper" Islamic taxation and mentioning quite specifically the jangali tax. Other objections focused upon the judicial practices in the kingdoms, which generally preferred fines over the corporal punishments suggested in Shari'a.[4]

Thus the scholars at the center of the jihad drew upon broader unrest in the kingdoms to mobilize support outside the narrow circle of the Fulani scholars of Usman 'dan Fodio's Toronkawa clan. In order to be effective for any length of time, however, such a disparate group needed to have some sense of common interest and identity. The identity of those following 'dan Fodio came increasingly to coalesce around issues and conflicts related to gender and dress. Dress was to become the symbolic focal point of conflicts between 'dan Fodio's growing following and the Hausa rulers at the court of Gobir. Whatever the original impulse was, it is clear that 'dan Fodio's following had begun to set itself off visually from other Muslims at the court by wearing turbans and veils. As the community grew, the clothing became a mark of resistance and defiance, prompting the king of Gobir, Sarkin Bawa Jangorzo, to eventually prohibit the wearing of caps and turbans. Sarkin Nafata after him extended the prohibition to the veiling of women.

The symbolic importance of dress in the conflict had a number of corollary consequences for women. As the jihad progressed, women began increasingly to take on veiling and seclusion. Whether they did so as a sign of piety or solidarity with the reformists, as a means of protecting themselves in a period of rampant slave raiding and continual warfare, or simply to support or protect their male kin would be difficult to determine at this point. However, it is clear that the jihad marked the beginning of a trend toward greater female seclusion and veiling. By the same token, as the segregation and invisibility of women became part of how the reformists marked themselves off from the "unbelievers," free women gradually began to move out of farming and into activities they could perform from within seclusion. Farming, which prior to the jihad had been practiced openly by freeborn commoner women, became associated with slave status (as female agricultural labor was replaced with that of male captives). Consequently, free-born status became associated with seclusion. By the time of the British conquest of the caliphate territories in the first decade of the twentieth century, to be a proper Muslim woman meant ideally to be secluded and veiled, although such was not possible for all women, and was certainly not possible for the slave population. This was a striking change from the pre-jihad kingdoms, in which free commoner women farmed openly, did not wear veils, and nevertheless might regard themselves as Muslim.

Although the crystallization of the sense of identity of the jihadists' community around dress, veiling, and seclusion had significant implications for women, the aim of the jihadists was not the subjugation of women. Some of the jihadists' critiques of the Hausa court system were intended to protect women. They objected, for example, to rulers "taking what women they wish without marriage contract," a reference to widespread concubinage within the court. They decried "the devouring of the alms of women who are subject to their authority" or the seizure of the property of widows by Hausa rulers. They also protested the practice of such unrestrained polygyny among the royalty that "the number of women of some of them amounts to one thousand or more."[5] Usman 'dan Fodio also sharply rebuked Muslim men who failed to educate their female dependents in Islam, laying the groundwork for a tradition of female scholarship and education in the caliphate, an issue to which I shall return in a moment.

The attack of the jihadists upon the religious foundations of the pre-jihad kingdoms, however, was to have profound implications for women's limited sources of power and income. In the centuries between the spread of Islam to the region in the fourteenth and fifteenth centuries and the rise of the Fulani scholarly class at the time of the jihad, a highly tolerant and syncretic variety of Islam had prevailed throughout the Hausa kingdoms. Over these centuries scholarship flourished in religious schools; mosques were built; rulers occasionally observed the Islamic injunction to visit the homeland of Islam in Mecca; and vocabulary entered the Hausa language reflecting the influence of Islamic law, trade, and religious practices. By the time of the Fulani jihad the kingdoms were deeply steeped in Islam, and the growth of a large following behind Usman 'dan Fodio was made possible by the tolerance, respect, and deference of the Hausa royalty for Muslim scholars within the kingdom. Indeed, the jihadists consciously set themselves apart from the large numbers of Muslim scholars closely identified with the Hausa court and supported by the courtly class.

The pre-jihad kingdoms had thus long been the locus of an extremely tolerant form of Islam, one which drew simultaneously upon the spiritual forces of the pre-Islamic religions of the region and upon the strengths of monotheistic Islam. The two could be reconciled because much of the Islamic world recognizes the existence of spirits, or genies. The pantheon of local powers that Hausa-speaking peoples had associated with geographical features such as rocks, trees, hills, and lakes were gradually reinterpreted as spirits far less territorially bound. These genies were celebrated in an urban spirit possession cult known as *bori*. The peoples of the Hausa kingdoms thus venerated one god, Allah, while at the same time working to reconcile themselves to other forces more immediate to their local environments and day-to-day experiences. A good ruler was one who was able to draw upon the support of Allah when such support was appropriate but who nevertheless maintained cordial relations with local spirits and those religious practitioners who venerated them, because at times it was these more immediate forces that would be most responsive to the needs of the kingdom. No conqueror of the Hausa kingdoms could rule effectively without also conquering and taming the local spirits.

Many of the practices associated with the bori cult were intimately related to women. Women made up a large number of the cult practitioners, much of the cult's appeal lay in its therapeutic efficacy in matters of concern to women such as fertility, and the cult was traditionally overseen by a titled woman of the aristocratic class (often a sister or aunt of the king). This pattern of important titled positions for women is quite common throughout West Africa: in many of the state systems of Sudan a parallel system of titles for women existed, formally recognizing female power and giving women visible political roles in the kingdoms. Women could act as regents; raise taxes; lead troops in war; and at least in the mythic past of the king lists of some of the kingdoms, serve as king. Thus the syncretic practices of the kingdoms prior to the jihad recognized and ensured women's roles in spiritual and indeed political life.

The jihadists, in attacking the syncretic Islam of the Hausa kingdoms, undermined some of the central sources of power and income available to women prior to the jihad. The titled positions for the aristocratic women heading the spirit cult were to be eliminated or transformed. Women were thus deprived of a leadership role and of representation in the administration of the judicial, military, and political life of the kingdoms. The activities of women as diviners, doctors, and dancers were forced underground. The leverage ordinary women could gain in their relations with husbands and other kin through their positions in the cult was threatened. And in general, women's recognized role in the health and spiritual well-being of the region was called into question.

Indeed, the war against many of the practices that the jihadists found most objectionable was fought on the domestic front, for women were in a sense the guardians of the syncretic practices through which the urban Islam of the court could be reconciled with the pre-Islamic spiritual beliefs of the farmers of the region. For example, the aristocratic women heading the urban spirit cult oversaw rituals performed in conjunction with rural priests to open and close the hunting and planting seasons. Merely conquering the territory of the Hausa kingdoms would not in itself eliminate the spiritual beliefs of the Hausa, and in particular it could not be expected to affect the beliefs and practices of Hausa women in their homes. In order to oppose these cult practices the jihadists had to rely upon the female scholars who were important figures within the Toronkawa camp.[6]

Although many of the beliefs of the jihadists restricted women's options, one important option that the jihadists opened up for women was training in Islamic scholarship. Muslim women within the jihadists' camp were often erudite scholars, poets, and historians. These literate, scholarly women were critical to the jihadists' ability to replace local spiritual beliefs with others more in accord with Islam as the Fulani scholars understood it.

Scholars such as Usman 'dan Fodio's sister Nana Asma'u wrote memorable poetry in Hausa to teach the women and children they came into contact with the "true" story of the jihad, proper religious practice, and proper female comportment. A religious movement for women known as 'Yan Taru emerged in the wake of the jihad, in which women visited the tombs of saints and studied religion together. The leadership of this movement mimicked and drew upon the authority implicit in the titled positions for women in the pre-jihad kingdoms, even as the jihadists worked to eliminate women's access to such positions within the conquered territories. The message to women was contradictory; although the support for women's education empowered them to lay claim to scholarship, women were simultaneously constrained by the seclusion that the settled Fulani practiced and that the symbolism of dress as a marker of community set in train.

THE SUCCESSES AND FAILURES OF THE JIHAD

It is important to recall, however, that the jihadists were not entirely successful in their reforms, whether political, judicial, or ideological. For example, the jihadists ended up retaining many of the taxes they themselves had criticized as un-Islamic, including the jangali cattle tax, which was merely renamed. They retained most of the titled positions through which the bureaucracy of the kingdoms had been administered, eliminating those reserved for women. Like the Hausa rulers before them, the jihadists discovered that they had to strike a balance between their Islamic ideals and the pre-jihad culture of the region. Shehu 'dan Fodio's successors complained bitterly that the communities within the new caliphates were not living up to the ideals of the jihad. His son Bello complained that Sokoto had attracted a new community, interested less in Islam than in power and property, and his brother Abdallah accused the new community of love of the same pursuits as the previous rulers: rank, concubines, clothing, horses, and the profits to be reaped from the abuse of office.[7]

If the political and judicial reforms were only partial, the ideological and cultural reforms also met with mixed results. One important measure of the limited success of the ideological war is that today the regions conquered by the jihadists speak not Fulfulde, the language of the Fulani

conquerors, but Hausa. Although those with access to positions of authority within governmental and religious structures are still characterized as
"Fulani," in significant ways they have become assimilated to Hausa culture. Even in the late nineteenth century before the arrival of the British
into northern Nigeria, the syncretic practices of the pre-jihad kingdoms
persisted, although they were substantially transformed by the elimination
of official recognition of female political titles. As official recognition of
female spiritual and political roles was denied, spirit cult dancing became
the province of prostitutes, who were not under the direct control of any
male. The sole remaining titled position for a woman (*magajiya*) became
the title for the woman who headed the local prostitutes rather than a titled
position for a woman heading the aristocratic class.

The British endeavored to uphold the version of Islam that the Fulani
had attempted to introduce, but they were no more successful in eradicat-
ing bori than the precolonial Fulani rulers had been. In an amusing and
telling anecdote, a Hausa woman named Baba told anthropologist Mary
Smith about how local bori adepts responded to the local Fulani administrator's edict forbidding spirit possession during the period of British colonial rule:

> Twenty days ago Fagaci [the titled position of the local Fulani ruler who
> administered Zarewa under indirect rule] forbade bori-dancing in the
> town. Then Tanko's wife went to Fagaci's compound to greet his wives,
> and as she came out from the women's quarters she had to pass through
> the room where he was sitting. She and her three co-wives knelt down to
> greet him, and as she was kneeling the bori came and possessed her—it
> was Baturen Gwari, the European from Gwari country. "Imprison me,
> bind me, call the police and lock me up! Isn't there an order forbidding
> bori? Very well, look at me, I have come. Lock me up then!" . . . She
> sang this "praise-song" right before Fagaci.
>
>> We are the end,
>> We are meningitis,
>> We are all the other illnesses,
>> We own the bit of earth behind the hut,
>> Laughing one, there's no cure for this illness,
>> Reveller, there is no rejoicing without us.
>> . . . The town is theirs, they went to Fagaci's compound and ap-
>> peared, they aren't afraid of him.[8]

In this anecdote Baba's friend is possessed by a European spirit, who cannot then be imprisoned despite having broken the edict. The bori family of
genies gradually integrated spirits that were not simply residues of the pre-
Islamic religions but rather reflected and embodied the changing composition of the political and social landscape, so that spirits might be Muslim
scholars, Arabs, or Fulani pastoralists. In this case the spirit is a European,
subject to different laws than the Africans Fagaci administers through
indirect rule. Bori practice was adaptive to new conditions and, as this

story attests, could become an arena through which resistance to the continued rule of the Fulani under indirect rule in the colonial period could be sustained.

Thus although the jihadists (and the Fulani rulers of the British territory of Northern Nigeria after them) consistently attempted to eliminate bori, they were unable to do so, for local understandings of illness made possession not an intentional act but something beyond the control of the adept. Possession could be tamed and perfected, but it could not be voluntarily abandoned except at peril to the health of the adept (and indeed, as the song above suggests, at peril to the health of the entire community). Health comes not from exorcism but from establishing a mutually satisfactory relationship between the spirits and the humans who inhabit the spirits' terrain.

SYNCRETIC PRACTICES IN THE MARADI VALLEY

If in the territories conquered by the jihadists, bori became an idiom of resistance practiced in defiance of the British and Fulani rulers, in the territories into which those who disagreed with the jihadists migrated, many pre-jihad institutions and practices were openly sanctioned and perpetuated. Thus in the Maradi valley the titled positions for women eliminated in the caliphates were retained; bori was practiced freely and indeed served to legitimate the rule of an aristocracy said to be intimately related to the spirit world ("they all have spirits"); women continued to farm openly whether slave or free; veiling and seclusion were limited to women of the aristocratic and scholarly classes; and in general the practice of Islam was far more syncretic and tolerant.

In part this last pattern reflected power relations in the region: the Maradi valley had long been a distant territory of the kingdom of Katsina, which governed with a light touch and made no effort to force local populations to convert to Islam. When the jihadists conquered Katsina, they attempted to rule the Maradi region far more directly and showed great arrogance and intolerance toward the non-Muslim Hausa of the valley. The unconverted Hausa-speaking population then invited their former Hausa masters to set up camp in the valley because they deeply resented their new Fulani overlords. Henceforth the indigenous population of the valley joined forces with the aristocracies of the defeated kingdoms to harass the Fulani emirates to the south, successfully disrupting trade and coming close several times to recapturing Katsina. In a sense, a tolerance for indigenous religious practice was a prerequisite to the continued presence in the valley of the ousted Hausa rulers.

In the Maradi valley, the most important and influential aristocratic woman heads the bori cult. Hajjiya Jeka explained this woman's role. Hajjiya had served in the court of Gobir as a messenger and therefore was intimately aware of the duties of the titled class. Since she had not herself ever been the head of the bori cult, her descriptions of that position were likely to be relatively objective.[9] When asked in an interview whether the titled position for women among the immigrants to the valley from Gobir (*inna*) was identical to a similar position for women among the immigrants to the valley from Katsina (*iya*), Hajjiya replied:

> Yes, well, they aren't the same. Both of them, their custom [*alada:* cus-tom, tradition, medicine] is that of the bori, of the *aljannu* [genies]. . . . As for the people of Gobir, wherever there is a woman who has been ini-tiated into the cult, who has received spirits on her head, she goes to greet the inna. At the harvest she would bring the inna a sheaf of grain, and they would do the same for the iya. . . . Even the King would do that, but he doesn't do the customs of the bori. Just the inna and the iya, that is their custom.

Thus the male ruler shows deference to the head of the bori cult by bring-ing tribute in the form of grain. When Hajjiya speaks of the spirits she uses both the Arabic loan word, aljannu (attesting to the Islamic recognition of such spirits or genies) and the Hausa word, bori. From personal observa-tions and from Hajjiya Jeka's further descriptions of the functions of these women, it seemed that they had important judicial responsibilities, and they seemed to act as a kind of *joji* (Western judge) or *al'kali* (Muslim judge) toward their adepts. Hajjiya responded:

> That's right. Each would come to greet her, and kneel in respect, just as they would before the King. Now the King only has power over men, he gathers the men, and if a man does something wrong he would be brought before the King, and if it was a matter for Shari'a law, then he would be brought to the Imam, he's the one who does Shari'a. Now the inna [or iya] does her own judging [*"Inna ke shara'a da kanta"*]. For her bori adepts.

Here the kind of judging or mediating the head of the bori cult does is likened to rendering a judgment according to the Shari'a. Men go to the king to resolve their conflicts, and if the conflict seems to require the in-tervention of a Muslim scholar, then they are referred to the imam. Women bring their problems to the iya or inna, and in particular women who are members of the bori cult come to her because if humans are governed by the Shari'a, spirits are subject to different but analogous law. This work of performing cult activities, mediating between women and adepts, and overseeing the spiritual well-being of the community is the responsibility of the aristocratic women heading the bori cult, and men of the aristocratic class have no part in it. As Hajjiya remarked, "It's women's work. It's none of the king's business." Hajjiya, a devout Muslim who has been to

Mecca, prays regularly, and composes songs praising Allah, sees no incompatibility between the practice of bori and the practice of Islam.

One further difference between the understanding of Islam in the northern Nigerian territories conquered by the jihadists and that which obtains to the north in Maradi bears repeating. Although women in northern Nigeria have gradually refrained from active farming as part of a trend toward greater female seclusion, rural Muslim women in Maradi farm as a matter of course. Women's farming activities, both on their own fields and on fields that meet the needs of the entire family, are an extremely important part of the agricultural economy of the region. Although many women would prefer to earn their livelihood in a less arduous fashion, the persistence of female farming in the Maradi region represents one more option available to women, providing them with a significant source of income and making a valued contribution to the economy. Their visible farm labor gives them some limited recognition as important producers and not simply as dependents or consumers. This option and the social recognition which it can imply is one which women in northern Nigeria enjoy much more rarely.

AFTER THE JIHAD:
THE COLONIAL AND POSTCOLONIAL INHERITANCES

As a consequence of the differential success of Usman 'dan Fodio's jihad, Hausa-speaking populations in this contiguous region may differ in their practice of Islam quite substantially, even today. In the early decades of this century, the British conquered the caliphates, whereas the French conquered the territories to the north of the caliphates. The French laid claim to the Maradi valley largely to obtain a resting place on the way to their territories farther east. The colonial boundary between Niger and Nigeria, then, reflected the animosities between the jihadists and those who resisted the jihad. As a consequence, many religious, political, and cultural practices among the Hausa in the Maradi region of Niger differed considerably from those in Northern Nigeria.

Colonial rule considerably complicated the picture of how Islam figured in the lives of the Hausa-speaking peoples. Both the French and the British attempted to rule their territories as cheaply as possible while reaping the maximum revenue from them, with the result that although the French were pursuing a policy of "assimilation," in reality their administration was quite similar to that developed by the British in Northern Nigeria, the paradigm of indirect rule. In both cases local hierarchies were left in place, outside influences that might have disrupted local peoples (such as Christian missionaries) were discouraged, and an economy based upon the export of peanuts and the import of European manufactured goods was encouraged. By relying upon local bureaucratic institutions and personnel, both the British and the French fixed in place an aristocratic class that benefited from colonial rule while extracting as much as possible from the peasant classes who performed most of the agricultural labor upon which the economy was built. And both the British and the French, perhaps inadvertently, placed the Hausa-speaking populations at a distinct disadvantage relative to other ethnic groups in the colonies at the moment of transition to independence. Other groups (the Zerma in Niger, the Yoruba and Ibo among others in Nigeria) were better equipped to step into positions of importance in the national and international arenas as a result of their earlier exposure to Western schooling.

Some aspects of French rule had the effect of bringing practices in Niger more in line with those in Nigeria: the peace enforced under colonial rule tended to erode the tradition of enmity between Maradi and the emirates to the south; the growth of transportation and communications infrastructures brought the former combatants into closer and closer contact with one another as regional trade grew; and finally, the French use of the Maliki school of Islamic law to regulate indigenous affairs (rather than the more flexible practices common prior to French rule) tended to formalize a relatively rigid interpretation of Muslim family law.

These developments had important consequences for women not only under colonial rule but also in the postindependence period. For example, as Maliki law was enforced, women in Niger began to inherit in fairly regular fashion from their fathers and husbands, which had not been the case prior to colonial rule. Today women in Maradi invest heavily in real estate, a pattern that built upon the new option to inherit land and houses and one with striking implications for women and for the economy as a whole.

As the economy became more and more centered upon the peanut trade from the 1950s to the mid-1970s, women found themselves increasingly marginalized from the most lucrative aspects of the agricultural economy because female farmers were virtually excluded from the information, credit, transport, storage, and trade institutions through which the peanut trade was conducted. Women came to rely more heavily on Maliki understandings of wives as dependents of their husbands in order to make up their loss of ground within the local economy and in order to stake a claim to an independent income from their farm enterprises. Although women had greater economic opportunity in urban areas, which were increasingly integrated into trade networks with Nigeria, they were also subject to the more orthodox Islam, which had been on the rise as trade ties grew. The net result today is that women's economic positions are becoming ever more precarious, and women are more reliant upon their dependent position as defined in Maliki tradition.

Finally, under colonial rule the significance of the titled positions for women began to erode because the colonial administration, blind as it was to female power in general, failed to support and draw upon the institutions women controlled. Although the titled positions for women continued to exist, some of their importance was undermined as alternate judicial, health, and male-dominated bureaucratic institutions emerged. Women's virtual exclusion from Western education until the postindependence era has meant that Hausa-speaking women, despite their prominence in the precolonial political system, have been largely absent from politics in the Nigérien state.

Since independence Maradi has progressively been drawn into regional trade circuits, relying upon a common Hausa cultural, linguistic, religious, and commercial heritage to build ties with more prosperous merchants in northern Nigeria. Northern Nigeria enjoys better conditions for agriculture than much of the Maradi region, has a more developed infrastructure as a consequence of Nigeria's oil wealth, and presents a huge market for Maradi's agro-pastoral products. Maradi's traders have consciously built strong ties with patrons across the border, particularly since the Biafran war of 1967–1970, during which time Hausa traders in Niger helped provision their neighbors who were cut off from their links to southern Nigeria by the war.[10] These ties have been reinforced through an idiom of common Muslim heritage. One of the consequences of the growth of regional ties is that seclusion, which until 1945 was restricted to the wives of the most conservative Muslim scholars within the city of Maradi, has been on the rise in the Maradi region. Although until quite recently rural women in Niger would not have been secluded because of their importance in the farming system, today the wives of prominent traders and those who aspire to be part of the merchant class may be secluded even if it is economically impractical. Practices in Niger are growing closer to those in Nigeria. One might argue that if the reformists did not succeed in the jihad against Maradi, they are winning the postcolonial peace.

Nevertheless it is important to note how differently Islam is constructed within the political economy of postcolonial Nigeria. Although northern Nigerian politicians were preferred by the British at the moment of independence, southern Nigerian politicians have had the advantage of Western education and better resources. Ethnic differences have coincided in a rough way with religious differences (Christianity in the south, Islam in the north) and with differences in access to resources. Particularly under military rule, it was impossible for civilians to express frustrations with these inequities that had begun in the different treatment of regions under colonial rule. Thus political discontent has often been couched in religious rather than overtly political terms. In the phrase of Jibrin Ibrahim, religion can be seen as the "ideology" of the "informal sector": "The importance of

religious movements in African society is linked to their capacity for providing 'democratic space' for subordinated actors."[11] The sense of embat-
tlement northern Nigeria experiences has been translated into a regional
nationalism couched in terms of Islamic identity.

The heritage of the jihad combined with that of northern Nigeria's relative isolation under colonial rule has meant that women in northern Nigeria have become icons in a virulent subnationalist movement. What distinguishes "northerners" from "southerners" is that the former are Muslim
and, in particular, that their women are secluded and veiled. This formulation, of course, effaces the significant Muslim Yoruba population in the
south and majority Christian enclaves in the north. The south, where Nige-
rians have had longer access to Western schooling and in some cases extended exposure to Christianity, is described by northern nationalists as the
debased realm of Western cultural imperialism and the source of corrupt
Western practices and values. Hence the advantages of the south become,
in this Islamist formulation, signs of moral and spiritual decay. Northern
regional autonomy and spiritual purity is thus to be safeguarded by protections for Shari'a in the constitution and in particular for those provisions in family law that most touch on women's lives: divorce, child custody, polygyny, and inheritance.

In Niger, by contrast, religion is not the idiom in which regional political tensions are expressed: although the Hausa region is disadvantaged
in terms of access to education and the resources of the state relative to the
Zerma-speaking populations around the capital of Niamey, the overwhelming majority of Nigériens are Muslim, and so regional/ethnic tensions do not coincide with religious differences. However, although a virulent Islamist movement has not developed in Niger, the fact that so much
of the population is Muslim means that much is taken for granted about
the status of women in family law. In Niger, anti-imperialist sentiment is
probably more significant than regional tensions in Nigériens' sense of
themselves as Muslim: structural adjustment, the recent devaluation of the
Communauté Financière Africaine (CFA, the regional franc tied to that of
France), and the precipitous fall in uranium revenues are felt to be consequences of Western intrusions and exclusions.

In both Niger and Nigeria, women are making use of prior history to
formulate arguments for female inclusion in positions of power, although
the grounds for those historical claims of necessity differ substantially.
Women in Nigeria are developing a women's movement that aims to reform Islamic practice from within, drawing upon a tradition of female
scholarship to claim the right to reinterpret Islam, Islamic texts, and Islamic practices. Thus the Federation of Muslim Women's Associations of
Nigeria (FOMWAN) attempts to evade the stigma of Western feminism
(characterized as "bra burning") by drawing upon Islam itself. Nigerian
women researching the religious and historical heritage of Nigeria have

consciously brought to light the important work of female scholars both during and after the jihad in an effort to gain public acceptance for prominent roles for women in religion, politics, and the economy.[12]

By contrast, Hausa women in Niger, who did not benefit from Usman 'dan Fodio's promotion of female scholarship, have instead drawn upon the institution of the iya, the bori cult, and the traditional female power both embody. This is a more difficult path to take because Islamist sentiment emanating from Nigeria is on the rise. The postcolonial state, more sensitive to local forms of power than the colonial state, has drawn upon some of the power of female titled positions in trying to garner support for its own programs and parties. Thus the woman in the position of iya in Maradi has been visible as part of national and state-directed women's groups since 1964. Women can build upon that tradition and upon their increasingly substantial history of political visibility since the establishment of a national women's association in 1975. Furthermore, the history of female participation in farming and trade makes it possible for Hausa women in Niger to be Muslim without necessarily being secluded. Hausa women in Niger, despite their relative lack of education, may be able to parlay economic power into increasing political power in ways that Hausa women in Nigeria cannot. However, Nigérien women's economic prominence must be constantly renegotiated as seclusion and northern Nigerian influence grow.

CONCLUSION

Barbara Callaway and Lucy Creevey, in their recent book, *The Heritage of Islam: Women, Religion, and Politics in West Africa*, argue that "throughout West Africa, Islam has had the greatest impact on women's lives among those who were converted earliest and who were relatively isolated for centuries thereafter from contact with other cultures," suggesting that the longer Islam is present, the more it will annihilate pre-Islamic customs favorable to women and the more subordinated women will become.[13] Conversely, in those regions that are exposed to Western ideas and that experience Islam more briefly, women will be less oppressed by Islam. I have attempted to sketch out here a picture of how Islam has been experienced and has developed within one contiguous ethnic/linguistic group in order to suggest that the picture is, in reality, much more complex and contradictory. Islam was present in Hausaland from the fourteenth century, but for four centuries it coexisted with a series of local political, economic, and spiritual practices, some of which favored some women (female titles, spirit cult practices, female farming) and others of which set back some women (the prominence of female slaves both for labor and as concubines; a sense that education in Islam is not urgent, particularly for women; a neglect of Qur'anic precepts that were intended to protect women's inheritance). The Fulani jihad of the nineteenth century represented a much more recent and more literal interpretation of Islam, and it could be argued that this brand of Islam has had the more constraining consequences for women in the longer term. Whereas some of the practices within the caliphates were favorable for women (notably the encouragement of women's education in Islam), many were less advantageous, particularly the exclusion of women from public office and from visible political and economic activities. The gradual crystallization of northern Nigerian cultural identity in the postcolonial period around female seclusion and veiling has had extreme consequences for women, and I argue that this nationalism is in large part a consequence of the particular form taken by Western colonial domination in Nigeria. Thus it is not Nigeria's "isolation" from the West that has promoted a particular vision of Islam but precisely the uneven and unequal intrusion of the West in the context of colonialism, which virtually guaranteed that an oppressive cultural nationalism would develop there.

In conclusion, then, the Muslim Hausa-speaking women in Niger and Nigeria are fighting to gain better protections under the law in their respective countries, but their experiences of Islam and the implications of their religion for the range of options and constraints they experience are quite different. These differences emerge not from any intrinsic qualities in Islam, but from the two regions' different relationships to the reformist jihad of Usman 'dan Fodio, their contrasting colonial histories, and their dissimilar situations within the postcolonial state. Thus if we are to understand the lives and experiences of Muslim women, we cannot begin with the assumption that Islam determines their options and constraints, but we must ask instead what Islam means for them, how it has developed historically in their region, and what role (if any) it plays in the interpretation of local, regional, national, and global conflicts and forces. I have attempted to suggest that although religion does figure among the forces that establish the limits and opportunities Hausa-speaking women experience, women are also themselves active in defining religion and history. As Marnia Lazreg remarks, "Religion cannot be detached from the socioeconomic and political context within which it unfolds. And religion cannot be seen as having an existence independent of human activity."[14] If the history and interpretation of Islam within one linguistic and cultural area displays this degree of richness and complexity, we should be extremely wary of generalizing about Islam and how women experience it across cultures, nations, and regions of the world.

NOTES

1. Marnia Lazreg, "Gender and Politics in Algeria: Unraveling the Religious Paradigm," *Signs* 15, no. 4 (1990): 756.

2. John L. Esposito, "Political Islam: Beyond the Green Menace," *Current History*, January 1994: 19–24.

3. The reader is forewarned that I am presenting here an unabashedly biased view of the jihad, as my own scholarly loyalties lie with the Hausa who resisted it. For an account from a scholar whose loyalties lie with the jihadists, see Mervyn Hiskett's engaging account of Usman 'dan Fodio's life, *The Sword of Truth: The Life and Times of the Shehu Usuman Dan Fodio* (New York: Oxford University Press, 1973). Hiskett has also written an extremely useful and comprehensive study of the history of Islam in West Africa, *The Development of Islam in West Africa* (London: Longman, 1984). No account of work on the Sokoto caliphate would be complete without mention of Murray Last's study of the jihad and the consolidation and administration of the caliphate, *The Sokoto Caliphate* (London: Longmans, 1967).

4. Bearing in mind that the primary sources for this claim come from the jihadist camp, it appears that among the most hated taxes were jangali, a tax on cattle much resented by cattle herders; *ku'din gari*, a tax on non-Muslims; *ku'din salla*, special taxes on Muslim festivals; and market taxes. None of these, according to 'dan Fodio, were sanctioned by the Shari'a. 'Dan Fodio advocated only one tax, the *zakat*, which was a kind of tithe. The jihadists also objected to arbitrary requisitioning of animals, food, and property and to obligatory conscription in wars. *Gaisuwa*, traditional voluntary gifts to rulers, were interpreted as bribery and condemned. See Mervyn Hiskett, "Kitab al Farq," *Bulletin of the School of Oriental and African Studies* 23, no. 3 (1960): 553–579.

5. Hiskett, "Kitab al Farq," 567.

6. Much of the following discussion of the importance of female scholars to the jihadists is drawn from Jean Boyd's groundbreaking and eminently readable book, *The Caliph's Sister: Nana Asma'u 1793–1865* (London: Frank Cass, 1989). See also Jean Boyd and Murray Last, "The Role of Women as Agents Religieux in Sokoto," *Canadian Journal of African Studies* 19, no. 2 (1985): 293–300.

7. Last, *Sokoto Caliphate*, 59, 66.

8. See Mary Smith, *Baba of Karo: A Woman of the Muslim Hausa* (New Haven: Yale University Press, 1981, originally published in 1954 by Faber and Faber), 223–224. This extraordinary and delightful book is one of the few full life histories available for an African woman who lived before and during colonial rule. This anecdote is typical of the kind of vivid story Baba tells.

9. Hajjiya Jeka, excerpts from an interview by the author, Maradi, Niger, April 13, 1989.

10. Emmanuel Grégoire, *The Alhazai of Maradi: Traditional Hausa Merchants in a Changing Sahelian City*, trans. Benjamin Hardy (Boulder: Lynne Rienner Publishers, 1992), 24–25.

11. Jibrin Ibrahim, "Pluralism and Religious Conflict in Nigeria: A Research Agenda," paper presented at the African Studies Association meeting, Boston, December 7, 1993, 3.

12. See for example, Rakiya Ahmed Sani, "'Dan Fodio Women in the Nineteenth Century," paper presented at the African Studies Association meeting, Boston, December 7, 1993. Whether these women would characterize themselves as "feminists" is an open question. However, it is clear that they are pursuing the betterment of women and issues of concern to women.

13. Barbara Callaway and Lucy Creevey, *The Heritage of Islam: Women, Religion and Politics in West Africa* (Boulder: Lynne Rienner, 1994), 188.

14. Marnia Lazreg, "Feminism and Difference: The Perils of Writing as a Woman on Women in Algeria," *Feminist Studies* 14, no. 1 (1988): 95.

3

When Modernity Confronts Traditional Practices: Female Genital Cutting in Northeast Africa

Noor J. Kassamali

Female genital cutting (FGC)[1] is a complex and controversial issue. It is a provocative subject that has caused emotionally charged debate, both in the West and in some of the developing nations where this practice is prevalent. This debate is a relatively recent phenomenon, for up until a decade or two ago there was very little awareness of this issue in the West. It was brought to the fore at an international level by the combined delegation of East and West African women, of which I was a part, in Copenhagen in 1980 at the nongovernmental organizations (NGOs) forum at the United Nations Mid-Decade Conference for Women. The very concept of excising a woman or girl's genitalia is repugnant to most of us, both in the West and the developing world. Although there can be no doubt that our efforts should lead to the eradication of this practice, this can only occur when the myths and misconceptions that surround it are understood and dispelled. Only then can appropriate strategies that are more likely to succeed be formulated.

Current discussion and critique of FGC encompasses not only cultural relativism, cultural hegemony, and feminism but also the rights of women and children and their right to healthy development. It has been discussed as a form of child abuse;[2] as an infringement of basic human rights, that is, as gender-based violence; and in terms of gender dynamics, as a deliberate attempt to curtail the sexuality of women in some patriarchal societies.[3] According to 1997 United Nations (UN) estimates, approximately 130 million women and girls worldwide are affected. This may be a conservative number since accurate statistics are difficult to document. The countries in which this practice is prevalent do not often have the means to gather meaningful data for several reasons, including the presence of largely rural populations and the disincentive to disclose the prevalence of a practice that is officially illegal. This custom is reportedly practiced in twenty African countries and is also found in the southern parts of the Arabian peninsula, namely Oman and Yemen. It has also been reported in Indonesia;

Malaysia; the Bohra sect of the Indian subcontinent; in parts of South America, namely Brazil and Peru; in the aboriginal peoples of Australia; and even in a Russian Christian sect known as the Skopti.[4]

Despite its widespread distribution and practice by geographically and ethnically diverse groups, the custom has in the last two decades been associated with Islam, both by the lay media and some academicians.[5] Is FGC an Islamic custom? If so, what are some of the religious sources that discuss this practice? What is the role of the primarily male, Muslim clerics in this debate? And of what relevance is the practice of this custom to the current discussion on the status of Muslim women? Such questions are indeed germane to the discussion of this topic, but an even more basic issue looms: the alleged association of Islam with FGC is regarded as an established fact in the Western media, which thrives on stereotyping Islam in the most negative light. Here, FGC is often portrayed as a violent custom whose aim is to subjugate women and girls. Such a depiction perpetuates the stereotype of Islam as a violent faith and of Muslim women as subjugated and submissive.[6]

In this chapter I attempt to clarify some of the issues surrounding the practice of FGC and its alleged association with Islam in particular. Given the widespread diversity of the practice of this ritual, the major focus here will be limited to northeast Africa because it is there that the most severe form, infibulation, is to be found, and it is also there that the incidence of this practice is the highest in the world. As it will become clear, my perspective on this subject is grounded in my East African upbringing and my subsequent medical training.

Female genital cutting encompasses several types of procedures, which may be broadly classified into the categories of clitoridectomies and infibulations. The former consists of the excision of the clitoris or the labia minora or both, whereas the latter is much more extensive and consists of the excision of the clitoris, labia minora and majora, and the radical narrowing of the vagina. There are thus five or six different variations of FGC depending on locale, ethnicity, socioeconomic status, and education levels. The medical consequences of this procedure, which are well documented in the literature, are significant and are all uniformly devastating. Since a significant majority of these procedures are performed by unskilled and medically untrained women, there may be profound long-term effects on a woman's subsequent health and mental well-being, aside from the initial pain and trauma of the procedure because of the lack of anesthesia and aseptic techniques. Given its negative effects, why has this custom persisted in these cultures over several centuries?

THE ORIGINS OF FGC

Understanding why a custom has survived is not tantamount to condoning it. On the contrary, a clear understanding of why such a deleterious practice has persisted may be the key to its eventual eradication. Although its tenacity cannot be used as a justification for its existence, it also cannot be ignored.

The practice of FGC dates back to antiquity, and although various theories have been advanced, its origins remain obscure.[7] Several sources attest that this custom first arose in the Nile valley in ancient Egypt. The historian Herodotus reported the practice in Egypt in the fifth century B.C.E. but noted that the Romans, Phoenicians, and Ethiopians also practiced it. In his travels to Upper Egypt in 25 B.C.E., the Greek geographer Strabo described the practice among the Egyptians. Some sources suggest that evidence from mummies of an even earlier period reveals circumcision, but this claim is difficult to substantiate because of their state of preservation. From its origins in the Nile valley, female circumcision spread to adjacent lands via the trade routes. Pietro Bembos's account, published posthumously in the 1550s, documents the spread of this practice. Later, several eighteenth-century travelers reported similar findings.

Initially the type of circumcision varied with class. Clitoridectomy was probably a premarital rite of the upper classes, whereas infibulation was more common in enslaved women. Infibulated women, mainly from Sudan and Nubia, fetched a higher price on the market because buyers assumed that they were less likely to get pregnant.[8]

The custom of female genital cutting, therefore, did not originate with Islam but predates it by at least 2,500 years. The custom continued in the Nile valley even with the Muslim conquest of Egypt in 642 C.E. Over the centuries, Islamic elements were appropriated into the custom. Nevertheless, the custom is not found among most Muslims, whether they belong to the majority Sunni or the minority Shi'a denominations. Notably, FGC is unknown in Saudi Arabia, the cradle of Islam. The practice is also absent in Iran, the country with the largest Shi'a Muslim population. Claims for the "Islamicity" of this practice need to be examined very closely. Although practicing Muslims are fairly uniform in their acknowledgment of the five basic pillars (*arkan*), there is substantial diversity of practices rooted in local traditions. Thus we have, in essence, many local "Islams." It is quite evident, then, that FGC is a local tradition and not a universal Islamic practice. The practice is confined to countries within the Nile basin or under its influence and in West Africa.

JUSTIFICATIONS FOR FGC

In 1985, the Working Group on Traditional Practices Affecting the Health of Women and Children reported that the three major reasons cited for the continuation of female circumcision were tradition, religion, and the diminution of women's sexual sensitivity.[9] More recently, a joint survey done in Cairo by the Department of Obstetrics and Gynaecology at Zagazig

University and the Department of Community, Environmental, and Occupational Health at Ain Shams University in 1991 substantiates these findings. Sixteen hundred Cairene women were interviewed about the practice
of FGC. According to the results of this survey, the most frequently cited
motivations for FGC were tradition (32.9 percent), religion (28.6 percent),
hygiene (18.3 percent), and diminution of libido (6.6 percent).[10] The en-
trenchment of tradition is also evident in the significant resistance encountered by sixteenth-century Roman Catholic missionaries proselytizing
in Ethiopia to their attempts to abolish this practice. They had to appeal to
the Pope for special dispensation to permit the continuation of the procedure. Mzee Jomo Kenyatta, the founding president of Kenya, also turned
to tradition when he urged the Gikuyu women to have FGC as a means to
oppose the British colonial authorities and adhere to their cultural customs.
His argument was based on the premise that the colonial power wished to
eradicate this custom in order to annihilate the Gikuyu's traditional practices. Kenyatta, an anthropologist, has written an elaborate account of this
practice called *irua* and the justifications for its continuation.[11] It is inter-
esting to note that the Gikuyu, who are Christian, have this custom,
whereas the Muslim population of the Kenyan coast does not.

Muslim groups that practice this custom often cite religious justifications and may precede the ceremony with a prayer or recitation of
verses from the Qur'an. Yet religion is not a determining factor. In Egypt,
where this practice is deeply entrenched, both Muslims and Christians
practice FGC. Esther Hicks's hypothesis that "the geographic area penetrated by Islam coincides with the general distribution of infibulation, and
all populations known to practice infibulation are (to one degree or other)
of the Islamic faith" is erroneous not only in the case of the Gikuyu
(which she acknowledges) but also in the case of the various West African tribes.[12]

The final frequently cited reason for the continuation of this practice
is the diminution of a woman's sexuality. This often enrages most of the
groups in the West dealing with FGC. However, efforts to control
women's sexuality are not limited to Africa and the less developed world.
In the mid-nineteenth to early twentieth centuries, clitoridectomies and
oophorectomies (removal of the ovaries) were advocated and practiced in
the United States and England as cures for female masturbation, hysteria,
and insanity.[13] As recently as 1936, L. Emmett Holt's text *Diseases of Infancy and Childhood* recommended removal of the clitoris as a treatment
for masturbation.[14] These practices died out in the West as education levels rose and as the medical justification for these procedures became un-
tenable. Therefore, surgical repression of a woman's sexuality is not
unique to Africa and was an acceptable practice in the West just sixty
years ago.

FGC AND ISLAM

Lawrence Cutner hypothesizes that "there seems to be an implicit cultural belief in Islamic countries that a woman's sexuality is irresponsible and wanton and therefore must be controlled by men." He argues that "in the Muslim culture the use of female circumcision has much to do with the social value system that honors the preservation of the female's virginity."[15] FGC, therefore, must have seemed like an adequate means to control the sexuality of women, analogous to the iron chastity belts used in twelfth-century Europe. Unfortunately, Cutner's hypothesis is echoed by many men, both the ulema (Muslim clerics) and laypeople in the countries where this practice is prevalent. The critique of this practice by female Muslim scholars is based precisely on these grounds, namely, that some ulema (who are primarily men) sanction FGC as being Sunna, or in the tradition of the Prophet, because the procedures diminish a woman's sexual desire. This is not to imply that there is unanimity among the ulema. The debate regarding FGC among them is rife with disagreements and contradictory opinions. In October 1994, the mufti of Egypt, Shaykh Muhammad Sayyid Tantawi, publicly declared that the Qur'an does not have any stipulations regarding FGC. He went on to assert that the hadith (reported sayings) attributed to the Prophet were unreliable and that there was no evidence to suggest that the Prophet had ordered his own daughters to undergo any type of FGC. He went on to state that "a young girl's modesty does not stem from 'circumcision' but rather from a good religious and moral education."[16] However, within days, Shaykh Gad al-Haq Ali of al-Azhar issued a *fatwa* (religious ruling) that "female circumcision is a part of the legal body of Islam and is a laudable practice that does honor to the women." Subsequently a lawsuit was filed against the imam of al-Azhar by the Egyptian Organization of Human Rights for the damage caused by this fatwa.[17] Marie Assad states that many Islamic jurists believe that "female circumcision is an Islamic tradition mentioned in the tradition of the Prophet and sanctioned by the Imams (religious leaders) and jurists, in spite of their differences on whether it is a duty of Sunna; they support the practice and sanction it in view of its effect on attenuating the sexual desire of women and directing it to the desirable moderation."[18]

In my view, the position of these religious leaders is not only contrary to the Prophet's teaching but also the Qur'an. Muslim women not only have the right to sexual satisfaction within the context of a marriage but also can initiate sexual intercourse (Sura 4:1). An account from the Prophet states that he granted divorce to a woman whose husband was sexually impotent.[19] This right to sexual gratification within marriage is recognized even by uneducated, rural women.[20] In Islam (in contrast to Christianity), sexual intercourse does not have the stigma of sin; within the context of a marriage, it is even considered to be a meritorious act. Hitherto, the predominantly male religious elite has had the privilege of interpreting the Qur'an and the hadith, primarily because literacy was confined to a privileged few. Some religious leaders have thus managed to claim Islamic authenticity for a custom that is local and, in my view, violates the spirit of the Prophet's teachings about the position of women in Islam.

The Qur'an, which contains numerous prescriptions for everyday issues, is conspicuously silent on the practice of female or male circumcision. There is some doubt whether female circumcision was practiced in pre-Islamic Arabia. If it was prevalent in pre-Islamic Arabia, one would expect a somewhat fuller discussion of this subject, similar to the ones on sexual intercourse (Sura 2:187, 23:10), menstruation (Sura 2:228, 65:4), or breast-feeding and weaning (Sura 2:233, 31:14) in the Qur'an or the hadith and the commentaries of early Muslim scholars. Dr. Said al-Naggar, an Egyptian scholar of the history of the life of the Prophet Muhammad, has not found a single reference on circumcision in his studies.[21] The practice of male circumcision, however, which is universal in Islam, is legitimized by the Qur'anic verse that recommends adherence to the practices of Abraham: "Follow, then, the community of Abraham, a man of pure faith, who was not a polytheist" (Sura 3:95). Although the Qur'an does not mention any specific practices, Abraham's account of his covenant with the Lord and the ritual of male circumcision are acknowledged and accepted by all Muslims.[22] Hence, only the male rite of circumcision, which is thought to originate from Abraham, is documented in the hadith. The Muslim position on this subject was best articulated by Dr. Hassan Hathout when he was at the Faculty of Medicine at the University of Kuwait: "It is incorrect to assert that female circumcision is sunna in Islam. Only male circumcision is sunna in Islam, a tradition taken from the Prophet Abraham which remained and is still performed in Judaism."[23]

How, then, is female circumcision justified by the Muslim groups who sanction it? The justification rests on one oft-quoted hadith of the Prophet to Umm Attiya, a woman of Medina who reportedly circumcised women. The Prophet is alleged to have said, "Reduce but do not destroy; this is enjoyable to the woman and is preferable to the man." Another version of the same hadith reads "Do not go in deep. It is more illuminating to the face and more enjoyable to the husband." This hadith (or its many variations) is not found in Muhammad al-Bukhari, whose collection of the hadith is regarded by most Muslims as the most extensive and the most authentic. It is doubtful whether this hadith, given its several versions, is authentic, This is also a view held by a number of Muslim scholars and clerics.[24] Haifaa Jawad asserts that in the absence of a Qur'anic reference, the hadith is too tenuous and the custom cannot, on this basis, be considered Islamic.[25] Similarly, Imam Deen Warith Mohammed reiterates that the "practice has no Qur'anic base and has no support in Sunnah."[26] Even if

the hadith is authentic, it clearly suggests, as many commentators have realized, an attempt by the Prophet to ameliorate the custom; it explicitly
says that excision should be minimized because it disrupts both male and
female sexual pleasure. Certainly, infibulation and clitoridectomy would
go against the supposed prophetic injunction.

Many commentators have sought to answer the questions: What then
are the conditions that make female circumcision acceptable to the Muslims who practice it? What "Islamic" sanctions do they cite in order to justify it? In the nineteenth century, Richard Burton suggested that the origins
of this practice lay in a domestic dispute in Abraham's household. According to his account, it was Sarah who, in a fit of jealousy, cut off
Hagar's clitoris while she lay asleep. (Hagar is generally referred to as
"the mother of all Muslims" because the mythic origin of the Arabs is
traced through her son Ishmael to Abraham.) God then ordered both Sarah
and Abraham to circumcise themselves.[27] This hypothesis is implausible,
for, if it were true, the custom would have been perpetuated on both Jewish and Muslim men and women. Barbara Stowasser, in her recent book,
has revived the Abrahamic connection and suggests that the religious le-
gitimization of female circumcision may have occurred with Hagar.[28] According to Stowasser, the account of Sarah's jealousy of Hagar prompted
the patriarch Abraham to order Hagar "to pierce her ears and have herself
circumcised." Hence, Hagar, despite her Egyptian origins, was not circumcised prior to joining Abraham's household. Stowasser therefore con-
cludes that female circumcision was introduced into pre-Islamic Arabia by
Hagar. Yet even if one accepts the myth of the Abrahamic origin of the
Arabs, one needs to bear in mind that the place where Hagar and Ishmael
sought refuge was an area near present day Mecca in Saudi Arabia. The
memory of Hagar's attempt to find water for her son by running back and
forth between the hills of Marwa and Safa is commemorated to this day
during the hajj. If Abraham's admonition to Hagar regarding circumcision
was the origin of the practice in certain Muslim populations, then we
should surely expect to find it being practiced in this region, but it is
not reported.

As increasing numbers of Muslim women gain access to both secular
and Qur'anic education, male-dominated interpretations of the Qur'an and
the hadith will be increasingly challenged. According to Mernissi, the original Qur'anic revelation regarding the *hijab* or veil has been interpreted
out of context.[29] In the case of the veil, the only specific recommendation
in the Qur'an, for both men and women, is to dress modestly. However,
the veil, which has its origins in the Byzantine empire, was appropriated
because it fit very well with the patriarchal system. Similarly, the Qur'an
emphasizes chastity for both the sexes. Therefore the religious leaders' es-
pousing the claim that female circumcision is necessary to curtail women's
sexual desire while turning a blind eye to male sexual desire is hypocritical.

As Nawal el Saadawi states succinctly, "female circumcision, like the veil, is a political issue rather than a religious one."[30] Both the veil and female circumcision were accepted and considered to be "Islamic" by certain Muslim groups because the former facilitates the segregation and seclusion of women and the latter ensures virginity by discouraging promiscuity (since infibulation severely narrows the vagina to only allow urination and menstrual flow, penetration during intercourse is very painful).

However, from a medical perspective, circumcision does not ensure virginity. Medically, it is far more difficult to reconstruct the vaginal hymeneal tissue than it is to recircumcise a sexually active woman. The procedure called *adla,* or tightening (also sometimes referred to as *adlat al-rujal* or "recircumcision for man"), is common because it simulates virginity (the vaginal introitus is narrowed, presumably to increase a man's pleasure). Many postpartum women undergo this procedure, as do divorced and widowed women prior to remarriage. Clearly then, the mere narrowing of the vaginal introitus does not guarantee virginity, nor does it discourage promiscuity.

The argument that FGC discourages promiscuity can, in fact, be used against the very premise that it is supposed to protect, as illustrated by O. Koso-Thomas's study in Sierra Leone.[31] She interviewed fifty women who had been sexually active prior to their circumcision and found that most of them had been unable to achieve the level of sexual satisfaction that they had experienced prior to circumcision. This led some to search for a sexually compatible partner, and in the process, many of these women lost their husbands and homes. Ironically, then, the very procedure that is believed to curb promiscuous behavior led to the opposite effect. Another study done among the Ibos of Nigeria reveals that the incidence of premarital coitus is increasing at an equal rate in circumcised and noncircumcised women. U. Megafu speculates that it is probably the influence of Westernization rather than circumcisional status that plays a major role in this change in sexual behavior. The same author reports that clitoridectomy did not diminish a woman's libido, contrary to the widespread belief that excision of the genitalia will suppress a woman's sexual desire.[32] This is only partially true because, in spite of painful intercourse as a result of circumcision, some Sudanese women did report the ability to achieve orgasm.[33] Similarly, a survey of Egyptian women reported that female circumcision did not decrease the women's libido, but it did affect their orgasmic ability.[34] Female circumcision neither curtails desire nor ensures chastity, yet the practice continues.

FGC AND PATRIARCHAL SOCIETIES

The peoples who perpetuate this custom have a number of traits in common: they live in patrilineal, nomadic pastoral, or agro-pastoral societies

in which women have very limited influence. Women are initially economically dependent on their fathers and, after marriage, on their husbands. To challenge such an entrenched custom, a woman would risk os-
tracism and even expulsion from the group; thus, she would need to be
economically independent.

In patrilineal societies, family honor is closely associated with the
(sexual) behavior of the womenfolk. FGC, therefore, may have seemed a
logical way to prevent women from having premarital sex. There is also
the widespread belief that FGC guarantees virginity. FGC would then seem
to be an appropriate measure to control women's sexual behavior. There
is also tremendous societal pressure on the men to marry circumcised
women only, and often the "proof of penetrating the bride" is publicly ver-
ified by the family matriarch's displaying a bloodied bedsheet. Some men
may experience considerable anxiety because intercourse is usually
painful, and sometimes, because penetration is impossible, the woman is
again cut open manually with a knife or blade. In a study done in Sudan,
difficulty of penetration was reported in 66 of the 231 women interviewed.[35] In another study from Sudan, A. A. Shandall studied 300 males
who had two wives each, one infibulated and the other clitoridectomized
or intact. The men unanimously preferred the latter because they could
share sexual gratification with them.[36] In spite of this, not enough men
have spoken up to oppose this custom. Unfortunately, in many of these
rural, patrilineal societies, much of the decisionmaking power rests with
the men, and unless the men can be persuaded about the futility of this
custom, it will continue to persist.

In addition, men in patrilineal societies want to be certain that their
children are indeed fathered by themselves and are not the progeny of their
wives' extramarital lovers. Paternity is a major issue for these groups because of their inheritance laws. Prolonged male absenteeism is another
feature of these pastoral groups. In this case, FGC is like the chastity belts
used in the West when the males were away from their homes for extended
periods of time.

However, even in patriarchal societies, the role of women themselves
in perpetuating traditional customs, be they harmful or benign, cannot be
underestimated. Women are generally considered to be the custodians of
tradition in most cultures. In the case of FGC, it is the women who make
the necessary arrangements for this rite, which is most detrimental to their
health and well-being. Regardless of the explanations offered for the continuation of this practice, it seems paradoxical that women sanction its perpetuation. Their low social status and their need for a larger community
identity over individual survival may explain why this practice has persisted. In the agro-pastoral, patrilineal societies where an individual
woman has virtually no authority, the practice may serve as a "collective
social identity."

SOCIOECONOMIC FACTORS AND FGC

FGC is clearly more prevalent among rural peoples, who tend to be poorer and less educated, than among urban groups. Statistics vary, from 50–70 percent of women in urban areas having been circumcised to 95 percent in the rural areas of Egypt.[37] Urban areas offer greater economic opportunities for women, leading to a decreased dependency on males and therefore a decreased incentive, for themselves or their daughters, to undergo FGC. Also, as women's level of education increases and they gain more economic independence, these practices decline (see Table 3.1). The lower prevalence of FGC—50 percent in urban Egypt compared to 100 percent in Somalia and 90 percent in Sudan, Ethiopia, and Eritrea—can generally be attributed to the higher levels of education and economic stability attained by the Egyptian women. Maternal and infant mortality rates are also higher in these countries because of a number of different obstetric complications that occur in women who have undergone FGC. The figures from Ethiopia and Eritrea may not be reflective of the current situation because there were significant changes during and after the civil war.[38]

FGC AND THE INTERNATIONAL DEBATE

The first discussion of FGC at an international level took place at the NGO forum at the United Nations Mid-Decade Conference for Women. The confrontational interaction between African and Western women revealed a disjunction between the priorities of these two groups as well as between their approaches to the eradication of this custom. The Western women, for

Table 3.1 Female Circumcision, Literacy, and Maternal and Infant Mortality in Selected Countries

	Percentage of Females Circumcised	Percentage of Female Literacy	Female Life Expectancy (male = 100)	Maternal Mortality (per 10,000 births)	Infant Mortality (per 1,000 births)
Somalia	100	6.0	109.1	1,100	215
Sudan	90	15.0	104.0	660	104
Ethiopia and Eritrea	90	46.7	106.8	N.A.	130
Kenya	60	49.0	106.9	170	68
Egypt	50	30.0	105.1	320	61
Nigeria	50	31.0	106.0	800	101
Mauritania	25	N.A.	108.9	N.A.	122
Tanzania	10	31.4	107.7	340	102

Source: Adapted from Minority Rights Group in Dorkenoo and Elworthy, *Female Genital Mutilation,* 22.

the most part, did not exhibit the level of cultural sensitivity conducive to meaningful dialogue. The African women wanted female circumcision to be discussed within the context of the socioeconomic conditions that allow for its perpetuation, not as a sexually repressive practice. Unfortunately, nearly two decades later, very little progress has been attained, which is due in part to differences in the analytical framework of these two groups.

Western analysis is dominated by two divergent approaches. Some anthropologists, not surprisingly, adopt a culturally relativist position and discuss female circumcision within the framework of gender identity and as a rite of passage. This would be a compelling thesis if female circumcision were performed only at puberty. However, this is clearly not the case. There is considerable variation in the age when circumcision occurs, both geographically and ethnically. In some parts of Mali, Mauritania, Nigeria, and Ethiopia, female babies are circumcised right after birth. Given that girls in some tribes, such as the Bambaras of Mali, are circumcised when they are infants, the gender identity framework is of questionable validity. These infants have not had the opportunity to interact with the world at large as members of the female gender. In most parts of Africa, male and female infants are treated equally; the differentiation of roles is not emphasized until puberty.

Viewing female circumcision as a rite of passage into adulthood is equally suspect. In some tribes of Kenya and Tanzania, the women are circumcised just prior to marriage or on their wedding night, whereas in other tribes such as the Gikuyu, it is clearly a prepubertal rite of passage. In some parts of Nigeria, women are not circumcised until they are about to deliver their first child because some tribes believe that the clitoris may actually harm the child as it traverses the birth canal, and it is therefore excised.[39]

Anthropological studies may, nonetheless, be useful in designing strategies for the eradication of female circumcision. Detailed ethnographies can allow for the understanding of this practice within its larger setting. This information can then be useful in devising eradication strategies that are group-specific and culturally sensitive. Fieldwork can also identify the various social forces at play and how they perpetuate this custom. All cultures are dynamic; they respond to external forces and appropriate other customs, cuisines, and vocabulary from those with whom they come into contact. Migration, for example, is already playing a small but serendipitous role in the eradication of female circumcision. Small numbers of Sudanese and Egyptians who have migrated to Saudi Arabia, the Gulf States, and other Muslim countries for economic reasons elect not to circumcise their daughters because they recognize that female circumcision is not integral to their identity as Muslims. Such knowledge may prove to be a powerful disincentive for those who have previously used religious justifications for the practice. The influence that Saudi Arabia exerts in the religious practices on the rest of the Muslim world should not be underestimated.

Another approach advocated by some Western feminists has been ve-
hemently opposed by the Africans. This approach is considered to be too
myopic because it focuses exclusively on sexuality and the sexual oppression of women. Much of their efforts are directed at the elimination of the
practice without trying to understand why the practice exists or if it serves
any function in the indigenous societies. Western critics of this approach
have recognized that the

> resurgence of campaigns to abolish female circumcision is in part an out-
> growth of the general concern about women's health and also of Western
> feminists' concerns with female sexuality. While the former has gener-
> ated an objective, analytical contribution to an understanding of health
> implications of female circumcision, the latter has in some instances
> sensationalized the issue by taking it out of general context of under-
> development and the oppression of women in under-developed societies.[40]

The efforts of the U.S. writer and more recently, filmmaker, Alice
Walker are a case in point.[41] Although well intentioned, her efforts cannot
belie a bias for the agenda of Western feminists. Walker has thrust herself
into the midst of this debate, and her actions have been criticized. Many of
the African women involved in the fight for eradication feel Westerners
have no understanding of the cultural nuances.

Regarding Walker's film *Warrior Marks,* Salem Merkuria, a filmmaker, and Seble Dawit, an Ethiopian human rights lawyer, say, "we do
not believe that force changes traditional habits and practices. Superior
Western attitudes do not enhance dialogue or equal exchange of ideas.
FGM does not exist in a vacuum but as part of a social fabric." Nahid
Toubia, a Sudanese woman surgeon and adviser to the Population Council,
had an even stronger reaction: "*Warrior Marks* is a portrayal by an outsider. . . . I, Alice Walker, save the beautiful children who are being tor-
tured by their own people. It's like saying Harlem women are giving their
children AIDS because they don't love them."[42]

Wilkista Onsando of Maendeleo ya Wanawake, the premier women's
organization of Kenya, states: "Let the indigenous people fight it according to their own traditions. It will die faster than if others tell us what to
do."[43] This has been a recurrent plea from African women to Western
agencies: do not dictate to us, but help us eradicate this practice in a manner that is effective in Africa. In 1979, Atawaif Osman, then the director
of the College of Nursing, Ministry of Education in Khartoum, Sudan,
who has devoted almost her entire life to this issue, declared: "Ultimately,
it is a Sudanese problem, a problem of which we are aware and which
must be solved by us. In every discussion with Sudanese, the importance
of greater literacy is emphasized, especially educational opportunities for
women."[44] This view is shared by a majority of women from the many

different countries. Many African women, including myself, feel there is an excess of sensational journalism regarding this issue and not enough support for ongoing grassroots efforts to eradicate this practice at the local level. The practice of FGC must be seen within the perspective of the tremendous economic hardships and other urgent health problems that exist in these countries. To focus solely on FGC would be counterproductive. Unless the issues of dire poverty, hunger, illiteracy, and unhygienic conditions are addressed and there are simultaneous efforts to advance the status of women through economic and educational means, the impact will be marginal.

There are two factors that will influence the pace of this transformation. First, the changes will occur at a rate that is acceptable to people involved in this process, which may not be the rate desired by outsiders; nonetheless, change will not occur any faster if there is coercion. Second, in attempting to eradicate such a deeply embedded practice, recommending alternative customs is necessary. An example of this would be to substitute a ritual of just nicking the clitoris or labia without excising any tissue. The ideal goal would be total eradication, but perhaps nicking would be a step toward this, recognizing that as more women have access to education and economic independence, that this practice, too, will fall into disfavor. This interim strategy has been advocated by some as a means to gradually phase out the practice.[45] However, the mere consideration of this view at a Seattle hospital serving a sizable Somali immigrant population created considerable controversy.[46] Many Somali and other African women who have undergone FGC and currently reside in the United States may be more receptive to performing only a ritual nicking of the clitoris on their daughters. The Somali women questioned in Seattle stated that this would satisfy their belief system. The transition from infibulation to no procedure is so drastic that few will be comfortable with it.

Symbolic nicking could also be advocated as a substitute procedure in Africa, which would maintain the tradition and the ceremony associated with it to a certain extent and would not jeopardize the health of the individuals involved. Such a transition phase would last, perhaps, one to two generations. Concurrent improvement in the level of education and economic status of the women over this period will eventually lead to a decline in FGC. The three UN agencies currently supporting a global ban against FGC are now cognizant of the fact that it may take three generations to eradicate this practice.[47] A long-term focus on the issue with concomitant change in the position of women and other underlying social factors, although slow, may be the most reliable method. Such slow change is evident in the decline of FGC in Sudan from 96 percent to 89 percent over the past decade. Even more encouraging is the recent trend toward the less severe (sunna, or clitoridectomy type 1) form, rather than infibulation.[48]

FGC AND LEGISLATIVE EFFORTS IN NORTHEAST AFRICA

In northeast Africa, female circumcision is practiced by animists, Muslims, Copts, Catholics, Protestants, and the Falashas (Ethiopian Jews). The most severe forms of FGC are practiced. Yet there are many contradictions. Here we find some of the more innovative approaches to eradication and, in Sudan, the longest history of legislative efforts to eradicate the custom, yet more than 90 percent of the women are circumcised in the most severe form. The initial campaigns in the Sudan to eradicate this practice were introduced by the British governor-general in 1943. This had little effect, so three years later, legislation making infibulation illegal was passed, which was done primarily to discourage the extensive procedure of infibulation in favor of clitoridectomy. The unanticipated consequences of this act were devastating. Many parents, fearing that the practice was about to be outlawed, rushed to have their daughters circumcised prior to the legislation going into effect, which resulted in a significant number of medical complications and deaths. The experience clearly demonstrates the complexity of eradication. Any approach to eradication must not only be multidisciplinary but also culturally sensitive. Previous legislation has been ineffective because it has been perceived as being introduced under Western coercion; legislation enacted in consultation with some of the women's organizations in the respective countries may fare better. It may not propose the drastic changes that some of us in the West desire, but it may be more acceptable to the indigenous peoples and therefore have a greater probability of success.

The eradication effort in Egypt did not fare any better. This custom, which is locally referred to as *khitan*, is deeply ingrained in the Egyptian milieu. After all, it is there that this practice is supposed to have originated. A resolution was passed in 1959 by the People's Assembly stipulating that partial clitoridectomy could be performed only under medical supervision. Thirty-five years later, this issue was still not resolved. In 1994, Ali Abdel-Fattah, minister of health, issued a decree to the effect that the procedure could only be performed by physicians at public hospitals; a significant reversal in the Egyptian government's policy.[49] A number of NGOs successfully filed suit against the minister for reversing the long-standing ban.[50] In the past few decades, as opportunities for Egyptian women have increased, there has occurred a decline in the practice by some of the more educated and affluent segments of the society.

Initially, like Egypt, Somalia started its eradication campaign by encouraging partial clitoridectomy, rather than infibulation, under medical supervision with use of anesthesia and antibiotics (today, all forms of female circumcision are banned). The Somali campaign was innovative because its message focused on the four premises associated with the practice: "it was not healthy, not clean, not Islamic and it did not even guarantee virginity."[51] In Somalia, the impetus to eradicate came from within: it was strongly advocated by the Somali Women's Democratic Organization. The measures advocated included the need for an educational effort throughout the country to present medical facts and reexamine traditional attitudes; cooperation with community leaders (religious leaders, doctors, etc.) to combat this practice; and use of mass media to encourage change and to establish a different relationship between the sexes. Eventually, one of the women leading this campaign and the author of *Sisters in Affliction: Circumcision and Infibulation of Women in Africa*, Raqiya Abdullah, became the deputy minister for health in 1983. The current status of the effort is uncertain because of the political instability after the overthrow of Siad Barre.[52]

The Ethiopian civil war, which ended in 1991, provided a unique opportunity to combat FGC. The Eritrean Peoples Liberation Front maintained the position of forbidding forced marriages and FGC and encouraged a significant number of young women to join its forces. This change in ideology and attitude regarding women's roles resulted in a permanent change in that society. Subsequently, once the civil war was over, these practices were no longer considered to be of any value and were eliminated.

Legislative efforts thus have had limited, if any, success in the eradication of female circumcision in northeast Africa. This is not to state that legislation is ineffectual, but we should be cognizant of its limited impact in the African milieu.

FGC AND LEGISLATIVE EFFORTS IN THE WEST

The recent influx of economic and political refugees from the different African countries to Europe and North America has brought the FGC debate to the West. Several countries have enacted legislation to ban this custom, such as Sweden (1982) and England (1985), and others such as Belgium, France, and the Netherlands have prosecuted the parents and practitioners who circumcise girls. In the United States, then Representative Patricia Schroeder and the Congressional Women's Caucus introduced a bill, with support from the American Medical Association, which made FGC illegal for girls under 18 years of age.[53] The bill also recommended that the Department of Health and Human Services fund programs to educate the immigrant communities that practice this custom about its deleterious effect on the health of the women and its legal ramifications. Representative Schroeder advocated that FGC be treated as a form of child abuse. Whether the legislative ban will be more successful in the West remains to be seen. The possibility that it will drive the practice underground cannot be discounted, nor can the parallel with unsafe abortions be dismissed. There is some anecdotal evidence that those immigrants practicing

FGC may be taking their daughters back to their countries of origin to have the procedures. To ensure compliance with the law, FGC would have to be a "reportable" condition that requires all medical personnel to notify police or social workers. The American Medical Association is currently lobbying state health departments and the Centers for Disease Control to make FGC a reportable condition (in the United States, there exist mandatory requirements for reporting of all cases of child abuse, with penalties for not doing so).[54] Such a step would also make life easier for those immigrants who are opposed to FGC and would provide them with a reasonable justification for avoiding it, that is, that the country of current residence forbids this procedure.

STRATEGIES FOR ERADICATION

Eradication attempts must be cognizant of the views of women affected by FGC as well as those who defend and perpetuate it. Unless we unravel and understand the several threads in the social fabric within which this practice exists, our probability of success in eradication will be fairly small. The role of legislation at both the national and international level, directed at the countries where the practice is prevalent, has been marginal. More often than not, legislative efforts have been viewed as neocolonialist or imperialist in inspiration. Experience has shown that attempts to outlaw the practice in isolation from its complex sociocultural milieu have only resulted in the exacerbation of practice. It is also essential that if legislation is to be enacted, cultural sensitivities must be respected. For example, to refer to the practice as a form of child abuse in Africa would only meet with resistance. Although it is true that it causes pain and a myriad of other problems, no mother subjects her child to this procedure with the clear intent of causing harm. Labeling the practice as child abuse is judgmental and rooted in cultural hegemonism. It reveals ignorance and a lack of understanding of the complexities of this debate. Such rhetoric ultimately impedes the process of transformation.

Recent efforts by international agencies such as the International Monetary Fund (IMF) and the World Bank to link economic aid programs with a national commitment to eradicate this custom, as in the case of Burkina Faso, have not been in existence long enough to assess their impact. It is possible that such external pressures applied to governments, particularly if these measures have been requested by some groups within that country, will be successful.[55] Many women's groups in Africa support such a strategy and find it preferable to the argument that FGC is child abuse and a violation of human rights.[56] However, such a strategy may be viewed as coercive, with economic aid as a reward for compliance.

In my view, if FGC were to be presented as a violation of the right to good health and be included under the broad umbrella of immunization and nutrition efforts, the chances for the eradication of FGC would be increased. This would be a persuasive argument because Article 15 of the UN's Universal Declaration of Human Rights states, "Everyone has the right to a standard of living adequate for the health and well-being of himself" and "Motherhood and childhood are entitled to special care and assistance." Similar articles are included in the Banjul Charter on Human and Peoples Rights, which was unanimously adopted by the Assembly of Heads of State and Government of the Organization of African Unity (OAU) and has been ratified by most of the African nations. Eradication attempts within this framework can then be represented as enforcement of African concerns. Most recently, three UN agencies, the United Nations Children's Fund (UNICEF), the United Nations Development Programme (UNDP), and the World Health Organization (WHO), will direct a joint, multidisciplinary plan to educate about and ultimately eradicate this practice.[57] These agencies will publicize the deleterious consequences of FGC and will target medical personnel, traditional healers, religious leaders, politicians, and at the local level, village elders and other leaders.

A number of African women, including Marie Assad, Asma El Dareer, and Edna Ismail, and the United Nations Working Group on Traditional Practices Affecting the Health of Women and Children have also recommended a multidisciplinary approach that includes education, health and family planning services, and vocational training programs designed for women. Both men and women need to be educated because in most parts of Africa, marriage is still vital to a woman's social status and survival. Unless the men in these cultures are sensitized to marrying uncircumcised women, these women will be ostracized and considered "unmarriageable." Men must be made to understand that these procedures do not ensure a woman's virginity and have a deleterious affect on fertility. The most compelling data regarding infertility come from Sudan. Approximately 20–25 percent of infertility in Sudan is secondary to chronic pelvic and tubal infections, a direct consequence of infibulation.[58]

In many of these societies, it is a stigma to be barren. It is therefore ironic that a practice that is supposed to enhance the fertility of women actually renders them sterile. Childbearing and motherhood are the primary functions afforded to women in these patriarchal cultures. Those unable to conceive are often considered to be deviant, and barren women will often seek to be labeled as *mazurin,* or possessed by spirits, to have their childlessness legitimized.[59] Infertility as a consequence of FGC should be emphasized in all the educational campaigns. This would be in keeping with the sentiment expressed in the Banjul Charter regarding the right of every woman and child to healthy development.

Many of the studies have focused on the medical complications from FGC, but the demographic consequences of this practice have not yet been adequately addressed. High infant and child mortality is a consequence of FGC. Somalia has the fourth-highest infant mortality rate in the world, and we may seek additional insight there. Omar Mohamud's study of female circumcision and its demographic consequences is the first to demonstrate these findings.[60] The two results of this study were that infant mortality is higher with infibulation and that there is an excess of female child mortality; both of these events can be related to FGC. Women who have been infibulated experience very prolonged and difficult labor because of the inelastic scar tissue resulting from the procedure. According to UNICEF and data from the Somali Ministry of Planning, Somali women routinely reduce their food intake in the third trimester of their pregnancy to prevent the baby from gaining weight. Although this facilitates their labor, it leads to infants of low birth weight in whom the mortality is extremely high. The prolonged labor also results in fetal hypoxia and stillbirths, and the lack of the protective labia predisposes them to increased infections, which are associated with premature labor. An excess of female child mortality was also noted in the 5- to 15-year-old age interval, which corresponds with the age when FGC is performed. One may then postulate that high female child mortality occurs in all countries that practice FGC. Gender-specific child mortality data should be utilized to facilitate the eradication effort, both by the respective governments and Western donor nations.

Women who perform circumcisions not only need to be educated about the subsequent health hazards but also must be retrained for other skills. Several studies have documented the position of authority and the social status enjoyed by these women in their societies.[61] The procedures also provide a significant source of income. It is therefore unlikely that these women will relinquish their status and income without adequate compensation. The model of a community health worker, generally a woman, has been successful in many developing countries. These women, who also at times function as traditional birth attendants, can conceivably have their roles broadened to include performing basic first aid, monitoring the growth of children, and encouraging immunizations and family planning. Ensuring an alternative means of earning their livelihood will be paramount in gaining their cooperation in efforts toward the eradication of FGC. Government subsidies in the form of training and direct remuneration (which may be more lucrative) may entice at least some of these women to abandon their profession. Western aid agencies can play a pivotal role here in funding some of these programs and ensuring their continued operation until the custom has declined substantially.

CONCLUSION

The complexity of the issue of FGC demands not only an understanding of the custom within the societies that practice it but also a willingness to compromise with these societies. FGC has been the norm for several hundred if not several thousand years. The West has stepped into this milieu only in the last century and initially with a judgmental and colonial attitude; such attitudes are surprisingly prevalent even today. A review of the nomenclature is illustrative: "female circumcision," which is the collective term for both clitoridectomy and infibulation, was abandoned by feminists for the more graphic and subjective "female genital mutilation." This term has now fallen into disfavor, and such nonjudgmental terms as "female genital cutting" or "female genital operations" are the preferred terminology. Perhaps this subtle change in nomenclature is associated with a change in the attitude of individuals involved in this debate. It is now recognized by both Western and non-Western institutions that the progress in this arena will be gradual. The previous approach toward eradication of FGC was analogous to the medical model for the eradication of smallpox—namely, we must eradicate the "disease"—and this had very limited success. The "social problem" approach has not fared any better. Condemnation of the practice by international and local organizations failed to discourage the abandonment of the custom, for it is difficult to abolish a practice that is not perceived as being harmful either to the individual or the society. A gradual transformation of the practice and the sociocultural environment in which it exists seems the most feasible eradication strategy.

Slow change may not be consistent with the goals of many Western agencies that advocate immediate eradication. But given the limited effect of earlier strategies, there is an urgent need to identify interventions that are most likely to succeed in the cultures that practice FGC. A multidisciplinary approach that promotes awareness about the health consequences (high maternal and infant mortality, infertility, and increased genitourinary problems) and increases education and economic opportunities for women is more likely to be effective. International agencies such as IMF and World Bank can be instrumental in the implementation of programs based on this approach.

Finally, religious and charismatic leaders who reflect the diverse religious, ethnic, and cultural backgrounds of the countries in which FGC is practiced can play a substantial role. One example is Shaykh Abdel Ghaffar Mansour from al-Azhar University, the oldest institution of religious and secular learning in the Islamic world. At the UN population conference held in Cairo he stated that FGC should be discontinued in the name of humanity.[62] Such leadership must convince the ulema who do not subscribe to this view of the facts that these practices are not the norm in Saudi Arabia and are not mentioned in the scriptures. Leaders should not hesitate to declare a jihad on this practice, which causes bodily and psychic trauma to half of their population. Finally, the entire society needs to understand that premarital chastity is not a physical but a moral issue and that life-threatening, at times fatal procedures performed under unhygienic conditions do not curb promiscuity or ensure virginity.

NOTES

1. As an African, I prefer the term "female genital cutting" (FGC) to the term "female genital mutilation" (FGM) because I find FGM to be derogatory and culture laden. The term "female circumcision" is too euphemistic for the extensive procedure that is often the norm in northeast Africa. "Female genital operations" (FGOs) has also been used, but as a physician, I feel that this is a misnomer because it implies a surgical quality that is clearly not present in a majority of the procedures.

2. Patricia Schroeder, "Female Genital Mutilation—A Form of Child Abuse," *New England Journal of Medicine*, 331, no. 11 (1994), 739–740; Kay Boulware-Miller, "Female Circumcision: Challenges to the Practice as a Human Rights Violation," *Harvard Women's Law Journal* 8 (1985), 170.

3. Lawrence P. Cutner, "Female Genital Mutilation," *Obstetrical and Gynecological Survey* 40 (1985), 438.

4. Ibid.

5. Esther K. Hicks, *Infibulation: Female Genital Mutilation in Islamic Northeastern Africa*, revised and expanded edition (New Brunswick, NJ: Transaction Publishers, 1996).

6. Sue Armstrong, "Female Circumcision: Fighting a Cruel Tradition," *New Scientist*, February 2, 1991; Dina Ezzat, "A Savage Surgery," *The Middle East*, January 1994; "Genital Mutilation: Stop the Butchering," *The Arizona Republic*, April 4, 1994; David Kaplan, "Is It Torture or Tradition?" *Newsweek*, December 20, 1993.

7. Hanny Lightfoot-Klein, *Prisoners of Ritual* (London: Haworth Press, 1989), 27.

8. I. R. Sami, "Female Circumcision with Special Reference to the Sudan," *Annals of Tropical Pediatrics*, 6 (1986), 100.

9. Report issued by joint WHO/FIGO Task Force, *European Journal of Obstetrics and Gynecology and Reproductive Biology* 45 (1992), 153–154.

10. "Female Genital Mutilation in Egypt," *Huqooq Al Insaan* (April 1995), 15.

11. Jomo Kenyatta, *Facing Mount Kenya* (London: Vintage, 1965), 125–148.

12. Hicks, *Infibulation*, 27.

13. G. J. Barker-Benfield, *The Horrors of the Half-Known Life: Male Attitudes Towards Women and Sexuality in Nineteenth Century America* (New York: Harper and Row, 1976), cited in Alison Slack, "Female Circumcision: A Critical Appraisal," *Human Rights Quarterly*, 10 (1988), 437–486.

14. V. Bullough and B. Bullough, *Sin, Sickness and Sanity: A History of Sexual Attitudes* (New York: New American Library, 1977), cited in Hanny Lightfoot-Klein, *Prisoners and Ritual* (London: Haworth, 1989), 180.

15. Cutner, "Female Genital Mutilation," 438.

16. "Female Genital Mutilation in Egypt," 15.

17. "Lawsuit Against the Grand Imam of Al Azhar," *Huqooq Al Insaan* (April 1995), 13.

18. Marie B. Assad, "Female Circumcision in Egypt: Social Implications, Current Research, and Prospects for Change," *Studies in Family Planning*, 11 (1980).

19. Fazlur Rahman, *Health and Medicine in the Islamic Tradition* (New York: Crossroad Publishing, 1989), 121.

20. Soheir A. Morsy, "Sex Differences and Folk Illness in an Egyptian Village," in *Women in the Muslim World,* ed. Lois Beck and Nikki Keddie (Cambridge: Harvard University Press, 1980), 611.

21. Ezzat, "Savage Surgery," 36.

22. Yahya Cohen, "Circumcision: Myth, Ritual, Operation," *Medical Journal of Malaysia,* 39 (1985), 213.

23. Efua Dorkenoo and Scilla Elworthy, *Female Genital Mutilation: Proposals for Change* (London: Minority Rights Group, 1992), 75.

24. The text of this hadith, in Ibn Dawud, *Kitab al-Adab,* Bab 45, hadith no. 4587, is "Sulayman b. al-Rahman al-Dimashqi and 'Abd al-Wahhab b. 'Abd al-Rahim al-Ashja'i told us: Marwan told us: Muhammad b. Hasan told us: 'Abd al-Wahhab al-Kufi said, from 'Abd al-Malik b. 'Umayr, from Umm 'Atiyya al-Ansari that a woman used to circumcise in Madina and the Prophet said to her: Do not be too vigorous as this is more enjoyable for the woman and more desirable to the husband. Ibn Dawud said: it is transmitted from 'Ubayd al-Allah b. 'Amr from 'Abd al-Malik with the same meaning and his (own) *isnad*. Ibn Dawud said: it is not a sound Hadith and it has been transmitted as *mursal* (missing the companion in the *isnad*). Ibn Dawud said: Muhammad b. Hasan is unknown and this Hadith is weak." I thank Whitney Bodman for this reference.

25. Haifaa Jawad, "Female Circumcision: Cultural Necessity or Religious Obligation?" *The American Journal of Islamic Social Sciences,* 11 (1994), 598.

26. Zakiyyah Muhammad, quoting Imam Warith Deen Muhammad in "Female Circumcision, or Let Us 'Purify' Women," *Islam in America* (fall 1994), 36.

27. Sir Richard Burton, *Personal Narrative of a Pilgrimage to Al-Madinah and Meccah* (New York: Dover Publications, 1964), vol. 2:19.

28. Barbara Stowasser, *Women in the Qur'an: Traditions and Interpretation* (New York: Oxford University Press, 1994), 147.

29. Fatima Mernissi, *The Veil and the Male Elite: A Feminist Interpretation of Women's Rights in Islam,* trans. Mary J. Lakeland (Reading, MA: Addison-Wesley, 1991), 85.

30. Nawal El Saadawi, cited in George Graham's article, "Pledge over Female Mutilation: World Bank and IMF Win Commitment by Burkina Faso," *Financial Times,* April 22, 1994.

31. O. Koso-Thomas, *The Circumcision of Women: A Strategy for Eradication* (London: Zed Books, 1987).

32. U. Megafu, "Female Ritual Circumcision in Africa: An Investigation of the Presumed Benefits Among Ibos of Nigeria," *East African Medical Journal* 40 (1983), 11.

33. Lightfoot-Klein, *Prisoners of Ritual,* 347.

34. M. Karim and R. Ammar, *Female Circumcision and Sexual Desire* (Cairo: Ain Shams University Press, 1985), cited in Hanny Lightfoot-Klein, *Prisoners of Ritual* (London: Haworth, 1989), 41.

35. Asma El Dareer, "Complications of Female Circumcision in the Sudan," *Tropical Doctor,* 13 (1983), 133.

36. A. A. Shandall, cited in Lightfoot-Klein, *Prisoners of Ritual,* 97.

37. "Female Genital Mutilation in Egypt," *Huqooq Al Insaan,* 4.

38. Figures for this table are from Dorkenoo and Elworthy, *Female Genital Mutilation,* 22.

39. Robert A. Myers, F. I. Omorodion, A. E. Isenabemhe, and G. I. Akenzua, "Circumcision: Its Nature and Practice Among Some Ethnic Groups in Southern Nigeria," *Social Science Medicine,* 21 (1985), 584.

40. B. Giorgis, *Female Circumcision in Africa* (U.S. Economic Commission for Africa, African Training and Research Center for Women, Addis Ababa, Ethiopia, 1981), 7, quoted in Esther K. Hicks, *Infibulation: Female Genital Mutilation in Islamic Northeastern Africa,* revised and expanded edition (New Brunswick, NJ: Transaction Publishers, 1996), 193.

41. Alice Walker, *Possessing the Secret of Joy* (Pocket Star Books, 1993); A. Walker and P. Parmar, *Warrior Marks: Female Genital Mutilation and the Sexual Binding of Women* (New York: Harcourt Brace, 1992).

42. David Kaplan, "Is It Torture or Tradition?" 124.

43. Ibid.

44. Dorkenoo and Elworthy, *Female Genital Mutilation,* 29.

45. Some commentators have drawn an analogy between slavery and FGC, arguing that just as slavery was a reprehensible practice and it would have been outrageous to suggest an alternative to its outright abolition, such an approach should also be rejected for FGC. This analogy is inapplicable here because slavery subjugates one group to another against their will, which is not the case for FGC. These procedures are uniformly carried out by women, regardless of the diversity of the groups that they occur in, with the consent, approval, and participation of the mothers of the female children.

46. Carol M. Ostrom, "Doctors at Seattle Hospital Consider Circumcising Muslim Girls," *News and Observer* (Raleigh, NC), September 29, 1996, 30A.

47. "Three UN Agencies Call for an End to Female Genital Cutting," *Boston Globe,* April 10, 1997, A29.

48. Celia W. Dugger, "Genital Cutting Embraced as a Rite of Passage in Some Cultures," *News and Observer* (Raleigh, NC), October 6, 1996, 21A.

49. "Female Genital Mutilation in Egypt," *Huqooq Al Insaan,* 15.

50. "Egypt Again Restricts Female Circumcisions," *News and Observer,* December 30, 1995, 11A. The remarks of Hassan al-Kallah, undersecretary of health, are pertinent: "People misunderstood us. They thought we are supporting the operation which is not true. We are against it, but we could not change the traditions of the society overnight. We are being attacked by people who did not understand Egyptian culture."

51. Dorkenoo and Elworthy, *Female Genital Mutilation,* 31.

52. Ibid.

53. Patricia Schroeder, "Female Genital Mutilation."

54. Christina Kent, "AMA Efforts Advance Ban on Female Circumcision: Culturally Sensitive Public Education Urged," *American Medical News,* October 28, 1996, 40.

55. The threat of the withdrawal of U.S. aid is thought to be a primary reason for the Egyptian government's reversal of allowing FGC to be performed in government hospitals ("Egypt Again Restricts Female Circumcisions," *News and Observer*).

56. There have been several attempts to view FGC as a violation of human rights in general and children's rights in particular. Even Efua Dorkenoo, the most outspoken African opponent of FGC, recognizes FGC does not neatly fit into the category of torture. It happens at home, is condoned by the family and community, and is culturally accepted. In a human rights context, it cannot be viewed as torture by authorities in power but only as citizen upon citizen abuse. See Efua Dorkenoo, *Cutting the Rose: Female Genital Mutilation, The Practice and Its Prevention* (London: Minority Rights Group, 1994), 70, quoted in Esther K. Hicks, *Infibulation: Female Genital Mutilation in Islamic Northeastern Africa,* revised and expanded edition (New Brunswick, NJ: Transaction Publishers, 1996), 3.

57. "Three UN Agencies," *Boston Globe,* A29.

58. *WHO Chronicle*, 40 (1986), 32.

59. Soheir A. Morsy, "Sex Differences," 602.

60. Omar A. Mohamud, "Female Circumcision and Child Mortality in Urban Somalia," *Genus* 47 (1991), 203–222.

61. Pamela Constantinides, cited in Slack, "Female Circumcision: A Critical Appraisal," 442.

62. Shaykh Abdel Ghaffar Mansour, cited in Barbara Crossette, "In Cairo, Please to Stop Maiming Girls," *New York Times*, September 11, 1994.

4

Cultural Diversity Within Islam: Veils and Laws in Tunisia

M. M. Charrad

Islam as culture worldwide offers both similarities and elements of diversity. With respect to gender, scholars have emphasized similarities. A trend in the scholarship on the Middle East and North Africa has uncovered the gender ideology of the major original texts of Islam.[1] This is an important side of the issue, because the texts, however open to diverse interpretations, have provided a common element throughout the Islamic world. It is only one side of the issue, however. We must remember that Islam has intermingled with many other factors such as local custom, politics, economics and historical conjuncture to shape the status of women in different ways in different times and places.[2]

Should one overlook the diversity within the Islamic world, one runs the risk of sliding toward a monolithic, essentialist, and static conceptualization of Islam. In his powerful critique of Orientalism, Edward Said has shown the intellectual shortcomings and political underpinnings of viewing Islam as timeless and monolithic.[3] The view leads to what Victoria Bernal has appropriately labeled Islamic determinism in the analysis of gender in the Islamic world.[4] Treating Islamic culture as frozen in place obscures the processes by which gender is historically, socially and politically constructed. It fails to locate Islamic societies within their proper historical and geographic context, and it ignores the particularities of time and place central to the making of culture.

As do other world cultures, Islam provides a general framework with a range of options for action. Within that framework, groups and individuals negotiate practices and symbols while engaging in social action and ongoing struggles. They may use the symbols in various ways at different times in constructing strategies of action. In the Islamic world, as in other cultural worlds, culture is best conceptualized as providing flexibility in how actors use any given symbol.[5] In this perspective, free-choosing, autonomous agents do not create cultural practices and symbols at will. Nor do rigid, frozen-in-place cultural values predefine the meaning of symbols for all times.[6] To use Ann Swidler's formulation, sociologists thus face the task not so much "to estimate how much culture shapes action" but to analyze "how culture is used by actors."[7] Whatever social actors we take—individuals, social groups, or nation-states—we find that units that share in the broader culture of Islam have developed very different cultural conceptions of gender.

In this chapter I aim to broaden the discussion on gender in the Islamic world by highlighting the diversity of meanings and symbols. I focus on Tunisia, considering it as an example of an Islamic country that exhibits elements of cultural diversity within Islam, and within that framework I analyze the veil and family law. These two issues have given rise to a wide range of interpretations and to a confrontation over cultural models within Islam. In Tunisia, as in other Islamic countries, the veil and family law in effect have occupied center stage in struggles over culture. Individual women confront the meaning of the veil in their own lives and grapple with sometimes difficult choices. In devising a family law, states make policies that mediate the interpretation of Islam. The Tunisian state has taken the lead among Arab-Islamic countries with respect to family law. It has made liberal reforms that expand women's rights. In so doing, it has provided an instance of diversity in state actions in the Islamic world.

The chapter is organized in two parts. Taking the individual as the unit of analysis, in the first part I examine the multiple meanings of the veil in women's lives. Turning to the state as the unit of analysis, in the second part I explore the cultural and social implications of the liberal family law reforms made by the Tunisian state.

A few words on the characteristics of Tunisia should help place it in the broader geographical and historical context of the Islamic world. A small country of 8.7 million people,[8] Tunisia is a republic. Colonized by France in 1881, it became a sovereign nation-state in 1956. Culturally and linguistically, Tunisia shares much with Algeria and Morocco, which were also colonized by France. Often perceived by Western powers as an island of stability in an unstable region, Tunisia is lodged between Algeria to the west and Libya to the east. Tunisians speak Arabic, and most of the educated population also knows French; Tunisian schools teach both languages. With an insignificant amount of oil, the economy is based in large part on agricultural products combined with increasingly successful industrial and manufacturing development in recent years.[9]

INDIVIDUALS AND MULTIPLE MEANINGS: THE VEIL

Veiling is best understood as an issue at the intersection of global culture, the quest for individual identity, and modern politics. To most people, the veil worn by women in the Islamic Middle East evokes images of passivity and subordination. It traditionally has been associated with notions of restriction, oppression, patriarchy, and confinement to female space. These associations hold much truth, and the literature on gender in the Middle East thus has understandably emphasized the symbolism of subordination.[10] Yet the veil has at times taken a very different meaning. It also has meant resistance, protest, empowerment, and entry into male space. The greater complexity of the veil appears when one sees it as part of individual efforts to construct personal identities within the broader cultural and political environment.

Struggles over cultural identification in the Middle East in recent years have involved the veil as a powerful political symbol. The burning issue at the center of the struggles has been posed in terms of identification with the West, or with an Islam true to its origins, or with other potential cultural alternatives in the making. As a result, in deciding whether or not to wear a veil today, women are not simply selecting a form of dress. A web of pressures and political symbolism surrounds the question of veiling.

Islamists, as Islamic fundamentalists are called in North Africa, have insisted that women are obliged to wear a veil. For example, an Islamist leader expressed the significance of veiling as a political statement in the turmoil of Algerian politics. In an appeal to Algerian women, he said that it was high time for them to wear the veil and stop "looking like cheap merchandise that can be bought and sold."[11] Although Tunisia has been spared the bloody divisions that have torn apart Algeria, the tide of Islamism has touched Tunisian shores. The growth of the Islamist movement has posed new challenges and elicited a range of cultural responses. Thus the richness of meanings connected to veiling finds its roots in the complex forces at work in contemporary struggles over cultural identification.

Two Kinds of Veil

Let us note at the outset that many Tunisian women do not wear a veil. Among those who do, there are two very different kinds of veil. The English term "veil" can be translated as either *safsari* or *hijab* in Tunisian Arabic. Women have worn the safsari, or traditional veil, for centuries. An all-white rectangular cloth, the safsari wraps around the body and covers it from head to toe. Influenced by local custom and history, it varies by region; there are many differences in the way of draping the cloth of a safsari around the body. To an outside observer, the differences may appear subtle or nonexistent. Many people in Tunisia claim, however, that they can recognize the region to which a woman belongs by the way she drapes her safsari.

In contrast, the hijab first appeared in the streets of Tunis in the 1970s and in large numbers in the 1980s. Literally, hijab means "protection" or "protector." A long scarf, often white or in austere colors, the hijab covers the head and shoulders. Women usually wear it over a long robe that leaves only the hands uncovered. The hijab looks basically the same throughout the Middle East, with small variations depending on income level or personal taste.

Women from a wide range of socioeconomic backgrounds wear a hijab: some are highly educated and have professional occupations. During visits to Tunisia, I saw women in hijabs studying at the university and receiving clients in law firms, coming out of factories in industrial suburbs of Tunis, and shopping in exclusive stores in the city. Women in hijabs live in wealthy and in poor neighborhoods. They drive cars, and some wear the long scarf over a dark and loose sweatsuit when jogging on the beach. In contrast, I have not seen women in a safsari work as lawyers, drive cars, or jog on the beach.

Apart from the fact that both are meant to hide the body, the safsari and the hijab represent very different forms of dress. They require different skills on the part of the wearer. Wearing a safsari requires the appropriate set of habits of the kind usually learned at a young age. It takes a long time to feel comfortable in it and to master the intricate ways in which it must be draped. To wear a safsari, one must belong to the cultural world in which safsaris are part of everyday life. For example, when a foreign woman visiting Tunisia plays at wearing a safsari, the game is obvious to all. She lacks the necessary cultural capital, in particular the proper body movement when walking. She also lacks the proper way of holding the safsari with one hand while doing something else with the other. In contrast, anyone may quickly learn to wear a hijab, and a woman can easily switch to it either from Western clothes or from the safsari. As a form of dress, the hijab lends itself to choice in a way that the safsari does not.

At present, it is the hijab, not the safsari, that carries a loaded political meaning. In the past, during the colonial period, the safsari did serve as a political symbol. While Tunisians were fighting against French colonial rule and especially at the height of the nationalist struggle from the 1930s to the 1950s, the safsari symbolized Tunisian cultural identity and separateness from the French. Since Tunisia became independent from French rule in 1956, however, the safsari has lost the political symbolism that it once had. Today, women usually wear the safsari because of tradition, as their ancestors did and without giving it any particular political meaning. It is now the hijab that constitutes a political statement. Depending on the particular context, it evokes a range of meanings from attachment to Islam as religion to identification with Islamism as a militant political movement. It is the potential identification with Islamism that makes the hijab a highly charged political symbol.

Reasons for Wearing a Hijab

In individual lives, the meaning of the hijab ranges from a form of empowerment for the woman choosing to wear it to a means of seclusion and containment imposed by others.[12] Even though some of the women are likely to succumb to pressures from others in putting on the hijab, other women put it on as a personal decision. Not all, but clearly some women in hijabs in Tunisia are in a position to make choices about the symbolism of their own appearance. In some cases, adoption of the hijab means that the woman has chosen to join the Islamist movement, or that Islamist relatives have coerced her into wearing it. Although little information is available about Islamist organizations, it is known among informed circles in Tunisia that the organizations include women. The hijab does not, however, necessarily imply a woman's participation in the movement as an active militant or even as a sympathizer.

The hijab may carry several other, more diffuse, meanings. For example, putting on a hijab may be a way of participating in a sphere of solidarity or may imply membership in a moral community of Muslims sharing a broadly defined cultural legacy. It may mean a rejection of the modern or Western world because that world has been found morally corrupt or wanting in some other respects. It may be a way of finding a safe place in a men's space by tracing clear sexual boundaries that men are not to cross or a shield under which women take on daring social roles. Or still, the hijab may be imposed by male relatives who want women to respect norms of modesty, without necessarily wanting them to participate in the political symbolism of militant Islamism. A female university student confirms the last reason: "When I wear the hijab, I get along better with my father. He trusts me more. Since I started wearing it, our endless fights about my whereabouts have came to a stop."[13]

Other women wear hijabs as a form of protection. A woman lawyer states: "When I wear a hijab, men in the street leave me alone. I can go out and do what I have to do more comfortably. The hijab gives a message to men. It tells them that a woman is not sexually available." And a produce stand attendant in a poor neighborhood declares: "To be on good terms with customers and because I don't want to be bothered by anyone, I wear the hijab." Finally, a woman who has a college degree and works as an administrator indicates that she made the choice to wear a hijab on her own. She says: "My choice is dictated by my conviction that I belong to a great and beautiful civilization with deep roots and a set of norms. It is this set of norms that I have adopted."[14]

The passions of struggles over cultural identification generate a delicate situation in which women have to negotiate their own identity. Tunisian women who wish to express an Islamic but not Islamist identity face a problem with no straightforward solution. ("Islamic" as used here refers to Islam as a world culture offering flexibility of interpretation, whereas "Islamist" refers to Islamic fundamentalism.) As a society in search of cultural identification, Tunisia offers few models with respect to women's appearance. In the last few years, some women have abandoned the hijab and taken on the traditional safsari, precisely to avoid identification with the Islamist movement. In other cases, the hijab provides a substitute for the traditional safsari, and a more practical one. Lighter and smaller than a safsari, the hijab has become the easiest form of dress for women who are not interested in adopting Western clothes.[15]

A Tunisian woman explains the dilemma:

> I have nothing to do with the political Islamists. It is true we wear the same kind of clothing. The traditional veil [safsari] is much more complicated to wear [than the hijab]. My father has accepted that I work outside the home under the condition that I wear a veil. My mother wears the safsari, so does my sister. We are a conservative family and women always go out veiled. . . . I don't see myself going to work with a safsari. The Women's Union should help us find a form of dress that differentiates us from those women who are involved in politics.[16]

By the "Women's Union," the woman making the statement refers to the National Union of Tunisian Women, a nationwide and government-affiliated women's organization. By "women involved in politics," she refers to Islamic fundamentalists. This woman offers an example of the apolitical choice sometimes involved in putting on the hijab.

A consideration of the struggles and choices surrounding the veil provides a window into the multiple messages that women give in wearing it. The veil has served as a potent political symbol, associated in particular with militant Islamism. In their everyday lives, however, Tunisian women have refused to let the hijab become exclusively an Islamist symbol. Many women have redefined it in ways that fit their own purposes, thus generating new cultural meanings that reflect the diversity prevalent in individual behavior under the umbrella of Islam. The diversity within Islam applies also to larger social units. In a similar way, states have taken actions that offer new models. We now turn to an examination of the family law policy adopted by the Tunisian state and to its implications for cultural models of gender.

THE STATE AND A DIFFERENT MODEL: FAMILY LAW

Family law represents an issue as divisive as the veil in the Islamic Middle East. It too has raised controversy about cultural identification. Islamists have preached a return to Islamic family law as rigidly interpreted in the original texts of the Shari'a. Others—women's rights advocates, human rights advocates, liberals, and democrats—have argued for reforms that alleviate the subordination of women sanctioned by conservative interpretations of the Shari'a. Since the law of a country defines behavioral norms for the entire population, the confrontation over kinds of law involves high stakes. In effect it comes down to a conflict over different cultural models within Islam.

In order to understand the discourse involved in conflicts taking place in the Middle East, let us keep in mind that different groups throw criticism at each other by accusing the other of "not being Islamic," of "not being truly Islamic," or of "distorting Islam." The definition of what is and is not Islamic varies greatly, depending on the political actors involved. There is no accepted and objective criterion to resolve the controversy over definitions, since cultural labels themselves are politically constructed. Both models, Islamist and reformist, are Islamic insofar as they draw on the Islamic tradition. The Islamist model increases women's subordination in claiming to return to rigidly understood patriarchal origins. Also placing itself within an Islamic framework, the reformist model decreases women's subordination in treating Islam as a dynamic civilization, able to adapt to changing conditions.

The Islamic revival of the past two decades has heightened the political significance of family law, which historically has been a feature of the Islamic world. As is dramatized by the Iranian revolution of 1979, the revival has been directed at personal as well as national issues.[17] It touches not only politics or the economy but also matters of individual conduct and family life. One should perhaps say that the revival touches especially matters of individual conduct and family life, since militant Islam very much preoccupies itself with these issues.

Reforms Within Islam

Taking the lead in the Arab-Islamic world, the Tunisian state has made liberal reforms in family law. Other countries, except Turkey (Islamic but not Arab), have taken more timid steps in that direction.[18] Many countries continue to apply conservative interpretations of the Shari'a, in some cases barely modified for several centuries.[19] In contrast, at the end of French colonial rule in 1956, the newly formed Tunisian state promulgated the *Code of Personal Status*, a major reform of family law.[20] A female member of the Tunisian League of Human Rights declared: "The Code of Personal Status is [Tunisia's] most beautiful accomplishment since independence [from French rule]."[21] In making the statement, she spoke the thoughts of most educated Tunisian women, who take immense pride in the code.

A key aspect of the Tunisian reforms has to do with timing. Tunisia reformed its family law in 1956, in a context very different from the current one, when militant Islam did not exist as an organized national or transnational movement. Additional reforms of family law occurred later, in the early 1980s and 1990s. They consisted in amendments to the initial code of 1956, which was the crucial reform. Had the initial step not been taken in 1956, it is doubtful whether it could have been taken later on.

The code, with its amendments, alters regulations on marriage, divorce, alimony, custody, adoption, filiation, and to a much lesser extent, inheritance. It leaves few, if any, aspects of family life untouched. The new laws give women greater rights in that they increase the range of options available to them in their personal lives and protect them from the most obvious forms of subordination. Most notably, the new laws abolish polygyny, or the right of a man to have as many as four wives. They also abolish repudiation, or the unilateral right of the husband to terminate a marriage at will without court proceedings. Instead, the code requires court proceedings and gives men and women equal rights in filing for divorce. Among other dispositions, the code raises the age at marriage (seventeen for women and twenty for men) as a measure against child marriage. It also improves women's chances to obtain custody of children after divorce.

Opponents of the code have read it as the introduction of secular norms into the legal system. Yet this is not the spirit in which the reforms were initiated. The Tunisian government of 1956 unambiguously described the reforms as Islamic in nature. Members of the government presented the code as the outcome of a new phase in Islamic thinking (*ijtihad*), similar to earlier phases of interpretation that have marked the history of Islamic legal thought. This contrasts with the reforms made in Turkey, where the government of Kemal Ataturk abandoned Islamic law altogether and replaced it with the Swiss code. In Tunisia, the policymakers emphasized the continuing faithfulness of the law to the Islamic heritage. Supporters of the code agree with this interpretation.[22]

The occurrence of the Tunisian reforms raises two major issues: the reasons for the reforms and their implications. The first question is beyond the scope of this chapter and is addressed elsewhere.[23] Suffice it to indicate briefly here that the beginnings of an answer reside in the particular historical conditions of the Tunisian state in 1956, following the end of colonization. The newly formed national state was able to make radical reforms because a modernizing faction faced no political challenger at the critical moment when it took the reins of power in 1956. Defeated in factional conflicts on the eve of independence from French rule, the political groups that could have spoken for a conservative interpretation of Islamic law and thus could have blocked the reforms had lost all political leverage at that particular time.

Cultural and Social Implications

The reforms embodied in the code have cultural and social implications. They confront Tunisians with a new cultural model with respect to the family, which in itself is significant. The code constitutes a major reduction of gender inequality before the law, although it does not institute equality. It also aims at protecting women and children from some of the worst abuses of male power, such as repudiation. Before the reforms, in the worst cases, women repudiated by their husbands would find themselves thrown out of their houses, separated from their children, and left with neither resources nor recourse. Now, a divorce can only occur in court, and women have a measure of protection.[24]

In discussing the implications of the code with Western audiences in a variety of academic settings, I have often encountered skepticism regarding its effectiveness. Scholars and students essentially state that laws may exist but stay on paper, forgotten and without effect; they wonder how much of an effect the new family laws have had in Tunisia. I can appreciate the skepticism. There is no simple way to measure the impact of a law anywhere. As a general assessment, however, I suggest that the new Tunisian laws matter a great deal, both within Tunisia itself and outside Tunisia in the Islamic world. Evidence shows that the code has not been a dead letter. On the contrary, it has offered what women's rights advocates see as a major benefit for women.

In considering the impact of the code on social conduct within Tunisia, it would be easier to show failure than success because of the difficulty of establishing causation. Suppose that we observe that the social conduct continues today much as it was before 1956. We then could conclude that the code had no effect. Even if social conduct has changed, however, the change could have resulted from other causes, such as women's expanding education or greater participation in the workforce, and not from the code.

Let us take the minimum legal age for marriage as a hypothetical example. The text of the code raises it. If the actual age at first marriage went down or remained the same, then we might conclude that the legal reforms failed to lower the age at marriage. In actuality, the average age at first marriage has gone up substantially since 1956. In the case of women, it went from 19.4 in 1956 to 23.9 in 1991.[25] This piece of evidence does not allow us to say that the code succeeded in raising the age at first marriage. We can safely say, however, that it did not fail to raise it.

In order to develop a more textured analysis of how Tunisians relate to the code, we must turn to other forms of reasoning and evidence. Some characteristics of Tunisia have facilitated the implementation of the reforms. Tunisia is a small country, where people and information travel relatively quickly from one end of the territory to the other. It has one law for all and a uniformly organized judicial system. Other characteristics have hindered the implementation of the reforms. Tunisia inherited from the colonial period large numbers of judges trained in religious schools and inclined toward a conservative interpretation of the code. These judges, often the first to apply the new laws, made more than a passing imprint on jurisprudence. Other judges have given the new laws a more reformist and liberal interpretation. This has resulted in fluctuations in the application of the law and uneven outcomes for women.[26]

Regardless of variations in judges' behavior, however, all Tunisians have to suffer the potential implications of violating some of the basic principles of the code. Many Tunisians may prefer to comply with the new laws rather than suffer the cost of not complying. For example, the legal abolition of polygyny does not prevent a man from marrying one woman according to the law and living with another without a marriage certificate. If the man has children with the second woman, the abolition of polygyny means, however, that Tunisian law considers these children illegitimate. The children therefore could be barred from inheritance. Should someone wish to engage in procedures to bar them from inheritance, that person will find support in the law. In another example, the abolition of repudiation does not prevent a man from throwing his wife out of the house, but the wife now has a legal recourse, should she be able and willing to use it.

Information about women's rights. Whether women avail themselves of their rights depends in part on whether they know of their existence. Women have a chance to hear about the new laws through television, the radio, and the press. A national survey indicates that 55 to 65 percent of Tunisian households have a television set. The figure ranges from a high of 88.5 percent for the capital city of Tunis to a low of 32.86 percent in remote regions. The average is 85.04 percent for all urban areas and 42.36 percent for all rural areas.[27] This suggests that substantial numbers of people in Tunisia, including in the countryside, have access to national television. In rural areas, transistor radios provide an additional connection with the rest of the country.

There have been mass media campaigns since 1956, on television, on the radio, and in newspapers, about the code. Women's associations, women's rights advocacy groups, and women lawyers have made sustained efforts to disseminate knowledge about the new laws. For example, a woman lawyer, profoundly dedicated to helping Tunisian women understand their rights, has a program on the radio in which she explains the laws in concrete terms. The text of the code appears as a small, readily available booklet. This is no obscure text hidden in dusty law books. Every lawyer knows about it, as does every judge, public notary, and educated person.

Literacy is a key factor in determining who knows, or knows of, the new laws. Availability of information alone does not guarantee that all women will hear the information, or hear it in the same way. As should be expected, women who are literate know their rights much better than illiterate women. The more education, the better the knowledge of existing rights and the greater the demand for more. For example, not only do college-educated women know about the code, but they want further reforms. A survey conducted in 1991 with a nationally representative sample of 1,000 respondents indicates that 72 percent of college-educated women wanted further changes to expand women's rights.[28]

Illiterate women have a shaky knowledge of the code. The same 1991 survey reports that, when asked whether they were aware of the Code of Personal Status, 70 percent of illiterate women said that they were not.[29] This brings the number of women who said they were unaware of the code to 41.5 percent of the total sample.[30] A survey conducted ten years earlier, in 1981, with a sample of 400 also designed to be nationally representative, found that 51 percent of the women in the sample were unaware of the code.[31] Not enough information is available to permit a comparison of the two surveys. Should we assume them to be comparable, the surveys would suggest a 10 percent increase in awareness of the code from 1981 to 1991.

Literacy trends over time provide a useful indicator for the likelihood that increasing numbers of women will know of their rights as the years go by. The trends show that younger women are more literate than their elders. Illiteracy has declined sharply, even though it has not been entirely eradicated. The rate of illiteracy has gone from 75 percent for men and 96 percent for women in 1956 to 26.4 percent for men and 48.3 percent for women in 1989, the last year for which data are available. Efforts in education and literacy have been overwhelmingly directed at the young. This shows in the sharp difference in illiteracy rates when one compares women in their seventies and those in their teens. Of girls aged ten to fourteen 13.3 percent are illiterate, whereas the rate goes up to 97.3 percent for women aged seventy and older.[32] If existing trends on literacy continue, we may reasonably expect the next generation of Tunisian women increasingly to know of their rights.

Illiterate women may not know the name of the Code of Personal Status, but some at least know the gist of its content. They know that their husbands can no longer repudiate them at will, thanks to some vague action that made women's condition somehow better than it used to be.[33] Some women in Tunisia refer to the code as Bourguiba's law, for the name of the president who initiated the reforms.

Women's opinions. Perhaps the most telling evidence about the significance of the code in Tunisia comes from women's statements about it. Women of different socioeconomic status see it as a source of positive developments in women's lives. I have not heard a Tunisian woman say that she would have been better off without the code. The only variation I have observed in women's opinions comes from Islamist women who find their loyalties divided between the gender ideology of the Islamist movement and their individual preferences. Otherwise, most women speak of the new laws as protection from potential tragedies. For example, a cleaning woman makes a contrast between "Bourguiba's law [the code], which has freed women" and "the tragedy of polygamy that she experienced in the house of her stepfather who had four wives and eighteen children."[34] An employee in a hair salon in a modest neighborhood speaks about repudiation and the images surrounding it: "I know an old woman that her husband repudiated without any prior notice. The shock was so traumatic . . . it gave her a stroke and left her paralyzed for the rest of her life."[35]

Most women treat the new laws as integral to Tunisian culture. They refer to it not as a policy to discuss but as a reality that is part of their lives. In addition, a generation of Tunisian women has grown up with the code. These women have never known any other law. Some take it as a point of departure to demand greater gender equality in all areas. Reflecting the spirit of some young, educated Tunisian women, one of them says: "What difference is there between my son and my daughter? She will be educated and she will work and she will never be, God willing, under the authority of anybody, and certainly not under her brother's authority."[36]

In comparing the Tunisian code to the laws of similar countries, a woman journalist says: "The dispositions of the Code are revolutionary relative to the laws of personal status in countries similar to ours."[37] The last statement captures the position of many Tunisian women's rights advocates who appreciate what they have when they compare women's rights in Tunisia and in the Islamic world at large. Women's rights advocates have celebrated the code for close to forty years, not only in Tunisia but also abroad. Family law reform in Tunisia has equipped women's rights advocates outside Tunisia with an example of such laws in an Islamic country. It has provided a model, not perfect, but good enough to serve as a basis from which to fight. If Tunisia has a set of laws such as the code, then this fact alone raises the possibility of similar laws in other Islamic countries.

Even though the code maintains forms of gender inequality, it nevertheless has served a symbolic purpose in the Islamic world. A woman active in Tunisian politics indicates what happens repeatedly at international conferences on gender in the Islamic world:

> The Code of Personal Status is a cutting edge body of legislation that many countries envy. I just came back from a meeting in an Arab country and I realized that, as soon as people speak about Tunisia, they speak about the Code of Personal Status. It is an excellent thing.[38]

CONCLUSION

The analysis of diversity within Islamic culture provides a counterweight to the often-encountered emphasis on Islam as monolithic or as a rigid determinant of action. It highlights the multiplicity of experiences in the

Islamic world. Like other world cultures, Islamic culture does not automatically determine action toward fully predictable outcomes; it offers a range of options for action. Within that range, groups and individuals make choices, are forced into accepting others' choices, or work out alternatives that combine elements of choice and constraint, depending on their particular circumstances.

In Islamic societies as elsewhere, states, social groups, and individuals renegotiate culture in the context of their particular social circumstances. Political groups that take widely different stands on gender issues all appeal to Islam as the ultimate source of inspiration for their particular position. This is true not only of the Islamists but also of liberal-minded groups and women's rights advocates who identify strongly with Islam as a religion while they fight for greater gender equality. Many women's rights advocates in the Islamic world demand empowerment within a changing Islamic culture.

Two key symbols of Islam as culture, veils and family laws, show aspects of diversity. The veil known as hijab remains a potent political symbol of Islamism throughout the Islamic world. Many Tunisian women who wear it refuse, however, any identification with militant Islam. Women have used the veil in multiple ways that reflect variations in how individual women relate to the veil as a cultural symbol. They have worn it because of tradition, to comply with pressures that others have placed on them, by choice as a form of empowerment in a male space, and as a practical and convenient form of dress. In their everyday actions, women are trying to retain the veil as part of their own culture, instead of letting it become the exclusive symbolic property of Islamism. In so doing, they are in the process of generating a wide range of cultural meanings for the veil.

New family laws in Tunisia show the diversity that exists among states within the Islamic world. No single aspect of the new family laws in itself is unique to Tunisia. Other countries have introduced partial changes in one aspect or another of orthodox family law. Rather, it is the entire body of legislation taken as a whole that differentiates Tunisia from most of the Arab-Islamic world.[39] The implementation of the new laws is by necessity imperfect and in constant flux. Women who can read and write have more information about the laws than those who are illiterate, and educated women are in a better position than others to avail themselves of their rights. Judicial authorities vary in their interpretation of the new laws, thus generating uneven consequences for women.

Despite all this, Tunisian law matters a great deal, both outside Tunisia and inside. Outside Tunisia, the code opens up the possibility of new cultural images within Islam. The very fact that Tunisia is different brings cultural diversity to the fore in the contemporary Islamic world. The law also matters within the country. Tunisian women, especially those who use it themselves or see it used by others, perceive it as a strong asset upon which to build the future. Women's rights advocates in Tunisia vigilantly protect the legal rights in existence. Although some want more, most women's rights advocates first and foremost want to keep what they already have.

At present, Tunisia thus offers an instance of diversity within the Islamic world with respect to women's rights, but the future is uncertain and policies are reversible. A degree of skepticism about the liberating potential of new family laws in an Islamic country is to be expected among Western audiences, barraged as they are with images of women's seclusion and subordination in Islam. Let us not carry skepticism too far, however. The protection of women's rights cannot be taken for granted anywhere in the Arab-Islamic world; therefore, those who believe in the value of the legal rights gained by Tunisian women must defend those rights. Any instance of diversity opens up a broader range of avenues for the Middle East in search of its cultural identity within Islam.

Whether the future brings greater uniformity or greater diversity in the condition of women in the Islamic world at large is difficult to assess. Many factors come into play in the social construction of gender, including internal and external pressures, local history, socioeconomic contexts, state policies, and social responses. As I suggest in this chapter, these factors all mediate the interpretation of Islam as culture that comes to prevail in a given country at a given time. They also mediate the many interpretations that come face to face with one another. It is risky to venture any prediction on how the factors may coalesce in the future. One may nevertheless suggest that, in all likelihood, diversity will continue to pervade the Islamic world, just as it has done so far.

NOTES

A Mellon Award from the University of Pittsburgh and a grant from the American Association of University Women provided partial support for the research that served as a basis for this article. I wish to thank Herbert L. Bodman, Michael Brenner, Betty Farrell, Linda Frankel, Mary Freifeld, Nayereh Tohidi, and anonymous reviewers for their comments on an earlier version.
    1. Fatima Mernissi, *Beyond the Veil: Male-Female Dynamics in Modern Muslim Society,* rev. ed. (Bloomington: Indiana University Press, 1987); Fatna A. Sabbah, *Women in the Muslim Unconscious* (New York: Pergamon Press, 1984); John Esposito, *Women in Muslim Family Law* (Syracuse, NY: Syracuse University Press, 1982); M. M. Charrad, "Repudiation Versus Divorce: Responses to State Policy in Tunisia," in Esther N. Chow and Catherine W. Berheide (eds.), *Women, the Family and Policy: A Global Perspective* (Albany: State University of New York Press, 1994).
    2. M. M. Charrad, "Policy Shifts: State, Islam and Gender in Tunisia, 1930s–1990s," *Social Politics,* 4, 2 (summer 1997), 284–319; Charrad, *States and Tribes: The Political Origins of Family Law in Tunisia, Algeria and Morocco,*

forthcoming; Leila Ahmed, *Women and Gender in Islam: Historical Roots of a Modern Debate* (New Haven: Yale University Press, 1992); Victoria Bernal, "Gender, Culture and Capitalism: Women and the Remaking of Islamic 'Tradition' in a Sudanese Village," *Comparative Studies in Society and History*, 36 (1994), 1; R. Bourqia, M. M. Charrad, and N. Gallagher (eds.), *Femmes, Culture et Société au Maghreb*, 2 vols. (Casablanca, Morocco: Afrique Orient, 1996); Lois Beck and Nikki Keddie (eds.), *Women in the Muslim World* (Cambridge, MA: Harvard University Press, 1978); Nadia Hijab, *Womanpower: The Arab Debate on Women at Work* (Cambridge: Cambridge University Press, 1988); Elizabeth Warnock Fernea (ed.), *Women and the Family in the Middle East: New Voices of Change* (Austin: University of Texas Press, 1985). On other aspects of diversity in Islam, see Clifford Geertz, *Islam Observed* (Chicago: University of Chicago Press, 1971).

3. Edward Said, *Orientalism* (New York: Random House, 1978).

4. Bernal, "Gender, Culture and Capitalism."

5. Ann Swidler, "Culture in Action," *American Sociological Review*, 51, no. 2 (1986).

6. Pierre Bourdieu, *Distinction* (Cambridge: Harvard University Press, 1984); and Bourdieu, *Outline of a Theory of Practice*, trans. Richard Nice (Cambridge, MA: Harvard University Press, 1977); Raymond Williams, *Problems in Materialism and Culture* (London: Verso, 1980); Clifford Geertz, *The Interpretation of Cultures: Selected Essays* (New York: Basic Books, 1993); and Bennett M. Berger, *An Essay on Culture: Symbolic Structure and Social Structure* (Berkeley: University of California Press, 1995).

7. Swidler, "Culture in Action," 284.

8. Tunisian Information Office, *Tunisia Digest*, Washington, D.C., June-July 1994. The following sources provide information on the history, politics, and economy of Tunisia: I. William Zartman and William Mark Habeeb (eds.), *Polity and Society in Contemporary North Africa* (Boulder, CO: Westview Press, 1993); I. William Zartman (ed.), *Tunisia: The Political Economy of Reform* (Boulder, CO: Lynne Rienner, 1991); John Ruedy (ed.), *Islamism and Secularism in North Africa* (New York: St. Martin's Press, 1994); Michel Camau (ed.), *Tunisie au Présent* (Paris: Editions du Centre National de la Recherche Scientifique, 1987); Francois Burgat and William Dowell, *The Islamic Movement in North Africa* (Austin: University of Texas Press, 1993).

9. Tunisia had a per capita income of $1,790 in the early to mid-1990s, which placed it ahead of a country such as Egypt, where the per capita income was $620. It also placed it ahead of Morocco, Jordan, and Syria. Morocco, for example, had a gross national product two-thirds that of Tunisia (CREDIF [Centre de Recherche, de Documentation et d'Information sur la Femme], *Femmes de Tunisie: Situation et Perspectives* [Tunis: CREDIF, 1994], 12). The Tunisian economy was similar to the Moroccan economy about thirty to forty years ago, but the Tunisian economy has done considerably better in recent years.

10. See, for example, Mernissi, *Beyond the Veil*.

11. *New York Times*, December 28, 1991.

12. To obtain data for this section, I combined interviews of a small sample of ten women in hijab in the city of Tunis with Tunisian studies that report on extensive and in-depth interviews, such as Souad Chater, *Les Emancipées du Harem: Regard sur la Femme Tunisienne* (Tunis: Editions La Presse, 1992); and Aziza Darghouth Medimegh, *Droits et Vécu de la Femme en Tunisie* (Lyon, France: Hermes-Edilis, 1992).

13. This and the next two quotations are from interviews I conducted.

14. Chater, *Les Emancipées*, 110.

15. Medimegh, *Droits et Vécu*, 134. The following sources discuss the meaning of the veil in other contexts: Leila Hessini, "Signification du Voile au Maroc," in *Femmes, Culture et Société au Maghreb*, R. Bourqia, M. M. Charrad, and N. Gallagher (eds.) (Casablanca, Morocco: Afrique Orient, 1996); Hind Taarji, *Les Voilées de l'Islam* (Paris: Editions Balland, 1990); and Arlene E. MacLeod, *Accommodating Protest: Working Women, the New Veiling, and Change in Cairo* (New York: Columbia University Press, 1993).

16. Medimegh, *Droits et Vécu*, 135.

17. Nayereh Tohidi, "Modernity, Islamization, and Women in Iran," Valentine M. Moghadam (ed.) *Gender and National Identity: Women and Politics in Muslim Societies* (London and Karachi: Zed Books and Oxford University Press, for the United Nations University, 1994).

18. A major difference distinguishes the Tunisian and Turkish reforms: In Tunisia, reforms were made within the framework of Islam. In Turkey, reforms consisted in a move away from Islam and in the adoption of the Swiss family code.

19. For example, Saudi Arabia, Algeria, Morocco.

20. *Code du Statut Personnel*, 1996 edition (Tunis: Imprimerie Officielle de la République Tunisienne), initially published in 1956 and periodically updated. Alya Cherif Chamari, in *La Femme et la Loi en Tunisie* (Casablanca, Morocco: The United Nations University and Editions le Fennec, 1991), offers an analysis of the code from a legal perspective. M. M. Charrad places the Tunisian code in the broader context of the Maghreb by comparing it to family law policy in Algeria and Morocco in the aftermath of independence. See "Formation de l'Etat et Statut Personnel au Maghreb: Esquisse d'une Etude Comparative et Théorique," in *Femmes, Culture et Société au Maghreb*, vol. 2, R. Bourqia, M. M. Charrad, and N. Gallagher (eds.) (Casablanca, Morocco: Afrique Orient, 1996); and "State and Gender in the Maghrib," *Middle East Report*, March-April 1990, updated and reprinted in Suad Joseph and Susan Slyomovics (eds.), *Gendering Political Cultures in the Middle East*, in preparation.

21. Quoted in Chater, *Les Emancipées*, 283. See also Susan Waltz, "Politique et Sens de l'Efficacité Parmi les Femmes Tunisiennes," in R. Bourqia, M. M. Charrad, and N. Gallagher (eds.), *Femmes, Culture et Société au Maghreb*, vol. 2 (Casablanca: Afrique Orient, 1996); and "Another View of Feminine Networks: Tunisian Women and the Development of Political Efficacy," *International Journal of Middle East Studies* 22, no. 1 (1990), where she discusses Tunisian women's involvement in politics.

22. For example, Naziha Lakehal-Ayat, *La Femme Tunisienne et sa Place Dans le Droit Positif* (Tunis: Dar El Amal, 1978).

23. Charrad, *States and Tribes*.

24. Charrad, "Repudiation Versus Divorce."

25. CREDIF, *Femmes de Tunisie*, 15 and 51. On the basis of data from the National Institute of Statistics, Tunis, Tunisia.

26. Charrad, "Repudiation Versus Divorce."

27. Institut National de Statistiques, *Enquête Nationale Population-Emploi* (Tunis: INS, 1989), 488, Table 18a; François Chevaldonne, "Peut-on Encore Parler de Radios et de Télévisions 'Nationales'?" in Camille and Yves Lacoste (eds.), *L'Etat du Maghreb* (Tunis: Ceres Productions, 1991).

28. Medimegh, *Droits et Vécu*, 68. Further amendments to the code were passed in 1993.

29. Medimegh, *Droits et Vécu*, 66.

30. Ibid.

31. Survey conducted by the National Union of Tunisian Women and the Institute El Amouri of Applied Psychology on the Image of Women in Tunisian Society, with a nationally representative sample of 400 subjects: Malika Zamiti-Horchani, "Les Tunisiennes, Leurs Droits et l'Idée qu'on s'en Fait," in Monique Gadant (ed.), *Femmes de la Méditerranée*, special issue of *Peuples Méditerranéens* 22–23 (January-June, 1983). Published in English as *Women of the Mediterranean*, trans. A. M. Berrett (London: Zed Books, 1986).

32. CREDIF, *Femmes de Tunisie*, 75.

33. Information gained from informal interviews of mostly illiterate women in rural areas in the mid-1970s, in Aly Chaouchi, "Vingt Ans Après le 13 Août 1956: L'Emancipation de la Tunisienne se Poursuit-elle avec Bonheur?" *Dialogue* 19 (1976).

34. Chater, *Les Emancipées*, 234.

35. Ibid.

36. Medimegh, *Droits et Vécu*, 69.

37. Chater, *Les Emancipées*, 238.

38. Ibid., 240.

39. Turkey is an exception. Some important differences exist between Turkey and Tunisia, as discussed previously.

PART TWO

The Middle East

5

Power, Ideology, and Women's Consciousness in Postrevolutionary Iran

Hisae Nakanishi

Exploring the dialogue between the Islamic Republic of Iran, which has been propagating an ideal Islamic woman since the revolution, and Islamic reformist women who advocate women's rights, this chapter examines the relationship between Islam as a state ideology and Islam reinterpreted through women's consciousness. Specifically, it investigates how the Islamic republic and women activists have debated women's rights in marriage and family in an Islamic society.

The impact of Islamist (or Islamic fundamentalist) movements on women's political and socioeconomic status has attracted scholars' attention in the last two decades. Some scholars have argued that Islamism has had a negative impact on women, enforcing women's veils only to secure the cultural and spiritual authenticity of the Islamic state and introducing an Islamic penal code that effectively reduced the legal rights of women. Other scholars have asserted that Islamist movements politicized and promoted women's political participation, granting some women new identities as Muslims and creating a path for their political, educational, professional, and economic advancement.[1] However, both these negative and positive viewpoints tend to be essentialist in their discussion of the concept of Islamism and its impact on women.

The government of postrevolutionary Iran has been commonly called an "Islamist" government. Thus, scholars often conceptualized women's issues by making the "Islamist" ideology of women the centerpiece of their discussion.[2] That is, when women's status is seen to decrease in postrevolutionary Iran, this decrease is generally attributed to the Islamism of Iran's government. Furthermore, the imposition of the *hijab* in Iran and of laws discriminating against women drawn from the adoption of the Islamic penal code supported the argument that Islamism, in general, brings about a regression in women's rights. However, one should raise two questions: Is Islamism itself antiwomen? Is Iran's government really Islamist?

If we broadly define the term "Islamism," Iran's case is a special one, in which the state power adopted Islamism as political ideology; Islamist movements elsewhere often opposed the established state power. Yet a more precise definition of "Islamism" is necessary to judge whether the republic is actually Islamist.

Islamism can be generally defined as an ideology in which Islamic values and principles constitute the most prominent features of the political system. Thus, whether the Republic of Iran is an Islamist regime or not depends on the extent to which Islamization policies are adopted and Islamic laws (the Shari'a) are practiced.

Islamization policies of the Republic of Iran are limited mainly to three areas: first, the ulema's monopoly on the acquisition of power in the political system; second, the introduction of the penal code; and third, the Islamization of social norms and morality.[3] Regarding the first area, Ayatollah Khomeini legitimized his power by institutionalizing the principle of *velayat-e faqih* (the guardianship of the Islamic jurist) and established other political organizations to ensure the absolute power of the clerical leadership in interpreting the Qur'an for legislation and to allow the ulema to enforce "Islamic codes of conduct" throughout the nation.[4] However, the velayat-e faqih is not intrinsic to the idea of an Islamic state in general. It is, rather, unique to Iranian Shi'i Islam, and more specifically to Khomeini's use of Shi'i tradition, in which the ulema have held strong state power since the Safavid dynasty.[5] Thus, Khomeini's Iran is more "Iranian" than "Islamic." Moreover, the application of the Shari'a in Iran is limited to the Islamic penal code. Thus, the third category of Islamization policies, the Islamization of social norms and morality, holds much significance in Iran's being "Islamist." Islamization of social norms and morality includes the imposition of the hijab for women and the abolition of the Family Protection Laws (FPL) which has directly affected women's legal and socioeconomic life. Thus the republic on the whole is based on "Khomeinism," rather than "Islamism," and the Islamic republic is more Islamist in its policies toward women than in other spheres of politics.

As we have seen, certain scholars emphasize the positive aspects of Islamism's impact on women, maintaining that women have recently achieved a certain level of autonomy in society by adopting the hijab and have become conscious of their identity as Muslim. However, this argument blurs different Muslim women activists into a single category of "Islamist" women. According to this viewpoint, veiled professional women active in the Muslim Brethren who criticize the secular system of government in Egypt and veiled women who raise their voices to question and criticize the state's discriminatory policies toward women in Iran are equally Islamist.[6] Islamism adopted as state ideology, as in Iran's case, and Islamism in opposition to the government, as in Egypt's case, should be differentiated in scholars' discussion of how Muslim women have responded to government policies toward women.

A few scholars maintain a balance, being neither positive nor negative. Eliz Sanasarian and Nayereh Tohidi identify the presence of "reformist" women, who debate the state's interpretations of the Qur'an, and distinguish them from other "Islamist" women.[7] Yet Sanasarian sees a contradiction in reformist women's arguments about women's rights, saying that "while they claim that Islam does not acknowledge separate rights for women (or any other category of people), they have focused on women's issues, negating their own stand."[8]

Like Sanasarian and Tohidi, I further explore how "Islamic reformist" women contest the state's ideology and politics on women. In other words, I examine the discourses between the Islamic republic and the "Islamic reformist" women on women's rights and roles in view of each other's "Islam." To do so, I single out the Women's Society of the Islamic Revolution of Iran (WSIRI) as Islamic reformist and analyze the society's biweekly newspaper, *Payam-e Hajer* (Hajer's Message).[9]

There are several reasons to consider the WSIRI as a representative Muslim women's group. First, this is one of the few women's organizations that has been able to survive from right after the revolution until today and that has continued to publish its newspaper. Whereas *Zan-e Ruz* (Today's Woman), one of the most important women's magazines, provides descriptive and narrative information of political and social events involving women in general, *Payam-e Hajer* presents a viewpoint and interpretation of social and political events based on a set of values. By advocating a certain ideology, *Payam-e Hajer* also informs women about what its editors and writers value as the "ideal" Muslim woman.

Second, although WSIRI follows what Khomeini advocated about political ideas as derived from his interpretation of Islam, it does not do so completely. Moreover, it remains independent of the Islamic republic's direct control, both structurally and ideologically. WSIRI, headed by Azam-e Taleqani, the daughter of Ayatollah Mahmud Taleqani, first sought the government's support through the political power of Ayatollah Taleqani as soon as the organization was established, but the society has remained independent of the government. In the summer of 1993, more than ten years after the establishment of the society, the Ministry of the Interior officially approved the activities of the society.[10]

And third, the organization locates women's issues within the wider political and socioeconomic context of Iran and seeks solutions in those spheres. Hence, the publication of this society is identified as the most suitable for comparing the government's views on "ideal" Muslim women with Muslim women's response.

Various women's issues are addressed by the republic's ideologues and then contested in many issues of this newspaper. The present discussion, however, is limited to the question of hijab and the institutions of marriage and family in an Islamic society. I attempt, first, to question the unitary category of "Islamist women," and second, to point out that an

"Islamic reformist" orientation will be an alternative weapon in the survival of efforts to improve women's lives in present-day and future Iran.

IDEALIZED MUSLIM WOMEN
VERSUS RECONSTRUCTED MUSLIM WOMEN

The hallmark stance on the advocation of women's rights taken by *Payam-e Hajer* is, in its own words, "the middle of the road." On the one hand, the publication denounces "West-toxicated" (*gharbzadeh*) women, accusing them of cultural alienation and a lack of self-identity. On the other hand, it attacks traditional (*sonnati*) women for blindly accepting what religious leaders preach as Islam.[11] These dual, opposing models of women appear frequently when *Payam-e Hajer* discusses the questions of hijab, women's participation in society, and women's rights in marriage and the family.

By denouncing both these extreme positions, *Payam-e Hajer* advocates an Islamic reformist orientation, emphasizing the reinterpretation of Qur'anic passages and other Shi'i texts such as *Nahj ul-Balagha* (the collection of Muhammad's son-in-law Ali's sayings and letters). The following sections will demonstrate how *Payam-e Hajer* responds to the Khomeinist ideology of Islamism on women's images and roles in postrevolutionary Iran.

The Question of the Hijab

The Islamic Republic of Iran imposed compulsory hijab on women as part of its Islamization policies. To dictate how Islamic women should behave, the government needed to manipulate images of women. The regime's ideal of Islamic woman is represented by the hijab. This dress code not only ordains what women are to wear but represents a graphic image of the regime's ideal woman. The prototype of this Islamic woman, as propagated by the government, is the veiled Fatima, Muhammad's daughter, Ali's wife, and mother of the two Shi'i martyrs, Hassan and Husain. What Khomeini and other prominent religious leaders said about Iranian women became the sole authoritative interpretation of Islamic women. The hijab, naturally, became the focus of the government's concern.[12] Thus, the question of the hijab has generated a threefold debate between the state and women activists, on the issues of Muslim identity, Islamic morality, and women's participation in society.

Muslim identity. Since the hijab became compulsory in 1983, Iranian women, unlike the female followers of Islamic fundamentalism in other countries, have no choice but to don it. So the presence of veiled women does not indicate the degree to which such women hold Islamic values.

This is quite peculiar to Iran, where the hijab is not a matter of personal choice but is backed by the state's Islamic ideology. Thus, veiled women are, to some extent, a repository of Islamic morality and the values that the government propagates. The propriety of the hijab has often been discussed in the media, and some "improperly" (*bad*, in Persian) veiled women have been accosted or arrested for their nonconforming dress.[13]

Payam-e Hajer advocates some kind of hijab as an identity for Muslim women. It criticizes *gharbzadeh* women who, ignorant of the fact that covering is indispensable in society, appear in public without the hijab. These West-toxicated women are also criticized, in *Payam-e Hajer*, for their lack of, or their confusion about, their identity. The infiltration of Western culture, especially during the Westernization period in Iran (from the time of Reza Shah to Mohamed Shah Pahlevi), caused people to believe in what was not their own, to blindly accept what other people had as desirable for them.[14] Thus, by adopting the sociological concept of alienation suggested by Ali Shari'ati, one of the ideologues of the revolution, *Payam-e Hajer* holds that the Iranian people were trapped in West-toxication and lost their identity. It also points out that Islam is not the sole basis on which people can restore their identities and that other sources will do, as long as they are rooted in one's tradition and culture.[15]

A series of essays in *Payam-e Hajer* also criticized traditional (sonnati) women for accepting blindly what religious leaders preach about Islam: these women wrongly identify the path of Islam with wearing chador (complete black covering from head to toe). Consequently, these essays maintain, traditional women blindly accept the idea that women are considered inferior to men and thus take no initiative in deciding what they want to do in their lives.

To project an image of the ideal Muslim woman, the newspaper turns to Ali Shari'ati's book *Fatima Is Fatima*. Though Iran's government also propagates Fatima as an ideal woman, *Payam-e Hajer*'s portrayal of Fatima differs from that of the government. The government's position emphasizes, first, Fatima's domestic role, and second, her role as a fighter against infidels, depicting her as a great "assistant" for Muhammad and Ali.[16] *Payam-e Hajer,* however, projects Fatima as an ideal woman who is never passive and subordinated, knows her identity as a Muslim, and takes initiative in learning and participating in society as an independent person, not merely as an assistant to a man. Thus, *Payam-e Hajer*'s idealized woman is neither a traditional type, who is passive and does not know what true Islam is, nor a Western woman who tends to lose her identity and to fall into consumerism and luxury.[17] As analyzed previously, the question of the hijab is debated around the issue of identity. For *Payam-e Hajer*, the hijab is important as a reification of Muslim identity that is deeply rooted in Iranian culture.

Islamic morality: Recognizing women as "human beings." On the ideological level, the Islamic republic emphasizes the idea of the complementarity of the sexes, which justifies the logic that, although men and women
are "equal" in relation to God, women have "different" roles because of biological differences.[18] The ideologues of the republic claim that whereas
men are rational, brave, conquering, and aggressive in their sexual urge,
women are emotional and sexually conniving.[19] Hence, the Islamic republic advocates women's hijab, so that men's strong sexual urges will not be
aroused by women's exposure of their beauty. Otherwise, the government
argues, society will become corrupt, and women will not be able to protect
their chastity.[20] Thus, wearing the hijab is a proof of women's chastity and
a matter of preserving the morality required by Islam.

The newspaper maintains that the issue of the hijab should be consid-
Anti-Western sentiment is strong in the government's propaganda of
the hijab. Western society, according to the ideologues, consists of corruption and excessive consumerism, where women are abused by appearing in
advertising and exploited as a commodity for consumerism. Thus, the hijab
is also a means to protect a woman's personality from Western corruption.

In response to this gender ideology of the state, *Payam-e Hajer* accepts the idea of the complementarity of the sexes, yet differs with the
government. It asserts that men and women are created in this world to
play different roles. The creation story in the Qur'an, it says, provides the
belief that the merit of woman lies in the quality of tranquility that God
granted her.[21] It maintains that "God made women so that she can get rid
of restlessness from a man, bringing tranquillity and peace."[22] Thus,
women fulfill an essential role in this world because of this attribute which
God granted only to women, which makes them equally important beings.
This is, according to *Payam-e Hajer,* the worldview of Islam, which
teaches us to recognize both men and women as human beings.

The newspaper maintains that the issue of the hijab should be considered in the broader context of this Islamic view of the world and the whole
philosophy of Islam, and "knowing a human being" (*insan shenashi*) in
particular.[23] Based on the aforementioned view of the world that *Payam-e
Hajer* interprets from the Qur'an, it asserts the hijab is a kind of covering
required by the sexuality of a person. To understand human nature is of
paramount significance in accepting the hijab. As long as one recognizes
this, the form of the hijab will be left to individual choice. Thus, the newspaper implies a criticism of the state's imposition of the hijab, which de-
nies individual choice.

Payam-e Hajer questions the manner in which the hijab has been institutionalized and practiced in contemporary Iran.[24] It maintains that the
hijab is not intrinsic to Islam and that the Qur'anic passage in the Chapter
of Light (Sura 24:31) refers only to covering the bosom.[25] It claims that
the ulema and jurists have distorted the meaning of the hijab throughout
history, misinterpreting it as an Islamic requirement.[26]

Payam-e Hajer also raises the question of men's responsibility for self-control of their own sexuality in order to maintain women's chastity and morality, if Iran is to be a true Islamic society.[27] Further, the newspaper claims that the extent to which women should cover themselves is an arbitrary human judgment rather than an Islamic dictum. *Payam-e Hajer's* criticism of the government's arbitrary ruling in the name of Islam leads it to engage in the debate on women's participation in society through employment and education.

Women's participation in society through employment and education. Based on the excuse that women are biologically, psychologically, and intellectually different from men, the Islamic republic barred women from the positions of president and judge after the revolution. In response, Fereshteh Hashemi, a woman activist in Iran, shares with *Payam-e Hajer* the view that "women should not be excluded from any activity because of femininity."[28] She particularly criticizes the fact that since the revolution women have been banned from judgeships, saying that no verse in the Qur'an prevents a woman from being a judge.

Payam-e Hajer insists that women's participation in political activities is an embodiment of the revolutionary spirit promoted by the revolutionary ideologue Ayatollah Khomeini. Here, the newspaper makes selective use of Khomeini's writings:

> According to Imam Khomeini, the family is the fundamental unit from which society grows. We raise our children so that they can fight against oppression and seek justice. In this context, the formation of the family, having and raising children by a couple, and the duty of husband and wife, all these issues are related and on the whole important. All these are necessary for the flourishing and perfection of individuals. Against the views of some opponents, Khomeini achieved women's participation in politics by giving women suffrage and the right to be elected. Muhammad considered that religion is politics, and politics as well as religion is for both men and women. Therefore, women should be involved in religious and political matters. If this is attained, we can solve the problems which the society and women are facing, such as divorce and the breakdown of the family. Empowering women, politicizing women, and educating women will provide women with motivation to be aware of the world while maintaining their role in the family.[29]

Women's participation in politics became an issue demanding a government response by early 1993. The WSIRI demanded that the government form a "Ministry of Women's Welfare and Aid," appoint a woman minister to head it, and agree that "discrimination should be removed with regard to women acquiring administrative positions including the directorship."[30] However, so far the government has not responded to these demands.

A bill restricting women's education abroad is still an ongoing debate in the Majlis (Iran's national assembly). The bill stipulates that a woman is allowed to study abroad only if accompanied by her husband.[31] *Payam-e Hajer* considers this bill a denial of women's independent personality, which contradicts the philosophy of the hijab: the hijab is a means by which women's personality can be valued.[32] The Women's Council in Iran's government asked women representatives in the Majlis to suggest sending women students to foreign countries, but this initiative has been rejected four times by the national assembly.[33]

Family and Marriage

One of the more drastic changes impacting women's legal and socioeconomic status in postrevolutionary Iran was the abolition of the Family Protection Laws (FPL) in 1982. The abolition of these laws meant a change in the content of the marriage contract, which is a legal document stipulating the conditions of marriage and divorce in Iran. The conditions of a marriage are generally determined at the time of sealing that marriage: for example, the provision to forbid a man's polygyny, the amount of money to be paid in case of divorce, and other conditions relevant to the marriage are decided in the form of legal contract.

The difference between what was stipulated in the marriage contract under the FPL and what was absent after the 1982 abolition strongly affected women's rights in marriage. Whereas women married in the era of the FPL possess a contract stipulating the conditions for polygyny and divorce, women married after the 1982 abolition require their husband's signature for each stipulation.[34] In other words, after the 1982 rescission, a husband has more authority and power to decide the conditions of the marriage: the husband can decide whether to sign or not for each claim. The following discussion deals with three aspects of the marriage and family that have been debated in postrevolutionary Iran.

Polygyny and temporary marriage. Polygyny was allowed even under the Shah's regime. Legally speaking, however, polygyny was more restricted during the later Pahlevi monarchy than in the postrevolutionary period, because the FPL required the permission of the first wife before another wife could be taken.[35] Moreover, the FPL required that conditions for polygyny (and divorce) should "be included in all marriage contracts irrespective of the husband's wishes."[36] But the present constitution of Iran allows up to four wives "in accordance with Islamic criteria."[37] In theory, the second Article of the Court stipulates that a man must notify the court each time he marries another woman. In fact, though, a man cannot actually be punished if he secretly engages in polygyny.

Moreover, the practice of "temporary marriage" allows men to engage freely in polygynous relationships. Temporary marriage was practiced before the revolution and has been relegitimized and further encouraged by the ulema since the revolution. Temporary marriage is a contract between a man and a *sigheh* (a temporary wife) to have a legal marriage. This type of marriage is possible for any length of time, typically less than three months, and requires the payment of *mahr,* or dowry. The marriage is terminated at the time previously agreed to by the two parties. Shahla Haeri's work on Iran's system of temporary marriage demonstrates that the temporary marriage rules, together with differing expectations of temporary marriage partners, result in many unanticipated disadvantages for women. In a society in which female virginity and chastity are traditionally highly valued, a woman who accepts a temporary marriage contract is socially stigmatized and can rarely become a permanent wife.[38]

The government's justification of polygyny and temporary marriage seems to contradict its justification for the hijab: polygyny is needed because men have an unbridled sexual drive, and society will become corrupt if women fail to satisfy these male urges. In reaction, Fereshteh Hashemi, together with *Payam-e Hajer*, criticizes polygyny and temporary marriage, calling them anachronistic: polygyny in particular was a social necessity at the time of Muhammad as a social welfare system for widows; it was not designed for satisfying men's sexual desire. *Payam-e Hajer* says:

> Using the excuse that there are more women than men, [early Muslim leaders] encouraged men to have many wives. Unaware that [such men] do not want to accept the guardianship of women, but actually want to misuse women, the men of God's law excluded, first women, and then children, from the guardianship of the law.[39]

Gohar Dasteghayb, a Tehran deputy in the national assembly, also objected to President Hashemi Rafsanjani's promotion of temporary marriage. She declared that to approve temporary marriage contradicts the principle of Islam, which upholds "women's rights and preaches developing their personality." Dasteghayb also attacked Rafsanjani for not "advising the believing men to praise chaste and modest women" as required by the spirit of Islamic law. She noted that women, being devoted to the glory of Islam and obedient to religious leaders during the war, do not deserve such oppression.[40]

Women's financial security. The question of women's financial security arises in two situations: when a husband is polygynous, and when a husband divorces his wife. The 1982 abolition of the FPL allowed these situations to occur more easily. We have seen that the abolition of the FPL meant that the stipulations restricting polygyny and divorce were removed from the marriage contract, and a women henceforth needed her husband's signature to stipulate each claim. Unless both spouses agree to stipulate the conditions relating to polygyny and divorce, a man can freely be polygynous, needing permission neither from his first wife nor from the court.

Although the abolition of the FPL also eroded women's right to initiate divorce, women activists have not debated this issue extensively. Instead, they have focused on the questions of women's economic security in marriage and compensation in the case of divorce, because reformist women do not want to become susceptible to criticism by ulema for promoting the "instability of the family." However, women's economic security is a vital issue, since a woman is not likely to be given much financial security when her husband is either polygynous or divorces her.

Many articles in *Payam-e Hajer* question whether the "Islam" practiced in the present Islamic Republic is "truly Islamic" and proceed from there to reconstruct what rights a truly Islamic society should guarantee for women. The newspaper contrasts the characteristics of Western and Islamic societies in an attempt to point out that Islamic society should secure women's subsistence in marriage.

In Western society, the notion of equality between men and women demands that men and women have the same responsibilities and freedoms. Women's employment is necessary in order for them to enjoy the same responsibilities and freedoms as men. However, in Islamic society, *Payam-e Hajer* asserts, men's employment is "natural," whereas women's primary role is motherhood; the husband has, therefore, a duty to provide subsistence for his wife and children.[41] Here, the newspaper employs rhetoric from the regime's doctrine of the complementarity of the sexes. The complementary roles of men and women, it asserts, "are needed for the perfection of the cell of their family."[42] It states that the Islamic regime's emphasis on the importance of the family as a fundamental unit in Islamic society should naturally lead to a guarantee of women's rights in marriage and to women's economic security.[43] Whereas the ideologues of the Republic use this doctrine to foster women's domesticity, *Payam-e Hajer* uses it to demand that women, in fact, have economic rights in Islamic society.

Within this context, the newspaper attacks West-toxicated women for confusing employment with equality.[44] Here, one can observe one aspect of the WSIRI's middle-of-the-road stance: it criticizes as overly feminist women who merely seek employment without careful reflection. The WSIRI certainly does not pursue equal rights for both men and women. Instead, it stays within the framework of Islam to prove that its arguments are rooted in its indigenous culture. For example, *Payam-e Hajer* argues that Islam grants mahr and *nafaqah* (alimony) to women for their economic security.

According to *Payam-e Hajer*, marriage consists of both spouses' responsibilities and duties. To pay mahr and nafaqah is the husband's duty, as stipulated both in the Qur'an and in the constitution of Iran.[45] This view is also held by other Muslim reformists such as Fereshteh Hashemi and Shahin Etezadi Tabatabai.[46]

Payam-e Hajer continues by saying that "dowry is not like the price in buying and selling, nor a part or condition of contract. It is what Islamic law orders [for men] for securing a women's life in case of divorce, and [should be paid] upon the request of women."[47] If this duty is neglected by the husband, it argues, a women could neglect her responsibility as a spouse without legal obstacle, because rights are always to be considered in relation to responsibility.

In reaction to such criticism of the reduction of women's rights in family and marriage caused by the changes in the context of the marriage contract, the post-Khomeini republic has made some effort to improve women's marital relations through the enforcement of the process of sealing the marriage contract. Indeed, since the revolution, some ulema have emphasized the importance of sealing the marriage contract as a form of protection for women.[48] Khomeini himself claimed that Islam granted women the right to condition their marriage by stipulating the marriage contract. Owing to the attempt by the Majlis to codify procedures for prenuptial agreements, all marriage contracts have allowed for prenuptial agreements since late 1991.[49]

However, the option of prenuptial agreements in the marriage contract protects only those women educated enough to demand them. One woman lawyer emphasized that only women who are knowledgeable about women's rights and prenuptial agreements are able to stipulate various conditions for their marriage, such as "not allowing the husband to take a second wife" and "specifying the amount and the time of payment of alimony in case of divorce." If a man breaks a marriage contract that prohibits him from having a second wife, his marriage to the second wife will be void and he can be executed for adultery.[50] But few women are aware of the possibility of requesting conditions in the marriage contract.

In 1985–1986, the Islamic republic issued a set of directives entitled "Conditions at the Time of the Marriage Contract," which were supposed to be read to both spouses before they sign the marriage contract.[51] These directives state, for example, that when a woman seeks divorce, she must "establish, at the court, one of the conditions signed which have been inserted in their marriage contract."[52] (A man can seek divorce without establishing any reason.) The number of conditions under which a woman may seek divorce has increased from twelve to sixteen between 1982 and 1986 and continues to grow.

On the surface, this increase in the number of conditions appears to signify more protection for women. However, for the conditions to have the force of law, both spouses must have signed for each stipulation. As Shahla Haeri and Ziba Mir-Hosseini maintain, to make each claim valid is very difficult. First, a groom will be less willing to sign as the number of conditions increases. Moreover, a husband will be aware of the risks he will incur to his prerogative to divorce. Second, the courts seldom consent to a woman's request. For example, they approve a woman's claim for divorce only when the husband is insane, withdraws his financial support, or has been missing for four years.[53]

The Ayatollah Ali Moqtadi, the head of the Supreme Court, announced that "women were not given the right to divorce because they are prone to emotional and irrational decision-making."[54] Thus, the government's effort to protect women by the aforementioned reforms has not substantially compensated for the loss of women's rights caused by the 1982 abolition of the FPL.

Compensation for divorced women. The financial security of divorced women has been one of the more contentious issues in the debate. Both *Payam-e Hajer* and Fereshteh Hashemi insist that women's financial security should be automatically fulfilled through marriage (even in the case of divorce) in an "Islamic society." What, then, do they mean by an "Islamic society"? The newspaper declares that women should know what the Qur'an says about the family in Islam before they think "there are no other solutions [to the problems they face at present] except the reinterpretations of Islamic jurisprudence in the Islamic system."[55]

Here we observe a fundamental criticism against the system of velayat-e faqih, in which the ulema monopolize the right to interpret Islam and impose their interpretations as absolute. Thus, *Payam-e Hajer* implies that present-day Iran, under such a system, is not actually "Islamic." The question whether or not Iran is an "Islamic" society is also raised by Zahra Shojai, director of the state-run Cultural and Social Council on Women's Affairs:

> Our society has inherited certain erroneous assumptions which are accepted in the name of religion. . . . Some people regard a good woman as chaste and submissive. Islam [in this country] has required women to work at home for free. But a woman deserves to be paid for doing housework.[56]

As one of the reforms to secure divorced women's financial security, Fereshteh Hashemi calls for setting up arbitration councils in the case of divorce:

> The law makers of an Islamic society should order the religious courts, taking into consideration religious principles, rational sciences, and the verse of the Qur'an [Sura 2:236, The Cow], to share economic resource with the woman in any divorce, according to tabulation or assessments based on the duration of the joint life, economic capacity of the family, and employment or unemployment of the woman.[57]

The demand in the above quotation has been partially realized, when a 1986 law allowed a divorced wife to receive half of her husband's property (or the cash equivalent, as decided by the court) when a husband sought divorce while the wife fulfilled her duties and if the divorce "is not prompted by the moral deficiencies of the wife."

The provision, however, is very ambiguous and subjective, requiring the court to judge whether a wife has been fulfilling her duties as a wife, or to determine whether the case involves the wife's "moral deficiencies." Moreover, this provision does not necessarily force a husband to pay half of his property or income because the outcome depends on the judge's objectivity. However, the provision does provide, at least theoretically, more financial protection for women than traditionally practiced in the case of divorce.

Furthermore, in December 1992, new divorce laws in Iran "granted women the right to seek compensation from ex-husbands for housework performed during the marriage."[58] Another provision of these new divorce laws authorizes female assistant judges to attend divorce court. Putting this law into practice, however, involves several difficulties. The Council of Expediency, which approved the bill containing the new divorce laws, has not specified a formula to determine a housewife's wages. Additionally, some judges may ignore these new 1992 laws, perceiving them as "un-Islamic." For example, female judges were barred in May of 1979, when the FPL was rescinded according to "the Islamic standard" by which women were considered more "emotional" and less "rational" than men.[59] In general, "women's participation in court proceedings are limited in Islamic Laws."[60] Thus, the government needs to fill the gap between what the regime originally banned as "un-Islamic" and what the regime newly considers as women's rights. This seems to cause tension between the government's need for "Islamization" and its need to negotiate over women's demands in present Iran. Moreover, it remains difficult in any case to measure the impact of the government's efforts on women's lives, since there is such a gap between theory and practice.

In addition to the reforms in the previously mentioned laws, the government has created several administrative councils specifically designed to ensure the welfare of women, among them the Cultural and Social Council on Women's Affairs, established in 1987. Directed by Zahra Shojai, this body, in cooperation with the High Council of Cultural Revolution, whose chair is appointed by President Rafsanjani, seeks to eliminate discrimination against women in work, education, and political representation.[61] It strives to create "educational and cultural cores in all parts of the country to allow women to understand their rights and to increase their protection in family and society."[62]

Another council, the Council on Women's Affairs, was established in early 1992, when Shahla Habibi became its director and a special consultant to President Rafsanjani. The entire purpose in establishing this council was, according to Habibi, to investigate women's difficulties in order "to fulfill the Islamic goals in the fields related to women based on the model of Fatima Zohra."[63]

Despite these apparent political gains, women have not succeeded in passing much favorable legislation. Women's issues have frequently been debated in the national assembly, but sectarian politics inside the government have revealed the opponents of the government's initiative to improve the socioeconomic status of women. Later in 1992, the plan to form the Special Commission of Women's Affairs was raised but did not pass in the Majlis. Then the formation of a similarly named Special Commission of Women's Affairs and Family was proposed to that body but again was not approved.[64]

Can we consider these trends a positive sign for the empowerment of women? There is some room for doubt. As Deniz Kandiyoti notes, "Governments that granted women new rights frequently proceeded to abolish independent women's organizations while setting up state-sponsored women's organizations that were generally docile auxiliaries of the ruling state party."[65] The pattern has been realized in the past under Mohamed Reza Shah Pahlevi's Women's Organization in Iran and under President Zia ul Haq's Women's Division in Pakistan.[66] Thus, one must entertain reservations in viewing the formation of state-run councils as indicative of improvement of women's status, for it is difficult to judge how much autonomy these councils may enjoy.

CONCLUSION

A gap exists, as we have seen, between Islam as interpreted by the Khomeinist regime and Islam as interpreted through women's political consciousness. The former's overall use of Islam or "Islamic criteria" has generated a double standard in determining the rights of men and women. In reaction, Islamic reformist women have maintained that Islam should, in fact, guarantee women's rights in marriage and family.

Payam-e Hajer, as analyzed above, is highly strategic in its discussion of women's rights in Islamic society. By criticizing both West-toxicated and extremely Islamist women, it proposes its reformist interpretation of the Qur'an. One theme of political rhetoric within the Khomeinist government is anti–West-toxication. It is under this very circumstance that *Payam-e Hajer* has sought to demonstrate that its agenda for improving Muslim women's rights is truly and "genuinely rooted in their own culture."[67] By criticizing West-toxicated women, *Payam-e Hajer* emphasizes the fact that it is not feminist. The WSIRI certainly contests the oppression of women caused by the interpretations and practices of the Khomeinist government. However, unlike Western-oriented feminists, the newspaper's authors do not deemphasize sexual differences, nor do they seek rights for women *equal* to those for men in the Western sense.

Simultaneously, by attacking extremely traditional (Islamist) women, who are the repository of the Islamist gender ideology of the regime, the newspaper criticizes the regime's practice of Islam. The WSIRI attempts to preach that the reinterpretation of the Qur'anic passages should be done by each individual, not just by the ulema. The newspaper shows how it is possible to define women's rights within the framework of Islam and that Islamic reformist women can reverse the logic of the regime's denials of rights for women.

This reformist orientation of the WSIRI seems to reflect the course of events of which contemporary Iranian history partook: the rapid Westernizaton policies of Mohamed Reza Shah Pahlevi and the Islamic theocracy of Khomeini's regime, which appeared as a reaction to the former. *Payam-e Hajer* proposes the moderation of the two extremes of these Iranian regimes. It ultimately suggests that reformist Islam is the place to which Iranian people can return. In this respect, the WSIRI may be truly Islamist in essence.

Payam-e Hajer's middle-of-the-road policy has made women's questions palatable to the state. It is not a coincidence that *Payam-e Hajer* and some women activists and deputies have focused their demands on the area of the marriage and the family, the area in which the government has recently started to make reforms.

The recent reforms made by the government, as analyzed previously, have not substantially compensated for the loss of women's rights caused by the 1982 abolition of the FPL. Furthermore, to what extent the recently established administrative councils for women will function for improving women's status in general remains questionable.

However, this reform-oriented posture of the government reflects the reality that to survive, the government must maintain a delicate equilibrium between the state's legitimacy and the mobilization of women in political and socioeconomic arenas. The tension will continue to grow between what "Islamic" shape the Islamic republic should and can take and what women seek to realize in an "Islamic" society. What is to be challenged now is the substance of "Islamic" in the Islamic Republic of Iran. The debate on "women's questions" in postrevolutionary Iran reveals one facet of this profound problem.

NOTES

1. Sherifa Zuhur, *Revealing Reveiling: Islamist Gender Ideology in Contemporary Egypt* (New York: State University of New York Press, 1992).

2. Guity Nashat, ed. *Women and Revolution in Iran* (Boulder, CO: Westview Press, 1983).

3. Hitoshi Suzuki, "Iran wa Genrisyugikokka ka" (Is Iran a fundamentalist state?), in *Isramu Genrisyugi towa Nanika* (What is Islamic fundamentalism?), ed. Masayuki Yamauchi (Tokyo: Iwanami Shoten, 1996), 149.

4. Sami Zubaida, "An Islamic State? The Case of Iran," *Middle East Report* 153 (July-August 1988): 3–7.

5. Nikki Keddie, *Iran and the Muslim World* (New York: New York University Press, 1995), 172.

6. Valentine M. Moghadam, *Modernizing Women: Gender and Social Change in the Middle East* (Boulder, CO: Lynne Rienner, 1993), 147, 156, 169.

7. Eliz Sanasarian, "Political Activism and Islamic Identity in Iran," in *Women in the World*, ed. Peter H. Merk (Santa Barbara, CA, and Oxford, England: ABC-CLIO, 1986), 214–219; Nayereh Tohidi, "Modernity, Islamization and Women in Iran," in *Gender and National Identity*, ed. Valentine M. Moghadam (London: Zed Books, 1994), 141.

8. Sanasarian, "Political Activism," 218.

9. The society organized as a permanent body by establishing its own constitution and programs in 1980. Like the Women's Organization of Iran, the WSIRI had offices in other parts of the country, such as Isfahan, Ahvaz, and Shahrud, but as early as 1981 the WSIRI had to dissolve its provincial sections. It engages in social work by establishing a kind of vocational school, which provides young women with the potential ability and opportunities to pursue education in order to meet society's needs. It aims at raising women's participation in society through increasing their understanding of Islam, politics, and economics and through upgrading their members' vocational abilities for employment in various jobs. WSIRI initiates voluntary partnerships with women nurses in war regions and related hospitals. The society also gets a part of its budget from production: it has a factory to produce cloth and watches.

10. "Activities of the Women's Society of the Islamic Revolution of Iran," *Iran Times,* July 2, 1983, 5.

11. "Neither 'Traditional' nor Foreign Woman?" *Payam-e Hajer* 177 (10 Tir 1369/July 1, 1990), 12.

12. *Zan dar Ayneh-e Defaq-e Muqaddas* (Woman in the mirror of defense of the holy place) (Tehran: Markaz Chaap-e Sepah, 1990).

13. The term *bad hejab* (wearing veiling wrongly) has appeared in Iranian newspapers, the women's magazine *Zan-e Ruz* (Today's Woman), and *Payam-e Hajer,* the biweekly newspaper published by WSIRI, since a few years following the revolution, when the government made ambiguous but strict regulations on wearing the hijab. There has been much discussion about what is "wrong veiling" and what is "proper veiling" among religious leaders, columnists, and others. See Nayereh Tohidi's article on Iranian women's positions in *Nimeh-e Digar* 10 (winter 1990): 51–95.

14. "Traditional or Foreign Woman: Which Type?" *Payam-e Hajer* 177 (10 Tir 1369/July 1, 1990), 12.

15. "Foreign Identity and Returning to Oneself from the Viewpoint of Ali Shari'ati," *Payam-e Hajer* 178 (10 Mordad 1369/August 1, 1990), 9.

16. *Zan dar Ayneh-e Defaq-e Muqaddas* (Woman in the mirror of defense of the holy place) (Tehran: Markaz Chaap-e Sepah, 1990), 21.

17. "Women's Role," *Payam-e Hajer* 137 (10 Farvardin 1365/March 30, 1986); "Fatimah," *Payam-e Hajer* 139 (10 Bahman 1365/January 30, 1987).

18. Abbas Ali Mahmudi, *Zan dar Islam* (Woman in Islam) (Tehran: Khir Khan, n.d.).

19. Ibid.

20. Ibid., 115.

21. "Traditional or Foreign Woman: Which Type?" *Payam-e Hajer* 177 (10 Tir 1369/July 1, 1990), 12.

22. "A Story About the Woman from the Viewpoint of Nahj al-Balagha," *Payam-e Hajer* 176 (10 Khordad 1369/May 31, 1990), 7.

23. "Hijab, Divine Value, and the Human Being," *Payam-e Hajer* 86 (10 Shahrivar 1363/September 1, 1984), 2–3.

24. The inconsistent position of *Payam-e Hajer* seems to reflect the fact that different authors expressed their personal opinions in their articles and that the newspaper had to modify its rhetoric depending on the political climate in the Islamic Republic.

25. The passage reads, "And say to the believing women that they can cast down their gaze and guard their private parts and do not display their ornaments . . . and let them wear their head-coverings over their bosoms. . . . " *Holy Qur'an* trans. M. H. Shakir (Qum: Anssarian Publications, 1990), 338.

26. "Are Iranian Women Going to Acquire Their Own Rights?" *Payam-e Hajer* 99 (25 Esfand 1363/March 16, 1985), 3.

27. Ibid.

28. Quoted in Azar Tabari and Nahid Yeganeh, eds., *In the Shadow of Islam: The Women's Movement in Iran* (London: Zed Press, 1984), 177, 186.

29. "Considering Woman's Role in Society," *Payam-e Hajer* 172 (10 Day 1368/December 31, 1989), 7.

30. "Activities of the Women's Society of the Islamic Revolution of Iran," *Iran Times*, July 2, 1983, 5.

31. Haleh Isfandiari, "The Majlis and Women's Issues in the Islamic Republic of Iran," in *In the Eye of the Storm*, ed. Mahnaz Afkhami and Erika Friedl (Syracuse: Syracuse University Press, 1994), 75.

32. "Why Should Women Marry to Seek Education Abroad?" *Payam-e Hajer* 100 (25 Farvardin 1364/April 14, 1985), 2.

33. "Women's Political and Economic Identity Has Never Been Recognized in Society," *Zan-e Ruz* 1449 (7 Esfand 1372/February 26, 1994), 7.

34. Ziba Mir-Hosseini, "Women, Marriage and the Law in Post-Revolutionary Iran," in *Women in the Middle East: Perceptions, Realities and Struggles for Liberation,* ed. Haleh Afshar (London: Macmillan, 1993), 59–83.

35. Moojan Momen, *An Introduction to Shi'i Islam: The History and Doctrine of Twelver Shi'ism* (Oxford: George Ronald, 1985), 183.

36. Nesta Ramazani, "Women in Iran: The Revolutionary Ebb and Flow," *Middle East Journal* 24 (January 1992): 417. Akbar Agajanian found that the divorce rate increased between 1981 and 1982, in contrast to the continuous decline of the rate since 1961. See "Some Notes on Divorce in Iran," *Journal of Marriage and the Family* 48, no. 4 (November 1986): 749–755. However, analyzing the cause of the increase is problematic.

37. This term is frequently used in the Constitution and in the sayings of Khomeini.

38. Shahla Haeri, *Law of Desire: Temporary Marriage in Shi'i Islam* (Syracuse: Syracuse University Press, 1989).

39. "Are Iranian Women Going to Acquire Their Own Rights?" *Payam-e Hajer* 99 (25 Esfand 1363/March 16, 1985), 3.

40. Foreign Broadcast Information Service–Near East Service (FBIS-NES), 19 April 1991: 52.

41. "International Laws of Rights Regarding the Family," *Payam-e Hajer* 106 (25 Tir 1364/July 16, 1985), 2.

42. Tabari and Yeganeh, *In the Shadow of Islam,* 176.

43. "The Creation of the Woman and Her Role," *Payam-e Hajer* 137 (10 Bahman 1365/January 30, 1987), 8.

44. "International Laws of Rights Regarding the Family," *Payam-e Hajer* 106 (25 Tir 1364/July 16, 1985), 4.

45. "Marriage from Islamic Viewpoints," *Payam-e Hajer* 86 (10 Shahrivar 1363/ September 1, 1984), 3.

46. Fereshteh Hashemi says that the economic rights of women at the time of separation, women's mahr, and their subsistence should all be guaranteed. See Tabari and Yeganeh, *In the Shadow of Islam*, 180.

47. "The Creation of the Woman and Her Role," *Payam-e Hajer* 140 (10 Ordibehesht 1366/April 30, 1987), 3.

48. John Esposito takes this position in his book *Women in Muslim Family Law* (Syracuse: Syracuse University Press, 1982).

49. Ramazani, "Women in Iran," 417.

50. "Rights of Women and Workers in Iran," *Iran Times*, May 10, 1992, 7.

51. Shahla Haeri, "Obedience Versus Autonomy: Women and Fundamentalism in Iran and Pakistan," in *Fundamentalisms and Society: Reclaiming the Sciences, the Family and Education*, ed. Martin E. Marty and R. Scott Appleby (Chicago: University of Chicago Press, 1993), 192.

52. Ziba Mir-Hosseini, "Divorce in Islamic Law and in Practice: The Case of Iran," *Cambridge Anthropology* 11, no. 1 (1986): 47.

53. Katayon Ghazi, "Teheran Journal: Helping Women Raise Sights in Islamic Society," *New York Times*, March 14, 1992, 2. See also Eliz Sanasarian, "Politics of Gender and Development in the Islamic Republic of Iran," *Journal of Developing Societies* 8 (1992): 61.

54. *New York Times*, March 14, 1992.

55. "Marriage from the Islamic Point of View," *Payam-e Hajer* 97 (25 Bahman 1363/February 14, 1985), 7.

56. "Iran Panel Backs Divorce Payments," *New York Times*, December 17, 1992, A12.

57. Tabari and Yeganeh, *In the Shadow of Islam,* 184.

58. "Women Get Divorce Rights," *Iran Times*, December 18, 1992, 1.

59. Nesta Ramazani, "Behind the Veil: Status of Women in Revolutionary Iran," *Journal of South Asian and Middle Eastern Studies* 4, no. 2 (1980): 28.

60. "Iran Panel Backs Divorce Payments," *New York Times*, December 17, 1992, A12.

61. "Women Get Divorce Rights," *Iran Times*, December 18, 1992, 1.

62. Ibid.

63. "Women's Political and Economic Identity Has Never Been Recognized in Society," *Zan-e Ruz* 1449 (7 Esfand 1372/February 26, 1994), 6.

64. *Zan-e Ruz* 1432 8 Aban 1372/October 30, 1983.

65. Deniz Kandiyoti, "Women, Islam, and the State: A Comparative Approach," in *Comparing Muslim Societies*, ed. Juan R. I. Cole (Ann Arbor: University of Michigan Press, 1992), 251.

66. *The Report of the Pakistan Commission of the Status of Women* (Islamabad: Government of Pakistan, 1985).

67. Valentine M. Moghadam, "Rhetoric of Rights of Identity in Islamist Movements," *Journal of World History* (fall 1993): 251–252.

6

Persisting Contradictions: Muslim Women in Syria

Bouthaina Shaaban

Two major problems are bound to face anyone making a comprehensive assessment of the status of Muslim women in Syria: First, there is an inconsistency on the one hand between important achievements made by women at many levels and, on the other, a still wavering social attitude that is not totally supportive of equal rights for women. The second problem relates to the image of Syria as a Muslim country where women are veiled, education is segregated, and public offices are filled with men to the near total exclusion of women, an image that bears no relation to reality. Thus, in any attempt to present an objective evaluation of the status of Muslim women in Syria, one has to swim against many currents, some of which are created by the nature of the subject itself, others by the frequent misunderstanding of it. In this chapter I can only highlight questions rather than provide easy answers.

The main theoretical contributions I seek to offer in this chapter are to emphasize the ambiguous relationship that is deliberately maintained between religious polity and secular society and to dwell upon the impact of this relationship on women's achievements in all domains. What appears to be coincidental or a result of a natural mixture of Islam and civil society is perhaps more a desired reality that some may find useful. My aim is to explore, analyze, and interpret phenomena in my endeavor to present a truly objective and realistic image of the position of Muslim women in Syria.

Legislative and institutional changes over the past thirty years have opened up large areas of opportunity for Syrian women, who are gradually entering the professions and government offices. Yet social attitudes have changed more slowly, leading to significant divergence between the ideal and the actual status of Syrian women, most of whom profess Islam but whose opportunities may be shaped as much or more by social class, education, residence, and economic means.

Several forms of Islam—Shi'i, Sunni, Alawi, Druze, and Isma'ili—are followed by Syrians. In addition, there exist a number of Christian sects forming about 10 percent of the population and a small Jewish community. Several ethnic minorities such as Circassians, Kurds, Armenians, and Assyrians are likewise present, each with its own social customs and traditions. Other differences among Syrian women may be found between urban and rural communities and even between Damascus as a capital city and the rest of the country. Moreover, class differences suggest varying codes of behavior. Syria is made up of many communities established along a variety of lines. The image presented in the Western media is a far cry from reality.

This reality is visibly reflected in the dress code of women, which ranges from the woman's body being enveloped completely in black, including face and hands, to the latest fashions freshly arrived from French and Italian boutiques. Such diversity may be discovered in the same family, one daughter wearing the most conservative black *hijab,* whereas another prefers to be attired in shorts or tight jeans.

Although Islam is the official state religion in the Syrian constitution and has been a formative influence in Syrian history for fourteen centuries, government policies over more than three decades have been guided by a secular philosophy. Such a historic revolution has brought about significant contradictions between laws on the books and the continuing relevance of the Shari'a as Syrian Muslims generally perceive it, not to mention the existential realities for Muslim women.

In "Rhetorical Strategies and Official Policies on Women's Rights,"[1] Ann Elizabeth Meyer explains many of the contradictions in the status of women. She argues that in Muslim countries as well as in the United States and the Vatican, "rhetorical strategies that proclaim support for women's equality are pursuing policies that are inimical to women's rights. The result is what might be called 'the new world hypocrisy.'"[2] Despite the generally accepted concept that Muslim women are the victims of inequalities, her article suggests that the status of Muslim women is not so different from that of women in the United States and the West. Just as Muslim countries use the Shari'a as an excuse for denying women full equality, the United States and the West generally agree that women should be equal but deny that their laws are discriminatory.[3] Thus, everywhere the opponents of women find it necessary to "adopt the doubletalk of the new world hypocrisy."[4] Such hypocrisy makes the battle for women's emancipation and equality particularly difficult.

In many Muslim countries the dividing line between the Shari'a and secular laws is left deliberately vague. Most of these countries maintain that their personal status law derives strictly from the Shari'a; therefore it is beyond their ability to alter anything in it to accommodate women's demands for full equality. New studies, however, have shown that personal status laws in certain Muslim countries propose very different interpretations of the Shari'a to suit their inherent stands on women's issues.[5] This aspect becomes even more confusing in a country like Syria where the state ostensibly pursues a secular policy yet Islam remains the official religion of the state.

GOVERNMENT POLICIES AND
PROGRAMS AFFECTING SYRIAN WOMEN

In the postcolonial era Syria went through a period of turbulent changes until the Ba'th Arab Socialist Party (still today the principal ruling party) seized office in 1963. In its own constitution the party describes itself as a secular party with a comprehensive social and political reform program. Pledging full equality between men and women, it promises full participation for women in the workplace. In 1970 the government adopted the party's program as a national program, and the general secretary of the party, Hafez Assad, became president of the republic.

Thus, Assad became the president of a Muslim country in which the president must be a Muslim, but at the same time he was—and remains—the general secretary of a secular party that strives to build a civil society. Since that time, compromises have been increasingly sought between Islamic policy and secular laws. This situation provides both secularists and Islamists with ready-made excuses for any program they dislike: each immediately lists its fear of the other as a pretext for its reluctance to act.

Women, however, were not sitting idly by through all of this; they were pursuing their own agenda. In 1967 women's welfare societies, educational associations, and voluntary councils merged into an organization called the General Union of Syrian Women (GUSW), which has a constitution, bylaws, and an infrastructure covering all parts of the country. This merger was inspired by the state, but the GUSW is not a state-controlled organization. The state may suggest to the GUSW the part of its agenda that is considered necessary for the general program of the state. Hence, the GUSW may be considered a quasi-governmental organization with a mandate to advocate women's issues in the country. The union aims to achieve equal opportunity for all women. In order to help women, particularly mothers, to engage in work and improve their standard of living, the union has given priority to opening efficient nurseries and kindergarten facilities on which working women may depend.

In 1989 the Syrian government passed a new law to ensure that ministries, schools, factories, and all public institutions provide nurseries and kindergartens on the premises for their female employees. All these services are partially subsidized by the government. They charge what might be considered an affordable rate to working mothers. For example, a mother whose salary is $100 per month pays $10 a month for her baby's nursery, with the fee including transportation provided by the nursery. The GUSW also offers training and handicraft courses for unemployed women seeking ways to support their families or to augment the family income.

Moreover, the GUSW has exerted considerable energy in the fight against illiteracy, which at its founding reached 80 percent among rural women. By 1981 the overall number of illiterate women stood at 55.2 percent, broken down into 41 percent for the 15- to 24-year-old age group and 67.7 percent for those aged 25 to 44 years. Because of intensive joint efforts of the GUSW and the Ministry of Culture, illiteracy among the first age group declined to 12.4 percent by 1992 and among the older women's group to 37.5 percent. Total illiteracy among Syrian women was reduced to 30.6 percent in that year.[6]

An important factor in the rapid reduction of illiteracy in Syria has been the extensive implementation of the compulsory education law. Since the law applies to the 6- to 12-year-old age group, it has opened the way for women to become literate and then to pursue their education, the topic to which we now turn.

Women and Education

Since the 1970s, government plans relating to education have adopted a truly radical approach in two main areas: rural education and women's education. In fact, the stress on opening schools in rural areas has by itself increased the percentage of women in education because in most villages people were eager to send their daughters and sons to school, never before having had this opportunity. Furthermore, since women work in the field alongside men, for girls to sit with boys at school desks presented no problem; villagers live a life of intimacy yet observe very strictly the customary morality codes. Such a demonstration by the state of understanding women's aspirations for education has encouraged them to push harder to pursue their university and even postgraduate studies.

A personal anecdote may be illuminating here. In 1971 I received my baccalaureate degree and ranked first in the province of Homs and fourth in Syria. My degree was in literature, not in science, simply because our village school lacked a science curriculum, as was the case in most Syrian villages. President Assad had issued a decree providing scholarships for the first ten students in the science field but for only the first three in the literary one. This meant that I failed to receive a grant.

Through the help of the highest political authorities in Homs, I managed to see the president. My argument to him was that since in most Syrian villages no science curriculum existed, it was unfair to give the sciences preferential treatment in regard to scholarships. Instead, the government should provide them for the first ten students in each branch. The president agreed and amended the decree to cover all students who rank first in their provinces in all branches: scientific, literary, industrial, commercial, and religious. In this manner the way for me as well as for hundreds of students over the years has been opened to continue university and postgraduate education. For me, both as a woman and as a citizen from a rural area, this incident signaled a new official attitude relating to education for women and for the rural areas of Syria.

It is in education, in fact, that Syrian women have made the greatest strides over the past three decades. In the first place, schooling in Syria is free, subsidized by the national government. Second, the government has launched school construction programs affecting every village, no matter how small. Even the bedouin, the nomadic pastoralists, have a mobile school complete with resident teachers moving with their flocks. As a result of this educational policy, the number of girls enrolled in primary, preparatory, and secondary levels doubled between 1980 and 1993.[7] As for university education, Table 6.1 is illuminating.

The number of women teachers at all educational levels has also increased from 47 percent in 1980 to 57 percent in 1993. In 1993 women teachers were 64 percent of the total in primary education (ages 6–12) and 45 percent in preparatory (12–15) combined with secondary (15–18) levels.[8] The figures are less impressive but still substantial at the university level, where in 1990 women constituted 20.75 percent of faculty members in various colleges.[9]

Yet instead of feeling satisfied with this rate of growth in the number of women students and teachers, one has to wonder, what do such statistics mean in real life? The status of women has not dramatically changed, and women are still regarded as the "weaker sex." These statistics might serve as a precursor to change or as an indicator that real change is now possible, but they hardly mean that the situation has completely altered.

In addition to this considerable entry of women into schools and universities, government educational plans have stressed the importance of coeducation as a means of changing attitudes and creating healthier social relationships. Here a difference between rural and urban areas must be considered. In rural areas all schools are mixed; no school is segregated by gender. In urban areas, too, some primary schools are coeducational, but

Table 6.1 Women in University and Postgraduate Education, 1980–1993
(percentage)

Level	1980	1993
Registered	26.12	39.10
Graduated	27.33	35.97
Postgraduate enrollment	8.86	22.00

the government plan specifies that by the year 2000, all primary schools in Syria will be coeducational. Moreover, a substantial number of preparatory and secondary schools in towns already serve both genders. This trend toward coeducation throughout the Syrian educational system will help to develop a more healthy relationship between men and women.

Such a quantitative upsurge in the number of women within the field of education has not, however, been matched by a qualitative change in Syrian society as a whole. Although becoming better educated has enabled more women to work and thus become financially independent, social attitudes lag behind. This is the dilemma of the developing world and perhaps the world in general. What should be changed first, the laws governing a society or the social conditions from which these laws emanate? Some laws have been changed only to be rescinded later because of a total lack of social cooperation in implementing the relevant laws. Women have assumed new positions in all fields without a concomitant shift in their family social status. These uneven results might be attributed to a number of factors, the foremost being that social attitudes are more difficult to change than laws and decrees. Other factors include the lack of representation of women at decisionmaking levels and the reluctance of most women who reach senior positions to take firm stands in defense of women's rights. Yet social attitudes are changing, but at a much slower pace than the realities affecting women.

Women in Politics

While the emergence of women into the field of education has been bold and impressive, their entry into politics has been slower. Women have no representation whatsoever in the National Front and the Regional Leadership, the two highest political bodies in Syria. Yet in 1976, Dr. Najah al-Attar was appointed Minister of Culture, a post she still occupies. The appointment in 1993 of Dr. Saleha Sunqur, a university professor and former dean in the College of Education, University of Dasmascus, to be Minister for Higher Education was symbolic, perhaps, of the impact of women in education. She was only the second woman minister in government during the past twenty years. There have been one woman ambassador and three women as chargés d'affaires in the diplomatic service, as well as one woman representative in the executive bureaus of trade unions, public organizations, and local party branches. In 1994, twenty-four women members of parliament out of a total of 250 were elected to serve during the fourth term of the Syrian Parliament, or 9.6 percent compared to 6.6 percent in 1981.

Although women's presence in such high political posts has symbolic importance, it must be apparent that such a small number of women will not significantly affect the process of decisionmaking. To make a true mark on political life, more women must be present. Moreover, even this small number of senior women is rendered almost ineffective by covert or overt pressure to behave like men in order to prove themselves worthy of the positions they occupy. Any woman trying to bring a feminist perspective into her work is accused of either being antimale or of trying to destabilize the institution in which she works. This constitutes a universal problem suffered by most women breaking new ground; they need courage and support to bring to bear their own perspectives rather than to fit into a mold that might contradict their vision and convictions. One might well describe the prevalent attitude of Syrian professional women as a false feminist consciousness leading those women in influential positions to ignore women's issues in order to avert being tarred with a feminist label.

In Syria as elsewhere, women can change their status only when they hold sufficient political power to amend those laws that hinder their efforts to shape a new identity and a new reality within which they can function. For women's participation in public affairs to be effective, their number must be sufficient to guarantee an influential voice in both legislative and executive positions. This requirement presents a special problem in those Muslim countries where women are barred from the legislature under the pretext that the Shari'a does not permit their participation. Otherwise, as occurs the world over—certain Scandinavian nations excepted—the presence of token women produces very little change in women's lives and destiny.[10]

In order to become part of a decisionmaking body, women must first understand the political system. Women in Syria and elsewhere still believe that hard work and dedication alone are decisive in climbing the political ladder. Men who have long been struggling for political power, however, know that the rules of the political game are quite different. Some sophisticated women might argue that women should not embark on changing their nature in order merely to become men's peers. Yet whether they play the game or rebel against it, women must attain a critical mass in influential posts to better themselves once and for all. In order to advance toward a brighter future, however, women in Muslim countries, including Syria, face an additional problem in the Islamists.[11]

WOMEN AND THE ISLAMISTS

The position of women in Islam has always been one of the most controversial areas of Islamic interpretation, partly because few interpreters over the fourteen centuries of Islamic history have been women. In his article, "Women in Islam," Mohammed Arkoun argues:

> In its essence, the problem of women in Islam is an interpretative problem, because the absence of women interpreters in our age, as is the case

in every age, constitutes a basic obstacle in the way of the Muslim woman's ability to liberate herself as other women in the world do.[12]

One of the few Muslim women interpreters of Islam is the Lebanese Nazira Zin al-Din, who wrote two books, *al-Sufur wa'l-Hijab*[13] and *al-Fatat wa'l-Shuyukh*,[14] in which she offers a thorough interpretation of the texts in the Qur'an concerning women's status, rights, and duties. Although these books were extremely well received and reviewed in different parts of the globe at the time of their publication in the late 1920s, they are hardly read or known today even by scholars on the subject.[15] The works of Zin al-Din, like all those of liberal Muslim scholars, have been marginalized and largely ignored. Unless such works are included in the educational curriculum or are integrated in one way or another into the mainstream literature about Islam, their effect is bound to remain limited. Even those rights of women that are clearly stated in the Qur'an are not properly emphasized in Syrian school and university curricula. To promote a national dialogue around such issues is a necessary prerequisite for changing laws relating to women.

Like Muslim women the world over, Syrian women are subject to different interpretations of their status. There are as many interpretations as there are interpreters. In most Muslim countries, enlightened readings of sections of the Qur'an concerning women continue to be marginalized.[16] During the past two decades, the Islamists have made such progressive views their prime targets and accuse these interpreters of being guilty of *kufr,* or heresy.

The Islamists assume the right to monopolize Quranic interpretation and have initiated campaigns of terror against anyone who dares to differ with them. Yet, as Abdullahi an-Na'im argues, according to the true spirit of Islam "all Muslims, men and women alike, have the right to debate among themselves the meaning of what the Qur'an says regarding the rights of women, or any other issue or question, challenge so-called 'orthodox' interpretations, and advance their own in this regard."[17] Abdol Karim Soroush, an Iranian scholar, totally agrees:

> Understanding of religion is all relative. It is not fixed for all time and place. Who can say what God meant? This opens the door to all kinds of new ideas, political as well as religious. . . . Interpretation of religious texts is always in flux. Those interpretations are influenced as well by the age you live in, so you can never give a fixed interpretation.[18]

An-Na'im makes the same point in different words: "It is the living community which should decide which view or interpretation of the Qur'an should prevail at any given time."[19] The Islamists, however, emphatically reject such views and seek to force their own reading of Islam on all Muslim men and women.

The two areas of interpretation that particularly affect women are the hijab and laws of personal status. Many liberal scholars have argued that there is nothing in the Qur'an that requires Muslim women to wear the hijab, whereas in many Muslim countries it is considered the most obvious duty of a Muslim woman.

The issue of the hijab has always been in flux in Syria. Because Syria is a plural society and because its Muslims come from very different backgrounds, there are some women who do not wear the hijab. But when the Muslim Brethren gained some strength in the late 1970s and early 1980s, the number of women in the streets and at work wearing the hijab dramatically increased, reaching record levels. Once this movement waned, however, the number of women wearing it just as quickly receded. Now the trend has reversed course again. The hijab is visibly in ascendance since the early 1990s. Yet this time it is a different hijab, modern, colorful, often worn with full makeup and Westernized clothes. In fact, the colorful hijab with matching outfit and makeup may render women more attractive than they would be without it. Some argue it is untrue that the number of women wearing the hijab has increased, merely that women who had never contemplated entering the workplace are now doing so and wearing the hijab to maintain their sense of dignity.

The essential point is not about what a woman wears, but rather what she does with her life. The nature of positions filled by women has changed. They now drive automobiles, manage their own businesses, and may need to keep open a supermarket or pharmacy until the early hours of the morning. Such women suggest that for them the hijab is a liberation rather than a restraint. Without it, in response to family or social pressure, they would be unable to engage in work outside the home. Under the circumstances, they prefer to wear the hijab and play the role of their choice rather than remain at home.

Collectively categorizing all hijab-wearing women is no less than egregious stereotyping, as is the historical classification of women as inferior to men. Muslim feminist scholars (both men and women) should engage in dialogue to prove that there is no text in the Qur'an making the hijab compulsory for women, and the Islamists must be made to engage in this dialogue as well.

PERSONAL STATUS LAWS

Issues that affect Syrian Muslim women's lives even more seriously are the laws of marriage, divorce, and child custody, all of which are encompassed in the personal status law. Most Muslim countries, Syria included, claim that such laws of personal status, particularly those in the above categories, are strictly derived from the Shari'a. However, since the Shari'a is interpreted by different male scholars from a variety of cultures and traditions, the ensuing laws also vary accordingly.

With regard to the question of polygyny, for example, we find that most Muslim countries recognize polygyny, claiming that God allowed it in the Qur'an. Yet Tunisia has passed a law declaring the practice illegal, citing exactly the same text but applying to it a different understanding. The laws of marriage and divorce also vary from one country to another, and the implementation of them diverges even more widely. In theory, women in Islam have the right to *al-usma,* which is the woman's right to a divorce, whenever she likes, but only if this provision is included in the marriage contract. This, of course, depends on the groom's concurrence. The reality of the matter is that very few Muslim women are aware of this right because it is not mentioned in schoolbooks or highlighted in, for example, the media. Even if a woman knows of this right and insists on its inscription in the marriage contract, very few men would agree to marry "such a woman" whose intentions, they would say, have to be dubious; otherwise, why would she insist on such an "unnecessary" right? What is more, since most judges are men who are not keen to empower women in any way, it is in practice much easier for a man to divorce his wife than the reverse. Such constraints on women seeking divorce, of course, may be just as valid in non-Muslim societies.

Theoretically, upon divorce the mother is granted custody of the children until a son is 7 years of age and a daughter 9, after which the children may choose to reside with either parent. In reality, it is often a simple matter for men to deprive women of this right. The man has only to testify that the mother of his children is unfit to care for the children for one reason or another, whereupon the court immediately transfers the right of custody from the mother to the father.

The Shari'a stipulates that the interests of the child should be paramount in such matters, but this provision is not always considered. The handicap for women is that in most cases they do not have an independent home in which to live with their children. Hence they end up relinquishing the custody of their children either because they lack a home or the means of support or both. In most cases the divorcee returns to live with her parents or her brothers, whereas the husband, who is the owner of the home, remains there with the children. Any sociologist studing divorce cases in Muslim countries would undoubtedly conclude that current practices are far removed from the spirit of Islam despite the fact that legislators claim the laws to be derived from the Shari'a. Moreover, there can be no doubt that the absence of women from the clerical hierarchy as well as from legislative and executive authority presents a further impediment to ensuring women their full rights. It is almost of no consequence what the laws are in Syria because what prevails are customs and traditions. Laws of personal status are implemented in a way consistent with these age-old standards.

In most cases women are helpless and end up securing no rights at all. The situation of women in most other Muslim countries does not diverge substantively from this situation.

Because Syria is in a different stage of development, urbanization, and industrialization, the family unit there is not comparable to that in Europe. The Syrian family consists not only of the nucleus, the parents and their children, but of the entire extended family as well. This traditional structure has its merits and demerits. The attention of the extended family often works as a mechanism of support that deters wife abuse and wife battering. In other cases, however, the lineage may interfere in the life of a happily married couple to its detriment. In Islamic culture the individual is supposed to subordinate all personal needs to those of the family, but Islam has also promoted the rights of the individual within the family. For a better understanding to develop between Muslim and Western cultures, these differences have to be acknowledged and candidly discussed.

The problematic relationship between Muslim and Western cultures originates in the fact that each sees the other through a distorted lens. Each one evaluates the other by its worst and most superficial qualities. To be properly understood in the West, Islam should be seen as having multiple shades of meaning, varied interpretations that naturally result in diverse practices. In Western cultures the separation of religion and state is a fundamental principle, but in Muslim countries personal status laws are derived from a religious canon subject to many interpretations. Hence there is a desperate need to build a true bridge of understanding between Muslim and Western cultures, a bridge based on mutual respect rather than the desire to prove the superiority of the one over the other.

SYRIAN WOMEN AT WORK

The number of women in the Syrian workforce remains quite low; in 1993 there were 2,858,000 men and 628,000 women working, a ratio of five to one. Of the 717,387 who work for the Syrian government, only 193,163 are women, or 21 percent. Official figures state that women make up a third of the labor force in agriculture, but it is well known that they assume no administrative positions and have no say in either land or crop management. As to their role in business, only 5,088 women, or less than 4 percent of the total, run their own businesses, compared to 126,194 men.

At least half of Syria's current population of fifteen million live in rural areas where the division of labor is very flexible. Here women are not counted as part of the formal, official workforce; they are housewives, mothers, and workers in the fields, part of the so-called informal sector. Yet more often than not, they are the pillars of agricultural production. In addition to bearing children and managing a home, women shoulder a substantial part of the work in the fields. In rural areas women probably constitute at least 50 percent of the workforce but lack any of the attendant benefits: no independent income, no pension, and no role in management. They form an unpaid labor force that contributes profoundly to the national economy.

In the urban environment the situation is different. In the past thirty years, Syrian women have significantly invaded the workforce, although their total proportion does not exceed 20 percent. Pressing economic needs have driven this change, but lingering traditional perspectives still persuade some women that they owe their salaries to those who allow them to enter the workplace, generally family members. It is only recently that some Syrian women have become aware that they are entitled to the rewards of their own labor and can claim their earnings as independent income.

The contrast between the prevailing situation in Syria and what is specified in the Qur'an is stunning. As stipulated in the Qur'an, women are entitled to their entire wages: "For men a share of what they have earned and for women a share of what they have earned" (Sura 4:32, known as al-Nisa). Islamic texts declare, moreover, that women are not obliged to perform any household services; they are wives and mothers, not servants. Women are not even obliged to breast-feed their babies should they choose not to do so. During the time of the Prophet, many women sent their babies to the desert to be breast-fed by wet nurses. This role of performing all the services of the home was dictated to them by men. Unfortunately, they accepted it and thus it became part of Islamic tradition and culture, but it has no basis in scripture.

Working women shoulder a double burden at home and at work. Although what a woman earns and what she inherits are legally hers according to the Shari'a, the new income she brings to the family does not reduce the burden of domestic services required of her at home. However, there can be little doubt that in the past twenty years, more services have been provided to enable working women to function outside the home. The widespread introduction of nurseries and kindergartens, as mentioned earlier, has been a step in the right direction. New mothers receive ten weeks of fully paid maternity leave, four additional weeks of pay at 80 percent, and up to a year of unpaid leave. They also get an hour a day for breast-feeding for the first eighteen months after giving birth. In fact, in a country in which the fertility rate is one of the highest in the world, Syria may accord too many privileges to mothers, encouraging them to go out to work and also to have more children.

Rural women, other than the teachers who enjoy nurseries and kindergartens at their schools, have no such benefits, however. Peasant women, of course, receive no maternity leave or child services other than the assistance of family members. The contribution of rural women to the Syrian economy, being informal, is neither recognized nor even noticed.

However, rural women are not exposed as much as urban women to the various waves of Islamism; their traditions are strong, and each village observes them in almost religious fashion. Whether the village is Muslim or Christian, the prevailing tradition applies to all, which means that culture and tradition are interwoven with religion. As women work in the fields and tend their cattle, they need to wear practical clothing that allows them to move freely yet maintain the appropriate level of modesty. In most villages women wear very colorful outfits and keep a variety of headcovers to protect them from the sun and dust as well as to observe modesty criteria. Since such women work with men both at home and in the field, there is no question of segregating men from women on any occasion. Thus in the village the question of gender hardly surfaces in peoples' minds. Both men and women are judged according to their adherence to ethical rules and moral standards.

Because of the efforts of the United Nations and its agencies and the rising level of human development, there is a growing, universal awareness of the importance of women's work in both rural and industrialized areas. The importance of acknowledging women's contribution to agriculture is a major theme in world conferences convened by the United Nations, the latest being the UN's Fourth World Conference on Women held in Beijing in September 1995. Even conservative Muslim societies are finding it difficult to ignore the pressing need for women's participation in the workplace. No less than the International Association of the Muslim Brethren, from its headquarters in Cairo, deemed it necessary to issue an Islamic edict in 1994 acknowledging the right of Muslim women to work and to assume senior government posts. In this edict, published in a booklet under the title "Muslim Women in Muslim Society,"[20] they argued that Muslim women's participation in running their country's affairs is not only their right but even their duty in order to inhibit non-Muslims from occupying such posts. The issuance of such an edict, considered revolutionary in the history of the Muslim Brethren, is a measure of the social pressure everyone feels to grant women equal opportunity in every domain. It also results from the feminist struggle and the mutual interaction of secular and Islamist movements, which goes on all the time, no matter how indirect or intangible it might be.

HEALTH CARE, FAMILY PLANNING, AND SOCIAL VALUES

Prior to the 1970s, most social and medical services were nonexistent in rural areas of Syria. Now, however, with the whole country electrified and roads paved, not only schools but also social and medical services have been extended to rural areas. Medical, dental, and family planning facilities not formerly known to villagers are now available at least in central Syria.

All medical doctors and pharmacists graduating from Syrian universities these days are required to work for two years in rural areas. Accordingly, health standards for both men and women have markedly improved.

Most helpful to women has been the opening of family planning centers. The Syrian government did not publicize them, although it worked hard but quietly to ensure that these centers attracted women's attention. As noted above, the rate of population increase in Syria, at 3.8 percent, is one of the highest in the world. Both the government and the people are tacitly concerned. No direct public discussion in this matter is enunciated for fear of raising a contentious argument with those in the country having strong Islamic tendencies. Articles appear in daily newspapers, however, about the danger to the health of the mother of closely repeated pregnancies. Women are urged to manage their pregnancies and space them, and since contraceptives are offered free of charge, women in both rural and urban areas are strongly encouraged to visit the centers. Recently, a few articles in the national newspaper, *al-Ba'th,* argued that family planning is in accordance with Islam and that the Prophet Muhammad advocated natural birth control even in his day. Quite wisely, the government does not want to start an unnecessary battle with Islamists who decry birth control; thus as with economic reform policies, it carries out its plans slowly but steadily, with minimal publicity.

A major contributor to this high birthrate in Syria may be the desire for male children. Many are convinced that they can manage only a small family, but they don't know how they can guarantee a son in a family of only two or three children. There are social as well as economic reasons for wanting a male heir to carry on the family name; otherwise the lineage dies out, a tragic outcome in a family-centered society. According to the Shari'a, the son is the one to establish the inheritance rights even of his sisters. A family having only daughters, for example, will find most of its property inherited by grandparents and uncles in accordance with Islamic law, leaving the girls a much smaller legacy than if they had had a brother. In a family with two daughters and one son, in contrast, the son inherits half his parents' estate, and the two girls share the other half. Since the law of inheritance, as previously noted, is spelled out explicitly in the Qur'an, it therefore cannot be changed—or so it is claimed. Yet any serious attempt to reduce the birthrate in Syria has to address the law of inheritance.

The need for a son also derives from cultural values: it may affect a man's social status. The father of girls is not considered as virile as the father of boys because the concept of the tribe, sons accompanying their father to war, persists in Syrian society even though men are no longer tribal warriors. In this case, local customs and traditions still affect the status of women. Thus, social attitudes are most impermeable to change. In fact, "change" is not a very positive word in the Syrian vocabulary. Few writers and intellectuals are prepared even to speak about change, not to mention

advocating it. Outmoded definitions of manhood and womanhood, therefore, remain today almost as they were long ago despite the actual dramatic changes in women's lives. Consequently women's achievements in
educational, cultural, and economic fields are not yet reflected in a new
cultural expression, perhaps because women's associations have focused
mainly on improving working conditions for women, without paying as
much attention to altering inherited perceptions of women to fit a much
improved reality.

CONCLUSION

Both government and nongovernmental organizations (NGOs) have devoted their efforts to changing the actual status of women without resort-
ing to theoretical and conceptual arguments aimed at transforming the
public image of women. By far the most important women's organization
in Syria, the General Union of Syrian Women, has a branch in every bor-
ough or village that offers services for women and their children and has
an impact that cannot be measured by its official membership alone. Other
NGOs, such as the Women's Educational Society, formed in 1946, still
exist, though only in Damascus where it consists of a certain group of
upper-middle-class women whose work can best be described as "charity"
for poorer and younger women.

Because of these groups' efforts together with legal and institutional
changes, women have achieved new positions in all fields. Yet these advances in economic, educational, and health opportunities in Syria have
occurred without a concomitant shift in women's social status within the
family. For example, a woman now pursuing her university or even postgraduate studies is expected to behave toward her brothers and father in
the same manner as an illiterate woman lacking any schooling. She is expected to consult even her younger brother in choosing a husband and, if
necessary, to submit to his will; thus she is hardly different from her
mother and grandmother. Her problematic status is a consequence of the
failure, through lack of courage, of women themselves to assert their new
identity. In the patriarchal Syrian society, they have not made it self-
evident that they reject being treated in an outdated fashion.

Such a discrepancy between tangible achievements on the one hand
and the transparent and persistent patriarchal attitudes on the other creates
tension and frustration among Syrian women. Their discouragement leads
them either back to the home or to enlistment in the forces of Islamism.
Working women who experience no radical changes in their personal lives
and social status are now weighing the value of work that leaves them with
a double burden and only marginal financial enhancement. The sweeping
desire of women to enter the workplace that appeared during the 1960s

and 1970s has markedly receded since then as women discovered that working neither reduced their traditional tasks nor significantly improved their social status. In the face of these contradictions affecting their lives, the challenge today and in the future for Muslim women in Syria is to strike the sensitive chord demanding a new status, without seeming to demean either their culture or their religion.

NOTES

1. Ann Elizabeth Meyer, "Rhetorical Strategies and Official Policies on Women's Rights: The Merits and Drawbacks of the New World Hypocrisy," in *Faith and Freedom*, ed. Mahnaz Afkhami (London: I. B. Tauris, 1995), 104–132.

2. Ibid., 104.

3. Ibid., 119.

4. Ibid., 123.

5. An example is Ann Meyer's article just quoted. Among studies of this kind that had a reputation among liberal thinkers in the Muslim world, see Muhammad Shahrur, *Al-Kitab wa'l Qur'an* (The Book and the Qur'an) (Damascus: al-Ahali, 1992); and al-Sadik al-Nayhum, *al-Islam fi al-Asr* (Islam as a hostage) (London: Riad El-Rayyes Books, 1991).

6. National Report of Syrian Women to the UN's Fourth World Conference on Women, held in September 1995, Beijing, 29.

7. Syrian Arab Republic, Ministry of Planning, *Annual Statistical Report, 1993*. Unless otherwise indicated, all statistics mentioned henceforth are taken from this report.

8. Ibid., 28.

9. Ibid.

10. Even in the United States, recent statistics relating to women in decision-making posts are disturbing. White women have nearly 40 percent of the jobs nationwide, but in the race for top management slots "women stumble or are tripped in the stretch: they typically constitute less than five percent of senior managers in industries across the nation." The report adds that "many middle and upper level [male] managers view the inclusion of women in management as a direct threat to their own chances of advancement." Peter P. Kilborn, "No Room at the Top in U.S. for Women and Blacks," *International Herald Tribune,* March 17, 1995, 1, 6.

11. I disagree with the word "fundamentalist" because a fundamentalist is one who refers back to the fundamental principles of Islam and abides by them. This is not what the Islamists do. To kill, maim, and terrorize in the name of Islam is to be an enemy of Islam. Therefore I shall call them "Islamists," a translation of the Arabic word *islamiyin* or *mutaslimin*, the latter meaning "those who claim to be Muslims" but do not adhere to the true ethics of Islam.

12. Mohammed Arkoun, "Women in Islam," *Al-Safir* (Beirut), October 21, 1994.

13. Nazira Zin al-Din, *al-Fatat wa'l-Hijab* (Beirut: Quzma Publications, 1928).

14. Nazira Zin al-Din, *al-Fatat wa'l-Shuyukh,* printed by Nazira Zin al-Din's father, Sa'd Bik Zin al-Din (Beirut, 1929).

15. For a full discussion of Zin al-Din's views, see my article, "The Muted Voices of Women Interpreters," in *Faith and Freedom*, ed. Mahnaz Afkhami (London: I. B. Tauris, 1995), 61–77.

16. To name just a few of these enlightened scholars and interpreters and their books: Mustafa al-Ghalayini, *Islam Ruh al-Madaniyya* (Islam: The spirit of

civilization) (Beirut: al-Maktabah al-Asriyya, 1960); Muhammad al-Ghazali, *Sunna Between Fiqh and Hadith* (Cairo: Dar al-Shuruq, 1989, 7th ed., 1990); Sadiq al-Azm, *Naqad al-Fikr al-Dini* (A critique of religious thought) (Beirut: Dar al-Talia', 6th ed., 1988); Abdol Halim Abu Shiqa, *Tahrir al-Mara' fi 'Asr al-Risalah* (The emancipation of women in the age of the Prophet) (Kuwait: Dar al-Qalam, 1990); Fatima al-Mernissi, *al-Harim al-Siyassi, al-Nabi wa'l Nisa'* (Political harem: The Prophet and women), trans. Abdol Hadi Abbas (Damascus: Dar al-Hassad, 1990); Muhammad Shahrur, *Al-Kitab wa'l Qur'an* (The Book and the Qur'an) (Damascus: al-Ahali, 1992); al-Sadik al-Nayhum, *al-Islam fi al-Asr* (Islam as a hostage) (London: Riad El-Rayyes Books, 1991).

17. Abdullahi an-Na'im, "The Dichotomy Between Religious and Secular Discourse in Islamic Societies," in *Faith and Freedom*, ed. Mahnaz Afkhami (London: I. B. Tauris, 1995), 53.

18. Robin Wright, "An Iranian Luther Shakes the Foundations of Islam," *The Guardian* (London), February 1, 1995, 10.

19. An-Na'im, "The Dichotomy," 53.

20. Published by the General Guidance Bureau of the International Association of the Muslim Brethren, Cairo, 1994.

7

From Two States to One: Women's Lives in the Transformation of Yemen

Linda Boxberger

A female religious scholar of fifteenth-century Hadramawt, Yemen, al-Shaykha Sultana bint 'Ali al-Zubaydy was well-known for her piety, knowledge, and teachings. One of her male counterparts, expressing the conventional opinion that religious scholarship and teaching were the domain of men, challenged her in verse: "But can a female camel compete with a male camel?" She completed the couplet, responding: "A female camel can carry the same load as a male, and produce offspring and milk as well."[1] Although her answer was appreciated by her challenger and by succeeding generations, the disparaging attitude toward women expressed by her interlocutor has for the most part prevailed.

According to the constitution of the Republic of Yemen, all citizens are equal without discrimination by sex.[2] Women have the right to obtain an education, vote, and run for parliament, and they do so. Some women are active in politics; some have positions in government, broadcasting, and private industry; some are doctors, lawyers, and engineers.

Yet many women are limited in their opportunity to participate in public life, largely due to traditional attitudes regarding women's nature and place in Yemeni society. The symbolic role of women as repositories of family honor leads to restrictions on women's autonomy. Early marriage is encouraged, and marriage choices lie in the hands of the family. A typical proverb advises: "Marry your daughter off at the earliest possible age, so you are guaranteed safe from problems."[3] Another proverb warns: "Don't put the gas next to the match," that is, keep women away from men. The responsibility for illicit sexual behavior, however, lies with the woman; it is said of the man, "A dog won't come unless it's called." Seclusion of girls and women thus becomes a symbol of female respectability as well as a means of maintaining it.

Derogatory attitudes toward women's abilities are transmitted through popular lore. A classic proverb holds that "women are deficient in intellect and religion as well as inheritance." Others warn that it is unmanly to take a woman's opinions into consideration: "If you follow a woman's wishes, you become one." Such commonly held views hamper women's participation in decisionmaking in the workplace and in government.

Despite the egalitarian language of the constitution of the unified Republic of Yemen, traditional social attitudes and practices regarding women do not change easily. Governmental fiat does not suffice to improve the conditions in which women live, as can be seen in the limited success of the former People's Democratic Republic of Yemen (South Yemen) when it attempted to radically transform the position of women in society by law. Complicating the matter of women's social position are the issues of poverty and underdevelopment that affect Yemen as a whole and that have been exacerbated in the political and economic chaos since unification. In a country where many live on the margins of survival, women find it particularly difficult to improve their situation.

Taking into account the economic and political conditions of recent years, in this chapter I examine women's issues in Yemen, focusing on their education, employment, and legal status. I consider how these issues were shaped by the policies and programs of the pre-unification governments and how they have been affected by Yemeni unification. In particular, I point out areas in which the reality of women's lives has differed from the policies and the stated goals of government, which is due in part to the traditional attitudes toward women illustrated above.

BEFORE UNIFICATION: THE TWO YEMENS

With a per capita gross national product (GNP) of $280 in 1994, Yemen is one of the poorest countries in the world.[4] The struggle to raise living standards is an arduous one. In May 1990, when the Republic of Yemen was created from the merger of the Yemen Arab Republic (the YAR, or North Yemen) and the People's Democratic Republic of Yemen (the PDRY, or South Yemen), the people of the newly unified nation anticipated a period of national progress toward social and economic development that would benefit all. Instead, its creation was followed by economic deterioration and political instability, which hindered such progress and led to civil war in the summer of 1994.

The two states forming the present Republic of Yemen both emerged through revolution in the 1960s. The Yemen Arab Republic was created in 1962 after the overthrow of an isolationist and obscurantist monarchy. A subsequent civil war between Republicans and Royalists, the latter supported by neighboring Saudi Arabia, lasted until 1967. In that same year, the state that was to become the People's Democratic Republic of Yemen proclaimed its independence from Britain. Previously, the port city of

Aden had been administered as a British Crown colony, while the numerous sultanates of the hinterland had been loosely federated as British protectorates.

The two emergent Yemeni states followed dramatically different political philosophies, with South Yemen taking a radical Marxist approach and North Yemen developing a conservative military government. Still, they had much in common: a heritage of relative isolation from the rest of the world and problems of underdevelopment such as poverty; lack of infrastructure; and lack of basic health and social services, including education. Agricultural productivity was low, relying on animals and human labor employing the simplest of tools. Aside from the British-built oil refinery in Aden, industry was limited to small artisanal workshops. The rugged mountains, barren plateaus, and harsh deserts hindered communications among and within regions. Modern health services were limited in urban areas and nonexistent in rural areas, which were served only by traditional talismanic healers, herbalists, and bonesetters. The colonial city of Aden had several schools, including a girls' school, attended by religious minorities and the local elite. The South Yemen hinterland had only a handful of modern private schools and North Yemen even fewer. Traditional Qur'anic schools taught recitation of the Holy Qur'an; basic religious duties; and some reading, writing, and arithmetic. Few girls had the opportunity for even this limited education.

Although both governments strove to develop modern economies, control their remote hinterlands, and provide government services to their citizens, life was generally a struggle to raise families in the harsh physical environment. Statistical estimates for government services reveal the difficult situation of the two Yemens in their early years. World Bank data for 1965 indicate the number of persons per physician in the PDRY as 12,870 and in the YAR as 56,150. They also indicate estimated percentages enrolled in education for the same year. For the PDRY, of the primary school age group, 23 percent of the total were enrolled and 10 percent of the girls; of the secondary school age group, 11 percent of the total were enrolled and 5 percent of the girls. For the YAR, of the primary school age group, 9 percent of the total were enrolled and 1 percent of the girls; no girls in the secondary school age group were in school. Lack of access to education was reflected in low literacy rates: in 1970, total adult literacy in the PDRY was 31 percent, but female adult literacy was only 9 percent. Illiteracy was even higher in the YAR: total adult literacy was 9 percent, and female adult literacy was a mere 1 percent.[5]

Both Yemens, faced with such massive development hurdles, undertook programs to provide health care and educational opportunities to their populations. With varying efficacy, the revolutionary Marxist PDRY sought radical change in social attitudes and practices in an attempt to create a more progressive, egalitarian, and economically productive modern society. One program that affected women was the universal literacy campaign of the 1970s, in which women government employees and schoolteachers temporarily left their regular work to teach illiterate women to read and write. The female government employees were also given militia training, a radical departure from traditional social expectations. For women in general, the greatest change in their status and expectations derived from the PDRY's progressive Family Law, which was passed in 1974 and remained in effect until the time of unification.

The YAR, a conservative military government, took a less interventionist stance on social issues while it sought to provide services to its citizens. With some assistance from international organizations, the government established rural clinics offering women's health care, including family planning, birth control, fertility enhancement, and prenatal care. The Gulf countries assisted in a massive educational development program: Saudi Arabia subsidized the building of schools, and Kuwait helped pay the salaries of teachers from Egypt and Sudan.

Although the two Yemens shared similar problems and aims, they remained at a political impasse. Both agreed on the goal of a unified state, but each aspired to absorb the other. Unsuccessful negotiations alternated with political assassination and border clashes. Intermittent civil wars between North and South took place until unification was finally achieved in May 1990.

MIGRATION BOOM AND BUST: EFFECTS ON WOMEN

For years, Yemenis have found relief from their homeland's economic difficulties and political problems through migration. The most recent wave began shortly after the revolutions of the 1960s and intensified with the financial boom of the 1970s in the oil-producing Gulf states, where the Yemenis provided labor for massive construction projects. Remittances had a dramatic effect on the livelihoods of the migrants' families and on the economy of both Yemens.

In the typical emigration pattern, men relocate on their own. They often perform labor they would consider demeaning at home, and they live in the most spartan of conditions in order to maximize remittances. Rarely is an emigrant joined by his wife and family. The workers send money and make periodic visits home, with the goal of eventually returning for good.

The more than a billion dollars a year sent home in the late 1970s led to a building boom in North Yemen and huge increases in consumer imports, dowry payments, land prices, and local labor costs. In the PDRY, as many as one-third of the able-bodied young men emigrated, their remittances amounting to 60 or 70 percent of the country's foreign exchange earnings.[6]

Women's lives were deeply affected. A few unfortunate women suffered abandonment by their emigrant husbands. In addition, the influx of remittances led to the development of new class differences. Cynthia Myntti's research in a community in southwestern Yemen found growing economic distinctions among households resulting from emigration, with newly well-to-do women abandoning work outside their homes while the poorest took up their labor for wages.[7] Local agricultural production suffered, since sharecroppers and hired laborers tended fields less carefully than women previously had tilled their family-owned lands. The community studied by Myntti was typical of Yemen as a whole in that women were left in the care of a male family member or neighbor who took over household decisionmaking. Women were left with heavier household and child-rearing duties without acquiring increased responsibility or power.

Emigration slowed considerably in the 1980s, when fewer opportunities for migrants were available in the Gulf. Then in the fall of 1990, in retaliation for Yemen's refusal to join the anti-Iraq coalition, Saudi Arabia's abrupt expulsion of Yemeni workers at the time of the Gulf War struck a grievous blow to Yemen's economy and society, the repercussions from which have continued to the present. The forced hasty departure from Saudi Arabia of Yemeni workers and small businessmen created heavy losses for many of the emigrants, and at home the ranks of the unemployed and underemployed swelled. Women suffered both from the loss of remittances and from the generally difficult economic situation that resulted from the loss of this important segment of national income.

THE TWO YEMENS: UNIFICATION AND DISUNITY

The attainment of Yemeni unification in May 1990 had fostered high expectations among all Yemenis that an end to wasteful political squabbles would create a new opportunity for economic and social development. Although the newly unified country would inherit the underdevelopment that plagued the previous regimes, it might finally be able to consolidate resources and energy to achieve common goals.

As a constitutional democracy with universal adult suffrage, the new republic prepared for parliamentary elections in a spirited atmosphere of political openness unique in the Arab world. New political parties emerged and the press flourished. The excitement of democracy was accompanied by a new promise of economic development, as oil companies competed for exploration concessions previously considered too politically problematic for investment.

Despite high hopes, the road to unification of the two Yemens was rocky. Incidents of tribal rebellion and urban terrorism were thought to be exacerbated by foreign influence in the unification process. Divergent domestic interests emerged as well. An Islamist group boycotted the national referendum on the new republic's constitution, objecting to terminology that indicated that the legal system was based mainly, rather than solely, on the Shari'a. Concurrently, women demonstrated in the streets of Aden, concerned that under the new regime they would lose the rights granted by the progressive Family Law of the PDRY.

Approved by referendum, the new constitution of the Republic of Yemen, while saying that Islam is the religion of the state and Shari'a the main source of legislation, holds that "All citizens are equal before the law. They are equal in public rights and duties. There shall be no discrimination between them based on sex, color, ethnic origin, language, occupation, social status or religion." In addition, it declared the universal right to get an education, to vote, and to run a candidacy for the House of Representatives.[8]

Yet the anticipated progress toward social and economic development failed to take place. The imposing task of integration of the two Yemens was disrupted by Saddam Hussein's invasion of Kuwait in August 1990. Highlighted by its role as a rotating member of the UN Security Council, Yemen's refusal to join the anti-Iraq coalition led to sharp cuts in aid programs by Western and Gulf countries. Education and health care programs that had benefited women consequently experienced steep reductions at the same time that the expulsion of the Yemeni workers from the Gulf countries severely damaged the economy.

During this difficult period, the transitional coalition government, which contended with extensive duplicate institutions, was unready or unable to deal with the social and economic problems facing the country. Government energy and revenues seemed channeled largely toward garnering support from tribal and other power groups for the impending elections. Moreover, the promise of new oil wealth faded; although significant discoveries were made in some fields, the overall increase in production was disappointing.

Fueled by high unemployment, inflation, and dashed hopes, a series of strikes, demonstrations, and riots revealed that the state, which had never been truly unified, had lost its ability to govern. Finally, a split between the president (head of the General People's Congress and former president of the YAR) and the vice-president (head of the Yemen Socialist Party and former president of the PDRY) led to the secession of the South in May 1994 and ultimately to open warfare between the two factions. Needless to say, during this period of conflict, women's issues fell by the wayside.

WOMEN'S HEALTH AND FERTILITY:
ISSUES OF SURVIVAL

Statistical estimates for life expectancy illustrate the many challenges to human survival in Yemen. According to World Bank figures, in both the

PDRY and the YAR in 1965, life expectancy at birth for females was forty-one and for males, thirty-nine. By 1988, it had improved in the PDRY to fifty-three for females and fifty for males, and in the YAR to forty-eight for females and forty-seven for males.[9] As for the unified Republic of Yemen, in 1992 female life expectancy was estimated at fifty-three and male life expectancy at fifty-two.[10] This rather low figure is due primarily to high infant and early childhood mortality. Yemen is among the countries of the world with the highest mortality rates under 5 years of age: 1995 estimates are 110 per 1,000 live births.[11]

Contributing to such high rates are nutritional deficiencies of mother and child; low birth weight; and diseases such as hepatitis, polio, and measles. The United Nations Children's Fund (UNICEF) and the World Health Organization have assisted in establishing immunization programs through government clinics, but they are difficult to manage and maintain. Travel is extremely slow in some rugged mountainous areas, and many villages have unreliable electricity or none at all, making it nearly impossible to keep vaccines adequately refrigerated.

Women's access to medical care is likewise limited by the rough terrain and by the custom of female seclusion. Although the government has built thousands of clinics throughout the country, a woman may not be able to make the arduous journey to the nearest clinic, particularly when ill or pregnant. Moreover, for respectability, she must be accompanied by a man or men from her family, so services such as prenatal monitoring, postnatal checkups, or infant immunization may require several family members to travel.

One of the greatest challenges to women's health is the high number of pregnancies most women experience. World Bank estimates for 1994 indicate a total fertility rate of 7.4 per woman (down from 7.9 in 1980).[12] Childbearing is risky due to the lack of available medical assistance in the case of difficult births, but the greatest effect on women's health is the toll that repeated pregnancies take on their strength. In addition to successful pregnancies, many women have numerous miscarriages. In rural areas, the physical stress of frequent pregnancies is compounded by hard physical labor and sometimes by low levels of nutrition. Many women become chronically anemic and complain of fatigue; some lose their ability to produce milk after birth.

The high fertility rate and the high infant mortality rate are, of course, related phenomena. The prospect of losing several children motivates families to have a large number of children in order to ensure the survival of some, yet having children in rapid succession jeopardizes that goal. A short interval between births requires the mother to wean the toddler early to feed the infant.

Birth control is increasingly available in the cities and in some rural areas, although a recent World Bank estimate that 10 percent of women of childbearing age were using contraceptives during 1989–1995 seems rather high.[13] Women hesitate to tamper with their ability to produce children, fearing that their husbands will divorce them or take a second wife if they practice birth control. Those women using birth control often state their goal as spacing births rather than reducing the number of children. If the trend toward birth spacing grows, both women and their children will benefit significantly.

FEMALE EDUCATION: GOALS AND REALITIES

Despite the achievements of both Yemen governments in facilitating universal access to education after their respective revolutions, education for girls—particularly after puberty—remains a problematic issue for many families. Social reality has lagged behind governmental goals; the data indicate considerable gender inequity in education. According to UNICEF estimates, in 1960 the ratio of students enrolled in primary school in the YAR was 14 percent for boys and zero for girls and in the PDRY 20 percent for boys and 5 percent for girls. A dramatic rise in enrollments during the 1980s has been followed by a continued increase in enrollment overall and an improvement in the proportion of girls enrolled, particularly at the primary level. For 1986 through 1991, primary school enrollment in the two Yemens was estimated at 111 percent for boys (enrollment of boys older than the usual age for primary study creates this unusual figure; this is due to the relatively recent access to schooling in remote areas) and 43 percent for girls; secondary enrollment was 47 percent for boys and 10 percent for girls.[14] Facilitating access to education continues to be a goal of the republic, and girls' schooling is increasing, but more slowly than that of boys. Girls' opportunities to study beyond primary school are greater in urban areas than rural areas. Many rural parents are tremendously proud to see their daughters as well as their sons learn to read and write, yet beyond the early grades of primary school a girl's further education often meets resistance.

Economic factors contribute to this resistance. Having so many children, most women rely on their older daughters to help with the younger children and with the myriad household chores. In some areas, herding and farming are traditionally female occupations, and girls spend the day with flocks or in the fields. In other cases, families decide that boys should study in preparation for a better future while girls assume agricultural tasks. Since few employment opportunities exist for educated young women outside major urban areas, girls' labor is often valued more than formal education.

Social factors also contribute to resistance to female education. Too much education may be thought to limit a girl's marriage prospects, especially in rural areas where the educational levels of men are also low.

Some Yemenis believe that an educated woman may be a less tractable wife and thus more likely to end up divorced and returning to her natal home, shaming the family and becoming an economic burden. In sparsely populated areas, primary schools may be coeducational, but by the time a girl reaches puberty it is unacceptable for her to be among unrelated males. Since the honor of the family relies so much on the pure reputation of its women, social pressure contributes to lower enrollment of girls outside urban centers.

Attitudes towards female education vary not only from family to family, but from region to region. In the strongly tribal northwest, family life is kept very private, women are quite secluded, and few girls study beyond the earliest grades. By contrast, in the densely populated and agriculturally productive southwest, organized by village rather than by tribal affiliation, the educational level in general is higher and girls are encouraged to study.

Whereas the YAR officially encouraged female education, the PDRY promoted female education aggressively as a means to transform South Yemen into a modern, egalitarian, socialist state. In cosmopolitan Aden, where some girls and young women had had the opportunity to study during the colonial period, society embraced female education and participation in the labor force. Girls were encouraged to study, and the lack of family supervision at school or at work was not thought to besmirch the family honor.

In the conservative hinterland of the former PDRY, however, parents resisted coeducation by pulling their daughters out of school at an early age. Even in provincial towns and cities, few girls studied beyond the earliest grades because families insisted on strict supervision of girls after the age of puberty. The identification of family honor with female respectability proved stronger than the mandates of the radical social reformist government of the PDRY.

The government of the Republic of Yemen continues to establish more schools for girls and promotes female education through messages in the broadcast media. Steadily increasing enrollment figures reflect the spread of education in urban areas, where a "critical mass" of schoolgirls renders it acceptable for even conservative families to enroll their daughters. Despite social and economic barriers, the trend toward increasing education for girls seems well established in Yemen today.

WOMEN'S ECONOMIC CONTRIBUTIONS: UNPAID AND PAID LABOR

Although women's labor in the home and within certain sectors of the informal economy is regarded as essential to family survival, women's participation in the money economy is more problematic. Local superstitions

warn against women's involvement in certain economic activities traditionally considered the domain of men. Sayings in Hadramawt caution that
a women nearing vats of indigo dye will prevent the dye from setting in
cloth and that if a woman approaches fish-processing tanks, the fish will
go bad. Similar lore exists for traditional industries in other regions.

Throughout Yemen, however, women perform work critical to the survival of their families. The idealized image of a woman's life as one of secluded leisure is far from reality. Women may need to work outside the
home to support their families, particularly in cases of widowhood, divorce, or abandonment. Even in families where the woman is not employed for wages, the daily task of food preparation requires a significant
amount of time and energy, with inconvenient, poorly ventilated kitchens,
few processed foods, and much manual labor. Gathering firewood in the
deforested countryside and fetching water from distant wells require
lengthy and difficult treks while carrying a heavy burden.

Tending animals requires considerable work from women as well. In
most areas, cattle are hand-fed sorghum stalks wrapped in alfalfa; cows
will not otherwise eat this diet. Women also herd sheep or goats grazing in
harvested fields and uncultivated areas. Among people considered
bedouin, women own herds and take them into marriage as an economic
asset that benefits the entire family. Pastoralists spin yarn and produce
ghee (clarified butter) for family use and for sale.

In the highlands, many women and girls work in the fields. Men do
the heavy work of maintaining terraces and plowing; women assist in
planting, irrigation, and harvest. In the Tihama, where large farms belong
to absentee landowners, women as well as men work in hired labor crews.
Although this lifestyle is considered less than ideal, the opportunity to earn
money is not disdained. In Hadramawt, where farm labor has long been
limited to an agricultural laboring class, women hired in crews or as part
of family labor units have specific tasks. Cynthia Myntti found in southwestern Yemen that family circumstances at a given time determined
whether families were self-sufficient, hired itinerant labor, rented to sharecroppers, or helped work others' land on an exchange basis.[15]

Women increasingly participate in the formal economy as well. Not
surprisingly, Aden surpasses other places in participation of women in the
workforce, as in other aspects of public life. Yet in other Yemeni cities as
well, increasing numbers of women work in banks, government offices,
and travel agencies, mainly as typists and clerks. Although some families
still resist the idea, many young women graduates want to work and would
be allowed to do so if more opportunities existed.

In the modern workplace, women maintain the traditional ideal of female respectability through modest dress. Most northern working women
wear a traditional black outer garment covering body and clothing and a
veil that covers their face except for the eyes. In the streets, an outer veil

covers the eyes as well. Southern working women often wear full-length raincoats with scarves covering their hair and neck; in the streets they may also wear a veil pulled down over the face. Adeni women accustomed to wearing Western clothing in public and leaving their hair uncovered have adopted more modest dress since unification, discomfited by the sometimes hostile scrutiny of the more conservative northerners.

In both states, women in the formal economy have been concentrated in clerical work, health care (particularly midwifery), and teaching. In the PDRY, the government had actively encouraged women's participation in the workforce in pursuit of its policy of modernization and in need of their labor to meet the goals of industrialization. Many women worked in the modern industrial sector, largely based in Aden. Research conducted by Maxine Molyneux in the 1970s found that women were mainly employed in low-skilled, low-paid jobs in the textile and food-processing industries but not in supervisory or managerial positions.[16] Molyneux also reported that the great majority of economically active women were agricultural laborers, but women did not play a significant role in the state farms and agricultural cooperatives.

Despite the obstacles facing them, women are increasingly entering the paid labor force. Yet after the shattering of earlier high hopes for Yemen's postunification economic development, women are finding it increasingly difficult to gain or maintain a foothold in a sharply reduced economy.

THE LEGAL STATUS OF WOMEN: SHARI'A AND THE STATE

The constitution of the Republic of Yemen states that the principles of Shari'a provide the basis for legislation, as had been the case in the former YAR. Shari'a principles regulating family matters are drawn from the Qur'an, which includes specific strictures on women and marriage, and from the Sunna, based on accounts from the lives of the Prophet and his companions. The Shari'a, as it has commonly been interpreted, determines a woman's share of inheritance to be half the share of an equivalent male relative and also establishes her inheritance to be an inalienable right. A woman's property is generally managed for her by a legal guardian, usually her husband or her brother, uncle, or another male relative.

The Qur'an allowed polygyny, limiting a man to four wives, but only if he could treat each equally. Financial considerations make it difficult for most men in Yemen to have more than one wife at a time, but the possibility is a continual threat for many women.

In marriage, men are expected to support and protect the family, and women are to take care of the home and raise the children. The man has a unilateral right to divorce. Unless the right for the woman to initiate divorce is written into the marriage contract, a woman can sue for divorce only on the grounds of impotence, insanity, or nonmaintenance. In Yemen today, many divorces initiated by women are on grounds of nonmaintenance, often in cases in which the husband has emigrated and failed to send support remittances.

The family law of the PDRY, in contrast to that of the YAR, was based on Marxist-Leninist political philosophy rather than Shari'a. The secular orientation of the Family Law of 1974, in effect until unification in 1990, is apparent. Although the traditional heading for a document in the Islamic world is "In the name of God," the PDRY Family Law began "In the name of the people."[17] This law transformed the legal situation of women in the PDRY by defining marriage in a radical new way: "Marriage is a contract between a man and a woman, equal in rights and responsibilities, based on mutual understanding and respect; its purpose is the creation of the cohesive family which is considered to be the foundation stone of the society." The ideal of equality between man and woman included the sharing of financial responsibility for the family.

The law required a woman's consent before her family could draw up an engagement agreement. It stipulated the age of the bride as no less than sixteen and twenty years as the maximum age difference between bride and groom. Dowry was limited to 100 dinars; subsidiary payments of any sort were prohibited. These provisions served to reduce family control in negotiation of engagement and marriage agreements.

A most radical departure of this law from Shari'a-based family law was its near-prohibition of polygyny. A man might marry a second wife only with permission from a special court that granted permission only in limited cases, such as female infertility. Moreover, the first wife had the right to appeal the decision or to sue for divorce if a second marriage was permitted. In divorce, women were granted the same rights as men, whereas men were denied the right to declare divorce unilaterally. Local people's committees mediated in divorce cases.

The Family Law, the most progressive in the Arab world, not surprisingly met with mixed reception and results. To ensure that women were informed of their legal rights, the government printed and distributed copies of the law throughout the PDRY. The many educated women of Aden prized the law, whereas in the more conservative areas of the hinterland people abhorred it and simply ignored it. In Hadramawt and other conservative areas, families retreated even more into their traditional privacy to preserve their system of family life.

Yet Molyneux's research indicated that women appreciated their new right of divorce.[18] Even in rural and remote areas, the divorce rate increased significantly as women who had been abandoned by emigrant husbands sued for divorce. A further increase occurred in 1978 when a new civil law awarded the house to a divorced wife with children from the marriage. Like many provisions of the PDRY Family Law, this law was honored in Aden more than in the hinterland. Even in Aden, though, the Family Law was not universally obeyed. The limitation on the amount of the dowry, for example, was considered to devalue women and their families. It was common for families to use gifts to supplement the standard dowry payment, thus subverting the letter and spirit of the law.

Upon unification, the radical Family Law of the PDRY was abolished, and principles of Shari'a became the legal standard for family law in all Yemen. The women of Aden felt hard hit by this change. Living in a city with a colonial rather than a traditional heritage, they had become accustomed to the exigencies of life in a revolutionary Marxist state, to the equal rights granted them by law, and to the salaries they earned. As in many other cases of sex role transformations around the world, however, parity had not been achieved. Although men and women both worked outside the home and men were helpful in child-rearing, most household tasks still fell to women. For these women, the rules have changed in the middle of the game; despite years of participating financially in relatively egalitarian marriages, they now fear that their husbands may divorce them unilaterally and arbitrarily or take a second wife. One Adeni woman said: "We were flying high for a while, but then this new government came along and clipped our wings."

CONCLUSION:
WOMEN AND THE FUTURE OF UNITED YEMEN

United Yemen confronts difficult tasks in fostering social and economic development while improving the standard of living of its citizens. This process, in particular the extension of government services to the countryside, has been made more difficult by recent political instability and economic problems.

Women, in particular, suffer because many of them have limited access to education, health care, and paid employment. Early marriage, continual childbearing, and hard labor make it difficult for many women to improve conditions for themselves and their families. Since women's respectability is critical to the maintenance of family honor, women's mobility and autonomy are often limited, making it difficult for them to pursue education and employment even where they are available. Because women traditionally have been limited to the domain of the household, their participation in public decisionmaking is curtailed, and their interests are easily ignored.

Although the national constitution forbids sex discrimination, traditional social attitudes and practices often foster it. Attitudes change very slowly, particularly when religion is used to justify customary practice. Governmental edict alone cannot change traditional attitudes, as was seen in the past by the failure of the progressive Family Law of the PDRY to radically transform women's lives and by resistance to female education in both the YAR and the PDRY.

Although women's access to education, health care, employment and participation in public life has increased over the past thirty years, women may have to struggle to maintain these gains. It remains to be seen if Islamist groups will gain greater power in government and influence in society, and what effect they will have on women's issues. In recent years, the removal from the bench of all women judges appointed by the former PDRY seemed to presage a loss of influence for women in public life. Yet women's activity as candidates, voters, and monitors in the 1997 Yemeni elections, in which two Adeni women won parliamentary seats, suggests that the women of Yemen will continue to defy limitations placed on them by tradition and assert their right to participate in public life.

NOTES

1. Ja'afar Muhammad Al-Saqqaf, "Biography of Sultana bint 'Ali al-Zubaydy," unpublished article in Arabic. While doing research in Hadramawt, I heard this anecdote from many people.

2. Found in A. P. Blaustein and G. H. Flanz (eds.), *Constitutions of the Countries of the World* (Dobbs Ferry, NY: Oceana Publications, 1971–).

3. Isma'il 'Ali al-Ikwa', *al Amthal al-Yamaniyat* (Sana'a: al-Jiyl al-Jadiyd Press, 1984). All proverbs cited are from this collection.

4. UNICEF, *The State of the World's Children 1997* (New York: Oxford University Press, 1997).

5. World Bank, *World Development Report 1990* (New York: Oxford University Press, 1990).

6. Jon C. Swanson, *Emigration and Economic Development: The Case of the Yemen Arab Republic* (Boulder: Westview Press, 1979); "Sojourners and Settlers: Yemenis in America," *MERIP Reports* 16 (March–April 1986): 5–21; and Fred Halliday, "Catastrophe in South Yemen: A Preliminary Assessment," *MERIP Reports* 16 (March–April 1986): 37–39.

7. Cynthia Myntti, "Yemeni Workers Abroad: Their Impact on Women," *MERIP Reports* 14 (June 1984): 11–16.

8. Blaustein and Flanz, *Constitutions*.

9. World Bank, *World Development Report 1990*.

10. World Bank, *World Development Report 1994* (New York: Oxford University Press, 1994).

11. UNICEF, *State of the World's Children 1997* (New York: Oxford University Press, 1997).

12. World Bank, *World Development Report 1997* (New York: Oxford University Press, 1997).

13. World Bank, *World Development Report 1996* (New York: Oxford University Press, 1996).

14. UNICEF, *State of the World's Children 1988* (New York: Oxford University Press, 1988); and *State of the World's Children 1994* (New York: Oxford University Press, 1994).

15. Myntti, "Yemeni Workers Abroad," 11–16.

16. Maxine Molyneux, *State Policies and the Position of Women Workers in the People's Democratic Republic of Yemen, 1967–1977*, Women, Work and Development Series, vol. 3 (Geneva: International Labour Organisation, 1982).

17. People's Democratic Republic of Yemen, *Law Number 1 of 1974, Pertaining to the Family* (in Arabic).

18. Maxine Molyneux, "The Law, the State and Socialist Policies with Regard to Women: The Case of the People's Democratic Republic of Yemen 1967–1990," in *Women, Islam, and the State,* ed. Deniz Kandiyoti (London: Macmillan, 1991), 237–271.

PART THREE

Central Asia

8

"Guardians of the Nation": Women, Islam, and the Soviet Legacy of Modernization in Azerbaijan

Nayereh Tohidi

A glamorous picture of a blonde, smiling Turkish beauty was plastered on the walls of many stores, offices, and homes that I visited in 1991–1992 in what was then Soviet Azerbaijan. Together with other byproducts of glasnost and perestroika in those last days of the Soviet Union were certain Western images openly promoted in almost all republics, particularly Russia, that were in sharp contrast to socialist ideals. In the context of Azerbaijan, however, this particular new image—a beauty queen from Turkey—conveyed not only certain gender-related messages but also important political statements concerning the growing ethnic and nationalist orientation of society.

Yet in less than four years, another new image entered into the fluid popular culture of the country, in sharp contrast to both the secular pro-Russian and pro-Soviet ideals of the past and the secular, nationalist pro-Turkish and pro-Western orientation of contemporary Azerbaijan. This most recent image, at times co-opting the Turkish beauty queen, portrays a demure young girl veiled in a white scarf, timidly looking down at a set of prayer beads she holds. The picture is accompanied by an arresting caption: a hadith concerning the virtues of prayer. Like the earlier one, this new image is loaded with messages regarding gender roles and the evolving identity of Azerbaijan. Although the previous image reflects the post-Soviet, postcommunist culture of display, emphasizing physical beauty, Western fashion, consumerism, and Turkish identity, the new one signals modesty, morality, Islamic values, and Muslim identity.

The popularity of such contradictory images is suggestive of, first, the complexity, diversity, and fluidity of national/cultural identity in post-Soviet Azerbaijan and, second, a thesis that here, as in many colonial and postcolonial contexts, gender issues are intertwined with variables like race, nationality, ethnicity, class, and religion. Through a demonstration of the interplay between such variables, I seek to explain in this chapter the

137

present dual nature of women's status in Azerbaijan. The specific questions to be addressed include the following:

- Despite two centuries of Russian influence in Azerbaijan (both under czarist orthodoxy and Soviet state socialism) and the Soviet legacy of equal rights by law, universal literacy, and high educational attainment and high level of employment among women, why is it that gender-related cultural patterns seem to have remained so similar to the ones in Muslim traditional communities? Is this simply due to Islam or Islamic traditionalism, as some Soviet scholars[1] have suggested?
- To what degree do the present gender issues and problems in Azerbaijan have their roots in the paradoxical impact of the Soviet model of socialist development and modernization?
- What has been the role of nationalism and interethnic conflicts in shaping gender roles under Soviet and post-Soviet contexts?
- How are the post-Soviet restructuring policies of the new nationalist state within a market economy affecting women's lives? What is the role of Islam in this new context?

While briefly reviewing three distinct periods in the modern history of Azerbaijan—pre-Soviet, Soviet, and post-Soviet—I analyze how Russian and Soviet officials, indigenous male elites, and Azeri women all attempted and attempt to manipulate gender issues for their own interests. During each period, gender roles have been constructed, contested, and modified in interaction with local customs, Islamic beliefs, state ideology and policies concerning socioeconomic development, and quasi-colonial, interethnic dynamics.

Azerbaijan provides an especially cogent case for revisiting certain theoretical problems concerning the study of Muslim women. One pertains to the nature, significance, and extent of the role of Islam in determining gender relations and women's status in a Muslim society. Azerbaijan, too, offers yet another example of the diversity of women's situation in the Muslim world, which defies commonly held Western stereotypes. It demonstrates, for instance, the fallacy of both culturalism, specifically Islamic determinism (i.e., an essentialist approach to Islam still popular among some orientalists), as well as the economic reductionism underlying gender ideology among many Marxist-Leninists and some advocates of developmentalism.

THE GEOPOLITICAL CONTEXT

As a Muslim people of the Caucasus, the mostly Shi'i Azeri Turks, who make up 83 percent of the diverse population of Azerbaijan, have been divided for the past two centuries between Iran, having about twenty million

Azeris, and the Russian empire and its successor, the Soviet Union. With the exploitation of the Baku oilfields and consequent modernization, Azeri intellectuals were influenced by nation-state formations in Europe and revolutionary movements in Russia, Iran, and Turkey in the early twentieth century. Thus with the collapse of czarist Russia, the first independent People's Republic of Azerbaijan emerged in 1918. In 1920, however, the Bolsheviks, supported by the Russian Red Army, conquered it, eventually replacing it with the Soviet Republic of Azerbaijan as one of the fifteen republics of the USSR.[2]

Seventy years later, the parliament of Azerbaijan was among the first to adopt a resolution of independence during the disintegration of the Soviet Union. With that declaration of August 30, 1991, Azeris found themselves in a position resembling their first republic of 1918–1920, facing many serious challenges. Situated in a most sensitive geopolitical region with abundant oil wealth, having ethnic and historic ties with Turkey, Iran, and Russia, Azerbaijan is likely to play an increasingly important role in the orientation of identity politics within the greater Middle East.

Already its postindependence position is seriously complicated by the armed conflict with Christian Armenia over the disputed territory of Nagorno-Karabagh. With some 20 percent of its territory under occupation, one of every seven Azerbaijanis has become a refugee or been internally displaced, of which 55 percent are women and children.[3] This war has devastated the economy and morale of both nations. It is in such an interethnic, war-stricken, and nationally and internally contested milieu that women and men in Azerbaijan are going through a semidecolonization process as they seek to reassess, reimagine, and redefine their identities.

This is, inevitably, a gendered process. Gender-related images and issues, especially women's place in this transitional society, are part of the ideological terrain upon which questions of national identity, ethnic loyalty, Islamic revival, and cultural authenticity are being debated.

THE HISTORICAL BACKGROUND

Women's status and roles have undergone significant changes through three different eras. By the turn of the twentieth century a limited level of oil-related industrialization had taken place, but it was mainly during the Soviet era that Azerbaijan developed into a modern agricultural and industrial society. The pre-Soviet socialization of Azeri women, too, was very limited and followed a slow pace.

The Later Czars

The political and social roles of Azerbaijani women outside the home date back to the years before the Bolshevik revolution. Women started to enter the public sphere through wage labor in the oil industry, garment work-shops, charity activities, women's publications, women's clubs, and broad political groups that promoted women's literacy, vocational training, legal rights, and improvement in their overall status.

In the modern urban life of Azerbaijan around the turn of the century, Azeri women, like their counterparts in Turkey, Iran, and Egypt, had al-ready become a "question." The growing oil industry and Russian-Euro-pean influence, especially in Baku, had further contributed to debate over the "woman question" and the socialization of women. As elsewhere, ten-sion between the old way of life, traditional views, and modernity mani-fested itself more clearly in women's role and gender relations.

Most reformers, including secular nationalists, social democrats, and Muslim modernists (Jadidists), saw the emancipation of women as a pre-requisite for the revival of Muslim civilization and Azerbaijan's economic, social, and cultural development.[4] People in intellectual circles and the new press, particularly writers like Mirza-Jalil Mammed-Qulizadeh (1866–1932) and his wife, Hamideh Javanshir (1873–1955), raised women's is-sues in their popular and influential journal *Molla Nasreddin* (1906–1930).[5] Through powerful satire and cartoons, the journal played a crucial role in criticizing the establishment, corrupt officials, and religious conser-vatives as well as denouncing compulsory veiling and seclusion, polygyny, wife battering, violence, and other oppressive practices against women.[6]

Founded by an Azeri woman (Khadija Alibeyova, 1884–1961) and her husband, the first journal for and by women in Azeri Turkic was published in Baku in 1911. This journal, *Ishiq* (Light), aimed at enlightening women regarding their rights to education and employment by emphasizing certain egalitarian passages from the Qur'an and hadith and by cautiously and in-directly criticizing conservative Islamic authorities. Nevertheless, the jour-nal lasted only a year because of pressures from conservative clerics and lack of financial support.

Along with intellectuals, the new industrial bourgeoisie of Azerbaijan played an important role in the modernization of Azeri society. The first school for Muslim girls, for example, was founded in 1905 by Haji Zeyno-labedin Tagiyev, an Azeri oil millionaire and philanthropist. Reformers like Tagiyev remarked on women's education among European women and Muslims of the Volga Tatars while postulating an egalitarian and progres-sive interpretation of the Qur'an.[7]

However, Russian colonizers, as in many other colonial contexts, were unconcerned about real emancipation of women and improvement in women's status. For instance, the Tagiyev school, the only existing school for non-Russian Muslim girls, was overcrowded and expensive. Azeris had to petition the city council of the czarist regime in Baku for money to begin a pedagogical course for Muslim girls at the school for Russian girls. Azeri representatives on the city council, one of whom made a rousing "down with the veil" speech on the need for education to make women good citizens and good mothers (the two roles being inseparable to him), had to fight vigorously for allocation of funds necessary to start another girls' school for Azeris.[8]

While Azeri bourgeois men and their wives contributed to the reform, modernization, and nation building of Azerbaijan, several women and men from the working class mobilized women for a more revolutionary agenda. As the social-democratic and Marxist movements grew throughout the Russian empire, Azerbaijani workers in the oil industry organized around a group entitled Himmat (Endeavor). Muslim, Christian, and Jewish women from the Tagiyev textile factory and other industries played a leading role in forming a women's wing of Himmat.[9] As early as 1904–1905 they raised specific demands for "maternity leave for women, time on the job for nursing unweaned children, and medical care for all workers."[10]

Azerbaijani female and male intellectuals today take pride in their short-lived independent republic of 1918–1920, formed upon the collapse of the Russian empire, characterizing it as "the first democratic republic in the entire Muslim world that provided universal suffrage guaranteeing all citizens full civil and political rights regardless of their nationality, religion, social position and sex."[11] Its brief yet inspiring existence also gave impetus to Azeri nationalism.

In short, this period in the cultural history of Azerbaijan is distinguished by the emergence of a sense of national identity, modernist and reformist Islamic and secular elites, elementary discourses on the "woman question," and a range of activities in support of women's emancipation.

The Soviet Era

The role of women during the seventy years of the Soviet era in Azerbaijan was characterized in several different ways as state policy and gender strategy changed from strict Marxist egalitarian ideological commitment and vigorous campaigning for women's rights to a later pragmatism centered on economic productivity.

An economistic perspective assumed that women's emancipation would automatically follow their participation in social and productive labor in the formal economy. Their massive entrance into the labor force was therefore encouraged. Universal access to education and gainful employment together with the establishment of equal rights in social and political domains—especially egalitarian changes in family law—did contribute to a rise in the overall status of women in both public and private spheres. Nevertheless, in reality women remained subordinated to men, unable to break away from dependence on male kin.

With no or little regard for the environment and sustainable human development, the Soviet state pursued, especially under Joseph Stalin, a strategy of modernization based on heavy and military industrial growth. This strategy called on women to mobilize and take an active part in social production. But in the sphere of reproduction and housework, the need for high quality child care, labor-saving household appliances, food cycle technology, and daily consumer goods, for example, did not constitute priorities for the state.

Other than egalitarian reforms of personal status law, the state paid only lip service to fundamental changes in gender ideology, the patriarchal structure of the family, and the gender-based division of labor in domestic and reproductive domains. The result was the notorious "double burden," a chronic stress on Soviet women's emotional and physical well-being so poignantly reflected in the words of "Kitchen Lines" by Nigar Rafibeyli (1913–1981), a prominent Azeri poet:

> I feel so heartsore
>   in this kitchen world;
> After all,
> There is something of a poet in me.
>   . . .
> Some are destined to occupy high posts,
> Others to wash dishes in the kitchen.
>   . . .
> But who is there to see
> That the cook burning by the stove
> Doesn't turn to cinders?[12]

Education is one area in which the state socialism of the USSR deserves undeniable credit. In contrast to women in many Muslim societies elsewhere, Azerbaijani women became universally literate. As of the late 1980s, over 42 percent of tertiary-level students were women, but they have been less numerous in educational fields relevant to better-paid and higher-level employment. Although women constitute over 65 percent of primary and secondary educators, for example, only 22 percent of school administrators are women.

According to the official statistics, the health of Soviet Azerbaijani women used to be better than that of its neighbors, Turkey and Iran, and far superior to many other Muslim states. Female life expectancy in 1989, for instance, was 74.2 years, compared to 69.4 in Turkey and 67.1 in Iran. Their fertility rate was lower at 2.7 children per woman (Turkey's was 3.6 and Iran's 6.1), and the maternal mortality rate of 29 per 100,000 live births compares well to Turkey's 200 and Iran's 250.

The reality of women's health, however, given the unreliability of Soviet statistics, was less encouraging. In Azerbaijan, as throughout the Soviet Union, the state's pro-natal policy, the lack of family planning, and the minimal access to contraceptives rendered abortion the primary means of birth control. The prevalence of abortion, usually carried out under morbid conditions, and particularly the frequency of induced and incomplete operations, was and remains a major gender issue neglected by Soviet and post-Soviet leaders alike.[13]

Compared to most other Muslim societies, the massive integration of women into the formal economy of Azerbaijan has been identified as another success story of Soviet state socialism. Yet a female participation rate of 44 percent reveals a different story when subjected to gender-sensitive evaluation. Their heaviest participation remained in agriculture and manual farm labor (52 percent in 1989 and 49 percent in 1993). On collective farms, moreover, women's labor was concentrated in nonmechanized areas since less than 10 percent were appropriately skilled. Only 1.3 percent held managerial or administrative positions. The overwhelming portion of hard manual labor in livestock, cotton, tea, tobacco, and vegetable farming was relegated to women.

Urban industrial women workers, 45 percent of the total, were also concentrated in the lower paid, lower rank, and lower skill grades. According to the laws of the Soviet state, no male-female wage differentials should have existed, but as a consequence of horizontal and vertical occupational segregation by sex, women's average earnings throughout the USSR have been estimated as about 30 percent lower than those of males.[14]

In the realm of Azerbaijani politics, this familiar pattern obtained. Based on the quota system, a proportional presence of women at local, regional, and national levels of formal politics was maintained in all three branches of government. In 1989, 39 percent of deputies in the Supreme Soviet of Azerbaijan were women, and until 1991 the parliament's speaker was a woman, yet their mere representation in the soviets failed to translate into women's empowerment. Not only were women and male deputies usually selected by the real source of power, the ruling Communist Party (CP), but women deputies held much less prominent positions than male deputies, suffered a higher rate of turnover, and were less likely to be party members.[15]

In sum, after over seventy years of the ostensibly egalitarian Soviet regime, the gender hierarchy, cultural ideals, gender-related ethos, and behavioral traits usually attached to Azerbaijani women seem to have remained similar to the ones in Muslim traditional communities elsewhere.

The Post-Soviet Era

Encouraged by the promising reforms (glasnost and perestroika) of the late 1980s, many Azerbaijani women joined the movement for democracy and independence. Through their participation in the flourishing free press, nongovernmental organizations (NGOs), new entrepreneurial opportunities, proliferating political parties, the war-related resistance, relief efforts, and peace initiatives, women have actively contributed to the post-Soviet developments.

So far, however, the adverse effects of transition on men and particularly women have overshadowed people's earlier optimism. The excesses and problems of the Soviet past and the exigencies of the return to capitalism are reinforcing regressive tendencies and strengthening old sexist attitudes. For example, with the advent of glasnost, it became an open secret that despite protective labor legislation, a widespread pattern existed of gender bias favoring men. Many women were experiencing hazardous working conditions, especially in the environmentally devastated areas of Central Asia and in some urban industrial regions of Azerbaijan such as Sumgait and Baku. Even officially conducted surveys of 1991 in Azerbaijan report that only half of employed women have been satisfied with their work.[16]

In their political rhetoric and ideological discourses, both secular nationalist and religious forces throughout post-Soviet republics, including Azerbaijan, blame the bygone Soviet system for what they call superemployment and abuse of women, especially in those jobs that are seen as disrespectful of women's "feminine qualities and motherhood as their primary duty." With the onset of marketization, the overemployment of women emerged as a central woman question, and some began to call for women to return to the family and free themselves from the double burden by abandoning the excessive toil in the sphere of production.[17] The respect toward women is thus increasingly correlated with their role as mothers.

According to many Azeris, although women have maintained their "respected" and "protected" position in post-Soviet Azerbaijani culture, its extent and parameters are changing. Following electoral reform and the elimination of the quota system during perestroika in 1989, women's presence in formal politics declined drastically, falling in Azerbaijan to 4.8 percent, then recovering to 6 percent in 1992 and 13 percent in the 1995 election. Any actual change in women's political roles, however, cannot be gauged from such quantitative shifts in state-oriented politics. A new civil society is emerging with an increasing number of informal and nongovernmental women's organizations, and women are active at this informal level as well as in formal political organizations. Whether they will have greater opportunities than previously to engage in decisionmaking as free agents of change with genuine representation is not yet clear.

Once relatively protected by the Soviet state, women now face the loss of its support together with an inevitably higher economic pressure as they constitute the majority of the newly unemployed in an ever more insecure and violent social atmosphere. Consequently, the need for male protection within the context of marriage has intensified the familial and kinship networks. So far, the process of marketization and democratization has not only failed to remove the disadvantages for women in the Soviet system;

it has actually intensified gender asymmetry. Simultaneously, prior female advantages have been jeopardized because of the disruption of the social safety net, soaring prices, rising unemployment, increasingly open sex discrimination, violence, prostitution, crime, and above all, the economic and moral devastation created by the war.

Such a context may be fertile ground for the revival of extremist ideologies that would declare a divinely or biologically determined patriarchal control over women and a return to strictly gender-based social arrangements as a presumed prerequisite for national and spiritual salvation. But can we attribute all the current gender-related problems in Azerbaijan to the restructuring policies of the post-Soviet nationalist state and market economy? In the following sections I attempt to show to what degree the present gender issues in Azerbaijan have their roots in the previous development strategy of the Soviet state on the one hand and the ethno-religious factors on the other.

THE PARADOXICAL IMPACT OF THE SOVIET STATE

In the Muslim peripheries of the Soviet Union such as Azerbaijan, the duality in women's status—formally equal, really unequal—seems to be accentuated by several interrelated factors. One is the Soviet state ideology and policies that prescribed a "statization" of the "woman question," a state-centered approach assuming that women's emancipation could be achieved through a deliberate top-down strategy of social engineering.

Under such a strategy, implemented largely if not solely by a male elite, the state became the primary actor instead of playing the role of facilitator of women's emancipation. A state-created or state-controlled women's organization declared itself the sole representative of women's concerns, replacing all women's autonomous movements and independent organizations. In practice, this strategy artificially homogenized women's diverse interests, undermined their genuine voice, and confined their real agency.

One may conclude that the more authoritarian the state, the more confined and auxiliary becomes the role of the state-oriented women's apparatus and the wider the gap between formal emancipation and real equality. When the originally desirable goals of women's emancipation (such as, for example, unveiling) are perceived as too closely associated with a repressive state, they eventually lose their credibility and appeal, especially among nationalists. Women, too, may not value or appreciate their controversial state-initiated rights when they themselves have had no role in attaining them. As a result, a backlash like the return to the veil and gender segregation may follow a statist, antisocialist regime such as the Turkey of Ataturk or the Iran of the Pahlavi shahs that desired larger roles for women.[18] Are such paradoxical consequences of Soviet statization likely in the similar post-Soviet Azerbaijani context?

The success or failure of recent regressive trends will be determined, to a great extent, by the nature of women's response and resistance. Unlike what some scholars have implied, Muslim women, in both the pre-Soviet and Soviet eras, were more than mere pawns, victims of ignorance and male oppression, and more than passive followers of the state and CP.[19] In the case specifically of Tatar and Azerbaijani women having a background in the Jadid or Muslim modernist and social democratic movements, one may argue that some women at times used the Communists' support for equality and the state's legal protection to fight patriarchy and religious re-action while promoting their own agenda. The play *Sevil* by the popular Azerbaijani playwright Ja'far Jabbarli, though fictional, illuminates the small number of women activists in the 1920s who pursued women's rights initially independent of CP influence.[20]

A careful analysis of the Zhenotdel, the Women's Department of the CP, both in its Russian and Muslim Azerbaijani contexts, reveals a contin-uous tension between the women members and the male party leaders. Zhenotdel's brief but stormy existence played a crucial role in the mobi-lization, socialization, and emancipation of Soviet women in general and Muslim women in particular. It had a mixture of native/local and Russian leadership in each republic. Besides press organs and publications aimed at literate women, local branches in Azerbaijan as elsewhere used sewing circles, conferences, women's clubs, and even public bathhouses for con-sciousness raising and mobilization of women.

The crucial role that local organs and indigenous mechanisms played in such mobilization attests to the native Azeri women's own enthusiastic involvement. Unlike the party organs dominated by Russian communists, the "women's clubs" were almost exclusively staffed by Azerbaijani women. One such club exemplifying Azeri women's agency in this period was the Ali Bayramov Women's Club in Baku, which predated Soviet rule and was radicalized in the early years of the Soviet state. Its press organ, *Sharq Qadini* (Woman of the East), played an important role in the politi-cal education and social integration of women in Azerbaijan.[21]

By 1923, many women had discarded their veils. As part of an antiveil campaign, certain activists removed their veils at the city theater during a popular play (like *Sevil,* Jabbarli's play). Yet many others, including some activists of the women's clubs, felt compelled or chose to retain some form of veil, often wearing, instead of the enveloping *charshab,* a compromise version in the form of a headscarf or *kalagaye,* originally part of an Azeri folk costume.

Nonetheless, the campaign promoting women's rights and opposing their seclusion, illiteracy, and so forth could not escape incidents of patri-archal resistance and even violent reaction from conservative mullahs. The growing association of the campaign with Russians, seen by many as the reincarnations of czarist imperialists in communist guise, further complicated the average Azeri's reaction to unveiling, for example, despite the active role of local women. Although they happened less frequently than in Central Asia, incidents of setting fire to unveiled women did in fact occur.

Reminiscences of ambivalence among many Azeris toward the process of women's emancipation may be detected even today. I noted, for instance, mixed feelings among some Azeri women and especially men toward the prominent statue in a Baku public square, the "Azerbaijan Azad Qadini" (The liberated woman of Azerbaijan), erected in 1950 by a popular Azeri artist. Symbolizing women's freedom from the veil, the huge Soviet-style figure of a woman in a dramatic unveiling gesture[22] signifies for a small number of Azeris, notably the more religio-nationalist ones, the "dishonoring of Azeri Muslims by infidel Russian Communists, a symbol of shame."[23]

Among contemporary male and female elites, including many nationalists, the women pioneers of liberation during the early years of Soviet rule are remembered with mixed feelings. Although they are respected and praised for their contribution to women's enhanced roles and massive integration into the processes of social modernization and economic development, their adherence to or collaboration with the communist system is remarked with resentment.[24]

Thus the party campaign for women's rights or the support given by the communist state to such institutions as the Ali Bayramov Women's Club was for Muslim Azeri women a mixed blessing. Although it accelerated the process of emancipation, it increasingly took away women's genuine voice and spontaneous role in the process. Furthermore, by statization and augmented Russification therein, it intensified people's resentment, if not actual resistance, to women's liberation.

INTERETHNIC AND NATIONALIST DYNAMICS

Especially in the Muslim republics, the Moscow-centered Communist Party's expectations of Zhenotdel—to be a docile instrument for implementing the party's policies among the female constituency—differed from those of many active women. An early tension grew into serious conflicts as many women members went beyond the party line in their actions and ideas for women's emancipation. This gender-related conflict intersected with interethnic tensions between Russians and Azeris. As Hokima Sultanova, one of the pioneers of the Azeri women's movement, well realized, solving the woman question among non-Russian nationalities of the USSR had become inextricably linked with solving the "nationality question."[25]

The ambivalent policy of Soviet Russians toward diverse nationalities, especially the compromise policy of "nativization" (*korenizatsiia*) proposed by V. I. Lenin, produced paradoxical results: a single state with an internationalist and universalist ideology under which emerged several distinct nation-states with acute nationalist sentiments.[26] This nativization compromise of the 1920s entailed the promotion of native elites, ethno-national culture, and local economies in each republic. In Azerbaijan the postrevolutionary compromise accelerated the process of nation building to a new level of national coherence and consciousness, the seeds of which had been planted during Azerbaijan's ephemeral republic of 1918–1920.[27]

Critical to this process was the role of the native intelligentsia, here the Azeri Muslim national communists, heritors of Jadidism. Muslim national communism was the product of a collusion between Russians and Caucasians, a synthesis of European Marxism, liberalism, Azerbaijani nationalism, and an Islamic outlook.[28] This native elite and Russian Marxist-Leninists concurred in the desire for socioeconomic change, including a modest improvement in the status of women.

By the early 1930s, however, Russian chauvinism revived under Stalin's personal autocracy. It destroyed Muslim national communism, severely punishing any hint of small-nation nationalism, imprisoning or executing thousands of ethnic communist leaders in the Great Purges, and promoting Russian culture as the most advanced in the USSR. Despite its egalitarian internationalist rhetoric, Soviet-style modernized industrialization, therefore, ultimately established a pattern similar to that in the capitalist imperial world: an "inequitable, hierarchical, imperial relationship between the center and the peripheral peoples,"[29] with Muslims at the bottom of the hierarchy.

Within such a paradoxical context, the Soviet Union ironically intensified popular nationalist passions. And these nationalist passions, I argue, have been of a gendered character and are expressed (if not held) in Azerbaijan with more intensity among women than among their male counterparts. For in retrospect, one can see that the woman question was an area over which the center (the Russian male elite) made a compromise with the periphery (the local male elite in Muslim Azerbaijan). As reflected in the voice of a leading Azeri woman activist of the time, Mina Mirzayeva, the implementation of this nativization was a mixed blessing for Azerbaijani women. It "had meant the promotion of Azeri men to positions of leadership in the Party, the government apparatus, the soviets and even cooperatives . . . rendering calls such as 'women should be given opportunities' absolutely meaningless."[30] The extent of this nativization compromise in gender issues was fairly limited under Lenin, partly because of the active interference of Russian and Azeri women revolutionaries. Rather than compromise on women's issues, Lenin advised "flexibility" and opposed the mechanical transfer of examples of women's political practices from the center to the republics.[31]

Yet again in retrospect, it seems that this Leninist flexibility was later transformed into a Stalinist compromise over women's liberation in general— and Muslim women's liberation in particular—as long as it did not threaten women's entrance into the labor force or their contribution to economic development. As far as the ruling male elite (basically the party members) was concerned, the Zhenotdel and women's clubs had outlived their state-determined purpose. During the very time (1930s) that the nativization policy terminated and the political autonomy of the local Muslim male elite eroded, it seems a subtle bargain or a tacit contract was made to leave intact the Muslim male's domination over his private territory, that is, women and the family. The local/native Azeri male elite, including the members of the Azerbaijan CP, showed an increasing unwillingness to attack traditional patriarchal norms.

It is no surprise that the timing of this change coincided with the abolition of the Zhenotdel (1930) and Azeri women's clubs (1933), leaving the "woman question" basically at the mercy of the local/national male elite. In so doing, the Russian male elite managed not to cross the sensitive border of Muslim *namus* (honor), despite the massive integration of Muslim women into the workforce. On the orders of the head of the Azerbaijan CP, the Ali Bayramov Women's Club and its journal were purged and several of its leaders removed, criticized for "Trotskyism" and "deviation from the Party line." By 1937, the club had become a mere shadow of the 1920s entity, turned into a *sa'adat sarayi* (palace of happiness) for the purpose of holding marriage ceremonies and wedding parties, an obvious reversion to the traditional family-oriented functions of a woman's club. One year later, the name of the main woman's journal, *Woman of the East,* was changed to *Woman of Azerbaijan,* and a new editorial board adopted a more traditional approach and noncontroversial language. Such a compromise is not unique to the Soviet context. Similar patterns have been observed elsewhere among opposing male elites:

> State elites have discovered that promoting male domination contributes to the maintenance of social order in a period of state formation. . . . [L]eaders of new states share a set of problems: how to eliminate rival sources of power and at the same time provide material resources for the state and allegiance to the state. A common solution involves offering a bargain to (some) men: in return for ceding control over political power and social sources to the state, they gain increased control over their families. Not only does this solution promote male domination, but it also establishes or strengthens *a distinction between public and private spheres, and subordinates the private sphere to the public.*[32] (emphasis added)

As Gregory Massell analyzes in the context of Soviet Central Asia, political institutionalization, stability, and uneven economic growth were purchased at the price of radical social transformation.[33] The liberation of women envisioned by Lenin himself and by earlier ideologues of socialism as well as their Azerbaijani counterparts was among the ideals that both Russian and Azeri male elites found the easiest to sacrifice.

In the entire Soviet Union, state mobilization campaigns reassured men that female employment would not interfere with women's domestic duties. But in the Muslim republics this reassurance had to go beyond domestic duties to encompass almost every behavior of women in public, especially those associated with ethnic identity, sexuality, and the code of honor—all seen as closely tied to Islamic religion.

THE ROLE OF ISLAM

At the time of the Russian conquest of Azerbaijan and other Muslim communities, the ulema were seen as the most likely leaders of opposition to Russian rule. In order to control and co-opt the ulema, the czarist regime created the Sunni and Shi'a ecclesiastical boards under state control. Each board had a president (called mufti for the Sunni, *shaykh al-Islam* for the Shi'a sects) appointed by the government.

Traditionally, mullahs (Muslim clerics) played important roles in Muslim society as prayer leaders, administrators, judges (*qadis*), and scholars. Russians had removed the qadis from the realm of civil and criminal law by the beginning of the twentieth century; they were confined to recording births, deaths, and marriages. During Bolshevik rule, civil structures took over registration of marriages. But even before then, Russians had succeeded in curtailing the power or securing the support of the ulema and mullahs either by military force or administrative cooperation and by granting rank and privileges such as land, titles, and tax exemptions.[34]

Hence, a century of Russian rule in Azerbaijan had considerably undermined Islam long before the beginning of Bolshevik de-Islamization. This, along with a higher level of industrialization and modernization, may in part explain why it has been secular nationalism rather than Islam that played the primary role in opposing the Soviet regime in the country. It is important here to distinguish official Islam from unofficial Islam and to note how each operated in everyday lives of Muslim women and men in both czarist Russian and Soviet contexts. Tension and distrust between many Azeri people and the religious authorities (official Islam) have long been apparent due to the latters' pro-state position, which even extended to confronting nationalists and democrats.

However, not in the Middle East, in the Russian empire, or in the Soviet Union has Islamic ideology reacted to Western modernization in any monolithic way. Although many Muslims shunned European secular modernity, those Muslims adhering to the Jadid movement sought change, reform, and modernization, particularly with regard to women's status. The reactionaries and traditionalists invoked Islam as the most effective and strongest means to resist change, including the emancipation of women. Yet the Jadids also resisted since they, for the most part, remained Muslim or maintained their Muslim identities; they sought change without detaching themselves from their people. After all, Muslims have long accepted the legitimacy of a periodic renewal (*tajdid*) of the community. But what that renewal means and should entail, particularly with regard to gender roles, has always been highly controversial.

Pressures on Islam in Azerbaijan intensified with the Bolshevik takeover after the October Revolution of 1917. Most mosques and other religious institutions were closed. Many Muslim nationalists and Jadidists who made up the core of the native elite in Azerbaijan eventually joined the Russian communists, albeit retaining their own interpretation of Marxism and their own agenda for socialist Azerbaijan within a Muslim national communist framework. This concept was foremost a blueprint for national liberation. Given the revolutionary mood among the Baku oil workers and the rising national consciousness and advocacy of modernity among the Azeri elite at the time of the Bolshevik revolution, Muslim national communism brought a necessary ideological metamorphosis for Azerbaijan.

Moreover, there has not been much animosity between Azeri secular modernist intellectuals and religion. They might criticize and ridicule mullahs and such practices as veiling and polygyny as incompatible with the true spirit of Islam, but they avoided denouncing Islam in its totality. To Muslim Jadids, many of the socialist ideas could easily blend with their own reform agenda. They believed that "Islamic culture or way of life and Marxism are not by definition incompatible ideologies. On the contrary, they could coexist and even complement one another."[35]

Eventually, however, such coexistence proved not to be free from paradoxes and conflicts. Consequently, a duality characterized most cultural aspects in the lives of many, turning them into "Soviets in public, Muslim Azeris in private."[36] This duality manifested itself most clearly in the realm of gender ideology, as reflected in the words of Betura Mamedova, an Azeri woman professor of English in Baku: "Socialism has affected our life externally; our character and psychology, however, have remained basically unchanged."[37] Another Azeri woman, Rena Ibrahimbekova, a prominent psychologist and director of the Center for Gifted Children in Baku, confirmed this observation while raising her deep concern about many Azeri women's "tendency to avoid practicing their officially constituted equal rights. . . . I am worried that in the post-Soviet era, we may go back to our *adat va an'aneh* [traditions] in official level as well as eventually resolving the present duality in favor of its pre-modern regressive side."[38]

THE PRIVATIZATION OF RELIGION

The ritualization of belief is apparently a common response for believers who have publicly had to come to terms with an antireligious order imposed by a dominant foreign force. Religion becomes essentially privatized and domesticated, displaying itself only through certain mores and rituals not seen as closely associated with religion, yet possessing an underlying base of religious feelings and emotions. The privatization of religion and other institutions of social life hinges upon the compartmentalization of public and private behavior, the latter being more authentic to one's nature and identity.[39]

Islam, like any other major religion, is a multidimensional institution with more than simply a corpus of directly spiritual beliefs and rites. It is, rather, a complex aggregate of cultural, psychological, and social traditions, attitudes, and customs governing a whole way of life.[40] One can argue, therefore, that the Soviet antireligious campaigns might have succeeded in minimizing its intellectual and ideological dimensions, but the experiential, consequential, and a certain level of the ritual dimensions of Islam, understood in a broad sense as the Muslim mode of life, have kept their vitality.[41]

Among the attitudes and practices that may be seen as Islamic mores and rituals, the ones associated with gender roles, sexuality, and life cycles maintained their relevance in Soviet Azerbaijan. Those related to male circumcision, sex-segregated mourning ceremonies, and means of testifying to a bride's virginity on her wedding night (*yengeh*), for example, might actually have been local customs preceding or superseding Islam but popularly viewed as Islamic. In fact, in a recent public lecture, Shaykh al-Islam Allah-Shokur Pashazadeh, head of the Islamic Directorate of Transcaucasia and the highest religious authority in Azerbaijan, reprimanded the custom of yengeh as non-Islamic and detrimental to marriage and the family.[42]

Unlike in many contemporary Muslim countries, the gender discourse in the Azerbaijan independence movement has not gained a doctrinal or ideological Islamist (fundamentalist) tone. So far, ethnicity, language, regionalism, and Islam—in its cultural, spiritual, and ritual forms—have served as the primary sources of national identity in the new republic. Nevertheless, the end result for women has been rather similar to the situation in those nations affected by Islamism. By turning the private or domestic domain into a bastion of resistance, gender roles and intrafamily dynamics have retained strong traditional and religious characteristics. In effect, women are expected to be the moral exemplars and primary carriers of this "religious load."[43]

Appearing in public without a male or an elder female chaperon, wearing pants, smoking or drinking in public, and driving cars are instances of behaviors widely viewed as unacceptable for an authentic Azeri woman. Ethnic loyalty and the observance of endogamy by women (but not necessarily men),[44] the cults of honor,[45] chastity, shame, prudery, and virginity before marriage are among the ethno-religious customs prescribed as essential female attributes. A woman is valued for her physical beauty, advanced education (especially among urbanites), endurance, self-sacrificing motherhood, docility and subservience toward her husband and in-laws, homemaking skills, hospitality, and delicacy. Such attributes constitute identity markers supposedly demarcating Azeris from "others," especially Russians and Armenians.

THE ROLE OF THE FAMILY AND ETHNIC VALUES

Compared to Russia and the northern regions of the former Soviet Union, the family has remained the most conservative and stable institution in Azerbaijan. Its divorce rate is one of the lowest, even though it has risen slightly in recent years to less than 15 percent in 1990.[46] Although the nuclear family is the norm, particularly in urban areas, people still rely heavily on extended family norms and networks. Men and women remain deeply family-oriented, women being usually identified by their kin, male kin in particular.

Children are seen as great blessings. Baby girls are generally welcomed, though with less joy than boys. Mothers have to start collecting dowry materials for a girl at infancy, since marriage remains the essential rite in the lives of Azerbaijanis. Ceremonies associated with it comprise the happiest, yet the most costly and demanding requirements of the life cycle. In addition to an engagement party, two lavish wedding ceremonies (*qiz toyi* for the bride and *oghlan toyi* for the groom) take place. In many regions of the country, traditional customs like *bashlig* (the groom's payment to parents for nurturing the bride), *mahr* (an agreed sum to be paid to women in case of divorce), and *jahaz* (the dowry of household appliances and furniture provided by the bride's parents) are strictly observed.[47]

Divorced women, but even more never-married single women, suffer a social stigma, since mothering is regarded as women's primary role and most important source of gratification. Laws protecting mothers (those providing paid pregnancy and maternity leave for working mothers) remain on the books, though they are increasingly ignored in the new market economy. Thus far, the egalitarian civil family law that had replaced the Shari'a since the consolidation of the Soviet state has remained in force in post-Soviet Azerbaijan, protecting women's rights relating to marriage, divorce, and child custody. Enforcement of such laws, however, is becoming ever more difficult in the current transitional society. Double standards in sexuality continue while the family structure still appears patriarchal. Although individual preference and love are important, particularly among urban dwellers, the choice of spouse is generally supervised, if not actually made, by the family.

As among other nationalities in the Caucasus like Christian Armenians and Georgians, the primary loyalty of Muslim Azerbaijanis is still centered on kinship groups and intimate friends. This traditional family and kinship system entails paradoxical implications for male and particularly female members.[48] On the one hand, it usually offers solidarity and trust. It can provide economic, political, emotional, and physical support during such difficult circumstances as the recent warfare. On the other hand, it operates as a repressive device, limiting women's independence, individuality, and personal growth. Hence, many urban educated women express ambivalent feelings toward their respected yet male-protected status, as is indicated by Kifayat, a 37-year-old nurse working in a town near Baku:

> One of the major difficulties in my life as a single woman is that I do not have any *arkha,* no father, no brothers. Russian women are luckier in this regard, as in their society a woman is accepted on her own. But in the case of an Azeri woman, people always ask, "Who is her man? Who is her guardian?" as if I am nobody without an arkha.[49]

The persistence of the extended family structure has reinforced patriarchal norms. Some scholars have also attributed the prevalence of the underground economy and corrupt political practices in the Caucasus to this traditional heavy reliance on close familial ties.[50] Powerful obligations to one's relatives, clan, and region, especially on the part of women, may have delayed the constitution of citizenship and national-civic identity. This in turn may have contributed to the duality and dissociation in Azerbaijan's modernization in general and women's emancipation in particular.

It can be argued, on the contrary, that under a repressive state lacking a civil society with its network of political institutions mediating between the individual and the state, the family network becomes a substitute. The Soviet state was never actually hegemonic over people's ethnic and familial practices in the private sphere, where familial and religio-ethnic norms rather than the Soviet state ideology established the vision of the good and moral, especially with regard to women's behavior. One may even argue that kinship networks have been intentionally organized to resist the state and to function as a buffer against politico-economic pressures. Rather than "public" versus "private" binaries, some important parts of the public or political life have actually been constructed by family and kin-related private, informal networks.

Political factors aside, certain economic constraints have obviously contributed to the persistence of the traditional extended family structure. As in Soviet Russia, but even more so in the Muslim peripheries of the FSU, the state's emphasis on production and the reduction of the woman question to its economic base made women's massive entrance into the labor force a priority without instituting corresponding social and economic provisions for transforming the family structure and gender roles. The backwardness in food cycle technology, the housing shortage that forced young couples to live for years with their parents, and the insufficiency of child care facilities made restructuring of the patriarchal and extended family infeasible. Azerbaijan has especially suffered in this regard: for example, its child care and preschool education attendance has been one of the poorest in the former Soviet Union (16 to 18 percent versus 71 percent in Russia).

Mamedova represents another Azeri voice contrasting with that of Kifayat and of Rafibeyli resentment earlier expressed in "Kitchen Lines." Such contrasts are indicative of the contradictory implications, or the mixed blessing, offered by the traditional family structure:

> We women are tenaciously clinging to our family and instead of getting weary of oceans of duties, we are energized by them. We are thought to be the backbone of the family and a buffer when things go wrong spiritually. We enjoy playing this role, because this is our life, and it is due to this family tenacity that Azeri people never forget their language, their culture and religion. One Azeri poet called it "blood memory" (*qan yaddashti*).[51]

As one can infer from Mamedova's comment, women are seen again as the guardians of the nation who have succeeded in playing this role thanks to "family tenacity." Her statement also implies that in a colonial or quasi-colonial, interethnic situation, the family would function as the bastion of resistance against assimilation (here Russification). The family thus becomes the *dar al-Islam* (domain of Islam) to be protected from the penetration of the dominant "other."

THE PLEASURE OF A PARADOX

To an outside observer, the hierarchical structure of the family and society favoring male domination in Azerbaijan may appear more paradoxical than elsewhere in part because of the equal rights guaranteed by law, women's high level of literacy, and their massive presence in social and economic arenas, but many Azeri professional women seem to perceive this paradox differently. According to Mamedova, they consider it to be to women's advantage rather than disadvantage: "Our way of life might seem paradoxical to foreigners, but I want them to believe that our women enjoy living the pleasure of this paradox."[52]

It may be that dual realities result in dual perceptions, or the distinction between constructed realities of men and women explains the pleasure of this paradox. Pusta Azizbekova, a prominent academician in her seventies and director of the Azerbaijan Museum of History, explains:

> Women's apparent subservient or male-dominated position is exactly that: apparent. . . . Why not? Like Russian and Western women, we enjoy

equal rights and legal protection. But we feel even more privileged as, in addition to what they have, we also enjoy the respect, pampering and protection we receive from our men and families. I enjoy having men open doors and wait for me to enter, pay the bill when we go out, and shelter me when we walk in streets and public places. What is wrong with that?

And in response to the idea that protection makes women dependent, she replies:

Oh, it just appears that way. Only men think that we depend on them and by thinking so they feel satisfied and powerful. Let them take care of us under this illusion. We know very well who in reality is the power here and who depends on whom. . . . God forbid a household without a man. A man to a household is like a gem to a ring, we Azeris say. But the gem stands on top, is nothing without the ring.[53]

Perhaps acting as assertive professional women in public, but showing docility and submission in private is a coping mechanism for Azeri women caught in the midst of the struggle against patriarchy on the one hand and the protection of their men's sense of masculinity in the Soviet quasi-colonial context on the other.

A further paradoxical observation is that some women seem to feel that the household is the only territory in which they can exert real power and that they are the owners of the entirety of their families. The husband is to be served in regard to everything, from bringing him a cup of tea to preparing the bathroom for his shower. At times there seems a deliberate attempt on their part to infantilize their husbands in order to keep them dependent on them in the household domain. Perceiving domestic responsibilities as empowering and gratifying rather than an oppressive burden is reflected in Mamedova's comment, not unusual from an Azeri woman:

The Azeri woman at work and at home is two, often radically different people. At work she looks confident, relaxed, and attractive. At home she is a busy bee because she has to see to a myriad of things: dusting, washing, cooking, sending children to school, checking their homework, scanning the daily newspapers (every family has to subscribe to newspapers), receiving uninvited guests. I can extend this list and you may stop believing me or you may ask what is the reward? And I will answer: the reward is *my* family and *my* children.[54] (emphasis added)

CONCLUSION

In Azerbaijan, both under the colonial rule of czarist Russia and within the quasi-colonial context of the Soviet regime, as well as during the recent post-Soviet nationalist and independent republic, Azeri women have been both objects and subjects of nation building and identity politics.

Along with the "kitchen lines," identity politics have further circumscribed women's role in Azerbaijani society. The definition of womanhood in Soviet Azerbaijan was construed in part in contrast to the perceived image of Russian womanhood. Since the complete takeover of Azerbaijan by czarist Russians in the early nineteenth century, the dynamics of modernity and traditionalism pertaining to gender roles as well as other realms of social life have taken place in a contested context of Muslim Azeri "us" and non-Muslim Russian/Soviet "them."

As in Algeria, Egypt, and Iran when confronting colonial domination or foreign intrusion, women's liberation in Azerbaijan has been held hostage to the prescribed responsibility of women as the primary repositories of tradition and national and ethnic identity. Certain traditional images, customs, and stereotypes of femininity dubbed as *asil* (authentic) and *ismatli* (chaste) have been preserved to function as identity markers defining Azeris' ethnicity and demarcating them from Russians. That responsibility of women as symbols of the ethnic/national community has complicated the process of change in gender roles and interfered with progress toward gender equality.

Among the main institutions offering Azeris the opportunity to resist complete assimilation were the family and religion. But religion, privatized and domesticated, could function and be manifested essentially through the family and women or women-associated rituals. Thus to preserve Azeri boundaries, women were designated as Azeri identity markers and moral exemplars. By upholding of ethnic traditions (*adat va an'aneh*) and the Islamic faith, women became the main agents for sustaining those boundaries. Women, thus, relegated as they were to the margins of the formal polity, did play a central role in the informal politics of identity by nurturing ethno-cultural variables.

Women generally do continue to play their prescribed roles in post-Soviet Azerbaijan, but with certain new distinctions. Although they do not seem to shun the assignment of cultural and national representation, they are seeking to expand, redefine, and at times subvert the parameters of Azeri authenticity and Islamic heritage.

This is perhaps the most challenging era for them. The state is not economically and legally as supportive of women's social and productive roles as it had been in the Soviet past, nor are free market rules female-friendly. Moreover, Islam is no longer only a matter of private life to be preserved and practiced mainly by women. It is becoming increasingly politicized in the hands of men and rival political entrepreneurs at both the national and regional levels and is being manipulated in accordance with or in reaction to the exigencies of the new capitalistic realities or the old patriarchal gender arrangements.

Another major distinction from the Soviet totalitarian past is the multiplicity and diversity in almost all spheres of life. Given the rich human and natural resources of Azerbaijan and notwithstanding the current economic deterioration, Azeri women have a substantial potential in the longer term for higher achievement in their social status. They can assert their agency by taking advantage of the fluidity that has characterized both the meaning of Islam and the parameters of national, cultural, and gender identities.

NOTES

I would like to express my gratitude to the Fulbright Foundation and IREX for sponsoring my research visits and to my departments at the Institute of Oriental Studies at the Academy of Sciences of Azerbaijan; the Pedagogical Institute of Foreign Languages in Baku; the Harvard Divinity School at Harvard University; the Hoover Institution at Stanford University; the Center for the Study of Women at the University of California, Los Angeles; and particularly to the Azerbaijani women and men who have been so generous and cooperative with regard to my research. I am especially grateful to Herbert Bodman for his most congenial and constructive cooperation and editorial help during the preparation of this chapter.

1. See, for example, Sergei Poliakov, *Everyday Islam: Religion and Tradition in Rural Central Asia* (London: Sharpe, 1992).

2. The name of Azerbaijan is a continual point of contention. In this article, "Azerbaijani" or "Azerbaijanian" is used in reference to citizens of the Soviet and post-Soviet republic of Azerbaijan who are members of different ethnic groups within this territory. "Azeri," however, is used only in reference to the majority indigenous ethnic group (Turkic and predominantly Muslim) from whom the Republic of Azerbaijan derives its name. Rather than referring to south or north Azerbaijan as designated by Soviet Azeris, average Azeris in Iran used to distinguish their brethren in Russia and the FSU as the ones living on "the other side" (*otayli*), that is, the other side of the Araz River that makes up the natural border between the two parts of Azerbaijan.

3. See the report by the Commission on Security and Cooperation in Europe, *CSCE Digest* 19, no. 1 (January 1996): 5–14.

4. *Jadid*, meaning "new" in Arabic, Turkic, and Persian, and *Jadidism*, derived from *usul-i jadid* (new methods), aimed at improving the curricula of the *maktab* (school) and their overall approach to teaching. In opposition to the conservative educators and ulema, known as *qadimists* (old thinkers), jadidism grew into a nationalist modernist interpretation of Islam because of the endeavors of the Crimean Tatar journalist Ismail Gasprinski. See Tadeusz Swietochowski, *Russian Azerbaijan, 1905–1920: The Shaping of National Identity in a Muslim Community* (Cambridge: Cambridge University Press, 1985), 30–35.

5. My book in Farsi (in progress) is based on Hamideh Javanshir's fascinating personal memoirs and observations on early twentieth-century Caucasia.

6. The journal was named after the legendary Molla Nasreddin (also called Nasreddin Hoja), a figure who appears in clever but didactic stories throughout the Middle East and Central Asia. The journal transcended nationality, and its articles were translated from Azeri-Turkic into many other languages. It was most influential in Iran, Turkey, Georgia, and Central Asia.

7. See Azade-Ayse Rorlich, *Volga Tatars: Profile in National Resilience* (Stanford: Hoover Institution Press, 1986).

8. See Audrey Altstadt, *The Azerbaijani Turks: Power and Identity Under Russian Rule* (Stanford: Hoover Institution Press, 1992), 56.

9. See Sabir Mamedova, *Put k progrecu* (Baku: Azerbaijan Dovlat Nashriyat komitasi, 1986), 4.

10. Altstadt, *Azerbaijani Turks,* 64.

11. Nasib Nasibzadeh, *Azerbayjan Demokratik Respublikasi: Magalalar va Sanadlar* (Baku: Elm, 1990), 44, cited in Tadeusz Swietochowski, *Russian Azerbaijan, 1905–1920: The Shaping of National Identity in a Muslim Community* (Cambridge: Cambridge University Press, 1985), 129.

12. For the full text of the poem, see Mirza Ibrahimov (ed.), *Azerbaijan Poetry: Classic, Modern, and Traditional* (Moscow: Progress Publishers, 1969), 374–378.

13. On women's education and health, see Nayereh Tohidi, *Situatsionniy Analiz Polozheniia Zhenshchin v Azerbaidzhane* (Baku: UNICEF, 1994).

14. Gail Lapidus (ed.), *Women in Soviet Society: Equality, Development, and Social Change* (Berkeley: University of California Press, 1982).

15. Mary Buckley, "Female Workers by Hand and Male Workers by Brain: The Occupational Composition of the 1985 Azerbaijan Supreme Soviet," *Soviet Union* 14, no. 2 (1987): 229–237.

16. On women's working conditions in Azerbaijan, see Tohidi, *Situatsionniy.* See also *Azerbaydjan Respublikaci Devlat Statistika Komitesi* (Baku: Azerbaidzhan Dovlat Nashriyati, 1991).

17. Valentina Bodrova, "Glasnost and 'The Woman Question' in the Mirror of Public Opinion: Attitudes Towards Women, Work, and the Family," in *Democratic Reform and the Position of Women in Transitional Economies,* ed. Valentine Moghadam (New York: Clarendon Press, 1993), 182.

18. For a comparable utilization of women as auxiliaries of the state and authoritarian statist modernization, see, for example, Suad Joseph, "Elite Strategies for State Building: Women, Family, Religion, and the State in Iraq and Lebanon," in *Women, Islam and the State,* ed. Deniz Kandiyoti (Philadelphia: Temple University Press, 1991), 176–200.

19. See, for example, Gregory Massell, *The Surrogate Proletariat: Moslem Women and Revolutionary Strategies in Soviet Central Asia (1919–1929)* (Princeton: Princeton University Press, 1974), xxiii.

20. Almaz is a young radical and devoted teacher in a small Azerbaijani village who organizes women into a literary club and tries to educate them about the oppressive customs of the time (1920s). One of her own male co-workers together with the village's mullahs and landlords mobilizes many villagers against her. She is eventually spared from the crisis by joining the CP. See Aydin Jabbarli, *Ja'far Jabbarli: Lyrika, Hekayalar, Piyeslar* (Baku: Yazichi, 1979).

21. For a detailed history of the club, see Azade-Aysa Rorlich, "The 'Ali Bayramov' Club, the Journal *Sharq Gadini* and the Socialization of Azeri Women: 1920–30," *Central Asian Survey* 5, nos. 3–4 (1986): 221–239; and Tohidi (in progress).

22. The statue is particularly associated with the memory of a young Azerbaijani woman who was set on fire by her father and brothers for "dishonoring" them by her act of unveiling and joining a women's club in the 1920s.

23. Such extremely negative views about women's unveiling under Soviet rule are rare and came out during my interviews with the leading members of the Islamic Party of Azerbaijan, August 1994.

24. See, for example, Fatma Abdollahzadeh, "Qadin va Jamiyyat," *Azerbaycan* (15 October 1994), 3.

25. Hokima Sultanova, *Sa'adat* (Baku: Azerbaidzhan Dovlat Nashriyati, 1970).

26. Ronald Suny, "Nationalist and Ethnic Unrest in the Soviet Union," in *The "Nationality Question" in the Soviet Union,* ed. Gail Lapidus (New York: Garland Publishers, 1992).

27. For a detailed history of nation building in Azerbaijan, see Swietochowski, *Russian Azerbaijan;* and Altstadt, *Azerbaijan: Turks.*

28. Alexandre Bennigsen and Enders Wimbush, *Muslim National Communism in the Soviet Union* (Chicago: University of Chicago Press, 1979).

29. Suny, "Nationalist and Ethnic Unrest," 28.

30. Rorlich, "The 'Ali Bayramov' Club," 232.

31. Mary Buckley, *Women and Ideology in the Soviet Union* (Ann Arbor: University of Michigan Press, 1989), 83.

32. Sue Ellen Charlton, Jana Everett, and Kathleen Staudt (eds.), *Women, State, and Development* (New York: State University Press, 1989), 180.

33. Massell, *Surrogate Proletariat,* 408.

34. Altstadt, *Azerbaijani Turks,* 57–62.

35. Bennigsen and Wimbush, *Muslim National Communism,* xx.

36. Nayereh Tohidi, "Soviet in Public, Azeri in Private," *Women's Studies International Forum* 19, nos. 1–2 (1996): 111–123.

37. Cited from her commentary on "Women in Azerbaijan," written at my request, December 1995.

38. Author's interview in Baku, February 8, 1995.

39. For an analytical elaboration on this, see Hank Johnston, "Religio-Nationalist Subcultures Under the Communists: Comparisons from the Baltics, Transcaucasia and Ukraine," *Sociology of Religion* 54, no. 3 (1993): 237–255.

40. Muriel Atkin, *The Subtlest Battle: Islam in Soviet Tajikistan* (Philadelphia: Foreign Policy Research Institute, 1989), 13.

41. My analysis here is based on a socio-psychological definition and theorization of religion originally formulated by sociologists like Charles Glock and Rodney Stark, *Religion and Society in Tension* (Chicago: Rand McNally, 1965).

42. I was present during this lecture delivered in Baku, February 18, 1995, at a conference on "Wedding Customs in Azerbaijan" organized by the National Committee of Women.

43. For a comparable analysis, see Gillian Tett, "Guardians of Faith: Women in Soviet Tajikistan," in *Muslim Women's Choices,* ed. Camillia El-Solh and Judy Mabro (Providence, RI: Berg Publishers, 1994).

44. See my discussion on endogamy, interethnic marriage, and nationalism in Tohidi, "Soviet in Public."

45. The notion of honor (*namus*), so prevalent in the Muslim world, is a very loaded, multidimensional, and gendered term. One of its most important connotations is women's chastity, even though it is usually used in reference to men, because in both Shi'a Iran and Shi'a Azerbaijan the responsibility for the protection of namus falls primarily on the men. A woman's misbehavior, especially sexual misbehavior, brings shame and dishonor (*namussislig*) not only to her but even more so to her male "protectors": father, brothers, and husband. The findings of my studies in Azerbaijan attest to the continuing strength of the cult of namus among Azeris. In my sample, male respondents ranked namus as the most important theme in their early socialization and even more frequently than females did.

46. Tohidi, *Situatsionniy,* 12.

47. Hassan Quliyev, "Toy Adatlarimiz," paper presented at the Conference on Women and Wedding Customs in Azerbaijan, Baku, February 18, 1995.

48. For patterns similar to those of the Caucasus, see Suad Joseph, "Gender and Family in the Arab World" (Special *MERIP* Publication, October 1994).

49. Author's interview (interviewee preferred not to be identified so withheld last name), Baku, August 29, 1994. The word "arkha" literally means "back," implying kin, primarily male kin, to lean on.

50. Ronald Suny, "Transcaucasia: Cultural Cohesion and Ethnic Revival in a Multinational Society," in *The Nationalities Factor in Soviet Politics and Society*, ed. Lubomyr Hajda and Mark Beissinger (Boulder: Westview Press, 1990), 231.

51. Comments received from Betura Mamedova, an Azeri woman who taught at the college, in reaction to the author's earlier draft of this chapter, December 1995.

52. Ibid.

53. Author's interview, Baku, June 12, 1992.

54. Mamedova, December 1995.

9

Between Lenin and Allah: Women and Ideology in Tajikistan

Shahrbanou Tadjbakhsh

The politicization of women's concerns in Tajikistan does not exist in a vacuum: it shares many similarities with the historical experiences of post-colonization and transition to democracy of the countries of the Third World, in addition to the experience of socialism that the countries of the Second World share. At the same time, one can place the characteristics of Tajikistan as the "East" within the East/West dialogue and as the "South" in the North/South debate.

Much has been written about Muslim women in the Third World. Women's experiences of socialism in the Eastern bloc countries have also been well documented, both during the Soviet period and in a growing literature relating to the effects of transition on the women of Russia and the Central and East European countries. The case of Muslim women under former socialist regimes, however, is underresearched, even though it presents a good opportunity for comparative thinking. The study of the experiences of women in Central Asia, Azerbaijan, and Afghanistan during the Soviet occupation can lead the way to a better understanding not only of Islam under socialism but also of the fate of traditional society under occupation. In this chapter I only begin to look at the historical experiences of women of Tajikistan while opening a path to the development of analytical thinking on a neglected and isolated field.

In order to identify and understand the real political power of women outside basic institutions, as argued in Haleh Afshar's edited volume, *Women and Politics in the Third World,* one cannot add women to the study of politics but on the contrary should reexamine the political process from a gender point of view.[1] The real political potential of women is recognized neither by political scientists trained to look at the number of women represented in high politics, nor by Western-style feminists who reject the concept of motherhood, especially as a political identity. Women's absence in the public space of high politics or reluctance to join

163

feminist movements does not mean that they do not have nontraditional paths to self-realization. Women participate in political activity in different ways from men; they have both different methods and different issues with which they are concerned.

Yet policy planners often simply add the "woman question" to mainstream politics. The Soviet regime, for example, as I argue in this chapter, believed it had solved the woman question by interjecting women in high politics through the introduction of quotas at the parliamentary and Communist Party levels and by creating Women's Councils acting like highly placed interest groups, even though women rarely appeared in the leadership positions of such echelons of power. In the conventional politics of the former Soviet Union as well as in Muslim countries, women have not been represented for various reasons ranging from the personal, such as demands at home, to the professional, such as competition and lack of opportunities. When they are represented in politics, they are mostly concentrated in the social spheres, such as education and health care.

Scholars of the Soviet system, in contrast, often divided society into the "public" sphere outside the home and the "private" realm of the household that could not be touched by the state. Often, it was only the public sphere that was associated with politics, and what was private, therefore, became apolitical. Hence, when scholars examined the status of Islam in the Soviet Union, they only saw the lack of official mosques, *madrasas* (religious schools), and outward signs of orthodox Islam in the public sphere and concluded that the Soviet regime had done away with political Islam. They often neglected to recognize the political aspect of Islam as practiced at home, within the household, because that was the private sphere. Yet this kind of thinking inevitably failed to recognize the political nature of women's activities because women featured, and continue to feature, predominantly in the private sphere.

Thus both the Soviet regime and those studying it, although they had very different perspectives, failed to recognize the real political potential for women's activities. Both often referred to the Tajik woman as a "Muslim woman of the Soviet East," an ambiguous term that in reality may not have amounted to anything more than a geographical attribute. It is indeed difficult to characterize the Tajik woman as a one-dimensional "Muslim," "post-Soviet," or "Eastern" woman. Her life has been shaped by a symbiosis between the word of Allah, the word of V. I. Lenin, and that of men, both Tajik and Russian, a mélange that has molded the contemporary history of Tajik society since the turn of the century. And yet Tajik women have tried to express their own cultural values and their own definitions of status and prestige, often regardless of the categories created by God, Lenin, and men.

The activism of women in Central Asia also cannot be categorized as traditionally "feminist." Feminist movements generally set as their baseline the political demands of equality between men and women and the rejection of patriarchal systems. Feminists would like to place women in the same categories that are traditionally male dominated. Yet women in Central Asia would join their voices with those of Third World and colored women, who in recent years have criticized traditional feminism on the basis that it relies on the experiences of white, middle-class women and does not take into consideration the problems of other women. In addition, women in Central Asia cannot join a feminist movement because of the mere fact that in postcolonial societies, such as Tajikistan, women often become bearers of the national cultural identity and thus are cornered into a position of having to disregard the interest of their gender in defense of the national identity of the nation.

IDENTITY AS A MYTH WITH A PURPOSE

Identity indicators, such as cultural symbols chosen as signifiers of ethnic, national, or gender identity, have a liquid existence that reflects their recognition by both outsiders and insiders within the group. Gender roles, defined as the social meaning given to differences between men and women, are distinguished from sexual functions that create universal, biological differences. Gender roles depend entirely on society's perception of men's and women's roles at a given time and place. In the same way that cultural elements chosen as relevant to ethnicity can be reinforced by ceremonies and repetition, the meaning given to gender identity is also subject to change. Gender identity, which in the Soviet parlance comes close to the "woman question" as opposed to "women's experience," can be created by women as a group or assigned to them by a dominant group, such as men in patriarchal society. Therefore, there is a distinction between what the group decides to do and what the outside imposes upon the group.

Gender identity is often used to stress the difference between groups when a situation may be threatening the existence of one group or the loss of its privilege. Gender identity can thus be a reaction to the negative evaluation of an outside group, an opposition. In the same way that colonial rule awakens nationalism when a group's existence is threatened, women as a category, when not in control of their own destiny, naturally want to unite to gain political authority in the name of gender. It is possible to argue that in the case of the Muslim republics of the former Soviet Union, there were sufficient indicators allowing for the existence of a coherent gender identity. These include the following:

1. A marked cultural history of women as a special interest group with events and symbolic benchmarks of the past relating to the experiences of women.

2. Ritualized, separate gender roles in society and within the household, including specific duties in the private and public spheres.
3. Reinforcement of differences between men and women by economic and political segregation and the existence of specific parties
   and unions targeting women only.
4. The transformation, in the context of the relationship between traditional Central Asian society and the Soviet state, of women into
   bearers of the Central Asian ethnic and cultural identity, whose
   contribution to the "struggle" was providing socialization and producing many children.

WOMEN AS A POLITICAL TOOL

Tajikistan is the only country in Central Asia in which most of the inhabi-
tants speak a language related to Persian rather than Turkic. They are primarily Sunni Muslims, although a small minority in eastern Tajikistan,
known as Badakhshan, are Isma'ili Shi'ite Muslims and speak a dialect be-
longing to the Eastern Iranian language group.

On August 25, 1990, Tajikistan, which borders Afghanistan, Turkmenistan, Uzbekistan, and China, declared itself a sovereign state and on
September 9, 1991, an independent country. Soon after, however, Tajikistan fell into turmoil: a slow and painful transition to a market economy,
the breakdown of institutions, and rising voiced dissent led to a civil war
in 1992, followed by a continued impoverishment of the country.

The modern history of Tajikistan can be divided into three distinct periods: the Soviet days (1924–1989), the post-Soviet reaction (1989–1992),
and the civil war and its aftermath (1992 to present). During Soviet times,
the state ideology of Marxist-Leninism tried to dictate the position of
women in Tajik society, and the Soviet state forced the socialist model on
women in Tajikistan. Because the emancipation of women could potentially play an important role in the disruption of traditional and presumably
anti-Soviet society, the Soviet government launched a campaign assaulting
practices that dealt with women's position in society, including outlawing
religious and customary laws and providing women with educational and
employment opportunities. It selected cultural symbols as well as state institutions to communicate its moral code regarding women's lives, status,
and behavior according to norms of an ideal Soviet woman. These Soviet
values and behaviors were adopted by a number of "Russified" and "So-
vietized" women in Tajik society, either because they were "modernized,"
or because they were chosen to act as leaders and organizers. However,
many customary practices and traditions survived in the family setting,
and Soviet ideology, because it stemmed from Russian society, considered
as "alien," was not effective in entirely changing the private lives of
women within the families in Tajikistan.

As glasnost and perestroika caught on in Central Asia, giving birth to nationalist and Islamist movements from 1987, an organized opposition to the official communist ideology advocated a return to traditional society, including a more conservative role and image for women. Between 1989 and 1992, intellectuals led discussions on a revision of history while Muslim clerics preached openly the need to study Islam. Members of the Tajik national front, known as the Rastokhez (Renaissance) and founded in 1989; the Democratic Party of Tajikistan (created in 1990); and the Islamic Revivalist Party (registered in 1991) all tried to dethrone the previous model and replace it with something more suited to representing Tajik society. Symbols and institutions of the Soviet past were deconstructed and replaced with new models derived from Central Asian cultural history as well as from the modern societies of the Middle East. The more radical side of the new Tajik identity opposed the emancipation of women because it was a Western, Russian idea and was carried out by either Europeans themselves or Russified Central Asian agents. In the process of returning to an Eastern, if not yet Islamic society, revisionists reevaluated the norms of Tajik society, including what an Eastern woman's role should be.

Beginning in the spring of 1992, however, the cultural demands of nationalist and Islamist groups became increasingly politicized, a process that eventually led to a full-fledged civil war. Members of the Democratic Party, the Islamic Revivalist Party, and the Rastokhez National Front fought a bloody battle with formerly Communist political leaders that lasted from the summer of 1992 to the beginning of spring 1993. The strife demonstrated the disunity of Tajikistan as a nation and its fragmentation on the basis of ethnic and regional identities. Up to 40,000 may have been killed in roughly six months of fighting, and 500,000 were displaced from their homes, one-fifth crossing the Amur River into Afghanistan.[2] Some 70,000 women and children became refugees, countless ones widows and victims of the civil war.

THE "WOMAN QUESTION": WHOSE CONCERN IS IT, ANYWAY?

At various times in the past seventy years, women's issues have been one of the decisive factors in the evolution toward a reborn Central Asian cultural identity. They have played an essential role in three periods of the history of Tajikistan: The first period, 1920–1989, coincided with the construction of the image, role, identity, and, eventually, culture of the Tajik Soviet socialist woman based on socialist laws and models adapted mainly from Russian society. The second period, during which the deconstruction of that model and its recreation on the basis of traditional society took place, corresponded with the beginning of organized political and cultural opposition to the Soviet regime in 1989 and ended in 1992 with the start of the civil war. During and immediately after that conflict, gender issues in this third period became once more a rallying point for efforts at reconciliation between feuding sides and reconstruction of Tajik society. Gender issues have also become a benchmark for the negative experiences of the transition period.

The question of the status of women, one can argue, has more to do with men's concerns than those relating to women. Both the Soviet state and the antistate movement used Tajik women as a myth, spoke for them, represented them, and used them more as a symbol than a reality. Power was found in the image of women: radical, liberated, and emancipated in one case, traditional in the other. Either they were seen performing men's duties, or they were presented as a caring mother of numerous children and a devoted wife and daughter. Women's representation by men, intellectuals and ideologists, in the Soviet as well as the post-Soviet periods, played a more crucial role in creating the myth of identity than their own voicing of their experiences. Meanwhile, women were caught confused among criticism of traditional patriarchal values in the home, images of emancipation, demands of industrialization, and discourses of nationalism and decolonization.

Between 1989 and 1992, the ideal model of women in Tajik society, once monopolized by communist ideology, faced strong competition from nationalist and religious groups. The image of beauty in society changed in popular culture, the media, and literature. The quiet, submissive, eastern girl with arched eyebrows on a moonlike face, the image created in the classical poetry of the Central Asian heritage, was during the Soviet times put behind tractors and in cotton fields and sometimes behind meeting tables in cosmopolitan settings. After glasnost, however, the favorite image became that of a village mother nurturing a large family, as portrayed in the poems of post-Soviet Tajik poetesses as well.[3]

THE SOVIET STATE
AND THE EMANCIPATION CAMPAIGN

Lenin claimed that before the 1917 October Revolution, the women of the Muslim areas of the Soviet Union were "the most oppressed of the oppressed and the most enslaved of the enslaved."[4] To aid the emancipation of the so-called women of the Soviet East, the new Bolshevik government set up trade unions, working women's clubs and workshops (*artel*), cultural and educational organizations, and evening and Sunday schools for adults, all of which operated as centers of agitation and propaganda for the new regime. The primary goal of the Soviet state was thus to organize women as a political and economic force and prepare them to be workers of the new socialist country. Moscow opened affiliates of the Women's

Department of the Communist Party (Zhenotdel) in the major cities of what was then Turkestan and Eastern Bukhara. By 1920, the Zhenotdel of the Central Committee of the Communist Party of Turkistan had organized provincial zhenotdels, nicknamed *jinotdel* (department of bad spirits) by its opponents, to carry out propaganda work among "women of the Soviet East." By 1921, forty-five local branches were active in Turkistan, with 16,000 Muslim women reportedly involved in their activities.[5] The primary function of these zhenotdels was to implement the new Soviet family laws that overruled the Shari'a.[6] In 1921, the Central Executive Committee of the Soviets of the Turkistan Autonomous Soviet Socialist Republic (the then administrative unit that became present-day Tajikistan) adopted a decree abolishing the payment of *kalim* (the groom's gift to the bride's parents, which the Soviets labeled as bride money) and raising the legal age of marriage from 16 to 18. The tradition of the *nikoh* (Islamic nuptials) was declared illegal; instead, ZAGS (Zapisi Aktov Grazhdanskogo Sostayaniya, or Soviet Civil Registry) offices were opened where marriages and childbirth had to be recorded. Once marital litigation was introduced in the Soviet courts, many Central Asian women were encouraged to initiate divorces.

To lend support to such endeavors, local zhenotdels organized informal gatherings in order to talk and work with women on an individual basis. At gatherings in women's clubs, support circles (*kruzhki*), and teahouses known as "red" *chaikhana*s, which had become centers for propaganda for the new communist regime, women, some still wearing *faranji* (the full veil),[7] rested and worked away from their families, all the while getting an internationalist political education. The first women leaders of these committees were Russian women, either functionaries dispatched from Russia or political workers demobilized from the Red Army. Yet this organization proposed to create a cadre of local women, and an entire class of convinced Central Asian and Tatar women communists were recruited to continue the propaganda work. Those who did well in local youth indoctrination schools were sent to higher party schools and political universities, often becoming propagandists themselves.

The movement of Hujum, or intractable assault on customs and traditions, was a decisive move adopted in 1926 to change the position of women in Central Asian society.[8] The first stage was meant to set an example by Central Asian communists, among whom veiling became forbidden. The second stage initiated an effort to engage the entire population, and by the spring of 1927, the machines of propaganda were set in full motion: the mass media, poets, and writers took up the cause of women's emancipation vigorously. On March 8, 1927, members of Central Asian Communist Parties were ordered to appear in a parade for Soviet Women's Day. Thousands of women joined in walking through the main streets of cities singing revolutionary songs. That evening, a mass unveiling was ordered simultaneously in the largest Central Asian cities. Apparently, in one day, 10,000 women burned their veils in Uzbek city squares alone. Although Hujum witnessed the initial expression of local communist women in Central Asia, it met with considerable opposition from local men, especially in the rural areas. Male relatives sometimes resorted to murdering liberated women and taking sides with the religious institutions in their sharp attack on the regime. In the much advertised case of Bibi Zeinab of Khujand in the mid-1920s, the local population assassinated an unveiled Central Asian communist worker, thus granting her the status of a martyred heroine.[9]

Meanwhile, Soviet efforts at emancipation were more marked in Uzbekistan than in Tajikistan, which during the 1920s had been the stronghold for the Basmachi, the anti-Soviet rebel movement. As a result, Soviet mobilization was less successful in the area, Tajik cadres less cooperative, and the population more under the influence of the religious and traditional values. Most of the activities of Zhenotdel among Tajik women concentrated on Khujand, Samarqand, and Bukhara, but it had very little influence in southern cities such as Kulob. By the early 1930s, Hujum had met with so much violence and opposition that it was abandoned. In 1930, the Zhenotdel, facing problems in Moscow, was dissolved both in the center and the periphery.

In the meantime, the assault of the Soviet regime on the extended patriarchal family continued with more subtle efforts of education and propaganda. Thus the Soviet regime gave what it believed to be fundamental rights to women, including medical care, protection of mothers, literacy, cottage industries, good hygiene and living conditions, an active role for women's journals, and legislation on women's equal rights.

Rights did not always translate into power, however. Despite all the efforts of the communist regime, many women, in the postcommunist period after the breakup of the Soviet Union, did not consider themselves free. Numerous educated Central Asian women were questioning whether emancipation had indeed taken place. They were counterposed to women who participated in the Hujum, and who, by the time of the sweeping reforms and nationalist movements of the post-Soviet period, were well into their late eighties and early nineties. The latter included Enoyat Hamroeva, a Samarqandi who, after moving to Dushanbe as a political appointee, was the first woman to burn her veil publicly in the new capital.[10] Maqdara Normurodova, after attempting to take off her faranji on two different occasions in Samarqand, was sent to Dushanbe to work in the sewing factories, where she learned Russian and became one of the first woman activist workers.[11] In defense of these women, Bibi Palvanova, a scholar of women's emancipation from Turkmenistan, decried attempts by the new revisionists to "chase women back home."[12]

THE QUOTA SYSTEM:
THE POLITICAL MOBILIZATION OF WOMEN

According to the 1991 census, women composed 51.2 percent of the population in Tajikistan. In 1989, 79 percent of women over the age of 15 had some education, and 39 percent of them were engaged in some kind of work.[13] Western feminists and Soviet Marxists both argue that women's activity in the community should be awarded political or economic recognition. Yet in the former Soviet Union, despite the quota specifically granted for the political, social, and economic participation of women, the latter enjoyed only low-level formal political activity. The number of women in key positions in the party and state hierarchy was meager; such women played only a symbolic role.[14]

Investigations pertaining to native women in the political elite of the republics show the hypocritical or purely decorative result of a policy to promote women to positions of higher authority. A study of the representation of women in the political elite of Uzbekistan from 1952 to 1981 demonstrated the lack of meaningful participation. Only sixteen out of the 457 individuals who held top positions in the Uzbek party and state apparatus in the period studied were women.[15] The numbers are similar, if not lower, in Tajikistan.

Yet in the tradition of the early zhenotdel affiliates, the new women's councils (*zhensoviet*) tirelessly carried out a campaign of agitation and propaganda to mobilize and direct Central Asian women toward a communist way of life by making them politically active and socially conscious.[16] The zhensoviets were dismissed by Western researchers as lacking the autonomy of women-only groups in the Western experience.[17] In general, they failed to produce genuine female leaders in the Communist Party of the Soviet Union (CPSU), even if they acted as autonomous consciousness-raising groups among women. By 1980 in Tajikistan, there were 1,310 local zhensoviets at the level of the village, town, district, region, and republic.[18]

The political reforms of the late 1980s and the easing of the quota system of the Communist Party had two effects on women's activities outside the home: fewer women were elected to the local soviets, and a wide range of independent women's groups were formed independent of the CPSU. At the height of the anticommunist, nationalist movement in Tajikistan, between the time the Communist Party was dissolved in 1991 and the conservative parliament staged a comeback in 1992, many communist women cadres lost their jobs. Those who had been chosen to fill the quota and work in local executive committees or as delegates to the Supreme Soviet found their jobs obsolete, or were replaced by younger "democratic" and politically correct men and women.[19]

In order to draw women into the sphere of production, the Soviet state had tried to provide day-care centers, pass legislative measures to increase salaries and ensure the protection of women and children, improve sanitary conditions, open kindergartens, introduce part-time work, and create flexible hours.[20] But as women were encouraged only to take agricultural, nonindustrial jobs, their participation in nonagricultural employment fell below average.[21] Tajik women pilots, cosmonauts, and even tractor drivers were the exception to the rule, while women cotton pickers outnumbered men by a large margin. According to the 1989 Tajikistan census, women directly engaged in the economy formed 38.8 percent of the total population of the country, out of which 48.3 percent worked in agriculture.[22] Of employed women, moreover, the primary reason they gave for working was to meet the needs of the family, not to be financially independent or to avoid limiting themselves to family chores.[23]

Any issue of the Tajik woman's magazine *Zanoni Tojikiston* from the 1960s or the 1970s would devote many pages to heroic women workers engaged in the cotton fields. They presented an image of a bold, hard-working, courageous fighter putting up with physical and psychological hardship. Women were encouraged by the state to enter the workforce in order to fulfill the quotas and to be transformed into producers for the Soviet state.[24] But the agricultural work praised in the official ideology lost its significance as a social value. Moreover, it became plagued with serious problems such as health hazards. For women engaged in unskilled manual labor in the fields, the countryside offered very difficult conditions deficient in health services and child care. Only in recent years have families been able to take full responsibility for the production of the farms they lease from the collective farms known as kolkhozes, most of which have now become privatized.

In fact, Central Asian women suffered from a double burden, not only because of the added responsibility of bearing and caring for numerous children and keeping house for a husband, but also because household duties are clearly segregated in Central Asia and men do not share housework such as cleaning or cooking. Women are responsible for all aspects of the private sphere, and men for the public. In rural areas, women not only work within the home but also tend the garden and look after the household cattle, while men spend their time at work outside the house. Readers complained in the press that men do easy jobs such as selling piroshki (fried meat dumplings), while women do heavy industrial jobs.[25] The humor magazines *Khorpushtok* in Tajik and *Mushtum* in Uzbek were inundated in the early 1980s with cartoons depicting women working hard in cotton fields, while men are busy entertaining themselves with food and music on nearby picnic carpets.

WOMEN AS KEEPERS OF TRADITIONAL CULTURE

During Soviet times, women became the keepers of honor and by extension of traditional culture and religion in Tajikistan. They preserved a culture that the Soviets tried to suppress. The duty of men was to protect the *nomus* (honor) of women by keeping them away from alien Russian cultural influences. The status of the family or the community depended, on the one hand, on the chastity, fidelity, and purity of women, demonstrated by the degree to which they abided by traditional customs of their ancestors, and on the other, on the "manliness" of men.[26] In Tajikistan, in accordance with the general glorification of virginity in the Middle East, families demanded to see the stained sheets of the young couple after the wedding night. If the girl was not a virgin, she was promptly returned to her parents' house and humiliated in the community. During the Soviet period, criticism of this practice appeared primarily in central newspapers such as *Izvestiia* and *Komsomol'skaia Pravda* and was cited as an example of the cruel habits of Central Asian families. But Tajik women themselves had accepted the practice as a reality of their everyday lives, and most did not protest out of humiliation or habit. The question of women's virginity was always debated more feverishly by the men, for whom the honor of the family was greatly at stake, than by the women themselves. Because a number of local practices and customs had passed the threshold from religious customs to national symbols, many women yielded who would have otherwise objected to them as degrading.

Gender divisions in most areas of Tajikistan are not as rigid as in more traditional Muslim societies. In Central Asian history, rural women have always been less restricted by patriarchal values than urban ones. For one, conditions in rural areas dictate mandatory field work for women, often side by side with men. Urban culture, however, created a physical separation within the architecture of the household and put women more predominantly at home under the influence of men and subject to the pressures of a tightly knit traditional society. In Tajikistan, a combination of rural culture and far-reaching Soviet efforts to draw women into the economy had many women working in the public sphere while at same time fulfilling the traditional role in the domestic arena. Men were not the only ones to dominate the Soviet element of village culture: even though the head of the kolkhoz was always a man, many women worked as brigadiers and older women led groups of other cotton pickers and exerted influence over them.

In order to prepare the ground for introducing the element of mandatory work as a patriarchal duty to the Soviet motherland, Soviet ideologists/ theorists had identified the rural woman as the key holder of traditions and had targeted her for atheist propaganda. S. Dadbayeva, the Head of the Department of Scientific Atheism of the Tajik Academy of Sciences, had in 1980 identified religious aspects of festivals and rites in the family, especially in the villages.[27] By describing the relationship between religion and education, the former "not just amount[ing] to views and convictions, but profoundly permeate[ing] peoples's sentiments, feelings and emotions," she argued that even the highly educated intelligentsia perform religious ceremonies. To promote atheism, she suggested that local clubs, workshops, and movie houses be set up in kolkhozes, even though she acknowledged that people spent more time reading and watching TV than going regularly to clubs or checking out atheist literature from rural libraries.

Whether in reality Islam had become a women's religion during the Soviet period in Tajikistan was open to different interpretations. Soviet ideologists, in an effort to downplay the importance of religion in everyday decisionmaking, had identified women as the principal bearers of religion, in the same way that in European Russia they stressed that only women went to Orthodox churches. Thus, by isolating women as the most religious sector of society, it was easier for ideologists to combat the influence of religion by directing atheist propaganda toward them. They saw Soviet atheist education as the best method for raising women's consciousness within the family.

Tajik nationalist males, in contrast, saw the protection of women in the private sphere as their way of exercising social control. To be able to point to the evidence that rural women were the most religious group was to prove victory over the Soviet propaganda assault. Orthodox Islam, based on the Qur'an, the mosque, and the religious school, was predominantly a male activity. Valid in the majority of Muslim societies where leading Islamic scholars and mullahs who conduct public prayers are more often than not men, this male dominance was even more important in Central Asian society where public, "official" Islam was inhibited by the critical eye of an atheist state. It was in their private lives that Central Asians were most successful in keeping their personal Islamic practices alive. Because women were the focal point of the home and because public manifestation of Islam was banned, religion moved into the private sphere. Women came to predominate in the private, "unofficial," and "popular" Islam, which coexisted parallel to orthodox, visible religion. As a result, Islam represented non-Soviet, non-Russian cultural values. The public sphere was communist and Soviet, whereas the private was a bulwark of local Central Asian, Tajik, and Islamic values.

During the seventy years of Soviet rule, Tajik women kept the core of religious activity, which took place in the private community or household, far from the eyes of the state. In the villages, middle-aged and elderly women had been observing Ramadan by fasting and praying since they were very young. In many Tajik village communities, women continued their group rituals in which a female learned in religious matters would lead others in prayers or in problem-solving ceremonies. At the tomb of the mother of the Sufi Shaykh Bahauddin Naqshband outside of Bukhara, groups of Tajik, Uzbek, and other Central Asian women tied knots around trees as they often did during their visits to other shrines (*mazars*) while praying for fertility or for the cure of a sickness. Among a certain number of religious families, mainly in the rural regions, the tradition of women saints and mystics had long been upheld. Religious education, until the few Islamic schools were opened for a short time between 1991 and 1992, was mostly given at home, taught by father to daughter, who in turn had become versed enough to teach other women in the community, the *mahalla* (neighborhood), or village. The emphasis placed on religious education for the new generation prompted the Board of the Muslims of Tajikistan, the Qadiat, to open special classes for 210 girls and women in 1992. These women, many of them professionals, schoolteachers, and journalists, were mostly urban women, members of the Islamic Revivalist Party, like their male relatives.[28] The subjects being taught at the school were hadith, *fiqh* (Islamic jurisprudence), the Qur'an, and *khat* (calligraphy).

Thus the process of glorification of the past in Tajikistan also brought forth an idealization of the values associated with rural life. In the Soviet period, the village had been the seat of traditional, non-Soviet values. The village thus represented the unadulterated purity of Tajik culture and tradition. Islam, which was mainly an urban religion before the Bolshevik revolution, became a major influence among families in the rural areas. Authentic Tajik women, in the revisionists' views, became the village women, keepers of religion in the private sphere far from the negative influences of Russian women in the cities.

THE FARANJI QUESTION

If the Tajik women were to be the heritors of a revived traditional society, their appearances therefore became subject to another important debate in pre-1992 society. Authors, mostly male, blackened many pages of local newspapers writing about whether women should wear the multicolored, striped national silk dress (*atlas*), with or without the pants (*e'zor*), or whether they should be clad in extremes, ranging from jeans and miniskirts to veils (called sometimes chador as in Iran, but more frequently by its Central Asian appelation, faranji). When nationalist zeal reached its intensity between 1990 and 1992, the atlas was declared the national dress preferred by many poets and politicians, who encouraged women to replace their Western clothes with the pride of Tajikistan.[29] At the height of political riots in February 1990 in Dushanbe, women not wearing the e'zor and the *rumol* (scarves) were harassed, and some were allegedly slashed with razors. Yet to wear or not to wear the e'zor was more than a debate over appearances. Although the debate carried symbolic value, it also became an escape from the real issues that were plaguing Tajikistan in its years of turmoil. In the stagnant Tajik society of the pre-perestroika years, there was emancipation for neither man nor woman. Under the circumstances, discussion of dress, because it was a distraction from serious problems, also became a means for the powerful to put pressure on the weak. The debate brought women down to levels manageable for nationalist and Islamist revisionists. Women became once again women and not that part of society over which the Soviet authorities had declared victory.[30]

The nationalist and Islamist elements of society reacted strongly to the question of women's dress in the post-Soviet, pre–civil war period. An article in *Najot*, the newspaper of the Islamic Revivalist Party, defended Islamist revisionists against accusations that during the 1991 February riots, Tajik men harassed women who wore European dress instead of the national atlas.[31] The author argued that what happened in February 1991 in Dushanbe was carried out not by Muslims but by hooligans influenced by their nationalist pride, because there was no need to force the Islamic dress on women.[32] Islam never allows such behavior, the author claimed. Believers should first lead people toward their ideas, faiths, and opinions of Islam without demanding changes in appearance. When the Tajik woman becomes aware of God's wish for her to wear the hijab, the author argued, she will do so without the use of force and even encourage others to do so. In another article, an Iranian apologist for Islam wrote for a Tajik audience that the comfortable dress of Islam was like a sign for new drivers: in the twists and turns of life, it acted as a guide to men and women.[33]

WOMEN'S RESPONSES TO THE
SOVIET AND POST-SOVIET DISCOURSES

Tajik women, in response to the role outlined for them by the Soviet, nationalist, and Islamist discourses, showed a variety of opinions and trends. Some were outspoken advocates of the Soviet system, whereas others defended the nationalist and even Islamist view on gender identity. Examining the role of the socialist cultural revolution in the spiritual growth of women of "the Soviet East," a leading Tajik philosopher with a number of books on the status of women criticized the traditional view of women in what she perceived as Islamic society: "The magnificent East sang the praises of its beauties with their starry eyes and moon-shaped faces, but sold them like goods and refused to think of them as people."[34] Another example of the socialist elite women of Central Asia is Munzifar Ghaffarov, who was a rector of the Institute of Art, professor at the Pedagogical Institute, and married to an intellectual husband, a philosopher. Urban, educated women like her were indeed the product of the socialist system, as well as the symbiosis of Russian and Tajik values. In the women's magazine *Zanoni Tojikiston*, a history teacher from Dushanbe pitied traditional families that sacrificed women's freedom for children. Yet she admitted that women like herself (presumably urban, educated women) were not properly in touch with the customs of the women in the villages, where, she said, women did not leave the house except with long-sleeved clothes and took their children to the mullah when they were sick. "It is now time to disrupt the superstition of religion," she urged other women. "In this time of perestroika [in Tajik referred to as *bozsozi*], a revolution is needed."[35]

Such advocates of the Soviet ideal may have spoken mostly out of loyalty to a system that while attacking the core of traditional life had rewarded its advocates loyally. They demonstrated their patriotic zeal by opposing their historical and religious customs and habits. Subsequently, a reverse transition from socialism to neocapitalism in the post-Soviet period left much to be regretted for those who had abided by the socialist experiment. These women of the "conservative" elite who were principally devoted to gender issues regret that, as Bibi Palvanova writes, "the way of thinking is being fundamentally changed, accepted views are challenged. There has been a reappraisal of spiritual values, of all that was achieved and fought for, including what was progressive and positive for almost the past three quarters of the twentieth century."[36] To the opponents of the Islamic and nationalist discourse, men who advocated these views were acting out their innate prejudice against women, chasing them back into seclusion, "hoping that female equality will be overthrown with the Soviet regime that brought it."[37]

Yet in the early 1990s the proponents of the nationalist and Islamist thinking in Central Asia generally were not only men but also women. A number of new women elites joined the movement for the revision of history in their societies, defending the religious cultural world and admiring the freedom and equality seen in Islamic society. The women's organization SIMO for example, organized by women of the intelligentsia and headed by a member of the Tajik Academy of Sciences, held a conference on "Islam and the Role of Women" in September 1992. There religion was deeply and favorably discussed in the way Soviet emancipation would have been a few years before. The role of the traditional woman in the education and upbringing of her children and family was often envied by the modern Central Asian woman, bent over by the modern Soviet-style double burden. A Central Asian historian, who could have also spoken for a number of Tajik women elites, wrote that emancipation *à la soviétique* promised to protect the political, economic, and human rights of the Central Asian woman, but that the totalitarian regime only needed women's labor.[38]

THE ISLAMIC REVIVAL: WOMEN'S DILEMMA

Often women were caught between two extremes. Disappointed with Soviet-guided emancipation, they did not subscribe to the view that Islam failed to grant women any rights. However, because the Islamic revival of the late 1980s and early 1990s was used as a political tool in an anticolonial discourse, many women felt that issues concerning what they should wear and how much they should work were being decided for them even after the breakup of the Soviet empire. Islam, for many, was being used as an excuse for political ambitions, and therefore was not pure enough to be proposed as a coherent alternative to the Soviet lifestyle.

In the ideological battle between men and women over the use of Islamic identity in society, many women felt that men were using the revival of Islam to draw women, with whom they were competing, out of the sphere they dominated. These women also feared that the trend to revive Islam would eventually lock them into a traditional, patriarchal society where men treated them as second-class citizens.[39]

For them, as for some critics of religion, Muslim women's support for an Islamic revival worldwide was, as once described regarding Iranian women's reaction to Islam, "a desperate venture in which they sacrifice themselves and their rights for the sake of independence from the West [and in this case, from the Soviet system] while they are still regarded as inferior to men by their rulers."[40] To critics of Islam, a return to Islamic values meant a return to passivity, a value not favored by feminists and strong individualists. To others, however, adherence to secular Western/ Russian values "empties the contents of the brains and spirits of the East," forcing women to leave their cultural models and adopt the characteristics of an alien people. "They made us believe that our religion was full of myths, was old fashioned and had no spiritual meaning, was reactionary, ugly and detestable."[41] The same kind of attitude was found among Tajik women who disclaimed the myth of emancipation in Soviet society.

But emancipation was never fully achieved in Central Asia under the Soviet regime. Beneath the surface of adopted Western/Russian values, society continued to function within its traditional rules. Instead, contact with Sovietization had brought about cultural disorientation, in which society became alienated from much of its own heritage. Thus, returning to the source, as an opposition tactic against the communist regime in the post-Soviet period, meant the reevaluation of Islam among the intellectual class who had hitherto dismissed it as superstition. In 1979, Iranian women had returned to Islam in protest against the shah's regime, claiming that freedom and salvation could only be granted to the public through a return to their own values, which they saw as rejecting the blind imitation of the West.[42] But if the prerevolutionary regime in Iran had manipulated the image of women in the mass media to promote the beautifully made up, consumption-oriented, mindless woman portrayed in *Zan-e Ruz* (Today's Woman),[43] the Soviet choice for a Tajik woman liberated from religion had painted her behind a tractor, building the new socialist society. This alternative was not that attractive. In replacing this image and propagating the rediscovery of Islam, women's magazines and the mass media began a discussion of the advantages of the new complementary and not necessarily competitive role of women in society after 1989. Many educated women showed their preference for letting their husbands work: Holding a job was considered against the liberation of their identity. Unlike their traditional, uneducated sisters, these women had seen the world outside and had rejected it.

Mehriniso (a penname) was one of the few women to join the authors of a wave of articles in Tajik newspapers between 1989 and 1992 that defended Islam in women's lives.[44] To answer critics of Islam, she suggested that religion be separated from superstition. She argued that according to the Qur'an and the hadith, women had the right to choose their partners and their place of living as well as to divorce. Mehriniso emphasized the same theme as the male Islamist revisionists, that Islam actually elevated the rights of women. When nationalist and Islamist zeal spread in Tajikistan between 1989 and 1992, even women like Qimat Rustamova, deputy director of the Executive Committee in the city of Kulob, known for conducting sessions of communist agitation and propaganda with fervor at the local sewing factory, proclaimed, "Alhamdulillah, I am Muslim" (Thank God that I am a Muslim), as if to legitimize her role in society.[45] A number of women intellectuals also claimed, as did the nationalist revision, that Islam was the national consciousness of a colonized East, an ideology of the anticolonial struggle: "[The] Muslim mode of life was understood as a national originality [*sic*] that should be defended from Western cultural expansion."[46] In fact, the Soviet cultural revolution targeted Islam as an ideology of resistance of a colonized East to the new Russo-Soviet empire.

"MUSLIM" PRACTICES
IN DEFENSE OF WOMEN'S RIGHTS

Islam, therefore, may have acted as a conservatory of traditions, customs, and norms of human relations; as a means of adhering to the ethnic culture; and as a subconscious resistance to alien cultural hegemony. A number of women in the postindependence period thus defended the same Islamic practices that the Soviet discourse identified as degrading to women. It is ironic that polygyny was not always viewed as a crime among Central Asian women. Tajik women familiar with Islamic laws maintained that polygyny was better than divorce for an infertile woman, and the Qur'an, although it allowed a man to have up to four wives, prescribed that they all be treated equally (Sura 4:3).[47] Often one wife tended to be favored, and interaction between two wives of the same husband was rare, although the situation was clear to all parties involved as well as to the village community. Many women in Tajikistan would defend the practice of polygyny as long as they shared equal treatment. In the few years after the introduction of market reforms in Tajikistan, many consumer-oriented Tajik women expressed the wish for their husbands to marry a second wife "only if she is richer than us."

The attitude of modern Tajik women is best summed up by Oinahol Bobonazarova, head of the law faculty at the Tajik State University in 1992, who declares: "Let's face it, polygyny exists in Tajikistan. If we make it legal, then the husband would have to be responsible, morally and financially to the second and third wife he already has."[48] After the 1992 civil war, in which thousands of young men perished in Tajikistan, the practice of polygyny became even more widespread, as many young widows married their brothers-in-law or other males in search of protection.

Women in Tajikistan also had an original view on the question of seclusion, raised by Soviet ideologists as the perpetuation of the victimization of women. Seclusion, to the extent that it reinforced a women's community (*jomeiai zanona*), could also work to the advantage of women in Central Asia. Women working and living together did not necessarily occupy a negative space of discrimination. In fact, local cultures continued the separation of the sexes even though the physical barriers had long been removed. In most ceremonies celebrating the cult of nature, such as the New Year festivities, Nowruz, women worked and entertained together in different sections of the space from men. Their get-togethers also served a specific function: to clean a new house and prepare it for habitation (*buriokubon*), to serve in weddings (*dugonatui*), and to provide institutional support in a variety of tasks. In cotton farms throughout Tajikistan, women worked together in brigades, giving each other support, creating a women's sub-mahalla, talking freely about issues they would otherwise not be able to cover in mixed society. The practice of kalim, which the Soviets criticized as bride price, was considered by many Tajik women as a deposit in case husband and wife were separated by death or divorce.

THE TRANSITION PERIOD:
MOBILIZATION FOR CHANGE

The post-Soviet transition from a centrally planned to a market economy especially disrupted the lives of women in Tajikistan. The breakdown of the state system led to increasing poverty, unemployment, and a decrease in political representation among women; chaos in the sectors of health, education, and social welfare; and the loss of maternal and child-care benefits. Violence, rape, and exile associated with the 1992–1993 civil war further aggravated the situation. The breakdown of the Soviet system meant an increase in massive population shifts around the country (both from urban to rural and vice versa) and a decrease in allocation of funds to sectors dominated by women. All this translated into a growing number of women in unskilled jobs, a shift in careers, and a move into private trade and small business initiatives as well as into the black market and other illegal activities. Loss of the quota system led to gender discrimination in the workplace.

Post-Soviet political events thus had a significant impact on women's lives, and women could no longer depend on the few members of their sex who had secured themselves a place in formal politics (and whose numbers were shrinking, at any rate) to defend their rights. The choice of using a conscious gender identity for sociopolitical gains is often presented to the elite women, those who have aspirations of recognition in society. In Tajikistan, for example, it was mostly the political, cultural, or economic elite who had created women's nongovernmental (NGOs) and associations, and their activities said much about their position in society. These organizations were often formed around women leaders who had already carved out for themselves a defining role in society. Among all women, political activity in the post-Soviet transition period falls into three categories:

1. As agents of the state: Women's organizations created by the state propagated the ideas and efforts of the state on a particular issue (including women's economic or political status). In Tajikistan, these semigovernmental organizations include the National Union of Women and the Women's Committee of the Council of Ministers.

2. As competition for the state: These organizations were created by those women leaders who were not formerly part of the political cadre but were members of the cultural or economic elite. They created competition for the state committees, either political, such as an organization of women members of the Democratic Party of Tajikistan and the Islamic Party, or nonpolitical, through competition for resources and recognition given by the state or increasingly by the international donor community. The mushrooming of NGOs in the postwar years has been largely in response to a combination of international donor interest and new opportunities for activism. Such organizations included the Association of University Women, the Women's Association of Tajikistan, SIMO, the Association of Business Women, the Association of Creative Women of Tajikistan, and the Association of Women Scientists.

3. As grassroots, spontaneous activists: Women's mobilization also occurred through spontaneous movements that did not necessarily put emphasis on the same demands as elite women's organizations but rather on what affected their immediate lives. These activities were not always recognized as political because the issues were considered to be in the "private" sphere and the methods were unconventional, involving the activities of women as mothers and housewives first and not as women. The issues were raised not through intellectualization of problems as in feminist movements or by their recognition by the state but out of actual situations, and the immediate needs of women, such as lack of food, the unemployment of

men, or the death of sons (Mother's Soldiers Association). Women working as a collective in Tajikistan, within informal structures such as mahalla
groups, work brigades, extended families, or small businesses, had a lot
of potential decisionmaking power. These activities were not considered
feminist, neither by the outside nor by the women themselves. Feminism
in the Third World has always been brought in by the outside world or
through its agents such as the elite or the middle class. Community organization is ingrown but has more to do with immediate practical concerns
than with the strategic consideration of gender.

CONCLUSION

At the beginning of this chapter I argued that gender identity, that is, identification of the self as part of a gender collective, is especially pertinent in
cases in which there are specific socioeconomic gains to be made. Gender
identity in Tajikistan was a reflection of the imposition of certain social and
historic roles on women by an outside group (i.e., the Soviet regime at first,
and nationalist men during the post-Soviet period). Only when it was ben-
eficial for women to stress their difference in order to gain access to resources allocated specifically for them, such as through the formation of the
women's NGOs in the transition period, did they emphasize their gender
identity. Trends in society in Tajikistan may have created the four indicators
of gender identity as outlined in the beginning of this chapter. However,
women may have chosen not to stress them in order to remain within the
mainstream of political activism, especially during postindependence times.
    During the years of discovery and openness of the post-Soviet period,
women's activism was carried out within specific categories, such as the
intelligentsia, a grassroots movement for democracy, an Islamic political
group, or a communist cadre. However, precisely because Soviet authorities had undertaken the task of emancipating women as a category, setting
them apart from the other half of the society, the concept of women's
emancipation as individuals may have been considered by both men and
women as a "foreign," imperial idea. When the state and the antistate opposition had already politicized gender identity, women were robbed of
their chance to create genuine feminist movements and to protest subjugation to patriarchal practices, which hampered their long-term strategic
gains as women. Thus, as in other Islamic societies influenced by European values, women were caught in the web of double loyalty: To express
their gender interest would have meant siding with the colonizers. To express their national interests, on the other hand, would have meant denying
their feminine identity. Women's dilemma in Tajikistan became the same
as that of women who participated in the early feminist movements in
Turkey and Egypt: they had to "choose between betrayal and betrayal."[49]

NOTES

1. Haleh Afshar, *Women and Politics in the Third World* (London: Routledge, 1996).

2. According to Tajik Interior Ministry figures, interview by the author, November 20, 1992.

3. As reflected in the satirical journal *Khorpushtok* as well as in the poetry of Gulchehre Suleimanova, Zulfiia Atai, and Farzona.

4. Yelena Yemelyanova, *Revolution in Women's Life* (Moscow: Novosti Press Agency Publishing House, 1985), 9. Ironically, a slogan that often appeared in the newspaper *Bidori Tojikiston* in 1928 read "Kori Ozodi Zanon Kori Lenin Bud," literally meaning: "The act of freeing women was the work of Lenin," but it could also be read as "In Lenin is the real culprit who freed women."

5. Yemelyanova, *Revolution in Women's Life,* 28.

6. John Hazard, "Statutory Recognition of Nationality Differences in the USSR," *Soviet Nationality Problems*, ed. Edward Allworth (New York: Columbia University Press, 1971). Also see Gregory J. Massell, "Law as an Instrument of Revolutionary Change in a Traditional Milieu: The Case of Soviet Central Asia," *Law and Society Review* 2 (1968).

7. *Faranji* comes from the word "farang," meaning France specifically but applied to describe the West. The original idea of faranji, which might have come to Central Asia from Europe in the eighteenth century, depicted a black lace face and hand covering used by aristocratic women, which rich merchants were said to have brought back for their urban wives. The veil, in Central Asia, was mostly worn by women in the cities and became a symbol of wealth.

8. Gregory Massell, *The Surrogate Proletariat: Moslem Women and Revolutionary Strategies in Soviet Central Asia, 1919–1929* (Princeton: Princeton University Press, 1974), 226.

9. Bibi Zeinab became a legend symbolizing the "free woman of the Muslim East." An opera based on her story was staged periodically during the Soviet period.

10. Interview by the author with Enoyat Hamroeva, August 1, 1990, in Dushanbe, Tajikistan.

11. Interview by the author with Maqdara Normurodova, September 25, 1992, in Dushanbe, Tajikistan.

12. Bibi Palvanova, in an untitled paper presented at a Conference on Women, Demography, and Family in Muslim Societies at the School of Oriental and African Studies (SOAS), London, July 6–10, 1992. View once again expressed in interview by the author with Bibi Palvanova, October 14, 1994, in Almaty, Kazakstan.

13. *Zhenshchiny I Deti v Tadzhikskoi SSR, Statisticheskii Sbornik* (Dushanbe: Gosudarstvennyi Komitet Tadzhikskoi SSR po Statistike [State Committee of the Tajik SSR on Statistics], 1991), 3.

14. Gail Lapidus, *Women in Soviet Society: Equality, Development and Social Change* (Berkeley: University of California Press, 1978), 228.

15. "Women in the Uzbek Elite," *Soviet Nationality Survey* 2, no. 6 (June 1985): 1–2.

16. A. Muzyria and V. V. Kopeilo (eds.), *Zhensoviet: Opyt, Problemy Perspektivy* (Zhensoviet: Experiences, Problems, the Future) (Moscow: Izdatel'stvo Politisheskikh Literatury, 1989).

17. Genia K. Browning, *Women and Politics in the USSR: Consciousness Raising and Soviet Women's Groups* (New York: St. Martin's Press, 1987); Lapidus, *Women in Soviet Society*; and Richard Stites, *The Women's Liberation Movement in Russia* (Princeton: Princeton University Press, 1978).

18. *Rabotnitsa*, no. 11 (1980).

19. Interview by the author with Qimat Rustamova, Deputy Head of the Executive Committee of Kulob, April 1, 1992, in Kulob, Tajikistan.

20. See Nancy Lubin, "Women in Soviet Central Asia: Progress and Contradictions," *Soviet Studies* (April 1982): 182–203; Michael Sacks, *Work and Equality in Soviet Society* (New York: Praeger, 1982).

21. Lapidus, *Women in Soviet Society*, 167.

22. *Zhenshchin I Deti v Tadzhikskoi SSR,* 13.

23. Ibid., 24.

24. Yemelyanova, *Revolution in Women's Life.*

25. Dzhonaid Abdul-Lakhanova, "Man's Work," *Trud* (August 1, 1984), as translated in *Current Digest of the Soviet Press* 36, no. 33 (1984): 16.

26. D. M. Heer and Nadia Youssef, "Female Status Among Soviet Central Asian Nationalities: The Melding of Islam and Marxism and Its Implications for Population Increase," *Population Studies* 31, no. 1 (1977): 155–173.

27. S. Dadbayeva, *Kommunist Tadzhikistana* (October 31, 1980).

28. Interview by the author with women students at the Islamic School, September 28, 1992, in Dushanbe, Tajikistan.

29. Shodmon Yusuf, chairman of the Democratic Party of Tajikistan, admitted in an interview with the author that he personally preferred the atlas to the European dress on Tajik women. The interview took place on April 3, 1992, in Dushanbe, Tajikistan.

30. Interview by the author with Mozaffar Olimov and Saodat Olimova, researchers at the Institute of Oriental Studies, July 20, 1990, in Dushanbe, Tajikistan.

31. Najmiddin Qurbob, "Hijob io Faranji" (Hijab or the faranji), *Najot*, no. 5 (spring 1992): 2.

32. Ibid.

33. Askar Rod, "Hijob Charo?" (Why the veil?), *Tojikiston* (July 3, 1992): 5.

34. N. Vishneva-Saranfanova, *Soviet Women: A Portrait* (Moscow: Progress Publishers, 1981), 40.

35. N. Anbaurzova, "Dar Panohi Shariat: Mutaassifona, Faqat Istisno" (Under the shield of the Shari'a: Unfortunately, only an exception), *Zanoni Tojikiston* (November 1988).

36. Bibi Palvanova, cited in ibid.

37. Ibid.

38. M. Tokhtakhodzhaeva, "Central Asian Society and a Woman," paper presented at Conference on Women, Demography, and Family in Muslim Societies at SOAS (July 6–10, 1992).

39. Mahdi Nodirzod, "Zan va Mushkiloti Jomea" (Woman and the difficulties of society), *Najot*, no. 3 (1992): 2. For example, he tried to explain and clear the name of Islam, which had offered women second-class citizenship, men four wives, and women hardship and work at home.

40. Minou Reeves, *Female Warriors of Allah: Women and the Islamic Revolution* (New York: E. P. Dutton, 1989), 158.

41. Ibid., 154.

42. Ibid., 12.

43. Some scholars argue that this "policy" was a conspiracy of the government against the advancement of women. See Reeves, *Female Warriors,* 104.

44. B. Mehriniso, "Zan dar Islom" (Woman in Islam), *Sadoi Mardum* (August 10, 1992).

45. Interview by the author with Qimat Rustamova, April 1, 1992, in Kulob, Tajikistan.

46. M. Tokhtakhodzhaeva, "Central Asian Society and a Woman."

47. Freda Hussein (ed.), *Muslim Women* (London: Croom Helm, 1984), 16.

48. Interview by the author with Oinahol Bobonazarova, chair of the law faculty, Tajik State University, October 6, 1992, in Dushanbe, Tajikistan.

49. Leila Ahmed, "Early Feminist Movements in Turkey and Egypt," in Freda Hussein (ed.), *Muslim Women* (London: Croom Helm, 1984), 122.

10

Kazak Women:
Living the Heritage of a Unique Past

Paula A. Michaels

As elsewhere in the former Soviet Union, the government of Kazakstan recognizes March 8 as a national holiday. Each year politicians deliver rousing speeches, workers take the day off, and families and friends gather to celebrate International Women's Day. Radio and television stations devote their programs to the unceasing praise of women's contribution to Kazakstani society. Be they ethnically Kazak, Russian, or any one of Kazakstan's 100 different minorities, all join in acknowledging the vital role women play both within and beyond the home.[1] Yet for most women this holiday, like all others, falls far short of a day of rest. Women spend International Women's Day in the kitchen preparing the feast their menfolk await, and their skills as hostesses must shine under the glare of male scrutiny. They rise early to prepare from scratch the dough for wide noodles served with large chunks of mutton for the Kazak national dish, *beshparmak*. Male and female guests alike offer their praise of the hostess's womanly gifts for cooking and entertaining. Basking in the recognition that her efforts to offer guests respite from daily worries were not in vain, the Kazak hostess accepts the compliments with pride. She may work as a university professor, a factory supervisor, or a doctor outside the home, but the source of her self-esteem and confidence on International Women's Day derives from her prowess in the most traditional arenas of women's work.

Despite the irony of this situation, Kazak women's lives repeatedly defy commonly held Western stereotypes about the reality experienced by Muslim women. The uninformed outsider might quickly dismiss the previous scenario as evidence of Kazak women's oppression at the hands of a patriarchal system that defines their value in terms of domestic skills. One might easily fit such an interpretation within the parameters of popular Western views on Islam and the position of women. However, closer examination unmasks a complex and subtle situation rich in meaning and beyond simplistic reductionism. The social system within which Kazak

187

men and women operate provides each gender with a role that lays down boundaries but provides flexibility, respect, and mutual accommodation. In the eyes of Kazak women themselves, the praise they receive signifies deep respect and veneration that does not exclude achievement in domains outside the home.

In this chapter I strive to show how Kazak women's lives represent the synthesis of diverse influences. The nomadic heritage, the adoption of Islam, Russian colonization, and the rise and fall of Soviet power all contributed to the construction of gender roles in Kazak society. How Kazak women understand their own culture and position within it recurs as a central theme.

Though Kazaks make up only 40 percent of the population of Kazakstan, and Russian, Ukrainian, and Uzbek women make important contributions to life in Kazakstan, in this chapter I refer exclusively to Kazak women residing inside the present-day borders of the Republic of Kazakstan unless otherwise specified. Within the country the experience of urban and rural women varies greatly, and traditions in northern and southern Kazakstan differ in meaningful ways as well. I limit my firsthand observations principally to educated, urban Kazak women. When useful, I compare the situation of Kazak women with that of their fellow Central Asians of the former Soviet Union.

KAZAK WOMEN AND ISLAM
PRIOR TO RUSSIAN COLONIZATION

Stretching from China in the east to the Caspian Sea in the west, Kazakstan encompasses desert, steppe, and mountains. To the north lies Russia's vast Siberian tundra, and Kyrghyzstan, Uzbekistan, and Turkmenistan fringe its southern rim. Situated on the crossroads of Europe and Asia, Kazakstan has found itself enticing to invaders from both worlds. From the Mongol invaders of the thirteenth century and the indigenous Turkic tribes emerged a people around the fifteenth century known to travelers through the region as Kazaks, who lived as nomadic pastoralists.

Kazak nomads organized themselves loosely into three hordes, or clan confederations. Although leadership roles within clans almost invariably fell to Kazak men, women were not automatically eliminated from consideration. As among other Central Asian nomads, if a woman demonstrated the ability to lead her own village, she proved eligible to ascend to higher ranks within the power structure.[2] Though women rarely took the reins of power, that the possibility to do so even existed distinguished them from their sedentary Central Asian sisters.

Beyond the confines of the formal political structure, Kazak women wielded influence in a variety of ways within traditional society. Customary law among the nomads did not bar women from property ownership, which gave them economic leverage not at the disposal of sedentary Central Asian women. Kazak folklore depicts women as worthy recipients of respect and as valuable contributors to society. Without fearing disregard of their opinions, women spoke out frankly at clan meetings. Older married women and widows exerted particular influence. To women also fell the vital duty of passing on legends and sagas of the clan's history to children.[3]

Religion played a significant role in traditional Kazak society. Prior to the arrival of Islam, one could label the religion to which Kazaks adhered as shamanism, a system of beliefs in powerful good and evil spirits that controlled human fate. Through worship of natural elements, such as the fire-god Tengre, and of their ancestors, Kazaks strove to forestall evil spirits and live out their lives in harmony with earthly and celestial forces. To mediate between the spiritual and earthly realms, Kazaks called upon shamans (*baqsilar*), believing them blessed with a special gift of communication with spirits. Only men served as shamans in Kazak society, although women in sedentary Central Asian cultures frequently fulfilled this role.[4] When traditional pharmacopoeia failed to heal an ill individual, the family turned to a shaman to expel the evil spirit at the root of the problem. On occasion, baqsilar resorted to beating the afflicted with a whip. Into the early twentieth century, whipping was also a common method of treating women experiencing difficulty in childbirth.[5]

Thus Muslim proselytizers on Kazak territory encountered an intact, strong, indigenous system of religious beliefs. One must view the arrival of Islam in Kazakstan not as an event but as the initiation of an Islamization process that continues to the present day. On the fringes of the Arab conquests, southern Kazakstan encountered Islam in the eighth and ninth centuries.[6] It penetrated northern and central Kazakstan only incrementally. As late as the close of the eighteenth century, many nomads in more remote regions had yet to join the community of believers (*umma*) at all or in anything more than a superficial way.[7] In the nineteenth century, Tatar merchants and missionaries from Russia's Volga region brought Islam into the Kazak hinterland. Tatars established religious schools for Kazak children, sent clerics into villages, and encouraged the construction of mosques.[8] Though only seventy-eight mosques stood on Kazak soil, by the early twentieth century virtually every villager could count a mullah among his or her neighbors.[9]

Many traditions from earlier times continued to endure under a veneer of Islam. The new faith merged with the preexisting one to form a syncretic religion, the line between Islam and shamanism becoming over time increasingly blurred. Taking over the role previously fulfilled by baqsilar, mullahs served as healers and exorcists. Muslim prayers replaced shamanistic incantations used to expel evil spirits. Kazaks believed that many of the spirits themselves adopted Islam and thus mullahs had the ability to communicate with these Muslim powers, whereas baqsilar continued to facilitate harnessing the influence of non-Muslim ones.[10]

In addition to the persistence of shamanistic rituals and beliefs, nomadic conditions and Islam's relatively late arrival led the Kazaks to express their faith in ways that differed significantly from those of their fellow Muslims. Nomadic life inhibited the construction of religious institutions, such as mosques and religious schools, which blossomed in sedentary areas of the Muslim world. If a mullah was not on hand to perform a ritual, such as marriage, Kazaks called upon an elder to fulfill this task.[11] No firm delineation between formal and folk religion ever fully emerged. The widespread belief that five visits to Hoja Akhmed Yassawi's tomb in southern Kazakstan equaled one pilgrimage to Mecca exemplifies this tendency. Both common folk and clergy propounded this unwritten formula, which tailored Islamic rules to Kazak conditions.[12]

Outsiders attributed the Kazaks' unorthodox religious expression to their "indifference" to Islam in particular and religion in general.[13] Such an assessment, however, judges Kazak religion against a presumed normative practice. Yet although ethnographers and travelers through the region routinely underscored the relative weakness of Islam as a force in Kazak life, Kazaks have for centuries described themselves as Muslim and see their expression of Islam as wholly legitimate. In their own consciousness, Kazaks defined themselves as faithful believers and would no doubt have bristled at the suggestion they were anything other than "true" Muslims.

In no significant way did the adoption of Islam impact negatively on the lives of Kazak women. Customs associated with Islam and commonly believed oppressive to women failed to take root in nomadic conditions. For example, Kazak women never adopted the veil. Although among sedentary Central Asian women seclusion became commonplace, Kazak women mingled freely in male company.[14] Nomadic life precluded seclusion, as conditions demanded women work in public view. Customary, not Islamic law (Shari'a) regulated Kazak life, and the relative lack of fixed property kept the question of inheritance at an insignificant level. For most Kazak women, Islam represented a source of comfort, not oppression. Those having difficulty conceiving children made desperate pilgrimages to holy shrines. If a beloved relative fell ill, they enlisted the support of the local mullah in prayer.[15] For Kazak women, Islam offered a source of strength, hope, and courage in the face of circumstances beyond their control and in no perceptible way impinged on their traditionally active public role in Kazak society.

With respect to marriage and married life, Islam left a mixed legacy difficult to evaluate. As was common in most of the preindustrial world, parents arranged their children's marriages. Considerations of wealth, mutual benefit, and political strategy played decisive roles in determining pairings.[16] Bride-price (*kalym*) dictated the presentation of livestock or other valuables from the groom's family to the bride's in exchange for their daughter. Outsiders have rejected kalym as "a barbaric custom, a vestige of the enslaved state of women, and her lack of rights,"[17] but in the eyes of Kazaks themselves it signified the respect a groom's family held toward his bride and her relatives.[18] One could also interpret kalym as recognition of the value of the girl's lost labor and contribution to the household's economic viability.

Traditional lives of Kazak women resist easy categorization as either free or oppressed. To comprehend their position, one must look at more than just Islam. Kazaks accepted Islamic practices that fit well with their way of life and rejected customs seen as incompatible with a nomadic lifestyle. Only by examining the entire socioeconomic system can one assess the position of women. Ultimately, nomadism played as critical a role as any other element in defining their status. Indeed, it determined the way Kazaks expressed their faith in Islam; one must consider both forces in tandem to understand traditional life for Kazak women and how this unique heritage influences their lives in modern times.

KAZAK WOMEN IN THE MODERN ERA

Kazaks and other Central Asians faced major external challenges as Europe moved into the modern age. Beginning in the 1740s, Russia slowly but steadily encroached on Kazak territory. As the conquest solidified, Slavic settlers flooded into Kazakstan. Disrupting traditional Kazak migratory patterns, Russians and Ukrainians took over the best pasture land and established sprawling farms.[19] Their settlements blocked customary migration routes, leaving many indigenous people without alternative pastures. This development forced some Kazaks to settle and take up agriculture, though they continued to maintain herds and engage in migrations during limited periods and over shorter distances.[20]

With the coming of revolution in 1917 and the disintegration of the Russian empire, Kazakstan achieved a brief period of independence before giving way to Bolshevik pressure. With the Red Army threatening attack, Kazak leaders had no choice but to accept Soviet control over Kazakstan. For the vast majority of Kazak men and women, these political changes at the top brought no immediate consequences for their daily lives.[21]

In Kazakstan and other precapitalist regions of the newly formed Soviet Union, Bolshevik leadership faced a fundamental problem in its political strategy. Marxist theory identified the proletariat as the disaffected class of society destined to bring about capitalism's downfall. The absence of a working class in less industrially developed areas of the country necessitated that the Soviet regime search elsewhere for what Gregory Massell labels a "surrogate proletariat."[22] Moscow looked toward women in

Central Asia and elsewhere to fulfill the role the proletariat donned in capitalist regions of the USSR. Believing that, like workers, women harbored dissatisfaction with their status in society, officials reasoned that they represented the closest approximation to the proletariat available in nonindustrial regions and targeted them for support of the new regime.

The state linked its antireligious campaign to propaganda against practices it perceived as oppressive to women. Marxist ideology defined religion as a false consciousness: all religions, including Islam, deluded the poor into collusion with their capitalist oppressors. Faith in Allah and the teachings of Muhammad supported the existing power structure, which the Bolsheviks sought to destroy. Communists believed that only by attacking practices such as kalym could the Soviet regime liberate "women of the East" and establish Soviet rule on firm soil. Thus by definition Soviet policy toward Kazak women became inextricably intertwined with a campaign to suppress the practice of Islam.

Soviet officials recognized, however, that attacking Islam alone would not bring about the collapse of traditional Kazak society. Although in sedentary regions such as Uzbekistan antireligious propaganda became a primary focus of the authorities' attention, in Kazakstan the campaign against Islam remained relatively muted. Moscow recognized that Islam found expression in somewhat vague forms in the Kazaks' nomadic society and therefore neither identified it as a significant problem nor saw a route for grappling with an intangible enemy. Authorities defined the clan structure as the single greatest challenge to Soviet power in Kazakstan.

Initially, the Soviets sought legal remedies to what European and a limited number of Kazak activists saw as discrimination against women rooted in traditional society. In 1920, the government issued the "Declaration of the Rights of the Working People of Kazakstan," enunciating the state's official stance on the position of women. Deeming liberation of women from their status as "slaves" a prerequisite for a free society, the declaration stressed the equal political and civil rights of women before the law.[23] On January 1, 1924, the state banned polygyny and kalym.[24] Legislators claimed that putting the law on the side of women's rights constituted the first, critical step to fighting the influence of wealthy clan leaders, the clergy, and others who sought to maintain "the old way of life."

When legislative methods alone failed to transform Kazakstan, the state turned to more interventionist measures to win the support of women. By the late 1920s, the government clearly had yet to penetrate deep into the steppe and reach out effectively to Kazak and other Central Asian women. In sedentary areas, the state endorsed the establishment of women's clubs, which it lauded as the most effective means for propagating Soviet values. For the nomads, so-called red yurts brought women's clubs to remote regions. First and foremost, these state-sponsored women's clubs offered adult literacy courses. After completing the course, women enjoyed access to books and newspapers in their native languages. European nurses and doctors sent by the government in Moscow provided basic medical care to women and their children. A variety of "circles" within each club emphasized developing marketable skills, such as rug weaving, that would draw women into work beyond the home.[25]

Only by bringing politically enlightened women out of the home and into the public sphere could the state revolutionize life in Kazakstan. To facilitate drawing women into work outside the home, the state developed a system of day-care centers. Child care constituted the single most important element in freeing women to contribute to what the state deemed "economically productive" work. By 1933, it had established a network that included space for 16,886 children year-round and for 81,796 children during harvest season.[26] Combined with legislative reform and literacy and political enlightenment campaigns, the state intended child-care centers to liberate women from their traditional roles, win their support for Soviet power, and destroy the influence of *bais* (wealthy clan leaders) and mullahs.

Yet despite its multifaceted effort to revolutionize the position of women in Kazakstan, the government faced a myriad of obstacles. Soviet attempts to uproot the traditional position of women met with responses that ranged from indifference to open defiance. Clerical authorities sought to meet each new challenge to their power. To discourage Kazak parents from sending their girls to state schools, in the 1920s mullahs established all-girl schools under mosque auspices. Further, the majority of Kazaks continued to reject state rhetoric against kalym and polygyny.[27] The government could not undermine such deeply rooted customs as easily as it hoped, and inexperienced propagandists had to cope with material and financial shortages, including insufficient reading materials in Central Asian languages.[28]

Despite overwhelming obstacles, developments in education slowly began to transform life for Kazak women. Soviet plans took far longer to bear fruit than intended, but the 1920s and 1930s set the stage for fundamental changes. In 1928–1929, the state set an objective of increasing literacy courses at women's red yurts by 30 percent. By the following year the number of "illiteracy liquidation centers" (*likpunkty*) rose by 35 percent and served eight thousand Kazak women. Among sedentary women in Kazakstan, numbers were still higher. Representing a 17 percent increase over the previous year, seven thousand women attended adult literacy classes in schools, red clubs, worker clubs, and other venues in 1927–1928.[29] When compared to Kazakstan's population of over six million in the 1920s, these numbers seem small but mark the critical beginning of profound social change.

Moscow also achieved incremental gains during the 1930s in its efforts to encourage Kazak women to seek wage labor outside the home. Party and state officials pressed for drawing increasing numbers of women into industry, collective farms, and state farms and for raising women to leadership positions in administration without delay. Such policies led to the proportion of women working outside of agriculture doubling from 1929 to 1935.[30] According to historian Janice Baker, however, "Kazak women comprised a disproportionately small percentage of the female workforce in all sectors of the economy with the exception of agriculture and construction."[31] Nonetheless, by the mid-1930s the number of Kazak women receiving wages had risen to 43,800, and eight out of eleven new women workers recruited were Kazak. Although Kazak women accounted for only 28 percent of female laborers in Kazakstan, the impact on Kazak society of women working outside the home could not but increase.[32]

Such gradual changes to Kazak women's lives in the public sphere found no immediate parallel in the home. Like women throughout the modern world, Kazak women increasingly accepted wage labor outside the home and yet continued to bear the bulk of responsibility for domestic duties. An expanding system of child-care facilities enabled women to work outside the home but in no way alleviated their obligation to cook, clean, sew, and tend to a vast array of other tasks at home. By 1935, Kazak women made up an average of 40–50 percent of the workforce in the agricultural sector, yet these women remained solely responsible for all household labor.

Political and economic catastrophes during the 1930s overshadowed the meager social developments nurtured by the Soviet regime. By the close of the 1920s, officials in Moscow under the guidance of Joseph Stalin had determined that only a path of rapid industrialization and collectivization of agriculture could pave the way toward socialism. For Kazakstan, this scheme meant the forced sedentarization of the nomadic population and their resettlement on collective and state farms. In resistance to settlement, some Kazak nomads took up arms against the state, while others slaughtered their own cattle rather than relinquish them to collective farms. The failure to settle the nomads and impel them to labor on farms led to a state-induced famine sweeping the Kazak steppe in the early 1930s. One-third to one-half of all Kazaks died in the 1930s as a consequence of violence and famine.

Despite the tragedies of the 1930s, propaganda lauded achievements to date, and below the surface the state seemed quietly to resign itself to incremental social change in Kazakstan. Publicly Moscow hailed "advances" the Soviet government had brought to the lives of Kazak men and women alike. Showing women working in the fields, listening to lectures, training as army field nurses, and agitating for the party, newsreels of this era depicted the world of the Kazak women as Europeanized, modern, and liberated.[33] Moscow's intent, however, appears clearer through its actions than its words and images. Authorities, confident that change was now underway, focused their efforts on continual, gradual movement toward the Russified, Europeanized society depicted in propaganda.

World events in the 1940s thrust Kazakstan into a whirlwind. In June 1941, German troops plunged deep into Soviet territory, and though far from the bloodshed, the war experience forever transformed Kazakstan, which played a key role in the Soviet Union's homefront efforts. To meet the German challenge, Moscow directed the dismantling of whole factories and their transfer safely behind the Ural mountains. Following their factories and laboring to turn out war supplies, skilled European workers moved eastward into Kazakstan and elsewhere. Refugees in flight from German troops poured into Central Asia and Siberia. In addition to the influx of workers, evacuees, and refugees, forcibly deported peoples further diversified Central Asian's ethnic composition.

For Kazak women, World War II brought significant changes to daily life. Processes set in motion in previous decades seemed to speed up dramatically. In particular, the number of women engaged in wage labor increased significantly. For example, on the eve of World War II, 488 women worked in industry in the central Kazakstan town of Ust-Kamenogorsk, but by June 1942, women comprised 2,213 of 4,941 workers.[34] The conscription of Kazak men into the armed forces and significant losses at the front no doubt required many Kazak women to seek at least supplemental income outside the home.

The state won cooperation on the homefront through a social contract with the population that included a cease-fire in the war against religion. In 1943 the state's desperation to win the masses' support translated into the founding of the Muslim Ecclesiastical Administration for Central Asia and Kazakstan (SADUM), which assumed responsibility for clerical training, managed organized religion in the region, and symbolized the high point in Moscow's retreat from its struggle against Islam. However, given the fact that historically Kazak religion found expression in noninstitutionalized venues, the impact of these changing policies on Kazaks proved difficult to gauge. Urban, educated Kazaks increasingly demonstrated signs of secularization, but in rural areas Kazaks preserved traditional values and beliefs. Kazak women's lives reflected these dual tendencies. Women worked outside the home and had learned to read but continued to profess Islam. Practices such as kalym survived in secret, particularly in rural areas.

With the end of the war in 1945, the Soviet Union's furious struggle for survival subsided, but the death of Stalin in 1953 and the increasing consolidation of Nikita Khrushchev's power by 1956 brought a new wave of upheaval to Kazakstan. A fierce, highly unpopular antireligious campaign constituted a focal point of Khrushchev's political platform. In Kazakstan this policy principally affected the Slavic population. Kazak religion continued to prove an elusive target, and given the absence of public religious institutions, the state saw little reason to fear Kazak adherence to Islam. Simultaneously, policies designed to foster Russification and secularization helped the state ensure that traditional Kazak values teetered on the verge of collapse. Kazaks had become a minority in their own republic; Russian became entrenched as the dominant language in Kazakstan. The seeds of social revolution that the state planted in the 1920s and 1930s finally seemed to bear fruit.

Kazak women experienced profound alterations of their lives in the post-Stalin era, particularly with respect to education. For the first time in their history, rural girls received universal elementary education. In urban areas, changes in women's lives were even more far-reaching. The 1950s and 1960s brought urban Kazak women ever-expanding access to higher education, professional work outside the home, and health care. Though still behind the Russians in education level, Kazaks began to put greater and greater distance between themselves and other Central Asians. In 1927, only 133 Kazaks, 184 Uzbeks, and 7 Tajiks were enrolled in institutions of higher education in the USSR. By the 1960s, such representation began to approximate more closely each nationality's proportion of the Soviet population (see Table 10.1).

For Kazak women, these changes meant going from essentially no access to higher education to enrollment almost equal to that of Kazak men.[35] For all the nationalities, these statistics demonstrate a remarkable expansion of educational opportunities for both men and women in Central Asia since the rise of Soviet power, but for reasons explained later, Kazak women seem to have benefited more than other Central Asians.

With respect to work outside the home, women's experiences increasingly diversified in the post-Stalin era. As seen in Table 10.2, Kazak

Table 10.1 Enrollment in Soviet Higher Education, 1970

	Total Enrolled	Women
Kazaks	100,300	45%
Uzbeks	150,700	33%
Tajiks	28,100	24%

Source: Adapted from Gail Warshofsky Lapidus, *Women in Soviet Society: Equality, Development, and Social Change* (Berkeley: University of California Press, 1978), 153.

Table 10.2 Central Asian Women Workers

	Kazaks	Uzbeks	Tajiks
Farm workers, 1986	38%	55%	52%
Blue- and white-collar workers, 1988	49%	43%	39%
Enterprise directors, 1989	5%	2.5%	2.7%

Source: Adapted from Judith Shapiro, "The Industrial Labor Force," in *Perestroika and Soviet Women,* ed. Mary Buckley (New York: Cambridge University Press, 1992), 17.

women held a higher proportion of management positions than any other Central Asian women. These statistics show that although Kazak women have not attained European levels in education and professionalization in the Soviet Union, they have outpaced other Central Asian women.

Of course, the dramatically higher Russian and Ukrainian presence in Kazakstan is in part responsible for the increasing "Europeanization of Kazak women," but Slavic settlement in Kazakstan alone fails to explain the gradual acceptance among Kazak men and women of new opportunities afforded women under the communists. Perhaps the answer lies in the Kazaks' distinctive heritage, which made them more receptive to Moscow's agenda. Unlike their sedentary Tajik and Uzbek neighbors to the south, women in traditional Kazak society, as we have seen, enjoyed extensive legal and social equality with men. Women played an open role in clan politics. Islamic practices common in settled, urban settings never took root in nomadic Kazak society. Just as the nomadic heritage of the Kazaks influenced their practice of Islam, so too it shaped the way they responded to communist policies. The very circumstances that made the institutionalized expression of Islam incompatible with traditional Kazak life led to the relative acceptability of Soviet policies. It is not surprising that the Soviet agenda, when combined with constant contact with vast numbers of Slavic settlers, met with considerably greater success in Kazakstan than in other regions of Central Asia.

Nonetheless, despite dramatic changes in educational and professional opportunities, women continued to bear a disproportionate share of the burden in family life. Domestic pressures on women increased. Though birthrates dropped, women increasingly became sole heads of households as divorce rates rose. More Kazak women took the lead in initiating divorce proceedings, liberating themselves from unhappy marriages.[36] However, freedom came at a high cost. Such women were often deprived of financial or emotional support from absentee fathers, becoming almost without exception the primary caretakers for their children. Unequal wages forced them to work for incomes lower than men employed in comparable positions. Throughout the former Soviet Union women earn on average only 70 percent of what men in similar jobs receive.[37]

THE POST-SOVIET EXPERIENCE

Following the Soviet Union's collapse and Kazakstan's independence on December 16, 1991, its citizens experienced a mixture of capitalism's positive and negative effects. Because of dramatic inflation, prices continue to rise at a rate dizzying to a people accustomed to state-controlled, stable costs. Although pensioners can barely afford bread, opportunities to earn money seem to abound for young people with knowledge of foreign languages, computers, or the drive to hustle for work.

No longer citizens of the powerful Soviet Union, Kazaks and others have sought to redefine who they are and look for the answers in their historical roots. As part of this renewed interest in Kazak history and culture, Islam currently enjoys a revival in Kazakstan as well. The government finds the revived interest in religion useful for purposes of national identity construction. Nauruz, the Muslim New Year's celebration that the Soviets repressed and replaced with a commemoration of the ban on kalym, has become reinstated as a state-recognized holiday, symbolizing the government's efforts to build contemporary national traditions by breathing new life into long-denigrated customs. In 1991, the Kazaks published a translation of the Qur'an in their native language, and an Islamic Institute was founded the following year for advanced religious studies. The capital's lone mosque is currently undergoing renovation, and a new one is being built. Funding from Iran, Turkey, and Saudi Arabia helps support these activities designed to foster Islamization among the Kazaks. In part, this new surge of interest in Islam represents a return to the past, but in a significant way departs from it. Although the once nomadic Kazaks observed Islamic rituals in a manner uniquely adapted to their way of life, the now sedentary Kazaks turn to more conventional expressions of faith. Prior to the revolution of 1917, few schools, newspapers, and religious institutions served the Kazaks, though today they are the hallmark of the "rediscovery" of the past.

The League of Muslim Women embodies the most vocal, public expression of Islamization among Kazak women. Since 1991, this organization has published a monthly newspaper, *Aq Bosagha,* the name of which reflects the league's mission. "Aq bosagha," or "white threshold," refers to the custom of laying a white cloth across the threshold of a home to welcome the arrival of a new bride to her husband's family. The title thus speaks of the purity of women, as represented by the white cloth, as well as the centrality of family in Kazak life. The league works for social causes and champions the sanctity of the family, and it attempts to enlighten women about Islam. The league's popularity, however, stays low. Although membership numbers remain in dispute, they do not exceed a few thousand. By definition, the league excludes from membership Russians and other Christians, who make up nearly 50 percent of Kazakstan's population.

For the majority of Kazak women, particularly in urban areas, Islamization has not translated into the institutionalization of practices historically absent from traditional Kazak society. In a March 1993 survey of Kazak students, when asked if Kazak practice of Islam differed from that of other Muslim cultures, 58 percent responded affirmatively and often cited the position of women as evidence.[38] The overwhelming majority of

women continue to seek careers outside the home. One finds no public, superficial signifiers of Islamization among urban Kazak women. Kazak
women find the suggestion of adopting the veil absurd, and almost no
urban women cover their hair. Thus, despite the fact that increasing reli-
giosity conforms to institutional patterns defined in the sedentary world,
the heritage of the nomadic past and the role women played within it remain meaningful.

Further, Islamization faces a significant challenge from other trends at
work in Kazakstan today. As one young Kazak woman described it, Kazak
youths find themselves drawn in one of three directions.[39] One group seeks
to get an education, earn money, and make the most of Kazakstan's fledg-
ling capitalist system. Others largely reject society and often turn to drinking to escape reality. The remaining small group finds the answers to
today's changing, confusing world in Islam. One of several choices, Islam
sparks the interest of only a limited number.

For women interested in social activism, alternatives exist to the
League of Muslim Women. The Women's League of Creative Initiative
(WLCI) seeks to foster equality for women in all spheres of Kazakstani
life. Founded in 1994 by a group of young artists, journalists, physicians,
and teachers, its membership includes representatives of a variety of ethnic groups who hope to appeal to women in the intelligentsia. Like the
League of Muslim Women, the WLCI intends to assist women and children forgotten by a government itself in severe financial straits; however,
it finds the answer to social ills not in Islam but in feminist ideology and
the development of a civil society. According to its charter, one of WLCI's
primary goals is to "study and spread the ideas of feminism," though the
members themselves grapple with defining feminism in the socioeconomic
conditions of contemporary Kazakstan.[40]

Women continue to play a high-profile role in the public sphere, such
as entering new university departments dedicated to fields like finance and
international relations, which should open up increasing opportunities in
the rapidly expanding business sector. Organizations such as the League of
Muslim Women and the Women's League of Creative Initiative give Kazak
women a platform from which to voice their social concerns. Simultaneously, financial problems continue to dominate the daily lives of most
women, who bear the burden of managing the family budget. Prices remain high relative to salaries, and inflation shows no signs of abating in
the near future.

Economically, socially, and politically, Kazak women's lives lie at a
crossroads. Pre-Soviet and Soviet influences have given rise to the multifaceted roles women play in present-day Kazak society. For now, renewed
interest in Islam seems to play only a modest role, and other factors, such
as the rise of the market economy, show signs of exerting a more dominant
influence on the position of women. Though one cannot foretell Islam's

potential political and social role, the historical absence of Islamic institutions in Kazakstan suggests that it will not be a significant factor, at least in the near future. One finds it difficult to imagine Islam emerging as a powerful political force and in any major way affecting the status of Kazak women, given the countervailing nomadic heritage. How these two legacies of the past express themselves in the future development of Kazak society remains to be seen, but both will no doubt play an influential role in how the history of Kazak women unfolds.

NOTES

Research for this article was supported in part by a grant from the International Research and Exchanges Board (IREX), with funds provided by the National Endowment for the Humanities, the United States Information Agency, and the U.S. Department of State. None of these organizations is responsible for the views expressed. I would like to thank Randi Barnes, Kari Bronaugh, Daniel Coleman, Susan Beam Eggers, Shahrbanou Tadjbakhsh, and Kathy Transel, for their helpful comments.

    1. Some clarification of the terms used in this chapter is necessary. "Kazakstani" refers to people who are citizens of the newly independent Republic of Kazakstan, regardless of their ethnic background. "Kazak" pertains to the indigenous ethnic group from which the country of Kazakstan derives its name (which means "land of the Kazaks"). After it achieved independence in 1991, the Kazak government officially changed the English-language spelling from "Kazakh" to "Kazak" in order to more closely approximate the indigenous, rather than Russian, pronunciation.

    2. "The Social Structure and Customs of the Kazakhs," *Central Asian Review* 1 (1957): 8, 20.

    3. B. A. Kuftin, *Kirgiz-Kazaki: Kul'tura i byt* (Moscow: Izd-vo Tsentral'nogo museia narodovedeniia, 1926), 10; "Social Structure," 20; Irene Winner, "Some Problems of Nomadism and Social Organization Among the Recently Settled Kazakhs," *Central Asian Review* 9 (1963), pt. 1: 249.

    4. V. N. Basilov, *Sredneaziatskoe shamanstvo* (Moscow: Nauka, 1973), 6.

    5. A. E. Alektorov, *Iz mira Kirgizskikh sueverii: Baksy* (Kazan': Tipolitografiia Imperatorskogo Universiteta, 1899), 3–8; A. A. Divaev, *Iz oblasi kirgizskikh verovanii: Baksy, kak lekar' i koldun. Etnograficheskii ocherk* (Kazan': Tipografiia Imperatorskogo Universiteta, 1899), 2–8; G. Kastan (Castange), "Iz oblasti kirgizskikh verovanii," *Vestnik Orenburgskago uchebnogo okruga* 3 (1912): 209–218; A. Briskin, *Stepi Kazakskie: Ocherki stepnogo Kazakstana* (Kzyl-Orda: Kazizdat, 1929), 109.

    6. For an excellent, brief survey of Islam in Kazakhstan, see A. K. Sultangalieva, "Islam v Kazakhstane," *Vostok* 3 (1994): 72–80.

    7. K. Shulembaev, *Obraz zhizni, religii, ateizma* (Alma-Ata: Kazakhstan, 1983), 82, 86.

    8. A. V. Vasil'ev, *Materialy k kharakteristike vzaimnykh otnoshenii Tatar i Kirgizov s predvaritel'nym kratkim ocherkom etikh otnoshenii* (Orenburg: Tipolitografiia P. N. Zaripova, 1898), 1, 14, 17.

    9. *Shkol'nyi al'bom Bukeevskoi ordy* (Astrakhan: Tipografiia gubernskago pravleniia, 1896), 11; Voitekhovskii, *Kirgizy Kustanaiskogo uezda, Turgaiskoi oblasti: Izvestiia obshchestva arkheologii, istorii i etnografii* (Kazan', 1910), 10.

10. Kastan, "Iz oblasti kirgizskikh verovanii," 78, 85; "Social Structure," 10, 16–17.

11. M. Lavrov, *Kochevniki: Zhizn' v kirgizskoi stepi* (St. Petersburg: n.p., 1914), 2.

12. F. Lobysevich, *Kirgizskaia step' Orenburgskago vedomstva: Ocherk* (Moscow: Kushnerev, 1891), 33; Efrem Eliseev, *Zapiski missionera Bukonskago stana kirgizskoi missii za 1892–1899 gg* (St. Petersburg: Evdokimov, 1900), 32.

13. Berotov, *Strana svobodnykh zemel'* (St. Petersburg: Izdatel'stvo A. N. Zarudnyi, 1908), 38; Lobysevich, *Kirgizskaia step'*, 34.

14. Fannina W. Halle, *Women in the Soviet East* (London: Martin Secker and Warburg, 1938), 104.

15. A. Ia. Smirnova, "Na smenu dikomu sueveriiu prikhodit meditsinskaia pomoshch'," *Kommunistka* 8 (1929): 27, reprinted in *Veliki oktiabr' i raskreposhchenie zhenshchin Srednei Azii I Kazakhstana, 1917–1936 gg: Sbornik documentor i materialov*, ed. Z. A. Astapovich (Moscow: Mysl', 1971), 415.

16. Winner, "Some Problems," pt. 1: 249.

17. *Bezbozhnik* (August 19, 1928): 3.

18. G. K. Gins, "V Kirgizkikh Aulakh: Ocherki Iz Poezdki Po Semirech'ia," *Istoicheskii Vestnik* 134, no. 10 (1913): 290; Halle, *Women in the Soviet East,* 227.

19. George J. Demko, *The Russian Colonization of Kazakhstan, 1896–1916* (Bloomington: Indiana University Press, 1969), 55, 109.

20. Edward Allworth, ed., *Central Asia: 120 Years of Russian Rule* (Durham, NC: Duke University Press, 1989), 283.

21. For a discussion of the revolution, civil war, and early Soviet period in Kazakstan, see Martha Britt Olcott, *The Kazakhs* (Stanford, CA: Hoover Institution Press, 1987), 129–165.

22. Gregory J. Massell, *The Surrogate Proletariat: Moslem Women and Revolutionary Strategies in Soviet Central Asia, 1919–1929* (Princeton, NJ: Princeton University Press, 1974).

23. Winner, "Some Problems," pt. 2: 362.

24. *10 let Kazakstana* (Alma Ata: Izd-vo gosplana Kazakstoi ASSR, 1930), 70.

25. A. Nurkhat, *Iurty kochevki: K rabote zhenskikh krasnykh iurt* (Moscow: Tsentral'noe izdatel'stvo narodov SSSR, 1929), 7, 9; Halle, *Women in the Soviet East,* 146.

26. N. N. Matveev, "Ocherednye zadachi na fronte zdravookhraneniia po KazASSR" *Meditsinskii zhurnal Kazakstana* 1 (October 1933): 6.

27. Rossiiskii Tsentr Khraneniia i Izucheniia Dokumentov Noveishei Istorii (RTsKhIDNI), fond 17, opis 25, delo 16, list 129 (hereafter, f. stands for fond, op. for opis, d. for delo, and l. for list); f. 17, op. 25, d. 18, l. 98.

28. "K predstoiashchemu vsesoiuznomu soveshchaniiu po rabote sredi zhenshchin vostoka," *Antireligioznik* (November 1928): 98; "IV vsesoiuznoe soveshchanie po rabote sredi zhenshchin Vostoka," *Antireligioznik* (January 1929): 97, 99; *10 let Kazakstana,* 69.

29. "Iz otcheta komissii po uluchsheniiu truda i byta zhenshchin pri TsIK Kazakhskoi ASSR (1930)," TsGAOR SSSR (presently Gosudarstvennyi Arkhiv Rossiskoi Federatsii [GARF]), f. 3316, op. 21, d. 685, ll. 79–81, reprinted in *Veliki oktiabr' i raskreposhchenie zhen shchin Srednei Azii I Kazakhstana, 1917–1936 gg: Sbornik documentor i materialov,* ed. Z. A. Astapovich (Moscow: Mysl', 1971), 424–425.

30. A. B. Tursunbaev, ed., *Kollektivizatsiia sel'skogo khoziaistva Kazakhstana, 1926–1941 gg.,* vol. 1 (Alma-Ata, 1967), 433; Janice Baker, "The Position of

Women in Kazakhstan in the Interwar Years," *Central Asian Survey* 4, no. 1 (1985): 77.

31. Baker, "The Position of Women," 81.

32. Ibid.

33. Central State Archive of Film-Photo-Sound Documents of the Republic of Kazakstan (TsGAKFF RK), newsreel series "Sovetskii Kazakhstan," ff. 488, 824, 765, 685, and 1255, for example.

34. "Spravka otdela kadrov TsK KP(b) Kazakhstana o podgotovke kadrov iz zhenshchin dlia promyshlennosti za 1-yi god velikoi otechestvennoi voiny," in *Kazakhstan v period velikoi otechestvennoi voiny Sovetskogo Soiuza, 1941–1945: Sbornik dokumentov i materialov*, ed. S. N. Pokrovskii, vol. 1 (Alma-Ata: Nauka, 1964–1967), 122; "Iz postanovleniia SNK i TsK KP(b) Kazakhstana o podgotovke zhenshchin dlia raboty na traktorakh, kombainakh i avtomashinakh," in *Kazakhstan v period*, vol. 1, 47.

35. Winner, "Some Problems," pt. 2: 363.

36. Vladimir Shlapentokh, *Love, Marriage, and Friendship in the Soviet Union: Ideals and Practices* (New York: Praeger, 1984), 208. The author refers specifically to an article based on the experience of Uzbek women, but the pattern holds true for Kazak women as well.

37. Hilary Pilkington, "Behind the Mask of Soviet Unity: Realities of Women's Lives," in *Superwomen and the Double Burden: Women's Experience of Change in Central and Eastern Europe and the Former Soviet Union*, ed. Chris Corrin (Toronto: Second Story Press, 1992), 183.

38. A. K. Sultangalieva, "Islam v Kazakhstane," 78.

39. Interview by the author, Jania Smagulova, January 1995, Almaty, Kazakstan.

40. Unpublished document, acquired from Asya Khairulina, president, WLCI, March 1995, Almaty, Kazakstan.

PART FOUR

South and Southeast Asia

11

Taslima Nasreen and Others: The Contest over Gender in Bangladesh

Dina M. Siddiqi

The ruling ideology of Bangladesh shifted dramatically within a few years of its birth in 1971, from socialism, democracy, and secularism to capitalism, military dictatorship, and Islamism. Underlying this shift was the inflow of foreign assistance under the auspices of the World Bank and the International Monetary Fund (IMF). Aid-driven integration into the global capitalist economy not only sustained successive military regimes but also precipitated conditions for the rise of Islamist politics. Simultaneously, nation building has become synonymous with economic development, and the imperative "to develop" possesses a near moral urgency.[1] Thus, competing visions of the nation invariably arise from disputes over the nature and implications of development interventions. In recent years, one of the most contested sites of such interventions lies in the realm of gender relations. Struggles to define ideal womanhood have become especially pronounced with the emergence of a multiplicity of Islamist groups that have increasingly challenged the direction of state and nonstate developmentalist practices.

In this chapter I analyze the relation of gender discourses to contests over national identity, development policies, and Islamist politics in Bangladesh. I begin with a review of the period prior to the country's independence, in which middle-class women's cultural practices were critical in delineating the boundaries of Bengali identity. In contrast, in independent Bangladesh the bodies of indigent rural women have become a new battleground, as strategies to "bring women into the development process" are implemented. Islamist groups have tapped into fears of unregulated female sexuality and the loss of patriarchal authority that such steps have generated. At the same time, impoverished village women affiliated with development programs figure centrally in the competition for patronage that marks the resource-scarce rural economy. I analyze the emergence of *fatwabazi* (the practice of issuing *fatwas* or religious opinions) against women in this context. I conclude with a consideration of the fatwa against the writer Taslima Nasreen, who came to represent, among other things, the dangers and excesses of uncontrolled developmentalism and Westernization.

This chapter is also intended to complicate conventional analyses of women in Bangladesh, which revolve around two major themes, purdah (female seclusion) and persistent poverty. As a recent World Bank report states:

> The overwhelming majority of women in Bangladesh are not only poor but also caught between two vastly different worlds—the world determined by culture and tradition that confines their activities inside homesteads and the world shaped by increasing landlessness and poverty that draws them outside into wage employment for economic survival.[2]

The story of women caught between two worlds is part of a larger narrative, recalling the conflict between tradition (here Bengali culture or Islam) and modernity (economic development, progress, and secularism). In orthodox development circles this clash is part of every modern nation-state's history. However, the implicit evolutionary movement from tradition to modernity glosses over the politics of representing Bangladeshi women. Conflicts that are ostensibly over purdah and poverty or tradition and modernity contain other larger struggles for power in many arenas.

It is in this context that I wish to situate my discussion of Taslima Nasreen. At the outset, I should say that despite her iconic status, Nasreen's plight is not representative of most women's lives in Bangladesh. Indeed, she stands at one end of a spectrum. Nevertheless, her predicament is emblematic of many of the tensions of contemporary Bangladeshi politics and so merits serious attention. In one sense, then, the title of the chapter is misleading, for although I discuss the Nasreen episode in detail, it is not my central focus throughout. I am equally concerned with the "others" of the title.

ENGENDERING THE NATION:
THE STRUGGLE FOR BANGLADESH

Contemporary feminist research has focused on the ways in which the bodies of women, often literally, are the sites of struggle relating to issues of identity and the reclaiming of territory and tradition.[3] Once the female body is constituted as a privileged signifier, various struggles can be waged over the meaning and ownership of that body.[4] Women can symbolize the space of the nation as well as its property; they are perceived at the same time to be the repository and transmitters of culture/tradition as embodied in their reproductive roles. Defined in these terms, women also become symbols of the community's honor and so need to be protected. Not all women are necessarily included in this category, however. Respectability and representativeness are usually embedded in the middle class, as is the nationalist project itself.

In this section, I examine how ambiguities over cultural identity were mediated through struggles to claim ownership of Bengali women's bodies and cultural practices in the period leading up to Bangladesh's independence in 1971. Although there was no specific women's agenda in the Bengali nationalist movement, middle-class women were critical in delineating the explicitly secular content of Bengali identity. Some women were mobilized in a highly visible fashion in the name of Bengali national culture—without any corresponding interest in women's rights in general. There were also a small number of women who took up arms and joined the underground resistance in 1971.

The creation of Bangladesh (formerly East Pakistan) directly repudiated the principle of Muslim religious unity on which Pakistan had been founded in 1947. Upon independence, the new constitution of Bangladesh instituted secularism (along with socialism, democracy, and nationalism) as a fundamental principle of state policy. Although Islam was not rejected as a component of the national culture, it was subsumed within a secular and syncretic concept of Bengaliness. The new state was characterized by one nation (Bangalee) and one language (Bangla). The minority of Hindus, Christians, and Buddhists,[5] it was assumed, shared a culture on the basis of linguistic and ethnic commonalities. The use of religious rhetoric in politics was banned, so that groups such as the Jamaat-i-Islami, the dominant Muslim party that had actively opposed the creation of Bangladesh, were forced underground.

Defining a syncretic Bengali culture specific to Bangladesh was complicated and potentially divisive. Indeed, reclaiming the cultural practices and beliefs of Muslims in Bengal as syncretic, Bengali, or un-Islamic (Hindu) has historically been problematic. "Orthodox" Muslims in other parts of South Asia characteristically interpreted the practice of Islam in Bengal as too Bengali (read Hinduized) and made it the object of various reformist movements over the centuries.[6] The combination of Hindu and Bengali in opposition to Muslim, therefore, has a long genealogy in Bengal, becoming particularly pronounced in the nineteenth century.[7] In practice, the categories of Hindu, Muslim, and Bengali are defined in relation to one another, their meanings constantly open to negotiation and appropriation. Efforts by the Pakistani state to establish distinct boundaries between Muslim Pakistanis and Hindu others were most visibly and effectively countered by the constant blurring of categories entailed in the production of a secular Bengali culture. The meanings of those categories considered by the Pakistani state as purely Hindu were constantly disrupted and reconstituted, most visibly in the cultural realm, most effectively by women:

> An important [aspect] of the nationalist movement was the Bengalis' re-
> sistance to Pakistani state ideology on the cultural front, and this fell
> more to women—in defiance they sang Tagore songs, put on tip [*teep*]
> (decorative spots on the forehead traditionally worn by Hindu women [to
> denote marital status]), wore flowers in their hair, sent their daughters to
> music and dance schools, allowed them to perform on stage—all these
> activities which seem so commonplace now, in the 50's and 60's were
> acts of dissent given the Pakistan government's branding of these as
> Hindu aberrations.[8]

Bengali nationalists appropriated the songs of Rabindranath Tagore, a Bengali Hindu poet much admired by educated and middle-class Bengalis, together with specific forms of clothing and adornment as secular signs of self-affirmation and resistance. To the Pakistani state these were too closely associated with the culture of (predominantly Hindu) West Bengal and so slipped into the category of Hindu aberrations. The extent to which the Pakistani regime was threatened by such symbolic resistance is betrayed by their injunctions against the public broadcast of Tagore songs in 1971 during the Liberation War and against women announcers wearing the teep on state-owned television.[9] In addition, the meaning of music and dress were not gender-neutral. Although there were plenty of male practitioners of Tagore's music and male versions of Bengali attire were available, it was women's practices that came to symbolize subversion and resistance. Certainly, it was not coincidental that the task of cultural resistance fell to women. Remapping or reasserting the place of women was a powerful mode of counteracting ambiguity for both sides in this cultural struggle. The bodily practices of middle-class East Pakistani women became a provocative and visible symbol of both state domination and ethnic resistance. Bengali women, most explicitly through their clothing (*sarees*) and adornments (flowers, teep), became the icon for Bengali ethnicity, a vehicle for marking cultural (and territorial) boundaries. Moreover, the image of women as reproducers of cultural traditions was enhanced by the assumption that it was they who allowed their daughters to be trained in traditional Bengali ways.

A more brutal instance of the mapping of women's bodies onto the nation occurred during the War of Liberation in 1971. West Pakistani discourses on the cultural and religious inferiority of their Bengali-speaking compatriots were derived from the perception of Islam in Bengal as inferior and impure. Not surprisingly, the West Pakistanis used the slogan of "Islam in danger" as the rallying point for the vicious military crackdown that marked the beginning of the War of Liberation in 1971. Sometime during the war, a fatwa originating in West Pakistan labeled Bengali freedom fighters "Hindus" and declared that "the wealth and women" to be secured by warfare with them could be treated as the booty of war.[10] Throughout the war, paramilitary groups primarily associated with the Jamaat-i-Islami collaborated with the Pakistani army, perpetrating mass killings, plunder, and rape. In the course of nine months, the Pakistani army and its supporters raped an estimated 30,000 Bengali women. Women who were detained in "camps" were released only after they had conceived and it was ascertained they could no longer terminate their pregnancies. The ideology underlying the systematic rape of Bengali women by the Pakistani army is chillingly similar to that used recently in the rape of Bosnian Muslim women in the former Yugoslavia. Rape was simultaneously a violation of the enemy's territory/honor and a sign of its inability to protect its space/ women. It was also a means of purifying the "tainted" blood of Bengali Muslims, of rupturing and refixing religious and territorial boundaries.[11]

In the collective memory of the nation, the figure of the raped Bengali woman is a powerful symbol of Pakistani lust and barbarism, yet it is a figure riven by ambiguity and irresolution. In popular plays on the theme of independence, for instance, the violation of individual women is often portrayed as a sacrifice, for the family as well as for the nation.[12] A standard plot revolves around the woman whose husband has been incarcerated by the military, who surrenders her body to the depredations of army personnel in order to secure her partner's freedom. Yet this sacrifice of her body can be redeemed only by the woman's subsequent exit from the plot, for her act signifies betrayal and shame as well as sacrifice. The choice of rejoining family and community is rarely exercised; ideally, she encounters death through suicide or accident. In other words, in this nationalist discourse women can only exercise agency within terms set by existing patriarchal structures. Moreover, in the stories about the "dishonored heroines" of the Liberation War, there are constant slippages between coercion and individual choice. This obviates the necessity of addressing the actual pain and contradictions of confronting the returned *birangona* (war heroine), as raped women were officially labeled by the new government of Bangladesh.

The euphemism of the title of birangona served only to underscore the socially unacceptable status of "dishonored" women. In contrast to male freedom fighters returning to a hero's welcome, women held in camps, symbolizing shame and social pollution, were rarely welcomed back into their homes or communities. The state initially attempted to rehabilitate these war heroines, but these half-hearted attempts were abandoned soon afterward.

ISLAM AND THE POLITICS OF THE AID REGIME

As the preceding section indicates, the majority of poor rural women remained distant from the nationalist movement. Since independence, state practices have pushed the rural populace, including indigent women, to the forefront of national politics. More specifically, the need to expand capitalist production by tapping the vast pool of rural labor has considerably redefined the "woman question." State policies toward women, as in many other domains, have consistently been mediated by the imperatives of an aid-driven economy. At the end of the Third Five-Year Plan (1985–1990), foreign aid accounted for almost 90 percent of the Annual Development Plan.[13] Aid disbursements have created a network of dependence that is deeply imbedded in the national administration, directly linking local systems of patronage with the international context.

Bangladesh emerged as an independent state at a time when the women in development (WID) school of thought lobbied to make women an explicit category of development theory and practice. With impetus from the United Nations Decade for Women (1975–1985) and pressure from women's groups, bilateral aid in many donor countries was tied to programs that recognized and promoted women's ecomomic empowerment.[14] The success of the WID lobby made women's programs a lucrative source of funding for aid-dependent nations such as Bangladesh. As we shall see, this strategy was not without its contradictions.

Although women's issues received little specific attention from the nation's first government led by Shaykh Mujibur Rahman, the constitution of 1972 gave women full political and legal rights—within the bounds of Muslim personal law. Socialist and secular in orientation, Mujibur Rahman's Awami League government also attempted to maintain political neutrality by soliciting aid from socialist bloc countries and India. His military successor, General Ziaur Rahman, who ruled from 1975 to 1981, rapidly embraced an explicitly market-oriented pro-Western agenda.[15] During this period, the configuration of donors changed; the significance of India and the socialist bloc was overshadowed by Muslim oil-producing states and Western capitalist nations. Ziaur Rahman attempted to reconstitute national identity in terms more acceptable to this new set of donors. Playing on the ambivalence of Bengali identity, Ziaur Rahman replaced the term Bengali with Bangladeshi in all official discourse, thereby distinguishing the Bengali-speaking population of Bangladesh from that of India. At the same time, through a 1977 presidential proclamation, he replaced the principles of secularism and socialism in the constitution with clauses on "absolute trust and faith in Almighty Allah" and a commitment to "economic and social justice," respectively.[16] This amendment to the constitution simultaneously legalized politics based on religion, thereby allowing for the rehabilitation of Islamist parties such as the Jamaat-i-Islami. The promotion of an Islamized Bangladeshi nationalism did not deter Ziaur Rahman from taking advantage of development assistance directed at bringing women out of the home and into the public wage labor sector.[17] Promoting himself as a modernist and a champion of women's rights, he tapped successfully into the extensive funding available for women's projects, thereby mobilizing yet another opportunity for political patronage.[18] The proliferation of non-governmental organizations (NGOs), mostly foreign funded and often aimed explicitly at working among rural women, occurred under his regime.[19]

Ziaur Rahman's policies of capitalist industrialization and state-sponsored Islamization continued under the military regime of his successor, General H. M. Ershad (1982–1990). At this time, Bangladesh adopted a structural adjustment program under the aegis of the World Bank and the IMF. With their support, in 1982 Ershad carried out a program of economic liberalization, based on export-led growth strategies and the promotion of the private sector.[20] These policies laid the groundwork for the unprecedented success of the export-oriented garment manufacturing industry, currently the largest source of foreign exchange earnings as well as the largest of employer of female industrial labor. Government officials and factory owners routinely express their satisfaction at being able to contribute to women's economic development, but Shelley Feldman turns a more critical eye on such growth:

> This initiative does not build on the specific employment needs of the Bangladeshi workforce but on parallel shifts in the international division of labor and economic restructuring. The point to emphasize here is that the political economy of Bangladesh has been restructured to better adapt to the state's need to maintain international credit, to generate foreign exchange, and to respond to the interests of multinational garment and textile firms in their search for cheap sources of labor.[21]

Even as such concessions to international capital promoted the visibility of large numbers of women in previously male spaces, Ershad moved to consolidate the Islamic bases of his regime. In 1983, the Ministry of Education attempted to replace English with Arabic as the second language of instruction. In the face of considerable opposition, especially from university students, the government was forced to abandon this plan. Nevertheless, through a constitutional amendment in 1988, Ershad declared Islam the state religion.[22] This too met with considerable opposition from some women's groups.

Playing the "Islamic card" not only secured specific sources of aid, but for military rulers eager to establish democratic credentials, it also provided a legitimizing ideology that was an alternative to both Bengali nationalism and the demands of an extreme religious right. This is consistent with the suggestion that both Ershad and Ziaur Rahman promoted state-sponsored Islamization to contain viable opposition from Islamist parties such as the Jamaat-i-Islami. Ironically, such policies indirectly nurtured and legitimized the growth of religious extremism at the national and local levels.

State policies such as the provision of government funding for local *madrasas* (Muslim religious schools), the training of imams, and the patronage extended to government institutions such as the Islamic Foundation have facilitated the operation of Islamist politics in rural areas.[23] The bulk of funding from Gulf states and Saudi Arabia is channeled primarily into setting up madrasas and mosques in the countryside to strengthen traditional Islamic values. Even multilateral aid agencies such as United Nations Children's Fund (UNICEF) have occasionally funded religious education that, because of resource constraints, is at the expense of secular education.[24] In the prevailing economic situation, in which access to scarce resources through patron-client ties is of paramount importance, such policies have effectively laid the groundwork for the rise of alternatives to Western-sponsored development. Moreover, the contradictory policies toward women implied in accepting aid from Western as well as Middle Eastern countries opened up a space for challenging the direction of national politics through contestations over gender.

The largest and only sizable party represented in parliament is the Jamaat-i-Islami, which has an estimated six million associated members.[25] Jamaat supports setting up an Islamic state with Shari'a applicable to all aspects of life. The party manifesto contains a special section on the protection of women's rights, which includes the provision of separate educational and work facilities for women, as well as a note on the "motivation of women to observe purdah."[26] This kind of movement must ultimately be located within the specific predicaments of modernity, in particular the tensions of the postcolonial nation-state and the contingencies of global capitalism. From this perspective, "political Islam" seems a more accurate term than "Islamic fundamentalism" to describe such movements.[27] The multiplicity of small and scattered religious extremist groups in Bangladesh are hardly fundamentalist, if the latter is taken to mean a return to the fundamentals of religion. Reflecting in part the belief of their patrons, such groups have sought to impose a monolithic version of Islam that is essentially authoritarian and patriarchal. Such claims to homogeneity leave no space for dissent or ambiguity, that is, for multiple interpretations of Islam.

Many of the religious extremist groups in Bangladesh rose to prominence in the early 1990s, when the Jamaat was being wooed both by the opposition and the government as a potential ally. The general environment of tolerance for Islamist rhetoric during this period allowed the more obscure groups, although not directly associated with the Jamaat, to operate unhindered. They launched virulent attacks on writers, journalists, or any intellectuals with views challenging a patriarchal Islamic social order. It should be noted that their influence seems to have abated somewhat, corresponding perhaps to a decline in the Jamaat-i-Islami's importance in national politics.

Moreover, successive elections indicate the relative indifference of the voting population toward Islamist politics, at least in terms of electoral representation. In the 1991 parliamentary elections (following the People's Movement that brought down the Ershad government in 1990), the Jamaat-i-Islami captured only 6 percent of the vote.[28] Its subsequent political prominence derived primarily from the swing votes it provided the newly elected Bangladesh Nationalist Party (BNP) to ensure a parliamentary majority. In fact, the Awami League, generally perceived as the more secular party, and the more openly Islamized BNP received almost equal shares of the vote, although the BNP won more seats. The significance of Jamaat and other Islamist parties declined further in the June 1996 elections, when they captured only three seats total. Nevertheless, as the 1996 election campaign revealed, a moderately Islamic ideological platform can resonate with the public.[29] In moments of political uncertainty, successive governments have not hesitated to take advantage of this, as the BNP did in the case against Taslima Nasreen.

There is, then, the danger of overstating the case for Islamist movements and their popularity in Bangladesh. Although support at the grassroots level is difficult to gauge and should not be underestimated, it is worth keeping in mind that state-sponsored Islamization rather than a people's movement has provided the primary impetus for the politicization of religion. In addition, the extent of Islamization in Bangladesh has been fairly superficial compared to countries such as Pakistan. Bangladesh is not an Islamic republic, and even the move to declare Islam the state religion is still under appeal in the Supreme Court. Political Islam is conventionally associated with a highly visible code of conduct for women, especially in the realm of dress and comportment and in family relations.[30] But the particular conditions under which Islamization has been sponsored in Bangladesh, by an impoverished state confronted with multiple sources of foreign aid and an increasing reliance on women's labor, have ensured that the state leaves untouched issues regarding women's deportment, dress, and working conditions.

WOMEN AND THE ECONOMY

Bangladeshi women have become the subjects of several national success stories in the last decade. The members of the Grameen Bank, the workers in the garment industry, and the women who helped to dramatically reduce the population growth rate all have been lauded for their contribution to the national project.[31] Nevertheless, for most women—and men—the situation remains bleak. In 1993, Bangladesh's gross national product (GNP) was only $224 per capita, twelfth from the bottom of the World Bank's national income table.[32] Although there has been a reduction in absolute poverty, the distribution of income has actually deteriorated.[33] The government uses three separate measures of the poverty line, a distressing sign in itself; such semantics are hardly able to gloss over the precarious quality of life for most Bangladeshis.[34] Liberalization and privatization have not significantly expanded the industrial base of the country. The predominantly agricultural economy is characterized by increasing landlessness and unemployment, the concentration of land ownership, and expanded social differentiation.

Despite its exclusion from the formal wage market, until recently women's farm labor was central to agricultural production, particularly in post-harvest processing. Working in their own homesteads or those of more prosperous neighbors, women from poor and middle-income families were able to contribute to household incomes while maintaining some level of purdah. Increasing landlessness, male unemployment, and the mechanization of agricultural processes have significantly altered the lives of most rural women. Conservative estimates suggest a 10.5 percent growth rate in the female labor force between 1974 and 1984.[35] The composition of households has also changed, with many women now seeking employment not to supplement family income but to provide any income at all. In addition, divorces and desertions by male income earners have risen sharply in the face of mounting economic crises, thereby increasing the number of effective female-headed households. Official figures from 1988–1989 estimate that about 14 percent of all households were headed by females.[36] The average monthly income from such households is 35 percent lower than that of male-headed households, reflecting the pervasive gender discrimination in the labor market.[37]

Many women have been forced to migrate to urban areas, often by themselves, in search of employment. Women migrants to the cities frequently seek work in garment manufacturing, the showcase of export-oriented industrialization in Bangladesh and the country's largest foreign exchange earner. Long hours, low wages, and uncertain terms of employment characterize the conditions of work for the approximately 800,000 women in this industry. In many ways, the lifestyle of garment workers breaches the limits of female "respectability." These young women often live alone, that is, without a male guardian, in slums or in women's hostels. They are forced to work until very late at night, sometimes all night, to complete factory orders. On both counts, their respectability is thrown into question. Moreover, many have developed highly visible modern consumer habits, such as wearing makeup, shopping as a pastime, and going to the cinema and the park for recreation. Thus their presence is marked even in their leisure time. The presence of young girls and women commuting to work has certainly shifted the tenor of urban public spaces that, even twenty years ago, were overwhelmingly male-dominated.

The encroachment of these "garment girls" on conventionally male social and economic spaces has generated widespread anxiety. By their very visibility, factory workers articulate both fears of unregulated female sexuality and the threat of the usurpation of male economic roles. My research indicates that in an economic context that marginalizes male labor, their high profile occupation renders garment workers permanently and peculiarly anomalous,[38] for factory workers call into question not only their own respectability but also the new social order configured by globalization and the feminization of labor. This is one explanation for the virulence of the hostility, mainly verbal, to which most garment workers are subjected in public places.

The social impact of rising poverty and inequality can be gauged by the growing incidence of trafficking, prostitution, and dowry demands since independence. Although a strictly causal relationship between poverty and violence against women is difficult to establish, violence against women has taken new and disturbing forms such as acid throwing, abductions, and dowry deaths.[39] The causes for the unprecedented rise in the demand for dowry and violence associated with such demands, relatively uncommon phenomena until the late 1970s, are still not clear.[40] In the early to mid-1990s, the form of violence against women that captured public attention most dramatically was associated with the Islamic fatwa. Spontaneous religious courts, which had turned their gaze on women, condemned to death by stoning or burning at the stake, among other things, those they declared guilty. Taslima Nasreen was the most prominent victim of the spate of fatwas that emerged at this time.

NGOS AND THE CULTURE OF THE FATWA

In order to understand the rise in the incidence of fatwas relating to women, we have to step back and examine specific development activities in Bangladesh. A prominent feature of development is the dominating presence of NGOs, particularly in rural areas. The proliferation of NGOs has gone hand in hand with the country's rising dependence on foreign aid. As of 1994, there were 15,676 registered NGOs in the country, of which 676 were authorized to accept foreign donations.[41] Unofficial estimates are much higher. Whatever the exact figure, it is safe to say that NGOs figure prominently in the rural economy, representing a significant proportion of available resources.

A primary focus of NGO activities in Bangladesh has been on women's empowerment and consciousness raising, mainly through the generation of income-earning projects. Women's projects are particularly popular because, as discussed earlier, targeting women is a relatively easy mode of soliciting external resources. Some indigenous organizations, such as the Grameen Bank and Bangladesh Rural Advancement Committee (BRAC), have attained high profiles internationally for their successful credit programs targeted at poor village women. Intended to generate income-earning activities and promote empowerment, Grameen Bank loans require no collateral. Grameen Bank loan recipients have been excellent debtors: the recovery rate of loans, which average $150, is over 98 percent.[42]

Unlike the majority of smaller NGOs, Grameen and BRAC have vast operations across Bangladesh; in fact, the former is no longer strictly an NGO since the government has a share in it. Thus, it would be misleading to discuss all NGOs in monolithic terms, for they are extremely heterogeneous in size, range of operations, and ideological orientation. With certain exceptions, however, their main activities—providing credit, creating income generating programs, offering educational, health, and birth control services—are designed primarily to alleviate poverty without initiating any structural transformations of society. Yet, with a presence in rural areas strong enough for one commentator to label them a parallel government,[43] NGOs have come to represent both the disruption and the consolidation of local systems of selective patronage and power.

> In keeping with the system of patron-client relationships NGOs are considered as new patrons bringing with them access to external resources. In a pervasive political system where accelerating aid-dependence has meant that governmental successes are measured according to the quantum of aid each government brings in, NGO resources are zealously sought after. Rather than promoting self-reliance, the NGO presence reinforces the patron-client relationship; either NGOs replacing old patrons or colluding with old patrons.[44]

At the same time, money channeled into the countryside to "strengthen Islamic values" offers alternative sources of patronage, enabling Jamaat and other extremist religious groups to build up a sustainable rural power base. As Feldman notes, it is not surprising that in competing for scarce resources, proselytizing is combined with social welfare to extend resources to the rural poor.[45]

NGOs, especially those with foreign affiliations, have been the sustained target of Islamist rhetoric. They have always faced some resistance from local religious leaders, but there now appears to be a much more concerted effort to galvanize opposition against NGOs in the name of Islam and of protecting women. Conjuring at once threats to Islam as well to the established order, NGOs are condemned as "anti-Islamic, anti-state and anti-people";[46] extremists claim they seek to destroy the Islamic way of life and compel women to act in an un-Islamic way. Occasionally, there are claims of forced conversions to Christianity.

The social order Islamist parties seek to protect includes hierarchical gender practices that clash overtly with the ideologies of NGOs. Regardless of the degree of their success, NGOs have become a powerful symbol of change in the domain of gender relations. Their intensive activities have opened up new opportunities for mobilizing women, making them literally more visible and offering possible alternatives to lives circumscribed by existing structures of domination. Women NGO staff in particular have been harassed and attacked by religious extremist groups. Schools set up by NGOs as well as their offices have been set on fire. Curiously, despite the anti-Christian rhetoric, no missionary schools were attacked, only those funded by NGOs.[47] *Khutba*s (sermons) in local mosques have directed men to divorce their wives if they worked with NGOs. In one instance, families sending women and children to schools set up by BRAC were declared social outcasts and told that their dead would be denied an Islamic burial.[48] On several occasions, horrifying forms of punishment— including stoning, caning, and burning at the stake—were sanctioned or condoned by men claiming to represent Islam and tradition.[49] No studies are available yet on the number, frequency, and geographical distribution of these fatwas. Most were scattered across rural Bangladesh and took place in the early and mid-1990s. Statistical significance aside, the violent censure of women who supposedly deviated from the prescriptions of correct Islamic behavior as laid down by local leaders was prevalent enough to indicate a crisis of major proportions.

The proliferation of fatwas against women—inevitably from disempowered backgrounds—partly represents the success of Islamist groups in generating support on a platform of pro-Islamic, anti-Western sentiment, drawing in at the same time the interests of the local elite. Attacking women's projects sponsored by NGOs has become an effective means of fighting NGO influence in general. The Coordinating Council of Human Rights in Bangladesh has suggested that economic factors may partly motivate clerics to issue fatwas against NGOs. Madrasas are losing students to NGO education programs; rural moneylenders, along with the clergy and large landowners from the local elite, are being replaced by NGOs that provide low interest loans.[50] This allows for the emergence of newly configured alliances between religious leaders and locally dominant figures. The intensification of corrupt patronage systems sustained by foreign assistance and the increasing presence of, and opposition to, NGOs provide a fertile ground for Islamist rhetoric.

Further, the inability of successive governments to establish political legitimacy by democratic means has produced a situation in which the official judicial system has been all but supplanted in many areas. Particularly in more remote regions, the groundwork has been laid for the dispensation of justice through newly reconfigured networks of power. Thus, for instance, the *shalish* has taken on a new life as arbiter of Islamic morality and justice. Essentially an arbitrating mechanism, the shalish has historically been a site for alternative dispute resolution, usually the mediation of family or land disputes. It has no legal sanction, and its opinions carry no legal weight. It is presided over by the male elders and religious leaders of a community. The former include large landowners, moneylenders, and traders as well as powerful local government office holders—chairmen and members of administrative units in charge of disbursing development resources. As a rule, women are excluded from membership, although the shalish is responsible for policing morality and preserving the social order. In practice, this frequently translates into maintaining class and gender domination:

> *Shalishkars* [members of the shalish] lay down prescriptive codes of approved behavior for the members of all classes belonging to their *shamaj* [community] groups, as well as censoring those, including women, who are deemed to have displayed forms of "deviant behavior." In other words, it is the male leadership of the dominant class which manipulates the rules of social institutions to restrict and regulate the movement and activities of all women, inclusive of those from the poorest classes (and whose men-folk are not in a position to become shalishkars). Male shamaj leadership is enthusiastically aided and abetted in this role by the religious functionaries at the village level. Often, the women concerned are simply placed in the role of "symbolic objects," and contentions about their position and honor (*izzat*) mask deeper conflicts about social political and economic issues between male leaderships of the shamaj groups concerned.[51]

Clearly, women of all classes and men who do not possess the requisite social standing are always in danger of being marginalized in shalish proceedings.

The shalish in contemporary Bangladesh has been reconstituted within the terms of modernity; it is not "a throwback to the obscurantism and barbarism of the Middle Ages," as one magazine characterized it.[52] Although the control of female sexuality and the maintenance of class domination have remained constant, the shift to exclusively Islamic judgments is new. Village religious leaders and other powerful figures are reformulating their legitimacy by setting up Islamic courts in the name of tradition. In the process, they are supplanting judicial authority. A placard at a women's rally in Dhaka put it succinctly: "Judges and magistrates stay home; the cleric now metes out justice."

One factor in the continued success of the extralegal activities of the shalish was the inaction and even covert support of the BNP government, during whose tenure fatwas against women became a serious problem. In fact, neither the government nor the opposition demonstrated very much interest in the issue at the time. The political climate was such that neither side wanted to alienate the public in a struggle that could be perceived as being anti-Islamic. The result was that women's bodies and sexuality continue to be contested terrain, especially in rural Bangladesh.

THE USES OF THE FATWA—TASLIMA NASREEN

It is not incidental that women's alleged crimes invariably involve the transgression of moral boundaries. As women have become more visible through the activities of NGOs, male anxieties about gender relations have been precipitated, feeding directly into debates on Islamism and developmentalism. Attacks on women and NGOs sexualize and criminalize women's activities within the disciplinary framework of an existing patriarchal structure. The Islamic rhetoric is easy to add on. From this perspective, the fatwa on Taslima Nasreen can be interpreted as another attempt to maintain a patriarchal social order threatened by the possibility of change.[53] The chain of fatwas on women that succeeded Nasreen's case bears witness to the danger she came to represent. However, the Nasreen case is more complex, a reflection of broader struggles for power within an increasingly polarized political landscape.

A trained physician, Taslima Nasreen is a prolific writer whose works were published by various Bangladeshi journals and presses for several years before she became an international celebrity. Nasreen had gained a respectable following for her courageous and blunt opinions on gender discrimination and sexual violence in society. At the same time, her open celebration of female sexuality as well as her anti-Islamic stance made her work the subject of widespread debates. She drew the wrath of many people for her explicit criticism of Islam, which she blamed for the plight of Bangladeshi women.

Ironically, it was not her writings on Islam that created the trouble but instead a novella entitled *Lajja* (Shame), which she wrote to protest communalism and fundamentalism on the Indian subcontinent. Published in February 1993, it was penned in the aftermath of the destruction of the Babri Mosque in India in December 1992 and the subsequent riots in which several thousand Indian Muslims were killed. Events in India led to a backlash in Bangladesh, where Hindu families were persecuted and Hindu property destroyed. *Lajja* is the story of a Hindu family born and brought up on the soil of Bangladesh but eventually forced to migrate to India because of communalism. The story is a mixture of fact and fiction, statistics and newspaper clippings, although the reader has no way of distinguishing fact from fiction. The novel sold for several months on the open market before it was banned by the BNP government in July 1993, on the grounds that it contained material "prejudicial to the state, which might create misunderstanding and mistrust among different communities living in exemplary harmony in the country."[54]

In September of 1993, a heretofore unknown group called the Council of Soldiers of Islam, based in northern Bangladesh, accused Nasreen of offending the religious sentiments of Muslims by writing *Lajja* and offered a cash reward for her death. Although the group retracted the fatwa, it continued to agitate against Nasreen, demanding she be tried for blasphemy. The writer's position became more precarious when, in an interview she gave in May 1994 to an Indian newspaper *The Statesman*, she was quoted as saying that the Qur'an should be thoroughly revised. Nasreen clarified her stand in a subsequent letter by stating that she had advocated a revision in the Shari'a, not changes in the Qur'an. Despite this, several extremist religious groups called for her execution.

In the meantime, the Bharatiya Janata Party (BJP), the right-wing Hindu nationalist party in India, began to distribute free copies of *Lajja* in northern India. Translated into Hindi, the bootleg BJP version included sections not in the original novel. Combined with widespread propaganda about the dangers of Bangladeshi Muslims "infiltrating" India, it was the perfect complement to the party's message of the dangers to the majority Hindu population from Muslims and of its construction of India as a homeland for Hindus: ultimately, all Muslims could be cast as outsiders. It is deeply ironic that, of all parties, the BJP was able to appropriate and exploit Nasreen's work so ably. After all, *Lajja* had been written in response to the destruction of the Babri Mosque, for which the BJP and its allies were squarely to blame.[55]

The Bangladeshi government, invoking an old colonial statute, subsequently charged Nasreen with the criminal offense of deliberately hurting the sentiments of some sections of the citizens of Bangladesh.[56] Nasreen went into hiding for two months until, in August 1994, under pressure from the international community, the government withdrew the warrant against her. She left for Sweden shortly thereafter, presumably with tacit government support.

Nasreen was not the first intellectual to speak out against discrimination toward minorities or to criticize Islam openly. It is the timing and the nature of her political interventions that allowed her to be so easily manipulated. Nasreen's facile use of orientalist imagery, without any reference to her own political location, made her texts perfect fodder for propaganda for both Hindu and Muslim religious extremists and for the Bangladeshi state. Her popularity in India coincided with a general rise in hostility toward Muslims there.

In the global context the attention she generated needs little elaboration. In the post–Cold War Euro-American imagination and foreign policy, "Islamic fundamentalism" had replaced communism as the major threat to Western democracy by the 1990s:

> Since the collapse of the Berlin Wall and the unanticipated demise of the Soviet Union it appears that both the U.S. State Department and Western media are on a hunt for an enemy. Unless an enemy is found, superiority cannot be established. To prove something sacred the profane needs to be

identified; an "other" needs to be created, not to mention a "demonic other."[57]

Nasreen's predicament, read as a conflict between democracy and Islam, served to justify such fears. Indeed, Nasreen was not only a "female Rushdie" but was better than Rushdie; she could expose the patriarchal as well as the authoritarian aspects of Islam. For in the arsenal of orientalist imagery, the fear of the abrogation of women's civil liberties under Islamic rule is elementary. Moreover, Western feminists who championed Nasreen's rights as a woman and a writer could lionize her as a heroic individual in an oppressive society and at the same time reaffirm their positional superiority.

At the national level, it is critical to note that Nasreen's arrest coincided with an emerging alliance between the Jamaat-i-Islami and the Awami League in an effort to bring down the BNP government. In turn, the government sought to deflect public attention and split the opposition by presenting itself as the custodian of religion and morality.[58] The effect was to provide covert support to the fragmented and scattered religious parties around the country. A motley crew of Islamists brought out massive demonstrations in all the major cities against the threat to Islam and to Bangladeshi sovereignty that Taslima Nasreen supposedly represented. The attacks on women and NGOs in the name of Islam escalated during this period, but neither of the two main political parties, the Awami League and the Bangladesh Nationalist Party, took a public stand against them. Neither side, it seemed, could afford to alienate the Jamaat-i-Islami and its supporters. The Awami League, despite its image as secular and progressive, remained silent on the issue of Taslima Nasreen as well. The major women's groups, other social activists, journalists, lawyers, and writers were those in the forefront of resistance to the Islamists.

One repercussion of these political maneuvers was that they allowed the grounds for further discussion to be set by the political agendas of the government and religious extremists. The ensuing debates came to be overdetermined by facile oppositions between secularism and Islamism, in which Islam stood for the antithesis of modernity and democracy. Islamists appropriated Nasreen as a sign of the most corrupting influences of Westernization and feminism, a sexual libertarian whose views threatened to usurp the social and moral order. To her supporters, Taslima Nasreen represented the forces of reason and progress, an iconoclast fearlessly exposing women's oppression that was all the more commendable for its personalized expression. In the highly charged political environment, public dialogue about issues of religion, secularism, or sexuality and violence were displaced by the pressure to take sides. In the circumstances, any criticism of Taslima Nasreen's opinions appeared to be a strike against progress and modernity or, worse, support for religious extremism. Both Islamists and secularists (these terms do not refer to two homogeneous and well-defined groups by any means) assume an opposition between Islam and modernity and often identify religion with fundamentalist politics. Yet the opposition is false: secularism and Islamism are both modernist terms, and both sides are contesting on the ground of modernity.

The Islamist identification of Nasreen with the dangers of feminism and the conflation of her views with those of any who spoke out on women's issues made activism on women's behalf much more difficult. In an atmosphere of bipolar possibilities, whether or not they shared her views, all "feminists" were potentially marked as "other Taslima Nasreens." This may partly explain the reluctance of feminist groups in Bangladesh to extend support to Nasreen. In an excellent essay on the subject, Ali Riaz has suggested that the silence of women's groups can be explained by examining the content of Nasreen's writings. Her focus is explicitly on the female body and sexuality, subjects that are taboo in public discourse. Feminist groups, according to Riaz, have chosen to operate within the constraints of a dominant discourse in which woman's control over sexuality is not an issue open for debate. The relative indifference of feminist groups can then be interpreted as pragmatic and rational.[59] However, it would be unfair to categorize all feminist groups in Bangladesh as "strategically puritanical." After all, if individual feminists could challenge a military dictator's decision to make Islam the national religion in the Supreme Court, as they had done under General Ershad's rule, they could come out openly in support of Taslima Nasreen. In this case, all feminists had a difficult time creating a middle ground for dialogue. Speaking from my own location as a Bangladeshi feminist on the outside of such events, it is precisely the content of Nasreen's writings that is problematic for feminist politics in general. Riaz states that in publicly discussing sexuality and sexual desire, Nasreen is indulging in a subversive act. I reproduce one of the examples he cites below:

> Although newspapers in Bangladesh regularly publish news about young girls in rural areas being forced by their parents to marry older men, hardly anybody investigates the causes. This is seen as a normal thing and justified on the ground that since older men need to have someone as company, they marry to have someone who would take care of them. Some even refer to the fact that the Prophet Muhammad also married at an older age. Nasrin, who is a medical doctor, challenges the common interpretation and presents a physiological cause. According to her, . . . after the age of fifty, every man runs the risk of prostate enlargement . . . which increases sexual drive, and that is why older men marry young girls. After a while, the sexual drive declines and the man becomes impotent. But the girl at the height of her youth faces a situation where she has to suppress her sexual desire. Nasrin contends that this behavior of older men should be viewed as a disease and treated, instead of being regarded as acceptable. I found her position with regard to sexuality quite close to that of Foucault.[60]

This is a rather extreme example of Nasreen's views, but I have chosen it to respond to those who would privilege the liberal framework in which she operates. On closer inspection, Nasreen's alternative interpretation appears neither subversive nor Foucauldian. In fact, she actively participates in reproducing what Foucault would call the "effects of modernity." Her understanding of the predicament of young girls rests on her superior understanding of physiological processes, and her solution, too, lies in medicine. Men are pathologized as victims of their bodies (they couldn't help it, right?), and women wait to be rescued by the truth revealed in science. Medicalizing the subject begs the question of why this is not a more universal problem. Moreover, not only does this analysis lack any historical or contextual specificity, it is indifferent to the social distribution of power. The language of medicine obviates the necessity to examine possible reasons that compel parents to force their daughters into such marriages. Poverty, dowry expenses, political coercion, all are displaced by her emphasis on sexuality as the driving force of life, a purely biological phenomenon empty of any social content.

For all of Nasreen's iconoclastic pronouncements, sexuality in her work is not as politicized as it is personalized. The narrow lens through which she views the world cannot contain the implications of her writing, either on Islam or on sexuality. Intended to open up discussions of the "unspeakable," Nasreen's interventions often have the effect of containing them in an essentialist framework.

CONCLUSION

The strategic deployment of the "woman question" in Bangladesh has been critical in local politics, nationalist rhetoric, and the international context. Women's bodies were invoked in the nationalist struggle to negotiate a specific set of meanings for a secular Bengali culture. In the contemporary period, a dismal economic landscape characterized by competition for resources and patronage has created a space in which Islamists and NGOs are pitted against each other, with control over women one ground for the ensuing struggles. Gender issues manifest most transparently the contradictions in state and developmentalist discourses as Bangladesh's march toward modernity clashes overtly with its desire to be part of a Muslim brotherhood. State-sponsored Islamization has been a highly selective process with respect to women. Officially, there have been no explicit steps taken to limit women to the domestic sphere or to enforce controls over deportment or work spaces. On the contrary, the perceived need to tap into women's labor both to access foreign funds and to promote effective development has meant that official rhetoric embraces the full participation of women in the public sphere. Nevertheless, confronted with a weak state structure that is precariously dependent upon foreign assistance, suc-

cessive regimes have created the conditions or have been directly responsible for increased Islamist activities in Bangladesh. In fact, by maintaining
silence on religious violence against women, the state implicitly endorses
such actions.

For the aid-dependent state, the situation involves negotiating potentially slippery territory, for it must remain accountable to its own social
and political context while mediating pressures from the donor community
and the global economy. These multiple and intersecting pressures are produced through shifting global and local interdependencies. On the one
hand, the state has to accommodate the demands of capital and profit entailed by aid-dependency, liberalization, and the export economy, a situation in which women's labor is deployed in a specific developmentalist
mode. On the other, it must recognize a variety of other lobbies representing the national interest, including the Islamists. National discourses on
gender, then, are constituted through these competing and not necessarily
converging claims.

NOTES

I should like to thank Koushik Ghosh, Manisha Lal, Pratyoush Onta, and the
anonymous reviewer for their comments on the first draft of this essay; Herbert
Bodman and Nayereh Tohidi for their patience; and David Ludden for many stim-
ulating conversations along the way.

1. See Sarah White, *Arguing with the Crocodile: Gender and Class in
Bangladesh* (London: Zed Press, 1992), 16.

2. World Bank, *Bangladesh: Strategy Paper on Women in Development* (Report no. 7899-BD, February 1990), 1.

3. For instance: Andrew Parker, Mary Russo, Doris Summer, and Patricia Yea-
ger, eds., *Nationalisms and Sexualities* (New York: Routledge, 1992); Kumkum
Sangari and Sudesh Vaid, eds., *Recasting Women: Essays in Colonial History* (New
Delhi: Kali for Women, 1989); Valentine Moghadam, ed., *Gender and National
Identity: Women and Politics in Muslim Societies* (London: Zed Books, 1994); and
Nira Yuval Davis and Floya Anthias, eds., *Woman, Nation, State* (New York: St.
Martin, 1989).

4. Lydia Liu, "The Female Body and Nationalist Discourse," in Inderpal Gre-
wal and Karen Caplan, eds. *Scattered Hegemonies* (Minneapolis: University of
Minnesota Press, 1994), 37.

5. The census of 1981 classified 86.6 percent of the population as Muslim,
12.1 percent as Hindus, and the remainder as Christians, Buddhists, and adherents
of "tribal" religions. Most Muslims in Bangladesh are Sunni and follow the Hanafi
school of jurisprudence. Figures quoted in Amnesty International, *Bangladesh:
Fundamental Rights of Women Violated with Virtual Impunity* (October 1994), 5.

6. See Rafiuddin Ahmed, *The Bengali Muslims: A Quest for Identity* (Delhi:
Oxford University Press, 1981); and Ashim Roy, *The Islamic Syncretic Tradition in
Bengal* (Princeton: Princeton University Press, 1983).

7. This period marked the crystallization of a predominantly Hindu nationalist
movement located in Bengal and was also critical in constructing "Hindu" and "Muslim" as fixed religious identities. For a variety of reasons, most nationalist leaders

were middle-class Hindu males, who consistently invoked "Hindu" symbols to construct and promote an indigenous Bengali culture. The implicit interchangeability of Hindu and Bengali in their discourse excluded to a great extent the participation of Muslims in the nationalist movement. The freezing of these terms was also greatly facilitated by the colonial production of knowledge and the perceived need of the British Raj to enumerate the various groups under their administration. Thus, the intersection of colonialist, orientalist, and nationalist discourses was responsible for the production of "Hindu," "Muslim," and "Bengali" as terms with relatively fixed and oppositional meanings in the nineteenth century.

8. Rehnuma Ahmed, "Women's Movement in Bangladesh and the Left's Understanding of the Women Question," *Journal of Social Studies* (Dhaka) 30 (1985): 47.

9. Naila Kabeer, "Subordination and Struggle: Women in Bangladesh," *New Left Review* (London) 168 (1988): 110.

10. S. A. Hossain, "Fatwa in Islam: Bangladesh Perspective," *Daily Star* (Dhaka), December 28, 1994, 7.

11. At the UN Conference on Women held in Beijing in September 1995, a member of the official Pakistani delegation suggested that the Pakistani government should formally apologize to Bangladesh for war crimes against women. Pakistan's Prime Minister Benazir Bhutto responded that she had no knowledge of such events in 1971 (as reported in *Bhorer Kagoj* [Dhaka], September 22, 1995), 1.

12. This has been a notable theme in plays commemorating independence and Victory Day, written for the state-run Bangladesh Television.

13. White, *Arguing with the Crocodile*, 12.

14. See Naila Kabeer, *Reverse Realities* (London: Verso, 1994).

15. Ziaur Rahman was chief of army staff from 1975 but did not formally take over as president until April 1977.

16. Proclamation Order No. 1 of 1977.

17. I do not mean to imply that there is necessarily an opposition between Islamization and women's public labor opportunities, only that donors such as Saudi Arabia might very well see the two moves as contradictory.

18. Kabeer, "Subordination," 114.

19. Shelley Feldman, "(Re)presenting Islam: Manipulating Gender, Shifting State Practices and Class Frustrations" (forthcoming), 16.

20. Kabeer, "Subordination," 91.

21. Shelley Feldman, "Crisis, Islam and Gender in Bangladesh: The Social Construction of a Female Labor Force," in L. Beneria and S. Feldman, eds., *Unequal Burden: Economic Crises, Persistent Poverty and Women's Work* (Boulder: Westview, 1992), 113.

22. Government of Bangladesh, Constitution of 1972, Article 2A, established by Constitution (Eighth Amendment) Act No. 30 of 1988. Islam is the official religion of the state; the measure does not declare Bangladesh an Islamic state enjoined to follow Shari'a law.

23. S. Amin and S. Hossain, "Women's Reproductive Rights and the Politics of Fundamentalism," *The American University Law Review* 44, no. 4 (1995): 1339.

24. National [NGO] Preparatory Committee for the World Conference on Human Rights, *Development, Democracy and Human Rights in Bangladesh* (Dhaka: National Preparatory Committee, 1993), 18.

25. Amnesty International, *Bangladesh: Fundamental Rights*, 3.

26. Jamaat-i-Islami, *Manifesto* (n.d.), sec. 12, 5.

27. See Joel Beinin and Joe Stork, eds., *Political Islam: Essays from Middle East Report* (Berkeley: University of California Press, 1997).

28. Ayesha Jalal, *Democracy and Authoritarianism in South Asia* (New Delhi: Cambridge University Press, 1995), 121.

29. Dina Siddiqi, "The Festival of Democracy: Media and Elections in Bangladesh," *Asian Journal of Communication* (Special Issue on Media and Elections) 6, no. 2 (1996).

30. Beinin and Stork, *Political Islam*, 20–21.

31. See, for instance, Susan Holcombe, *Managing to Empower: The Grameen Bank's Experience of Poverty Alleviation* (Dhaka: University Press, 1995).

32. World Bank, *Bangladesh: Recent Economic Developments and Priority Reform Agenda for Rapid Growth* (Report no. 13875-BD, 1995), 1; see also Rehman Sobhan, *The Crisis of External Dependence: The Political Economy of Foreign Aid to Bangladesh* (London: Zed Press, 1982).

33. Between 1973–1974 and 1988–1989, the aggregate share of the bottom 40 percent of the population declined from 18.3 to 17.5 percent of total income. The corresponding figure for the top 10 percent increased from 28 to 31 percent: Government of Bangladesh, Bureau of Statistics, *Household Expenditure Survey 1988–89* (Dhaka: Government of Bangladesh), 31.

34. The absolute poverty line is defined by minimum energy requirements as recommended by a joint World Health Organization/Food and Agriculture Organization group for South Asia for each age group. Adjusted for the age and occupational profile of Bangladesh, the weighted average per capita daily intake corresponding to the absolute poverty line is estimated at 2,122 calories. The cutoff for the hard-core poverty line is 85 percent (1,805 calories) of this intake: see ibid., 31.

35. Sobhan, *Crisis of External Dependence*, 73.

36. Government of Bangladesh, *Household Expenditure Survey*, 41.

37. Ibid.

38. Dina Siddiqi, "Women in Question: Gender and Labor in Bangladeshi Factories" (Ph.D. diss., University of Michigan, 1996).

39. See Roushan Jahan, "Hidden Wounds, Visible Scars: Violence Against Women in Bangladesh," in Bina Agarwal, ed., *Structures of Patriarchy* (London: Zed Press, 1988).

40. See Rahmuna Ahmed and Milu Shamsun Naher, *Brides and the Demand System in Bangladesh* (Dhaka: Centre for Social Studies, 1987).

41. Cited in *Grassroots: An Alternative Development Quarterly* (Dhaka), July-December 1994: 10.

42. Grameen Bank, *Annual Report* (Dhaka: Living Media India, 1994), 13.

43. *India Today*, June 30, 1994, 112.

44. S. M. Hashemi and S. R. Schuler, "State and NGO Support Networks in Rural Bangladesh: Conflicts and Coalitions for Control," Development Research Centre Working Paper 8 (Dhaka, June 1992), quoted in Rosamund Ebdon, "NGO Expansion and the Fight to Reach the Poor," *IDS Bulletin* 26, no. 3 (1995): 51.

45. Feldman, "(Re)presenting Islam," 19.

46. As reported in the *Dhaka Courier*, June 17, 1994, quoted in Amnesty International, *Bangladesh: Fundamental Rights*, 9.

47. I owe this observation to Jude Fernando, who is currently completing a dissertation in NGOs in Bangladesh at the University of Pennsylvania.

48. Amnesty International, *Bangladesh: Fundamental Rights*, 10.

49. Amnesty International, *Bangladesh: Taking the Law into Their Own Hands: The Village Salish* (October 1993), 5.

50. Ibid., 9.

51. S. Adnan, "Birds in a Cage: Institutional Change and Women's Position in Bangladesh," *ADAB News* (Dhaka) 16 (January-February 1989): 6–7.

52. Soutik Biswas, "The Fear of the Fatwa," *India Today*, June 30, 1994, 113.

53. Shelley Feldman makes a similar point in "(Re)presenting Islam."

54. Amnesty International, *Bangladesh: Fundamental Rights*, 14.

55. See David Ludden, ed., *Contesting the Nation: Religion, Community and the Politics of Democracy in India* (Philadelphia: University of Pennsylvania Press, 1996).

56. Under Section 295A of the Bangladesh Penal Code of 1860, which says: "Whoever, with deliberate and malicious intention of outraging religious feelings of any class of the citizens of Bangladesh, by words, either spoken or written, or by visible representations insults or attempts to insult the religion or the religious beliefs of that class, shall be punished with imprisonment . . . for a term which may extend to two years, or with a fine, or both."

57. Ali Riaz, "Taslima Nareen: Breaking the Structured Silence," *Bulletin of Concerned Scholars* 27, no. 1 (1995): 22.

58. For details, see ibid.

59. Ibid., 26.

60. Ibid., 25–26.

12

Urban Minangkabau Muslim Women: Modern Choices, Traditional Concerns in Indonesia

Lucy A. Whalley

Minangkabau as a people and their homeland in West Sumatra, Indonesia, are well known to Western anthropologists because of their system of matrilineal descent and unique traditions known as *adat,* which survived over 100 years of Dutch colonialism, the introduction of a capitalist economy, and the establishment of a modern nation-state after 1948.[1] Beginning in the 1970s, Minangkabau women were increasingly recognized by Western anthropologists as being powerful decisionmakers in family, lineage, business, and community affairs. This observation challenged an older model of matrilineal society in which men were viewed as maintaining control over women in their roles as mother's brother. Despite the burgeoning literature on Minangkabau, the integration and significance of Islam in contemporary Minangkabau daily, symbolic, and spiritual life has been virtually ignored by Western scholars.[2]

When I first traveled to Minangkabau in 1982, I was struck by the high profile of Islam in Minangkabau life, the influence of Islam on the moral values recognized as adat, and women's devotion to Islam. Islam was as much a part of Minangkabau daily life and sense of identity as adat. Women were essential agents in upholding the tenets of adat and Islam and conveying them to future generations. Maintenance of tradition continued to be a dynamic and challenging process for Minangkabau women. Modern Indonesian society presented many choices and dilemmas for generations of young women who were coming of age during the post-1965 New Order of Indonesia's President Suharto, a time of dramatic social, political, and economic transformations.

In this chapter I focus on how both adat and Islam influence the lives of young (15 to 35 years of age), educated, professional, married, and unmarried Minangkabau Muslim women in the urban centers of West Sumatra. While I was living in the cities of Bukit Tinggi, Padang Panjang, and Padang,[3] young women talked to me about their concerns—women's roles, family and kinship obligations, the moral order, religion, and ethnic identity—as they searched for meaning and equilibrium in their changing world, where Islam and matrilineal traditions meet. Their concerns were echoed in the discourse of the national government and the local Minangkabau community. Such discourse is symptomatic of an increasing Minangkabau fear that modernization will result in the sacrifice of moral values based on perceived traditional strengths of family, kinship, and female responsibility bolstered by Islam and adat. Part of the struggle for modernity in Minangkabau has to do with new questions on the meaning of life arising from the influence of the Indonesian educational system, as well as from media images of life, including Muslim life, in other countries. Women as players and symbols are at the center of this struggle for meaning.

Young women, many of whom had grown up in the villages of their mothers, represented the first generations to reap the full benefits of increased educational opportunities supported by the national government in the 1970s. Government-sponsored middle schools and institutions of higher education were located in or near urban areas in West Sumatra and elsewhere in Indonesia. Opportunities for professional or clerical employment were also concentrated in urban areas, with a small number of appointments being available in rural areas. During the 1970s and increasingly into the 1980s, a greater number of women took advantage of various educational programs that prepared them to be teachers, university faculty, technocrats, nurses, dentists, and office workers. These women, like their sisters in much of the Muslim world, have been affected by their participation in mass education. Encouraged by modern instruction, questions arise such as, What is my religion? Why is it important to my life? How do my beliefs guide my conduct? How do I fit into my parents' world of village and tradition?[4]

Young educated women were participants in and purveyors of a national culture that encompassed all citizens of Indonesia regardless of their ethnic origin. In discussions with me, they saw themselves as facilitators of national development and as modern women with lives different from those of their mothers, who had married and had children by their midtwenties and continued to live in their ancestral villages. Instead, they wanted to have an active say in choosing a husband, rather than accepting the choice made by a mother and mother's brother in the traditional way. For these young women, work was a job outside of the home for which they received a wage or a salary. At the same time, these young women respected the lives and traditions of their mothers. The latter represented the cultural heritage of the Minangkabau people, whose ancestral lands and houses were handed down through the lineage from mother to daughter since time immemorial and who were well known since the seventeenth century throughout the Indonesian archipelago for their devotion to Islam.

Young women graduating from high school or a university in the 1980s aspired to enter the newly emergent middle class, characterized by an increasing number of urban professionals who were employed by the government or private businesses.[5] In Minangkabau they contrasted with members of an older middle class who were members of the civil service or were merchants or owners of home industries; this older middle class had developed in the nineteenth century in the Dutch colonial market and administrative centers that later became the cities and towns of the new Indonesian nation.[6] Members of the new middle class in Indonesia were exploring new expressions of material wealth, democracy, Islam, and gender roles. These developments were the most striking in Jakarta, the capital city of Indonesia, but were apparent in the cities of West Sumatra as well.

THE FUTURE OF TRADITION

In this environment of perceived change, young urban Minangkabau women were reassessing the strength and relevance of their traditions. Adat coexists with orthodox Islam and with the traditions developed by the teachers of Islam since the early seventeenth century. An often repeated Minangkabau proverb states that adat sits side by side with Islamic law, which is based on the Qur'an. Minangkabau people view themselves as essentially Muslim. In the areas of etiquette and morality, adat appears to have melded with Islamic teachings. For example, before entering a house, the Muslim greeting is called out to those inside. Also, moral conventions demand that the virginity of unmarried women and the fidelity of married women be preserved.

Since 1600, when Islam is thought to have been introduced into West Sumatra, the teachers of Islam promoted the fundamentals of the faith while accommodating local traditions. The challenge of Islam for Minangkabau continues to be tolerating or expelling local traditions depending on whether or not they are antithetical to Islamic teachings. Minangkabau reformist movements in the early twentieth century, such as the Kaum Muda (Young Group) and the Muhammadiyah, which had its origins in West Java, advocated a return to the original teachings of the Qur'an and Sunna and the use of Islam as a model for the development of modern society.[7] In Minangkabau, at least since the influence of the reformists of the early twentieth century, women have been instrumental in integrating Islam into everyday life while upholding the traditions that continue to distinguish Minangkabau from their neighbors. For example, the first Islamic school for girls in the Indonesian archipelago, the Diniyah Putri, was established in a Minangkabau town by a Minangkabau woman in 1923.

During the 1980s a renaissance of Islam developed among the urban middle class of Indonesia, Minangkabau included.[8] The older Minangkabau middle class—that developed in the highland market towns and administrative centers created by the Dutch—supported the transformations in Muslim practice and education advocated by the reformists. The new middle class sought to revive interest in Islam by focusing on the observance of major events in the Islamic year: the fasting month (Ramadan), the community prayer after the end of the fasting month (Idul Fitri), feasting and visiting following the fasting month, the feast of sacrifice (Idul Adha), and the pilgrimage to Mecca (hajj).[9] Family celebrations commemorating a child's first recitation of the entire Qur'an were escalated into community events with the graduating class parading about the village or neighborhood.[10]

The promotion of Islam was also apparent in the public secular schools.[11] In Minangkabau a religion course on the history and teachings of Islam was required of high school students, the majority of whom were Muslims. At the request of the Muslim students, some public high schools created rooms where students could pray while school was in session. There was a significant increase in the wearing of Muslim dress among high school girls, a practice not allowed by the national government in other Muslim areas of Indonesia.[12] These girls abandoned the short-sleeved white shirt and knee-length gray skirt for a gray head covering that fell over the shoulders, a long-sleeved white tunic, and an ankle-length gray skirt. This alteration in the school uniform was an additional expense for the girl's family, suggesting that middle-class families were more inclined to have the funds to indulge their daughters' increased attention to religion.

During the 1980s the Indonesian state created a favorable environment for conservative religious development, which encouraged religious expression among middle-class Minangkabau. Although the Indonesian state subscribes to a separation of religion and state, it supports monotheistic religions and encourages all its citizens to register themselves as adherents of a religion recognized by the state, that is, Islam, Christianity, Buddhism, or Hinduism. In West Sumatra, government office buildings were outfitted with a special room in which to conduct daily Muslim prayers; female civil servants, mostly Muslim, were encouraged by their division heads to wear Muslim dress; and all government rituals began and ended with an invocation to God. To gain support for the government party GOLKAR (Joint Secretariat of Functional Groups) in the 1987 elections, the government provided funding to build a record number of mosques. Through the Department of Religion, the national government sponsored Qur'anic arts competitions at the district, regional, and national levels. Crowds paying assiduous attention to wearing Muslim dress turned out to observe these competitions. The national government sponsored a savings plan through local banks for accruing money to fund the pilgrimage to Mecca, one of the five pillars of Islam, and arranged transportation and accommodations for the participants.

FAMILY AND KIN

In Minangkabau religion is thought to nurture strength and protect family ties, and adat is intricately tied to maintaining family relations. Therefore Islam is perceived to support adat. Young people in Minangkabau grow up immersed in family relations that maintain adat. Female children learn that women are responsible for the welfare of the household and for the maintenance of relations that define the household. Family in Minangkabau refers to the conjugal unit of wife, husband, and children and the kindred of the wife and husband.

In the 1980s the members of the conjugal unit were the immediate focus of concern in everyday life. A wife has certain obligations to her father's side of the family and to her husband's kin that are expressed on ritual occasions such as births, weddings, and funerals. However, her major kin obligations are to her mother and her mother's siblings together with their children.

Male authority in Minangkabau does not follow the same lines as in those societies in which Islam has been superimposed on patrilineal systems that favor the authority of fathers, husbands, and brothers,[13] or in Malaysia where Islamic law has supplanted adat.[14] In these cases, marriage implies a transfer of male control over women, from father to husband. In the Minangkabau case, marriage does not necessarily mean the subordination of women to male authority. In Minangkabau Islam is thought to strengthen the bonds of marriage and to advocate complementarity in the roles of husband and wife. Islamic law is applied to certain aspects of marriage and divorce. However, any male authority that can be construed by the Minangkabau or their scholarly interlocutors as having been granted by Islam is mediated by adat and Minangkabau practice.

A Minangkabau man marries into his wife's house and resides with her as well as any of her closest female relatives and their families who may choose to live in the same structure. Since the early twentieth century, many Minangkabau nuclear families have preferred to live in separate houses, although the houses may be built in close proximity on the wife's lineage property. Even when a family house is built with contributions from a husband's income on new property in an urban area, the house is considered to be the property of his wife and her daughters.

In the past a husband retained more responsibilities to support his own matrilineage than his wife's family. His children belonged to his wife's matrilineage. During the twentieth century, the investment of the husband in his wife and children has led to more stability in marriages in Minangkabau. The rates of divorce and polygyny are thought to have decreased during the twentieth century.[15] With the growth of economic opportunities resulting from the influence of the Dutch regime and later the development of the Indonesian nation-state, men were able to make greater financial contributions to their households. This factor, coupled with the rise of nuclear family households, the acceptance of the practice of a father's willing to his children his personal property (as distinct from lineage property, which is not his for disposal), and the increasing ability of a father to pay for the education of his children, together served to encourage male investment in stable marriages.

A number of practices were said to be common among an older generation (ages 50 and older) of Minangkabau, such as polygyny, particularly among the aristocracy; unequal treatment of wives by polygynous husbands; the disappearance of husbands after their migration to faraway urban areas; and the offering of incentives by parents for desirable young men to marry their daughters regardless of their earning power. I observed that these practices were still carried out by some Minangkabau, though far less frequently according to my consultants. They were all viewed as undesirable among the young, educated, female generation aspiring to be middle class in urban Minangkabau. Furthermore, according to Indonesian law, civil servants received compensation for one wife and two children only. A Muslim wife, whose husband could potentially have as many as four living wives, must give him permission to take an additional wife. The husband must be able to demonstrate that he can adequately support an additional wife and family.

I cannot definitively state whether the increased investment of a husband in his conjugal family resulted in a decrease of women's power in Minangkabau. In their studies relating to Malaysia, Aihwa Ong and Ingrid Rudie argue that the modernization of Muslim Malay society did result in an increase in male authority consequent to the rise of the nuclear family and male control over the family income. In Minangkabau, however, the rise of the nuclear household has led to the husband contributing more subsistence for his wife and children, allocating inheritance to his children, providing for the education of his children, having moral authority over his wife and children, and having a voice in whom his daughters marry. On the surface, this echoes Ong's discussion of the dependence of Malay masculinity on a man's economic power and moral authority over women. However, I believe that the distribution of power in Minangkabau households is more complex because of the effects of matriliny and adat as well as women's control over social and economic resources.[16]

Households that are solely dependent on a husband's income are a minority in urban and rural Minangkabau. Nevertheless, a husband who is able to contribute monetarily to the household and reside with his family is viewed as having more to say about the affairs of his children. A husband's involvement in household and lineage affairs is also dependent in part on the age of the marriage itself.[17]

Islamic doctrine says that males are responsible for women's welfare, are the spiritual and social leaders of women, and are guardians of the moral order. Generally in a Minangkabau household, the husband has no absolute authority over his wife's affairs. The wife controls the income for household expenses. Her husband's authority is mediated by the concerns of her kin and lineage and by the power of the wife herself in household matters. Yet the wife's concerns extend beyond her husband to the children and her kin. She must strive to have a part in the affairs of her matrilineage. In fact, she may actually spend more time with her children and kin than she does with her husband, unless she and her husband work together. Her parents are frequently taken into her household if they are aging and need to be supported. Representatives of her matrilineage renew their claims to the children through visiting and continued interest and participation in their lives. The husband tends to stay out of his wife's kin's affairs, unless his input or expertise is solicited by her or her kin.

If a husband does not do his share in contributing to the family income, or disappears, his wife can appeal for help from her kin, generally from a brother or her mother's brother, who may be able to contribute monetary aid or help her to find a new, more reliable husband. Should a Minangkabau woman be unhappy in her marriage, she can appeal to her matrikin for support to help her maintain or end the marriage. In the latter case, she may have recourse to Indonesian marriage and Islamic law as well as adat practice. In short, a Minangkabau wife cultivates her relationships with kin, which may have the result, intentional or otherwise, of mediating a husband's power in the household.

Some husbands in Minangkabau forbid their wives to work while they are bearing and raising children, based on a stringent interpretation of the authority of religion. From what she observes in other households, a wife involved in such a marriage, particularly if educated, may complain that she is capable of contributing to the income of the household or that she has a right to self-development. But in many more Minangkabau households, a wife's contribution to the family income, either with money or labor, is considered necessary for the economic security of the household.

The power of husbands is also mediated by senior Minangkabau women who have authority in everyday practice and in planning for the future. Decisionmaking within the household and lineage is ideally based on consensus, even though both male and female leaders and experts are recognized. However, senior women guide decisions for the future regarding the management of household and lineage assets that may affect their status and material success. They profoundly influence those decisions that shape the lives of the household members—which schools to attend, which professions to choose, whom to marry. In consultation with the mother's brother, senior women decide about lineage matters such as marriage arrangements, the management of lineage land and assets, the building and maintenance of lineage houses, the disposition of lineage land, and the timing and organization of rituals.

Through their ability to influence major decisions in the lives of the lineage and household members, these senior women set and maintain the moral standards of Minangkabau society. Younger women anticipate that they will have to gain sufficient knowledge to attend to these matters. Their elders view these matters as their business until they become too old to perform effectively.

Urban upper-middle-class and upper-class practice in Minangkabau does favor the scenario of a husband who can fully support his family so that his wife does not have to work, a lifestyle common to wealthy businessmen or high-ranking government officials. Perhaps in these cases, the husband can claim superior authority in the household or, at least, expect deference from his wife. In the cases of the husband who forbids his wife to work so that she can fulfill her duty to raise their children or of the wife whose husband's income enables her not to work, a strengthening of male authority might be possible in Minangkabau similar to that found in Malaysia by Ong. However, the power and wealth of the wife's lineage would still serve as mediating factors in any calculations of domination. Within the sphere of her lineage, a wife has access to domains in which she can exert power and influence. In short, by upholding Islam and deferring to her husband on certain matters, a woman neither relinquishes power in her household and matrilineage nor the support of her kin.

AN INVESTMENT IN WOMEN

The foregoing discussed the social legacy of young Minangkabau women that supports women's power. Yet despite a woman's level of schooling or status in a profession, full adulthood was considered to be achieved only upon marriage and childbearing. A woman who passed childbearing age without marriage but enjoyed a full professional career was still perceived by the majority of Minangkabau women and men to have a flawed life. She had not fulfilled her calling as a woman to marry, bear female children, and pass on her superior talent to her children. This corresponds to Islamic teachings that counsel that the proper destiny of both women and men is to marry and produce progeny.

For Minangkabau women graduating from high school, enrolling in the tertiary educational system, or working in a profession, life choices appeared different from those available to their mothers. Many women who came of age in the nineteenth and early twentieth century in Minangkabau had achieved literacy in religious schools, of which more were built locally than colonial schools and, later, national government-supported public schools. A few exceptional young women had graduated from a university and entered a profession. In the 1980s higher numbers of young women could expect to graduate from high school, and women entering professions were much more visible.

Sending young women away from home to attend a university or to accept a job had become a more acceptable practice in the 1970s and 1980s, as families became more affluent and more young women became qualified to pursue a tertiary level education. Families were still hesitant, however, to allow their unmarried daughters to accept jobs in areas of Indonesia far from home where no relatives resided to guard the welfare and reputations of their daughters. Daughters preferred to visit their mothers frequently and to attend to their welfare, particularly if the mother were widowed or divorced.

Beyond producing children, young women represent another kind of investment to their families and lineages—an investment in raising the status of the lineage.[18] The primary source of a Minangkabau woman's identity is the "house," which consists of a woman's matrilineage and two affinal groups, namely, those who gave husbands to her lineage (her father's and father's father's matrilineage, etc.) and those males from her lineage (her brothers) who were received as husbands by other lineages.[19] For a Minangkabau house, the potential of its women and the quality of husbands that it is able to attract enables the house and, by extension, the mother's lineage to increase its rank. Husbands instead of wives are exchanged symmetrically among lineages of equal rank and asymmetrically among lineages of different rank. A woman's marriage rank depends upon the limits, on the one hand, of the lowest-ranking lineage from which her lineage will agree to invite a husband and, on the other, of the highest-ranking lineage into which male members of her lineage can be invited to marry. Thus a woman's present and potential rank is determined by the history of husband exchanges with lineages who have given and received husbands to and from her own lineage.

Minangkabau, whether they have achieved or are aspiring to wealth and power, have a long tradition of concern for rank, expressed in the complicated politics of marriage and ritual life. Marriage represents an exchange between two lineages in which both sides may gain, maintain, or lose rank depending upon the perceived assets of the male marriage candidates that have been exchanged between them.

Differences in hierarchy and status among matrilineages fuel the making of marriage alliances. The Minangkabau recognize a hierarchy of aristocracy, commoners, and former slaves who were assimilated into matrilineages. The rank of aristocracy is measured by lineage ownership of land, political titles held by males, and wealth. Houses of less rank try to marry up, that is, prefer to acquire husbands from aristocratic houses, which means a loss of status for the aristocratic house. But by receiving demands for husbands from lower houses, the aristocratic house gains status. Houses of the former slave rank, however, must marry among themselves and can never expect to acquire a husband of aristocratic status.

Rank was traditionally defined within the village hierarchy; each village functioned as a separate political unit prior to the Dutch restructuring of indigenous government in the late nineteenth century. Village endogamy in the arrangement of marriages is still commonly preferred by many Minangkabau because a lineage's rank can be investigated more thoroughly among those who are better known to those contemplating the marriage. The majority of urban-dwelling Minangkabau continue to identify themselves with their home village and maintain close relationships with their kin through exchanges of news, material items, money, and often visits. Among urban Minangkabau who have become middle class, markers of status generally gained in an urban environment, such as higher education and professional employment, are figured into calculations of rank. Particularly well-to-do merchants and the professional elite rival the old landed aristocracy in the villages in terms of their income and prestige. However, many of these urban Minangkabau continue to seek to legitimate themselves with reference to their village hierarchy by carrying out rituals and claiming titles that may confer on them aristocratic status.

Differences in rank are not readily apparent in daily Minangkabau life and are only alluded to indirectly in everyday speech. However, distinctions in rank become apparent in the fine calculations and negotiations of making a marriage choice and in the process of marriage ritual.

I observed a trend among urban, educated, professional, middle-class parents of allowing their children to marry outside their home region if all other qualifications—such as religion, education, potential earning power, and moiety exogamy (marrying outside one's own group or related lineage)—were judged to be equal or compatible. Following the teachings of Islam, Minangkabau parents were adamant in their refusal to allow their daughters to marry non-Muslims because women were thought to be strongly influenced by their husbands, and mothers feared the loss of their daughter's children, who are of their own blood, to an infidel religion. Parents seemed slightly less concerned with the prospect of their sons acquiring a non-Muslim wife because men were said to possess the strength to convince their wives to convert to Islam. Nevertheless, the contemplation of such a marriage would be a matter of serious conflict, particularly if the boy was the only son.

More broadly, women bring to a marriage economic value, traditionally in the form of landholdings and more recently through their business interests or professional employment and the social ties that they control and maintain. Men bring to a marriage the fecundity of their seed and the titles that convey the rank of their matrilineage. In addition, a wealthy but middle-rank husband can invest money in his wife's matrilineage to allow her to acquire land, thus gaining status and access to higher titles, and thereby giving his children the potential for making higher status marriages. A husband can therefore be an asset to his wife's matrilineage and can contribute to his children's abilities to aggrandize the matrilineage.

Women are particularly active in maintaining close ties with kin and retain a lively interest in assessing the potential marriage pool for themselves (if they are unmarried) or for their own children. Previous researchers emphasized the roles of the mother's brother and more recently the father in the making of marriage alliances.[20] Although the father and mother's brother may play important roles as guardians of the process, more recent gender-sensitive research shows that senior women of the lineage, and particularly a girl's mother, are the principal actors.[21] Rural- and urban-dwelling Minangkabau women gather information on potential marriage candidates, determine the timing of the marriage, initiate the marriage negotiations, make the marriage proposal to the representatives of the groom's lineage (his mother and the mother's senior brother), and organize and provide the labor for the entire marriage ritual.

Minangkabau women are very sensitive to upholding the reputation of their houses. Although level of education and employment are included in calculations of a woman's contribution to a marriage in the urban context, the common perception remains that a woman's status can only be activated through marriage, which links her to the reproduction of her lineage. Marriage provides access to a social universe within which women operate with power and authority. A woman's wealth is traditionally reinvested in her children, her younger siblings, and her mother and on ritual display for the purpose of potentially increasing the status of her lineage. Minangkabau women have considerable motivation to invest in adat and its transactions. Thus, educated, professional women, despite their distance from the rural context, endeavor to maintain their reputation in the village.

Losing control over adolescent women and, by extension, access to grandchildren was considered to be a great tragedy for an entire family and lineage. High school and university students did experiment with dating and sex, particularly if they had left their home areas to attend schools in the city. However, most young women and men eventually acceded to the wishes of their parents because they were aware of their identity as lineage members and did not want to jeopardize the future status of their house. Young women were less likely than young men to strike out on their own because they felt that they had much more to lose; their strengths and security were with household and family in the home village.

University-educated women had a tendency to put off marriage until a later age (25 years or older), which they viewed as a form of resistance: a statement of their independence, of their control over their own lives, of personal achievement. However, the longer a woman waited to marry, the more precarious became the balance between self-expression and finding an appropriate husband. Women who were thirty-something and not yet married were considered to be less attractive marriage candidates because their childbearing years had decreased, their physical attractiveness had declined, and their character was less malleable. Minangkabau women and men perceived that there was an optimal time in a person's life to marry. Those women who spent more time in the educational system and worked to establish themselves in a profession before marriage were pushing up against this understood boundary of optimal age for marriage. They tended to marry men of similar abilities and interests even if they were not the ideal choices of those in the village. Older Minangkabau women and men (40 years or older) related to me that a woman's ability to contribute to the reproduction and success of her lineage are considered to be more important than her educational or professional achievements. Such divergent perspectives created conflict and dilemmas for younger, educated Minangkabau women who wished to pursue their personal careers but also to fulfill their obligations to their families and relatives.

Often a Minangkabau's only recourse to escape the demands of adat is to marry out of the region, to establish distance from the heavy and expensive family relationships, or to move to distant Jakarta and assume a new cosmopolitan identity. Yet significantly, a large number of Minangkabau, even when they had moved to urban areas, chose to keep up with calculations in rank, make traditional-style marriage arrangements, and expend large amounts of both money and time to perform a marriage ritual for the aggrandizement of the status they claim. The pathway to marriage and family life was not a clear one for those women who had chosen to develop a contemporary career in a society that placed so much emphasis on a successful marriage. Young women who were making life choices viewed the demands of adat placed on them by their elders as limiting, even though in theory they valued the strength of their traditions.

THE GLORIFICATION OF WIVES AND MOTHERS

In the 1980s in Indonesia, young Muslim women were also receiving the message, both from the national government and from female Muslim leaders in Jakarta, that women's primary roles should be those of wife and mother. As development became one of the major goals of the state, women were enjoined to take responsibility for its success. Government discourse in the media extolled women as the primary educators of the children of the nation and the upholders of a moral order based on family. During the late 1980s, seminars that discussed the dilemma of womanhood as being a choice between family and career were very popular among civil servants at universities and the government Department of Religion at both the regional and national levels. Government representatives participated in the

Muslim discourse that proclaimed women to be the pillars of the family, community, and nation, an exhortation taken from the Prophet Muhammad.

The glorification of wives and mothers also became a dominant theme in the rhetoric of some female Muslim leaders in Jakarta. For example, Zakiah Daradjat, a well-published Minangkabau psychology professor at the prestigious University of Indonesia, was frequently asked to speak on the status and education of Muslim women in Indonesia. Daradjat emphasized that Muslim women have a critical role to play in society as wives and mothers. As wives, for example, women must be willing to create a tranquil, secure, and pleasant atmosphere in the home, following the teachings of Islam.

Both female Muslim leaders and representatives of the national government emphasized the attention the Qur'an and Sunna devote to the roles of women as wife and mother. For instance, an oft-quoted saying of the Prophet Muhammad was, "Paradise lies at the feet of mothers." Another favorite saying used by government officials and female Muslim leaders arises from Qur'anic teachings that women are the primary educators of their children; hence, to educate one woman is to educate an entire family. Although this provides a reasonable argument for the education of women, the founder of the first Islamic girls' school in Minangkabau, Rahmah el Yunusiyah, argued more broadly that "to develop society without the participation of women is like having a bird who wants to fly with only one wing. The education of one woman means the education of all of the people."[22] This educational tradition fits better with Minangkabau perspectives of women filling a wide variety of roles in society.

Examples abound in Minangkabau of accomplished women who have had careers in addition to making a successful marriage—from the small-town entrepreneur to the founder of a popular Muslim girl's school. Islam was not believed to limit women's potential. The prevailing view among young, educated Minangkabau women was that Islam places no restrictions on women for achieving their potential in society. The second head of Diniyah Putri, the first Islamic school for girls in Minangkabau, established in 1923, once explained that she hoped that an education at Diniyah would at least produce individuals who had acquired a knowledge of Islam for themselves. "If they have more to contribute let them be good mothers and educators of their children. Or better yet they can become teachers. At the highest level we hope that some of our students will become leaders in society," she says. Graduates of Diniyah have chosen a wide range of careers in addition to the traditional ones of wife, mother, daughter, sister, and aunt.

Women's education was promoted by reformist Muslims in the early twentieth century, and the reformist perspective that Islam can strengthen modern social life remains popular among urban Minangkabau. As a result of the efforts of early twentieth-century Minangkabau reformers, such as

Rahmah el Yunusiyah and her brother Zainuddin Labay, women were allowed access to Western- and Islamic-style education, acquiring skills enabling them to develop their capabilities in a modernizing society while
being active participants in the Muslim faith. In Minangkabau the impetus of Muslim reform created new opportunities for women, whereas custom counseled that women remain in the domestic domain.

In contemporary Malay society affected by resurgent Islam, the re-
placement of adat with Islamic law, and industrialization, Aihwa Ong sees
the increase of social control and moral authority of males over females.[23]
Unmarried and divorced females are viewed as a danger to the moral order
by resurgent Muslims. Thus a woman's body must be contained and controlled by strict Muslim dress, a visible sign that the moral order has been
reasserted. Certainly, morality and moral authority are major concerns of
the Muslim community in Minangkabau, particularly with regard to unmarried adolescent females. The covering of a woman's body with traditional Minangkabau Muslim dress is regarded as a sign of moral and religious correctness.

The dress preferred by Malay Muslim reformists resembles the *hijab*
advocated by Muslim fundamentalists elsewhere in the Muslim world. In
Minangkabau, however, very few women adopt the more Middle Eastern
style. Instead, new Muslim dress is expressed by the incorporation of the
jilbab, a triangular fabric secured under the chin that covers the body from
the head to below the shoulders, into traditional Minangkabau Muslim
styles, which include a long-sleeved, loose tunic, a sarong, and a filmy
head scarf. The use of the jilbab is popular among university and high
school students. Although for some young women wearing the jilbab may
be merely adopting a new fashion, the jilbab also expresses a new awareness of being Muslim.[24]

For many young, educated, urban Minangkabau women in the 1980s,
adopting the jilbab was viewed as an unnecessary expression of Muslim-
ness and a challenge to their own sense of themselves as devout Muslims.
They tended to wear Western-style dress that eschewed sleeveless tops,
miniskirts, and shorts, while adopting traditional Minangkabau Muslim
dress for special occasions or when they went home to the village. Like all
Minangkabau women, for prayer they wore a clean, white, hooded garment
that covered their bodies from head to knees and a checked pattern sarong,
similar to those worn by men, which extended down over their feet. Although the majority of Minangkabau Muslim leaders agreed that women
should cover themselves except for their faces and hands as directed by the
Qur'an, many young women felt that modest dress, proper demeanor, and
morally correct behavior conveyed a similar message—that Muslim women
should be respected in public and do not deserve to be harassed by men.

In the Minangkabau case, the guardians of morality are the elders of
the matrilineage, mothers and fathers, Muslim leaders, Islamic institutions,

and learned adult community members, both female and male. The foundation of morality in Minangkabau is perceived to be both adat and Islam. There appears to be no fundamental sense in Minangkabau that men are morally superior because of their proclivity to use reason over passion or because of their guardianship role with regard to women, as Ong finds in Malaysian society, even though such concepts exist within Islamic doctrine.

If anything, women are thought to be equally or more morally worthy in Minangkabau because of their idealized function as pillars of the house, family, and community. Minangkabau women are granted moral authority by adat if they demonstrate the strength of character counselled by adat. This ideal woman is honest; intelligent; skillful in the use of language for leadership and instruction; practiced in social interaction; respectful of others; humble; patient; knowledgeable in the practice of etiquette; and in general, vigilant in remembering and upholding adat. These are the same qualities of character advocated for an adat leader such as a lineage leader or mother's brother.

As Ong's findings for Malay society suggest, women can lose power when they are incorporated into the rationale of the capitalist workplace. In Minangkabau the workplace is a location in which relations between men and women do not follow Minangkabau conventions. For example, in local government offices, the head of the department is usually a non-Minangkabau, generally a Javanese senior male, because the national government prefers to hire people from different groups to diffuse the development of regional politics. Such men expect that women will accord them deference because of their higher positions and also because of Javanese domestic conventions that women are caretakers who flatter men rather than productive partners. Although according to Minangkabau tradition, people of power and position should be respected, an obsequious show of deference is viewed as inappropriate. Those in power are supposed to have a democratic spirit, a humble demeanor, and a sense of the perspectives and needs of their constituents.

THE FUTURE OF ADAT

In the two cities of Minangkabau with which I am most familiar, Padang Panjang and Bukit Tinggi, youth organizations and activities were vigorously promoted at the local mosques and prayer houses. I speculated, along with several Minangkabau elders, whether these strident attempts at Islamic education of Minangkabau youth would overtake or diminish their identification with adat. They felt that adat was losing ground in the realm of social control. For instance, the elders told me that a young man used to leave the coffee stand if his mother's brother appeared there, out of respect and fear for the man's power in his matrilineage, yet nowadays the young man calmly remains seated.

In Minangkabau Islam pervades every aspect of mundane life and orders the yearly ritual calendar. At prescribed intervals five times a day, the call to prayer emanates from the numerous mosques and prayer houses in the neighborhoods and villages. Before each prayer the supplicant must bathe in a prescribed manner. If a husband and wife have had sexual intercourse, both the man and woman must bathe completely, including washing their hair. A woman must not pray or fast during menstruation. After her menstruation ends, she must bathe completely before she resumes praying. Islam also has a presence at birth, marriage, and death. Circumcision for boys is an established Muslim practice that occurs somewhere between 10 years of age and puberty. The fasting month divides the year in half. Marriages are held before the fasting month, whereas divorces take place after the fasting month. For many Minangkabau, Islam is a part of daily and ritual life as well as an expression of faith.

Opportunities for Minangkabau children to learn about Islam and to make Islam a part of their daily lives abound in Minangkabau, particularly in the cities. Minangkabau villages, with their men's prayer houses and Islamic schools, were once known as the heartland for Islamic development in the nineteenth century. From the early twentieth century onward, however, Islamic development in the form of the establishment of schools, organizations, and activities centered in Minangkabau cities and in progressive villages.

During the 1970s and 1980s, Minangkabau youth experienced a revolution in education in which the majority of youth were exposed to formal, Western-style secular education and a sampling of products resulting from commerce with the West. Those of the older generation, their teachers, parents, and grandparents, worried that the younger generation had lost its respect for and knowledge of both adat and Islam. In the late 1980s, Minangkabau elders and educators were absorbed in attempting to reclaim their youth from the perceived grasps of a Westernized, secular modernity. Perhaps their concern was fired in part by the government investment in Islamic education and its strategies for luring the support of conservative Muslims and by a general questioning among Muslim intellectuals in Jakarta and Java of the relevance of Islam for addressing the needs and problems of a modern society. This perceived strain with modernity caused some university students to adopt a reformist approach to Islam and to make a concerted effort to apply Islam in their daily lives.

Minangkabau elders, however, were also concerned that young people would not be moved to replicate their elders' command of the knowledge of adat. In 1988, one prominent Minangkabau scholar conducted a project funded by a private Japanese organization, whereby he traveled to Japan to study how the Japanese have so successfully maintained their traditions and preserved their traditional fine arts in a postindustrial society. His interest in the project mirrored the concerns of his Minangkabau colleagues and elders, who were also publishing articles in Minangkabau journals and newspapers and participating in seminars that addressed the fate of Minangkabau adat and the problem of instructing youth in the intricacies of adat in an urban context, in which old systems for the transmission of knowledge appeared to be attenuated.

Islamic outreach in Minangkabau was countered by the encouragement of an appreciation of adat arts among school children. Such a program can be seen as part of the government's attempt to transform ethnic ritual into salable ethnic art and to replace its local meanings. However, urban schoolchildren who rarely had an opportunity to see an actual performance of traditional music and dance were given the opportunity to develop an interest in Minangkabau adat, even if the music was provided by cassettes and the dances had been standardized for the stage. Some Minangkabau traditional performances, such as songs accompanied by a flute or *randai,* a group performance that relates Minangkabau fables through music, song, and synchronized movement, remained popular among youth and adults alike. And yet, these same youth, who were seemingly disenfranchised from their Minangkabau roots and who could not recite a ritual speech nor relate the sequence of wedding gifts and protocol, were willing and curious participants in every family adat ritual. Often young women contributed their labor to the production of these adat rituals. Does this crisis of Minangkabau youth merely exist in the active imagination and discourse of a few outspoken, hysterical Minangkabau elders? After all, this kind of dialogue concerning the plight of adat has been conducted in Minangkabau since at least the beginning of the nineteenth century.

On the part of youth, a lack of knowledge of the particulars of adat is balanced by a continued commitment to adat that will ensure its preservation in some form in the future. Amid this perceived crisis of adat, urban middle-class Minangkabau were hosting great marriage festivals that juxtaposed the entertainment of local rock bands with all the intricate observances of high adat. And lineages that had neglected to fill the official lineage leader position, who must be a male according to adat, either because they were relatively newly created (and thus had not been qualified to have a lineage leader) or had allowed such a position to lapse because of the cost of the inauguration, were funding the inauguration of a lineage leader. The inaugurations were carried out with all the great pomp and circumstance of adat. After the inauguration ceremony was completed, the lineage leader returned to Jakarta to live. A deputy was appointed as his proxy in the homeland. Thus, the lineage has achieved a statement of rank in the hierarchy of the home village, and adat has been revived, researched, and reinvented in the process.

CONCLUSION

Women's relationship with adat and Islam in Minangkabau exhibits conflict and ambiguity, particularly for young urban women between high school and university age. Educational and work opportunities have presented new choices for young women that do not always fit well with a lifestyle that had its roots in the village, centered around the household of one's mother and grandmother. Generational differences in women's experiences are apparent. Senior women are accustomed to having considerable control over the life choices of their daughters.

Young women are struggling to find a balance in which conflict is minimal and in which all the people for whom they are responsible are at ease. Adat is a lived tradition, the way of mothers, grandmothers, fathers, and mother's brothers. Islam is the Minangkabau religion that is fully integrated into social, moral, and spiritual life. In the 1980s in Minangkabau, given the favorable political environment, Islam could be promoted as an answer to reestablishing order in a society perceived to be threatened by Western-style values and influences. Women were seen by some as having a major role to play in the reestablishment of the social and moral order as responsible wives and mothers. Yet Minangkabau women also were encouraged by a tradition promoted by reformist Islam that women could serve their communities and God by becoming educated and working outside the home. As is evident from the example of Minangkabau, the interpretation and expression of Islam in society changes through time and can be used as an inspiration and rationale for women's personal and social development.

NOTES

1. The Minangkabau traditions called *adat* are distilled in rules and proverbs that outline the operation of matrilineal descent, inheritance of property, marriage alliances, political and social authority, and rituals. The practice of these traditions in daily life is imbued with moral values, such that "the way we as Minangkabau poeple do things" is perceived as the right way to do things.

2. Scholars have written about contemporary Islam in other areas of Indonesia, for example, John Bowen, *Muslims Through Discourse: Religion and Ritual in Gayo Society* (Princeton: Princeton University Press, 1993); Robert Hefner, *Hindu Javanese: Tengger Tradition and Islam* (Princeton: Princeton University Press, 1985); and Mark Woodward, *Islam in Java: Normative Piety and Mysticism in the Sultanate of Yogyakarta* (Tucson: University of Arizona Press, 1989). However, scholars of Minangkabau have focused on the historical development of Islam prior to the establishment of the modern Indonesian state, for example, Taufik Abdallah, *Schools and Politics: The Kaum Muda Movement in West Sumatra (1927–1933)* (Cornell University: Southeast Asia Studies Program, Modern Indonesia Project, Monograph Series, 1971); Abdallah, "Modernization in the Minangkabau World: West Sumatra in the Early Decades of the Twentieth Century," in *Culture*

and Politics in Indonesia, ed. Claire Holt (Ithaca: Cornell University Press, 1972), 179–245; Abdallah, "The Pesantren in Historical Perspective," in *Islam and Society in Southeast Asia,* ed. Taufik Abdallah and Sharon Siddique (Singapore: Institute of Southeast Asian Studies, 1987), 80–107; Christine Dobbin, *Islamic Revivalism in a Changing Peasant Economy: Central Sumatra, 1784–1847,* Scandinavian Institute of Asian Studies, Monograph Series no. 47 (London: Curzon Press, 1983); and Deliar Noer, *The Modernist Muslim Movement in Indonesia, 1900–1942* (London: Oxford University Press, 1973).

3. This chapter is based on doctoral research reflected in my 1993 Ph.D. dissertation, "Virtuous Women, Productive Citizens: Negotiating Tradition, Islam, and Modernity in Minangkabau, Indonesia." The research was conducted in West Sumatra from 1986 through 1987 (funded by Fulbright-Hays) and from 1987 through 1988 (funded by the National Science Foundation).

4. Dale Eickelman discusses the effects of mass higher education on religious knowledge and authority in contemporary Arab societies, in "Mass Higher Education and the Religious Imagination in Contemporary Arab Societies," *American Ethnologist* 19, no. 4 (1992): 643–655.

5. On the development of the new middle class in Indonesia, see Richard Tanner and Kenneth Young, eds., *The Politics of Middle Class Indonesia* (Clayton, Victoria, Australia: Monash Papers on Southeast Asia 19, 1990).

6. For a historical perspective on the development of the middle class in Minangkabau, see Dobbin, *Islamic Revivalism;* Clifford Geertz, *Agricultural Involution* (Berkeley: University of California Press, 1963); and Joel S. Kahn, *Constituting the Minangkabau: Peasants, Culture, and Modernity in Colonial Indonesia* (Oxford: Berg Publishers, 1993).

7. For the history of the development of Islam in Minangkabau, see the works by Taufik Abdallah previously cited in note 2; Dobbin, *Islamic Revivalism;* and Noer, *Modernist Muslim Movement.*

8. For a discussion of a revival of Islam among Indonesian middle classes, see Robert Hefner, "Islam, State, and Civil Society: ICMI and the Struggle for the Indonesian Middle Class," *Indonesia* 56 (1993): 1–35.

9. The names of the festivals are those in use in Indonesia. The Indonesian national language, *bahasa* Indonesia, employs the Latin alphabet.

10. This Islamic revival among the Indonesian middle classes was superseded by a general florescence of Islam in urban Indonesia led by university students in the 1970s, which was inspired by a number of developments throughout the Islamic world. The Iranian revolution of 1979 raised the consciousness of Muslims in Indonesia and other areas of Southeast Asia, as discussed by Fred van der Mehden in *Two Worlds of Islam: Interaction Between Southeast Asia and the Middle East* (Gainesville: University Presses of Florida, 1993). Exposure to new Muslim interpretations was possible through the increasingly available Middle Eastern works in translation in magazines and newspapers, and by contacts with other university students from the Middle East, Malaysia, Australia, and the United States.

11. From the early nineteenth century Minangkabau was known for both its traditionalist and reformist Islamic schools, as discussed by Abdallah in *Schools and Politics* and "The Pesantren in Historical Perspective"; and by Noer in *Modernist Muslim Movement.* In the 1980s in Minangkabau, approximately 40 percent of the high school age students attended either private or government-sponsored, public Islamic schools.

12. According to Suzanne Brenner in "Reconstructing Self and Society: Javanese Muslim Women and 'the Veil,'" *American Ethnologist* 23, no. 4 (1996): 673–697; and Hefner in "Islam, State, and Civil Society," the Indonesian state raised its ban on the wearing of Muslim dress by high school girls in 1990 in

response to much protest and several court cases. Perhaps Muslim dress was tolerated for high school girls in Minangkabau because it closely resembled traditional Minangkabau Muslim dress.

13. See Sondra Hale, "The Politics of Gender in the Middle East," in *Gender and Anthropology: Critical Reviews for Research and Teaching*, ed. Sandra Morgen (Washington, DC: American Anthropological Association, 1989), 246–267.

14. Comparisons made with the influence of Islam on women's lives in the Malay society of Malaysia rely upon the work of Aihwa Ong, "Japanese Factories, Malay Workers: Class and Sexual Metaphors in West Malaysia," in *Power and Difference: Gender in Island Southeast Asia,* ed. Jane Atkinson and Shelley Errington (Stanford: Stanford University Press, 1990), 385–422; Ong, "State Versus Islam: Malay Families, Women's Bodies, and the Body Politic in Malaysia," *American Ethnologist* 17, no. 2 (1990): 258–276; and Ingrid Rudie, *Visible Women in East Coast Malay Society* (Oslo: Scandinavian University Press, 1994).

15. Based on comments by my consultants and Tsuyoshi Kato's research published in *Matriliny and Migration: Evolving Minangkabau Traditions in Indonesia* (Ithaca: Cornell University Press, 1982).

16. Rudie (*Visible Women*) argues that among Malays in the Malaysian state of Kelantan, one of the effects of economic change in the 1980s has been men's increasing ability to obtain higher-paying jobs than women. Therefore, men are more able to become sole providers for their families. These Malay women, similar to Minangkabau women, are accustomed to being producers, controlling resources, and relying on a network of family and kin that counterbalances a husband's ability to exercise authority in household affairs.

17. Based on R. J. Chadwick, "Matrilineal Inheritance and Migration in a Minangkabau Community," *Indonesia* 51 (1991): 48–81; and Nancy Tanner and Lynn Thomas, "Rethinking Matriliny: Decison-making and Sex Roles in Minangkabau," in *Change and Continuity in Minangkabau: Local, Regional, and Historical Perspectives on West Sumatra*, ed. Lynn Thomas and Franz von Benda-Beckman (Athens: Ohio University, Center for International Studies, Monograph in International Studies, Southeast Asia Series, no. 71, 1985), 45–71.

18. The discussion of the influence of considerations of rank and status on marriage alliances is based on Ok-Kyung Pak, "Lowering the High, Raising the Low: The Gender, Alliance and Property Relations in a Minangkabau Peasant Community of West Sumatra, Indonesia," Ph.D. dissertation, University of Toronto, 1986.

19. Claude Levi-Strauss developed the concept of the "house" in *The Way of the Masks*, trans. Sylvia Modelski (Seattle: University of Washington Press, 1982).

20. Compare Franz von Benda-Beckman, "Property in Social Continuity: Continuity and Change in the Maintenance of Property Relationships Through Time in Minangkabau, West Sumatra," *Verhandelingen van het Koninklijk Instituut voor Taal-, Land-en Volkenkunde*, no. 86 (The Hague: Martinus Nijhoff, 1979); and Kato, *Matriliny and Migration*.

21. Noted by Evelyn Blackwood, "The Politics of Daily Life: Gender, Kinship and Identity in a Minangkabau Village, West Sumatra, Indonesia," Ph.D. dissertation, Stanford University, 1993; Ok-Kyung Pak, "Lowering the High"; Joanne Prindiville, "Mother, Mother's Brother, and Modernization: The Problems and Prospects of Minangkabau Matriliny in a Changing World," in *Change and Continuity in Minangkabau Sumatra: Local, Regional, and Historical Perspectives on West Sumatra,* ed. Lynn Thomas and Franz von Benda-Beckman (Athens: Ohio University, Center for International Studies, Monograph in International Studies, Southeast Asia Series, no. 71, 1985), 29–43; Tanner and Thomas, "Rethinking Matriliny"; and Whalley, "Virtuous Women."

22. Quoted from Isnaniah Saleh, *Peringatan 55 Tahun Diniyah Putri Padang-panjang* (Commemorating 55 Years of the Diniyah Putri Padang Panjang) (Jakarta: Ghalia Indonesia, 1978).

23. Ong, "Japanese Factories," and Ong, "State Versus Islam."

24. Compare young women's rationales for adopting the jilbab in Java presented by Brenner in "Reconstructing Self."

13

Muslim Women in India: A Minority Within a Minority

Shahida Lateef

The status and role of Muslim women in India is inextricably linked to the political, economic, and social survival of the Muslim community in India; to developments in Indian society; and to the position of all Indian women.[1] In recent decades these factors have intensified the underlying struggle in the Muslim community between women and men, both over the interpretation of the tenets of Islam regarding women and over the community's relationship to a secular, democratic Indian state. This struggle is complicated by political and economic developments in the nineteenth century and since independence in 1947, which have directly and indirectly influenced the actions of all Indian communities and the current position of Muslim and all Indian women. In this chapter I examine the position of Muslim women in contemporary Indian society in the context of historical and postindependence developments and as a minority within the minority Muslim community.

In the past two decades, political, economic, and social changes have led to an escalating conflict within the Muslim community and with Hindu communities that has focused on Muslims' political and economic strategy and on the rights of Muslim women. Three divisive issues epitomize the triangular predicament: the right of Muslim women to maintenance after divorce; the preservation of Muslim women's rights in the Indian constitution; and the demolition of one mosque as a means of catapulting Hindu nationalist parties into political power. Although Muslim men and women tend to be similarly affected by the threat to places of worship and by economic and political marginalization, the current Muslim leadership's lack of support for advances in their rights have set women against men. These three issues represent the still unresolved struggle for political and economic power between communities and between sexes despite the egalitarian political and constitutional changes instituted after 1947. The resurgence of Hindu nationalism underscores the anomalies inherent in the position of the Muslim community. The creation of Pakistan on Muslim demand in 1947, which partitioned the country and dismembered the Muslim community, had an impact throughout Indian society. However, its long-term consequences on Muslim women have been particularly deleterious. The current position of Muslim women can best be understood in the context of historical and contemporary changes that influence community action and the status of women.

Political and economic changes in the nineteenth century served to formalize and organize community and regional ties, which intensified community rivalry even as the broader goal of independence was collaboratively pursued by both secular and partisan political parties. After independence in 1947, political, social, and economic changes flowed from a secular constitution and democratic institutions that formed the basis of the Indian state. It is the majority Hindu and the minority Muslim communities' response to these changes before and after independence that has shaped the current position of all Indian women.

The Indian Muslim community, although just 11 percent of a population of 929 million, is represented in all Indian states and constitutes from 7 to 30 percent of each population, except in Kashmir (97 percent).[2] The Muslim community's heterogeneity because of linguistic and cultural differences manifests itself in marriage and family customs, in attitudes toward women, and in chosen occupations and education. These differences, however, are underplayed by the community's leadership, intent on presenting a unified front to overcome the political and economic disadvantages of being a minority. As a minority within a minority, Muslim women have been and continue to be subject to the same political and socioeconomic factors that influence the status of all Indian women, yet their position is affected by the community's history and its minority position. In recent decades the status of Muslim women has been subject to political pressures from the predominantly conservative Muslim leaders in the community.

Policymakers and community leaders have generally tended to disregard the socioeconomic problems of Muslim women, which is manifested in the lack of accommodation to women's rights within the community and, specifically, in the postindependence resistance to legislative changes in the Shariat Application Act of 1937 and the Dissolution of Muslim Marriages Act of 1939. Moreover, the community's conservative leadership was instrumental in inducing the Indian government to pass the Muslim Women's (Protection on Divorce) Act of 1986, enacted to overthrow a landmark Supreme Court judgment granting indigent Muslim women maintenance by invoking secular law. Muslim women have been increasingly turning to Indian courts to redress marital and financial issues. In this struggle Muslim women are ironically pitted against conservative Muslims and supported by Hindu conservatives. They have become a pawn in the anti-Muslim campaign waged by Hindu right-wing groups. The rights of Muslim women have thus become an issue in Indian politics because religion and caste factors continue to be important to electoral outcomes.

The arguments advanced by organized Muslim conservatives on the All India Personal Board have been couched in religious terms, emphasizing the inviolability of the Shari'a and hence their opposition to any accommodation for Muslim women even under secular law. The Congress Party in power at the time tried to limit the electoral fallout from this issue by enacting legislation that would stop Indian courts from using certain secular laws in reference to maintenance for separated or divorced Muslim women. An alliance of Hindu right-wing groups led by the Bharatiya Janata Party (BJP) has characterized the accommodation thus extended by the Congress to the Muslim community as antisecular.[3] Hence the struggle of Muslim women for a change in their legal status has come to represent a power struggle in Indian politics between the minority Muslim community and right-wing elements in the majority Hindu community. The former strives to retain perceived symbols of the community's identity and exclusiveness and to resist absorption, whereas the latter is attempting to isolate and marginalize the Muslim community. Yet for Muslim women these changes in their legal status are essential to equip them to deal with current economic and social conditions.

PRIVATE AND POLITICAL RELIGION

Since the nineteenth century, most Indian communities have used religion and caste to distinguish their political and economic interests. In order to represent their interests before the British colonial power, communities sought to minimize regional differences as they organized on a religious or caste basis. The forging of political ties based on caste and religious commonality led to a dichotomy between private and political religion. Private religion is the belief in and the practice of religion by individuals, accommodating and adjusting to changes in society and allowing for each individual's rights and needs. Political religion, in contrast, is a group mechanism employed to unify the community politically and establish its exclusivity and control over its own members. Political religion can result from either internal or external pressures. Although the divergence between private and political religion was initially a mechanism employed to unify Muslim communities politically, its effect has been to stifle the rights of women.

The contrast between private and political religion has had profound implications for Muslim women. Although the resistance to change in Muslim personal law has created ascriptive differences between the status of Muslim and Hindu women, the achieved status of women in both communities primarily reflects socioeconomic factors and educational attainments subsumed in class differences in India. For Muslim women in postindependence India, this difference has led to an escalating legal struggle in response to changing social and economic conditions, even as their socioeconomic position reflects the economic and political travails of their community. The concerns of Muslim women, however, are not represented in those political forums where conservative leaders continue to pursue cohesion, ignoring the socioeconomic struggle of women. Such neglect is due in part to the quality of leadership and to the paucity of institutions that could more effectively synthesize and represent the interests of women. It is also due to the nature of the Indian political process itself.

Changes underway in India since the nineteenth century have transformed inter- and intracommunity relationships. Not only has the concept of political parity altered communal relations from the hierarchical to those representative of numerical strength and political efficacy, but this transformation underscored the economic leverage and social ascendancy enjoyed by a community. These changes, once instituted, became potent factors in the struggle between communities adjusting initially to British rule and then to political independence. The Muslim community was at the center of this struggle because of its traditional political dominance in Delhi and in certain other states that resulted from more than three centuries of Muslim rule and hegemony under the Mughal emperors. After the British takeover in 1857, Muslim leaders, confronted with the loss of political and economic power, endeavored to lower their expectations and realistically assess their minority status. These fundamental changes together with consequent adjustments in the response of the Muslim and other communities, therefore, form continuous points of reference in this chapter.

The triangular struggle between Muslim women and conservative Muslims and Hindus over the rights of Muslim women demonstrates the imperfect and discriminatory nature of the existing laws relating to the rights of Muslim women and of the Indian political process as well as the unequal position of all Indian women. In this article I focus on societal transformation in India and its impact on all Indian women, on the Indian Muslim community, and on Muslim women while drawing on an analysis of historical factors that have shaped the current position of Muslim women.

CHANGE AND CONSOLIDATION, 1857–1947

The political dominance of the Muslim community in Delhi and certain princely states was directly affected by the consolidation of British colonial power in the nineteenth century. The resulting changes disrupted existing hierarchies, forcing community leaders, both Muslim and Hindu, to seek ways to minimize its adverse consequences. An emphasis on numerical strength and cohesion became important in influencing government policies and actions. Communities were compelled to collaborate with co-religionist groups in other regions to exercise greater leverage.

The importance of interregional cooperation within groups thus encouraged the revival and maintenance of those traditions and customs specific to each group, even when these conflicted with the rights of women or with current regional practices.[4] Initially the push for Muslim unity was a reaction to the loss of political power and took the form of efforts to persuade Muslim communities to accept British rule and English education, which had become prerequisites for political access and employment. These developments were also taking place in other communities, as caste, language, and religious affiliations became the basis on which each organized politically. This process of organization was to become the mainstay of Indian political development.

In the nineteenth century, Islam provided Indian Muslims not just with spiritual and social succor but with a refuge, a rallying point designed to reorient the community to meet the challenges confronting it. The loss of political power and a decline in Muslim economic fortunes impelled the ulema not only to encourage religious observance but also to urge political and economic initiatives to guide the community. Such political activism led to a convergence in the religious and political agenda of the community.

Scholars and theologians such as Shah Wali Ullah (1703–1762) and his son Shah Abd al-Aziz (1746–1864), quoting Islamic law, the Qur'an, and the Sunna, advised Muslims to free themselves from blind acceptance of the four traditional schools of jurisprudence; to distinguish between pure, universal religion and local Arabic coloring; to learn English; and to acquire technical skills from the British. They also sought to make the Qur'an more accessible by having it translated into Persian and Urdu.

Later, Shibli Nomani (1857–1914), writing on Islamic law pertaining to women, noted that "every permitted thing is not capable of being practiced" because of accompanying restrictions. Shibli stressed the importance of freedom and rights for women, including the right to divorce and to participate in sociopolitical aspects of life, because anything else would be a violation of the Shari'a. Ashraf Thanvi (1863–1943) held similar views on the rights of women, including his conviction that Muslim women had the right to divorce and to receive maintenance throughout their lives if they did not remarry. Although upholding the injunction to modesty, he did not subscribe to the full body covering that has become customary for Muslim women living in predominantly Muslim areas in India.[5]

This effort to synthesize Indian Islam with the requirements of new and adverse conditions could have resulted in a holistic approach to such problems. However, political events, political organizations, and the actions of other Indian communities competing for economic and political advantage increasingly separated the private aspects of religion from the political use of religion necessary to organize and unite the community. In the struggle among the conservative and liberal ulema and political leaders over strategy, political and economic survival rather than the rights of women or the interpretations of Shari'a were primary concerns. The Muslim League, formed in 1905 to represent Muslim political interests, supported voting and legislative rights for women but favored political separatism to ensure the community's political rights. Its separatist policy was ultimately to result in the partition of India, despite the opposition of the Jamiat-ul-Ulema-i-Hind, the successor to the theological movements of the nineteenth century, which steadfastly resisted separatism as a viable Muslim strategy.[6] In postindependence India, without the issue of separatism, it is the religious conservatism of the Jamiat-ul-Ulema-i-Hind that continues to shape the agenda of current Muslim political leaders, making the possibility of synthesis between private and political religion less achievable.

Although the core beliefs of Islam—monotheism, daily prayers, fasting at Ramadan, charity, and pilgrimage—pertain to both men and women and link regionally and ethnically disparate communities, specific customs and traditions vary between culturally diverse regional Muslim communities. The Qur'an placed the obligation for being morally responsible on women and men individually since there is neither church nor clergy to enforce compliance. Differences exist among Islamic scholars on the interpretation of certain Qur'anic passages, as in the case of purdah (i.e., whether the reference to modesty in dress and behavior for men and women necessitates the head to toe covering imposed on women in some Indian Muslim communities).[7] From injunctions against female infanticide and provisions for marital and property rights, however, there is little doubt regarding the intention of the Qur'an to elevate the status of women. The reference to polygyny is solely in the context of the Battle of Uhud in Muhammad's day. The injunction urges correct behavior toward orphaned or widowed women and forbids seizing their property or forcing them into prostitution or adultery. It is in this context alone that marriage with more than one may be deemed permissible, and then only if the wives could be treated with equality.

The translation of this Qur'anic vision, which merged spiritual beliefs and socioeconomic conditions, was left to four schools of Islamic jurisprudence whose interpretations have historically differed. These differences have been used by some Muslim societies to legislate reforms, particularly in laws relating to women. In the preindependence period in India, laws in accord with the Shari'a were enacted to give Muslim women access to marital and some property rights. This codification, which brought all Indian Muslims into its purview, has come to be regarded as defining the community. Therefore, it cannot now be easily changed without appearing to compromise the community's integrity.

Indian women were not political players in the nineteenth century. Social reforms occurred initially at the behest of men who focused more on such glaring inequities as child marriage, child widows, and the complete lack of control women had over their lives. Despite many centuries of Muslim rule, the Shari'a had remained more an aspiration than a reality for Indian Muslim women; rather, regional culture and customs determined the rights and position of women. Hence Muslim women were seldom encouraged or able to utilize either marital or economic Shari'a rights. It was not until the 1920s that the women's movement, a coalition of Hindu and Muslim women leaders and groups focusing on the rights of women, created a constituency among Muslim political leaders sufficient to reestablish the marital and property rights of Muslim women. Legislation to this effect was politically expedient since it would define and unite all Muslims under one law.

Western education was the avenue communities and groups used to benefit from the political and economic changes instituted under British rule. The purpose of education and the medium of instruction were thereby altered. In regions previously under Muslim rule, regional languages, such as Bengali and Hindi, gained importance over Urdu as they became the medium of instruction in vernacular schools, and English replaced Persian, the court language of Muslim rulers, for groups seeking patronage and employment by the colonial power. Though neither professional nor government employment was a possibility for women in the nineteenth century except for teaching, reformers regarded education for women as a means of delaying marriage and creating opportunities. By the end of the century, there was general acceptance of the importance of women's education, and because of the campaign of Muslim leaders for acceptance of Western education by the community, Muslim women's education met with little resistance.

Regional variations and occupational differences determined the participation of Muslim men and women in education. The activities of Syed Ahmad Khan in the United Provinces (now known as Uttar Pradesh), Nawab Abd Al Latif and Amir Ali in Calcutta, and Badruddin Tyabji in Bombay contributed to the social and political transformation of the Muslim community. The Muhammadan Educational Conference of 1888 passed a resolution urging the education of women. By 1896 the conference created a separate section to promote their education. The Fourth Quinquennial Review of Education (1897–1902) indicated that public school attendance by Muslim girls was comparable to that of Hindu girls except in Bengal and Punjab, where the Muslim population was mainly rural and agricultural.[8] This was also true at the secondary and collegiate levels; later reviews of education confirmed these findings.

The custom of purdah, or seclusion of women, was part of the control the family and community exercised over women. Although the custom was often attributed to the advent of Islam in India, there is evidence to suggest that such constraints had always existed apropos the Hindu caste system.[9] Hindu women practiced seclusion, or purdah, within the family, covering head and face from men in the household, whereas Muslim women wore an overgarment outside but discarded it within the family circle. This differentiation stemmed from Hindu marital taboos within kin groups and the Muslim encouragement of such ties.

Thus the deleterious effects of purdah were felt by women of each community. Both men and women reformers regarded purdah as an obstacle to women's education and to social interaction. The active involvement of both Hindu and Muslim women in organizing and lobbying for changes in women's rights led them to campaign against the custom, which though less formal in the south than in the north, was nevertheless responsible for a purdah mentality that assigned women specific roles within the family and society. Despite the formality and pervasiveness of Muslim purdah, social changes at the turn of the century prompted Muslim writers such as Hali and Nazir Ahmad and the activists in the Muhammadan Educational Conference to advocate greater freedom and control for Muslim women. The Begum of Bhopal, very much involved with the women's movement and Muslim education, rejected the religious basis for purdah and symbolically removed her veil at the 1929 session of the All India Women's Conference.

The response of the Muslim community to social legislation pertaining to women and instituted by Hindu reformers in the nineteenth century was mainly supportive. They were able to distance themselves from the more iniquitous customs being targeted by reformers and missionaries by citing the rights Muslim women had under the Shari'a.

The similarity of views expressed by Muslim and other communities in the same region suggests that attitudes toward women's roles and rights were less affected by religious considerations than by regional ones, as indicated by evidence presented before British appointed committees whenever legislative changes were proposed in the rights of women. The evidence presented to a government committee on the proposed 1869 legislation to legalize marriage between members of different communities was protested by representatives of the Muslim community on the grounds that it sanctioned dissent from established religions and contravened the stated policy of the British government on noninterference in religious matters. Hindu protest centered around the divine nature of Hindu laws, which could not be changed by a legislature.[10] Although the evidence portrayed the rigidly organized social structures in which the rights of both men and women were secondary to the interests of the family and community, it also expressed concerns for community cohesion and unity. Promoting community solidarity on the basis of shared traditions and experiences in the Hindu and Muslim communities served to politicize religious or caste ties and to establish the always marginalized rights of women as a symbol of that continuity. Although the right of Muslim women to later marriages, education, and remarriage after widowhood were generally accepted by political parties, both Muslim and Hindu conservatives opposed legislative changes, citing religious traditions.

Social legislation and public policies were often scrutinized through the prism of differentiation rather than on the merits of a specific issue. This was demonstrated in the evidence gathered by the Sarda Committee, appointed by the government in 1927–1928 to elicit public opinion on proposed legislation to raise the age of marriage for both girls and boys. The evidence gathered across the country indicated that although the proposed legislation was either supported or opposed by members of the Hindu community, Muslim opinion included a third aspect, which expressed concern that Muslim identity and exclusiveness could be compromised as a result of the uniform legislation, even though no credible religious objections could be advanced against the legislation and it was supported by the Muslim League.[11] The passage of the 1937 Shari'at Act pertaining to the inheritance rights of Muslim women and the 1939 Dissolution of Muslim Marriages Act, however, combined the twin objectives of providing Muslim women with rights while uniting the community under one legislation. That the two laws did not include the right of women to landed property, as prescribed in the Shari'a, showed that Muslim leaders were more interested in unity than women's rights per se.

The participation of Muslim women in the Indian women's movement created a cadre of women leaders who, unlike male Muslim leaders, were able to focus solely on securing women's rights and education. In this both Hindu and Muslim women leaders were able to disregard religious and political differences in order to right historical inequities. This collaboration provided women leaders with a platform from which to fight for an agenda that came to be accepted by the government and by political leaders of all spectrums. By acting in unison, women were able to replicate the power of lobbies representing other important groups. Such a convergence of interests was to lead to the support by Hindu and Muslim women for each others' rights. Hindu women leaders were thus able to laud the rights Muslim women had gained through the two acts.[12] The debates in the Legislative Assembly, on the other hand, were an indication of the way in which male Muslim and Hindu legislators viewed the push for women's rights, focusing on additional women's religious interpretations rather than on the intrinsic importance of their rights. However, in the debate on women in the National Planning Committee in 1948, Hindu and Muslim women leaders and some Muslim men leaders were able to agree on the need for a uniform civil code that would not be compulsory but would be an alternative to the personal laws that governed both communities.[13]

POSTINDEPENDENCE DEVELOPMENTS

In many ways the dilemmas of a century ago continue to beset the contemporary Muslim community in India. Debates continue on the rights of women, the minority position of the community in India, and the problems associated with political and economic underrepresentation. Democracy and economic development in India in more than four decades of independence have created significant new conditions that have touched all segments of society. Adjustment to such changes has depended on historical circumstances and the socioeconomic differences existing among Muslim communities. For Muslim women, regional disparities, political and economic pressures associated with a minority community, and the emphasis on maintaining symbolic cultural and religious differentiation have created specific concerns and pressures. Unlike in the earlier period, political and economic changes have intensified communal politics, making it more difficult for Muslim women to find support either from the women's movement or the Muslim political leadership. The acquisition of secular constitutional and legal rights by all women and the passage of the Hindu Code Bill of 1956, giving Hindu women marital and property rights, eliminated the broad-based national agenda that had included all Indian women. Now microlevel socioeconomic issues are pursued by a proliferation of women's and nongovernmental organizations (NGOs), though the specificity of some of the issues espoused may exclude certain groups and women not directly targeted.

With independence and partition, the problems of the Muslim community were exacerbated. Regional Muslim communities separated by both political and economic circumstances tended to be dominant in certain geographic areas and occupations. At the time of partition, those migrating to Pakistan were mainly urban, northern, and young.[14] This eviscerated the traditional urban Muslim centers. The outbreak of intercommunal violence and the Evacuee Property Act of 1950 deprived Muslim families of property rights when some members of the family migrated to Pakistan and eroded the economic base of the vast majority who stayed on in India.[15] Muslim women were deprived of the leadership that had represented their interests so effectively in the Indian women's movement, one that had fought against the separatist stance of the Muslim League. The lack of male and female leadership thus created a vacuum to be filled by conservative, semireligious, feudal leaders. To them, the political nuances of the pre-partition period, whereby political religion was confined to political separatist demands and not to the denial of women's rights, were incomprehensible. This current leadership has come to regard the imperfect 1937 and 1939 acts as constituting Muslim identity in India and has challenged the right of the Indian parliament to change the acts.

Although the Indian Constitution and its institutions provide all citizens with rights and representation, the functioning of political parties continues to be based on consolidating votes by caste and religious cohesiveness. There is economic, criminal, and social legislation that is uniform and secular and applies to all Indian citizens. However, certain legislation such as the Special Marriages Act of 1954, when invoked, would negate personal laws and would bring marriage, divorce, and inheritance under secular nationwide laws.

A strong role for the state in the area of economic development was incorporated into formal five-year plans. Legislation was introduced to regulate labor relations, to set labor standards in the workplace, and to act as an instrument of social policy. These government initiatives empowered many previously neglected groups and encouraged less organized elements to strive for greater cohesion in order to take advantage of political and economic opportunities.[16] The struggle among them for political and economic representation resonated within political parties, which cultivated them in search of a reliable political base.[17]

After 1947, the Congress Party's rhetoric in support of secularism and the rights of religious or caste minorities did not always translate into either physical security or justice for the lower castes or minorities because of entrenched vested interests.[18] Policymaking, decisionmaking, and implementation increased in complexity as the Congress Party, which traditionally had accommodated ideologically diverse groups under the banner of nationalism, sought to mobilize the rural masses after independence, thus vastly increasing the number of vested interests jostling for power within the party.[19] The rise of the BJP and regional parties has undercut the Congress Party's traditional base, prompting party strategists to vie for the "Hindu" vote, in effect validating the Hindu right-wing approach. The damage has been further compounded by the Congress Party's subdued defense of secularism as had been interpreted and practiced by successive Congress governments. As a consequence, the Congress Party has lost the support of both the lower castes and the religious minorities and reinforced the sense of insecurity of both. Its neglect has made the Muslim community in particular amenable to the political religion that is the mainstay of the established conservative leadership.

Hindu extremist groups have reoriented their goals from pursuing an ideological social agenda aimed at unifying the Hindu polity to gaining political power through the BJP.[20] These groups, active before independence, have sought to underplay caste or gender issues within Hinduism by tapping into the latent animosities toward the Muslim community.[21] Harking back to perceived historical wrongs and transferring the blame for the ills of the Hindu community to Muslims, the extremists seek to contain the underlying tensions among Hindus. Their attacks on the Muslim community have been accompanied by efforts to belittle secularism and those Indian institutions that support pluralism. Although Hindus are currently fragmented by caste, a unified Hindu majority could propel these extremist groups to national power.

The combination of political, social, and economic factors, in conjunction with the community's minority and historical position, creates a specific context for Muslim women. If these factors are disregarded, then the achieved and ascriptive differences in women's rights, the asymmetry between private and political religion, and the diversity and flexibility of the Muslim community's response to modern Indian conditions all tend to become invisible. If, for example, Islam is the only factor considered, current differences among Muslims cannot be explained. Nor would an Islamic analysis explain the similarities based on class differentials that primarily account for the current status of all Indian women, including Muslim women. Class differentials in India subsume nutrition, education, and training, all essential factors that affect women's control of their lives. Conversely, it is the persistence of social and institutional factors in both the Hindu and Muslim communities that accounts for the adverse demographic, political, and economic conditions that continue to hamper the progress of women.[22]

THREE DIVISIVE ISSUES

Since the late 1980s, three issues illuminate the escalating conflict both within the Muslim community and between Hindu and Muslim communities. First, the controversy over the Babri Masjid/Ramjanam Bhoomi, a religious structure in Ayodhya, was an issue tailored to polarize the two communities by playing on "religious" sentiments favorable to the electoral success of the Hindu right-wing groups. Its destruction on December 6, 1992, unleashed widespread riots across the country in which Muslims, especially women, were targeted. Second, the Shahbano case regarding the maintenance of divorced Muslim women made clear the more destructive aspects of political religion, since it induced the Muslim right-wing to cause Muslim women to lose certain constitutional rights. Third, the struggle of Muslim women to regain constitutional rights and to have unilateral divorce declared unconstitutional continues unabated. Each of these issues demonstrates the impact of new circumstances on communities and on individuals. The use of political religion to maintain communal integrity was often a response to the actions of other communities and could be at the expense both of women and the moderating effects of private religion.

The Babri Masjid controversy's relevance to this chapter lies in its effect on that minority of minorities, Muslim women. It was set in motion when the Congress Party, to attract Hindu voters, allowed the Babri Masjid issue to be reopened. This mosque, built by the sixteenth-century Mughal emperor Babar, was such a bone of contention between Hindus and Muslims that it had been closed by the British in 1938. Certain Hindu groups claimed that it was built on the site of a temple commemorating the birth of Lord Rama, a claim Muslims denied. Its reopening in 1985 led to confrontations between the parties and uncertainty in the Muslim community regarding the intentions of the Congress Party government at Delhi. The government left the settlement of the issue to the "give and take between religious leaders and non-party organizations whose legitimacy and representative status are open to question . . . [and] are not democratically accountable."[23] This strategy, while keeping the pressure on the Muslim community as villains of choice, threw the concept of secularism and its validity into question while encouraging proponents of a Hindu *rashtra* (theocratic state).

Hindu emotions were whipped into an anti-Muslim frenzy as the BJP and its right-wing Hindu allies gathered in massive numbers at the Babri Masjid on December 6, 1992, and demolished it under the watchful eye of the law and order authorities, the media (both foreign and domestic), and internal intelligence agencies. The Congress government had chosen to trust the BJP leadership's assurance that the gathering was going to be peaceful. The aftermath to the demolition led to Hindu-Muslim riots all across India in which Muslims' homes and businesses were targeted and destroyed, in many instances with the compliance of the police and government authorities.[24] Indian Muslims were profoundly disturbed by the seeming collaboration of the Indian government in these events.

Muslim women's struggle for constitutional rights has been a continual issue throughout the twentieth century. They had almost never had the full protection of the rights accorded them in the Shari'a until the enactment of the 1937 and 1939 acts. The Shahbano controversy was triggered by the Supreme Court decision in the Mohammad Khan versus Shah Bano Begum case in 1985. The case demonstrated the anomalies still inherent in the position of Indian Muslim women. Shahbano, a Muslim woman separated from her husband, applied for maintenance under civil law. Her husband divorced her and paid her 3,000 rupees ($75), claiming this to be her dower and refusing further payments, citing Muslim personal law. The case went all the way to the Indian Supreme Court. His position had the support of the conservative Muslim establishment. The Supreme Court had earlier settled cases granting Muslim women maintenance under Section 125 of the Criminal Procedure Code of 1974 on grounds that women were indigent.[25] In adjudicating the Shahbano case, Chief Justice Y. V. Chandrachud not only granted maintenance but also delivered a homily on the necessity of enacting a uniform civil code, which in his opinion "will help the cause of national integration by removing disparate loyalties to laws which have conflicting ideologies." The judgment was exploited by both Hindu and Muslim conservatives. The former demanded changes in Muslim laws, and the latter demanded that the judgment be legislatively countermanded. Neither was particularly concerned with the problems of Muslim women. The political controversy between Muslim conservatives opposed to the ruling and its supporters led to the passage of the Muslim Women's (Protection on Divorce) Act of 1986. The act in effect deprived

Muslim women of their constitutional rights by excluding them from the purview of Section 125 of the Criminal Procedure Code.[26]

Despite such difficulties, Muslim women have continued to take marital and property cases to Indian courts. The All India Muslim Women's Association has hailed such cases, noting that they would help focus on Muslim women's rights and would curb the use of unilateral divorce, as well as suppressing its misuse as a means of evading the ceiling placed on landholdings. False divorce has been used to pretend that the family property was divided between husband and wife, who in essence continue to be married and retain the property beyond the ceiling limit.[27] In many other cases the misuse of unilateral divorce violates the protective aspects of Shari'a, such as a strict waiting period. After the Shahbano case, women's groups and scholars appear prepared to challenge the conservatives on Muslim women's rights.

These three issues are indicative of the continuing relevance of religion and caste in the Indian political process, as political parties and community groups use both to define constituents and socioeconomic interests. That the Muslim Women's Act was in the best interests of Muslim women and minority interests was a "secular" argument advanced by the conservative Muslim lobby and the government to justify the sectarian passage of the legislation. Its use has created uncertainty regarding the government's objectivity and support of secularism. It has also left religious communities open to exploitation by practitioners of political religion. A case in point is the exploitation of caste rhetoric by "backward" castes and other minority groups as a means of extracting political and economic concessions from the upper Hindu castes and government.[28]

THE POLITICAL ECONOMY OF WOMEN

In 1951, the government introduced a series of economic measures with a view to reshaping the economy and society. These were linked by Jawaharlal Nehru, the first prime minister of India, to the Fundamental Rights and Directive Principles of State Policy in the constitution, when he stated:

> the State shall strive to promote the welfare of the people by securing and protecting as effectively as it may a social order in which social justice, economic and political, shall inform all institutions of national life, and shall direct its policy towards securing among other things, that the citizens, men and women equally, have the right to an adequate means of livelihood.[29]

Successive five-year plans and legislative changes, such as the Minimum Wages Act of 1948, the Equal Remuneration Act of 1976, and the Dowry Prohibition Act of 1961, have increased the participation of women in education, in the labor market, and in the professions.

From 1972 to 1974, the National Committee on the Status of Women in India examined the role and status of all Indian women, noting that the attainment of equality was one of the specific objectives implicit in the Fundamental Rights and Directive Principles of State Policy.[30] It studied social and religious institutions, the direction of government economic and social policies, and the impact these have had on women in the postindependence period.

The analysis of successive census data from 1901 to 1971 revealed that an adverse male-female ratio had not changed, and mortality, literacy, and education levels for women continued to lag behind those of men despite the rights conferred on women and their representation at many levels since independence. Until the report was made public, it had been widely assumed that the acquisition of legal rights had effectively equalized the position of women and that planned economic changes aimed at accelerating economic growth would automatically reduce poverty and benefit women. The report, however, revealed that women at lower socioeconomic levels had seen their lot worsen in relative and sometimes even in absolute terms.[31] These findings triggered efforts through government economic planning and legislation and by various women's groups to identify and reverse the causes of these demographic and social inequities.

Women's labor participation rates in the formal sector between 1911 and 1971 declined as a result of mechanization, lower literacy rates, and competition for jobs, pushing women into the informal sector where they lack the protection of laws regulating and protecting their working environment. This situation has continued despite legislation to secure rights and government intervention.[32] The 1991 census indicated that the average male-female population ratio declined steadily from 1901, when it was 972 females per 1,000 males, to 929 females per 1,000 males. The 1991 ratio varied from 1040 per 1,000 males in the state of Kerala, to 861 per 1,000 in Arunachal Pradesh. The female literacy rate has gone up from 9 percent in 1951 to 39 percent in 1991, but male literacy has risen from 27 percent to 64 percent. Regional variations in literacy ranged from 87 percent for females in Kerala to 21 percent in Rajasthan.[33] Although an increase in women's labor participation rates in the organized sector, particularly in urban areas, has brought them into the regulatory purview of the Equal Remuneration Act of 1976, the majority of women working in the unorganized sector were untouched by this legislation.[34]

Gender roles are conceived, enacted, and learned within a complex of relationships: within the family, the community, and the region. The intervention of political religion has affected the gender roles of women of all castes and religions. It has revitalized the struggle to control the rights of women through an appeal to custom and tradition. Even after more than a century of social change, the attitudes toward women have remained essentially patriarchal. This is evident in the continuing importance of dowry and resistance to marriages outside the preferred caste groupings.[35] And it is the legal and economic processes set in motion, directly or indirectly, by political parties and the government, that have reinforced traditional notions of family and community.[36]

Through the determination of the BJP and its allies to create a specifically Hindu platform, for example, the role of women, family, and community is increasingly identified with Hindu customs and traditions, whereas individual rights and achievements are treated as less significant.[37] The BJP's ideology, implemented where it has held power, supports the Hindu image of women as dutiful, sacrificing, chaste, and pure and the equally traditional dominant role for men, thus justifying the party's differential treatment of men and women.[38] The Babri Masjid/Ramjanam Bhoomi controversy, as well as other incidents, created opportunities for right-wing agitation by invoking the image of a Hindu woman endlessly raped or threatened by Muslims. Hindu women are also portrayed as liberators of an endangered motherland.[39] However, discussion of gender, caste, or class issues, which could be contentious and thus weaken the party, is discouraged.[40]

Indian social, political, and economic changes have affected all communities irrespective of religion, caste, and regional associations. For the Muslim community in particular, the manipulation of caste and religious sentiments by political parties has intensified a patronizing and frequently hostile scrutiny that has been most tellingly directed at the status of Muslim women by the Hindu right-wing. It castigates the community for treating the retention of Muslim personal law as an entitlement and accuses the ruling Congress Party of cultivating the Muslim vote and compromising secularism. For Muslim women, the physical threat of Muslim-Hindu riots and disruption of economic and social conditions has created fear and uncertainty.[41]

CHANGES IN THE STATUS OF WOMEN

Most studies of Muslim women in India have related women's role and status to Islam without reference to Indian regional, social, political, and economic conditions, such as were associated with women's roles in other communities. In my 1990 study of Muslim women, I sought to set women's roles within the context of relations among Indian conditions, women, and Islam, using Indian historical events to demonstrate the continuities and pressures that had influenced the position of Muslim women and the community. The study distinguished between the ascribed and achieved status of women and the evolutionary process undergone over the century by Indian women. It also explored the differences between regions, between women observing purdah and those who did not, and between women employed outside the home and homemakers. For Muslim women, the economic and political position of the community remained of paramount importance since it determined the institutional support extended to Muslim women by government, the Muslim community, and the women's movement; the interplay between political and private religion; and the extent to which political considerations dominated the Muslim agenda, which after the passage of the 1937 and 1939 acts directly affected the status and role of Muslim women.

My findings were based on historical research, an interregional and stratified survey, and a field trip to the nine cities covered by the survey— Ahmedabad, Bombay, Calcutta, Cochin, Delhi, Hyderabad, Lucknow, Madras, and Srinagar—each chosen to reflect regional differences, language, customs, and culture. The survey differentiated between states with a history of communal tensions and those that were better integrated in terms of language and culture and were at that time relatively free of Hindu-Muslim discord. (In the eight years since the study, the anti-Muslim BJP campaign has affected every region.) The survey was stratified to include two categories of housewives in the upper and lower groupings (defined by type of house and amenities), career women, women working outside the house, and students, and the questions were aimed at exploring marital and familial relationships, linked as these were to the access women had to the community and, beyond that, to the Indian community. Regional differences were considered important because of the contrasts that exist in literacy, cultural attitudes toward women's roles, customs and traditions, and occupational differences among Muslim communities. However, although each of these factors contributed to variations in responses to questions on education and literacy, they tended to be superseded by factors relating to socioeconomic strata. In sum, the survey revealed that socioeconomic strata and personal income, rather than regional differences or purdah observance, were the primary considerations that influenced respondents' attitudes toward personal decisionmaking, including attitudes toward rights in marriage and inheritance, education, and purdah.

Comparing the results of respondents practicing purdah with those who did not indicated that the former were generally in the lower socioeconomic strata, had lower educational levels, and participated less in family finances or decisionmaking. Yet family relationships, attitudes toward the education of sons and daughters, and expectations for improvements in the status of Muslim women all tended to negate the effects of purdah. The study demonstrates purdah's flexibility in the urban environment and was also suggestive of the shifts that have taken place in urban nuclear families, in which respondents appeared to react to socioeconomic pressures rather than to some arbitrary "Muslim" position. Muslim communities and individuals were preoccupied with economic survival and lingering illiteracy. Purdah practices were blamed on poverty and unemployment, rather than on resistance to change. The responses of career women and wage earners, on the other hand, did reflect their greater input into family finances and decisionmaking.[42]

The increase in Indian women's literacy rate over the last decade may be traced to the recognition being given to it by the government and the family. The increase between 1951 and 1991 is subject to wide regional variations. According to the 1991 census, literacy varies from 21 percent in Rajasthan to 87 percent in Kerala, with Uttar Pradesh at 26 percent and Maharashtra at 52 percent. The enrollment of girls as a ratio of total enrollment is 41 percent at the primary level. This falls to 37 percent at the middle level and 33 percent at the secondary and upper levels. Clearly, the government's 1986 National Policy on Education, which was formulated to fulfill the constitutional directive of providing free education to all children up to fourteen years of age, has not yet met its goal.[43]

The ascriptive differences in the status of Muslim and Hindu women because of personal laws have been seen as demonstrating the supposed relative traditionalism or modernity of each community. This conveniently overlooks the similarities that are imposed by class, region, and culture and that influence the achieved status of all Indian women.

Greater opportunities for education and employment were the primary changes survey respondents wanted to see among women in the community. Few respondents mentioned abolition of unilateral divorce or dowry or changes in legislative rights as being important, realizing that education and employment would be the most liberating to women. In doing so, they were expressing the aspirations not just of Muslim women but of Indian women generally. In recent years the increase in personal law cases brought by women, including an appeal by Muslim women to the Supreme Court to render unconstitutional the Muslim Women's (Protection on Divorce) Act of 1986, reveals their impatience with the political dominance of conservative Muslim leadership, which has stifled debate on social issues in the community while failing to ensure the community's political, economic, or security needs.

CONCLUSION

The current status of Muslim women is attributable to historical factors; to current social, political, and economic conditions confronting women and the Muslim community as a whole; and to the position of Indian women generally. Religion, important for commonly held beliefs and worship, is transformed when it is used politically to motivate a community for political and economic gains. The political use of religion creates a dichotomy between private and political religion, which in the case of Indian Muslim women has led to leaders' resistance to legislative changes. Whereas private religion continued to moderate the actions of community members as they adapted to changing socioeconomic structures, political religion required adherence to symbols of Muslim identity and unity espoused by conservative Muslim leadership as a means of resisting absorption into the majority Hindu community. The inability of the state to physically protect the Muslim community, to rebut attacks on the workings of Indian secularism, and to ensure an objective law-and-order machinery on the basis of which various communities could compete for political and economic progress has created uncertainty for all communities.

The position of Muslim women in India differs from that of women in predominantly Muslim societies in that the struggle to redefine women's legal and societal roles in those societies is juxtaposed against the power of the state and the pressure of Muslim conservatives. This is unlike the triangular struggle that prevails in India, where Islam was used in the colonial period and subsequently to differentiate the interests of the Muslim community from those of other communities. This stultified change and served to widen the gap between private and political religion. In recent years, the rights of Muslim women have become the focus of a political power play between the Muslim and Hindu communities, and yet this has never been over civil or criminal laws that would affect the rights of men.[44]

In the struggle over the rights of women, the Shari'a remains the point of reference. That each society in the Muslim world has evolved its own set of laws and references to the Shari'a suggests the juridical differences in Islam and its inherent flexibility. Yet conservative groups seeking political and economic power have used violence and intimidation to oust governments and threaten women into complying with rituals they deem in keeping with Muslim tradition. Instead of opposing this by pointing out the essentially revolutionary message of Islam and its intrinsic elasticity, its lack of church or clerical hierarchy, and its individualism, several governments and politicians have instead played to the "religious" galleries. This has been equally true of the relationship between the Indian government and Hindu right-wing groups. Motivated by the pressures of electoral politics and by latent prejudice against Muslims, the government has given considerable latitude to Hindu groups, which have used the opportunity to express anti–women's rights sentiments, denigrate Indian institutions, and attack minorities verbally and physically. The government has simultaneously caved in to the Muslim right-wing by depriving Muslim women of certain constitutional rights. This duality has created uncertainties in both communities regarding the intentions of government.

Stripped in the nineteenth century of its once dominant political position, the minority Muslim community endeavored to secure its place in India despite the political hostility it faced from the British government and Hindu communities. Cooperation between Muslim communities focused on political and economic dispossession and on maintaining Muslim identity. To fashion regionally diverse Muslim communities into a unified political entity able to fight for economic goals and social position, Indian

Muslim leaders have both competed and cooperated with Hindu leaders. Both before and after independence, overcoming the inherent prejudices that have influenced the course of both communities has been difficult. Contemporary Muslim political leaders, evolving as they did from the antiseparatist and pro–Congress Party stance of the preindependence Jamiat-ul-Ulema-i-Hind, have found it hard to separate the need for political cohesion from that for social and legal change. The existing leadership has been little challenged, since political parties uninterested in addressing Muslim economic or political issues have confined their attention to not alienating the conservative constituency. The institutional support for an alternative point of view has only just begun to emerge, as Muslim nongovernmental organizations and groups proliferate across the country and are beginning to speak out.[45]

Although the ascriptive rights of Hindu women are superior to those of Muslim women, the achieved rights appear to be a factor of region and socioeconomic strata for women of both communities. Successive censuses, labor participation rates, dowry customs, and educational and literacy levels document the unequal status of women in India, irrespective of religion. Patriarchal attitudes and social mores continue to impose constraints on Hindu and Muslim women. In recent years this has been complicated by the resurgence of right-wing politics in both communities. The attack on women's rights and on minorities has polarized communities and groups of women and kept them from jointly pursuing the interests of all Indian women. The support extended by some women's groups to Muslim women has been so condemnatory of the community and even of religion that Muslim women have been put off. Although there are some Muslim women's organizations, they are area-specific and involved in promoting economic or educational activities. No national organization exists that is able to discuss issues of importance to Muslim women knowledgeably or with authority, despite the extensive mobilization during the Shahbano case. This has given the Muslim right wing, well funded and organized, the appearance of speaking for all Muslims. Change may be approaching, however, as the interests of Muslim women and men continue to diverge.

The resolution of the security and legal issues for Muslim women can come through better governance. That in itself may ease the Muslim community's concerns relating to security and the objectivity and fairness of the law-and-order machinery, thus enabling it to pursue more important economic and social issues at the center of women's grievances. Muslim women can benefit through organizing locally and nationally to pressure government, the community, and the judicial system into working in their favor.

It is evident in the Indian situation that the issue of Muslim women and their rights is not simply a controversy over conflicting interpretations of the Shari'a. Although the conservative Muslim leadership is always ready to invoke the "religion and community in danger" response as a symbol of the community's identity and tradition, Muslim women at the very center of the community's organizational and cultural base have already assimilated societal changes, as demonstrated by judicial actions and academic studies. This cannot be reversed, though women's aspirations can be suppressed and they can be intimidated by conservative pressures. The struggle, then, is over the need for Indian society and the Muslim community to acknowledge the right of Muslim women to be the equal partners they were meant to be in both.

NOTES

1. "Community" has been defined as "a body of people forming political or social unity, or . . . having race, religion, etc. in common" (*Little Oxford Dictionary*, 4th ed. [Oxford: Clarendon, 1969], 104). Although all Indian nationals share political and certain social institutions, regionally diverse Muslims have been compelled by virtue of shared religion, sociopolitical history, and minority position to unify and differentiate their political, economic, and social concerns from those of other Indians.

2. "Muslim Population Growing Fast: Study," *Indian Express*, November 8, 1995, 7, quoting from "Paper One of 1995—Religion," published by the Census Commissioner of India.

3. Amulya Ganguli, "The Future of Hindutva," *Times of India*, January 4, 1993.

4. Shahida Lateef, *Muslim Women in India: Political and Private Realities* (New Delhi: Kali, 1990), 17.

5. Furqan Ahmad, "Role of Some Indian Muslim Jurists in Development and Reform of Muslim Law," *Journal of the Indian Law Institute* 34 (October-December 1992): 563–579.

6. Zoya Hasan, "Minority Identity, State Policy and the Political Process," in *Forging Identities: Gender Communities and the State*, ed. Zoya Hasan (New Delhi: Kali, 1994), 61.

7. Shahida Lateef, "Islam in India" *Seminar* 416 (New Delhi, April 1994): 17.

8. Lateef, *Muslim Women*, 79, 50.

9. A. S. Altekar, *Position of Women in Hindu Civilization from Prehistoric Times to the Present Day* (Benares: Motilal Benarsidas, 1956), 169.

10. Lateef, *Muslim Women*, 59.

11. Ibid., 67–68.

12. Shahida Lateef, "Defining Women Through Legislation," in *Forging Identities: Gender Communities and the State*, ed. Zoya Hasan (New Delhi: Kali, 1994), 46.

13. K. T. Shah, ed., *Report: National Planning Committee* (Bombay: Vora and Company, 1948), 219.

14. Zafar Imam, "Some Aspects of the Social Structure of the Muslim Community in India," in *Muslims in India*, ed. Zafar Imam (Delhi: National, 1975), 76.

15. Ibid., 83.

16. Atul Kohli, *Democracy and Discontent* (Cambridge: Cambridge University Press, 1990), 6.

17. Harish Khare, "Beyond Vote Banks—Help the Muslim Underclass," *Times of India*, December 15, 1992, 10.

18. T. V. Satyamurthy, "Indian Impasse," *The Statesman*, February 13, 1993, 8.

19. Kohli, *Democracy and Discontent*, 5.

20. Pradip K. Datta, "VHP's Ram at Ayodhya: Reincarnation Through Ideology and Organization," *Economic and Political Weekly*, November 2, 1991, 2518.

21. Tanika Sarkar, "The Woman as Communal Object: Rashtrasevika Samiti and Ram Janam Bhoomi Movement," *Economic and Political Weekly*, August 31, 1991, 2062.

22. Lateef, *Muslim Women*, 102.

23. Praful Bidwai, "Countering Majorityism," *Times of India*, January 4, 1991, 10.

24. Edward Gargan, "Trust Is Torn: Police Role in Bombay Riots," *New York Times*, February 4, 1993, 1; Jan Breman, "Anti-Muslim Pogrom in Surat," *Economic and Political Weekly*, April 17, 1993, 737–741.

25. Vimal Balasubramanyam, "Personal Laws and the Struggle for Secularism," *Economic and Political Weekly*, July 27, 1985, 1260.

26. Lateef, *Muslim Women*, 193.

27. Planning Commission, *Progress of Land Reform* (New Delhi: Government of India, 1963), 62–64; Seema Alavi, "Talaq Ruling Has to Be Supported," *Indian Express*, May 9, 1994, 8; Asghar Ali Engineer, "Laws of Islam and Triple Talaq," *Times of India*, May 12, 1994, 10.

28. Ambrose Pinto, "Caste Conflict in Karnataka," *Economic and Political Weekly*, July 11, 1992, 1465; Sumit Sarkar, "The System of Caste, Gandhi, Ambedkar and Hindutva," *Times of India*, June 11, 1994, 12; Neerja Chowdhury, "Long March to Kanshi Ram," *Economic Times*, January 16, 1994, 11.

29. V. S. Mahajan, ed., *Studies in Indian Planning* (New Delhi: Deep and Deep, 1988), 21.

30. Indian Council for Social Science Research, *Synopsis: Towards Equality, Report on the Status of Women in India* (New Delhi: ICSSR, 1975), 1.

31. Government of India, Ministry of Social Welfare, *Towards Equality: Report of the Committee on the Status of Women in India* (New Delhi: Ministry of Education and Social Welfare, December 1974), 152.

32. Ravindran G. Nair, "Law and Women in the Unorganized Sector," *Economic and Political Weekly*, May 15, 1993, 962.

33. Ashish Bose, *Demographic Diversity: 1991 Census* (New Delhi: B. R. Publishing, July 1991), 50, 51, 59.

34. Padmini Swaminathan, "State and the Subordination of Women," *Economic and Political Weekly*, May 15, 1993, WS35.

35. Jyoti Punwani, "Beyond the Purdah," *Times of India*, May 28, 1994, 17.

36. Kamala Ganesh and Carla Risseuw, "Gender Between Family and State," *Economic and Political Weekly*, October 12, 1993, 2332–2333.

37. Veena Poonacha, "Hindutva's Hidden Agenda: Why Women Fear Religious Fundamentalism," *Economic and Political Weekly*, March 13, 1993, 438–439.

38. Ratna Kapoo and Brenda Crossman, "Communalising Gender/Engendering Community: Women Legal Discourse and Saffron Agenda," *Economic and Political Weekly*, April 24, 1993, WS38.

39. Sarkar, "The Woman as Communal Subject," 2061.

40. Lalita Panicker, "Sita Cannot Cross BJP's 'Laxmanrehka,'" *Times of India*, February 15, 1993, 8.

41. Bhava Mehta and Trupti Shah, "Gender and Communal Riots," *Economic and Political Weekly*, November 21, 1992, 2522–2524.

42. Lateef, *Muslim Women*, 186–187.

43. Bose, *Demographic Diversity*, 61.

44. Deniz Kandiyoti, "Introduction," in *Women, Islam and the State*, ed. Deniz Kandiyoti (Philadelphia: Temple University Press, 1990), 7.

45. Kirti Singh, "The Constitution and Muslim Personal Law," in *Forging Identities: Gender Communities and the State,* ed. Zoya Hasan (New Delhi: Kali, 1994), 102.

PART FIVE

Conclusion

14

The Issues at Hand

Nayereh Tohidi

As studies of the status, roles, and contributions of women have broadened from Western societies to the entire world, those relating to Muslim societies have until recently focused primarily on Middle Eastern women, usually emphasizing the presumed Islamic ideas about gender relations. This collected volume accords with the recent trend of corrective scholarship on women in Muslim societies.[1] Aimed primarily for a nonspecialist audience, it undertakes to modify the contemporary perspective on "Muslim women." Through the scope of their inquiries into various Muslim societies in Africa, South and Southeast Asia, Central Asia, and the Middle East, the contributors call attention to diversity, multiplicity, and change in women's lives in Muslim societies. Connecting themes throughout the chapters are the importance of the following: the internal dynamics of the historical moment, the nature and extent of socioeconomic development, religion and local customs, and state policies in defining the status of Muslim women. Other recurring central themes are the extent of women's power and agency and the opportunities or constraints they may experience.

As a correction to a simplistic, negative stereotypical image of Muslim women as passive victims presented in popular media, this book stresses women's agency and the less appreciated fact that women in Muslim societies constitute important agents of change and progress. At the same time, we have tried to avoid falling into any one-sided perspective, such as those labeled "misery research" and "dignity research."[2]

DE-ESSENTIALIZING ISLAM AND MUSLIM WOMEN

Among other things, this book intends to problematize and demystify the very notion of Muslim women and disallow any tendencies to discuss Muslim women while relying on evidence from a single region or society.

Although recent works of serious scholarship and even some journalistic reports on the Middle East have become refreshingly more nuanced and sophisticated, orientalist approaches to Muslim women still appear in school curricula, mass media, movies, and even the feminist-activist press in both Western and non-Western Muslim communities. The problematic implications of the very categorization of Muslim women used in both the Muslim and non-Muslim Western popular press can be put in perspective by comparing it to the much less seen categories of "Christian women" or "Judaic women." The categories of "Western women" or "Jewish women," though not free from methodological and political flaws, denote a broader and more inclusive conception encompassing ethnicity, nationality, and religion.

The notion of "Muslim women," however, is more reductive because it diminishes the composite identity of millions of nationally, ethnically, economically, and geographically diverse women to a single element, that is, the religion of Islam. What usually underlies such a unidimensional identification is an essentialist perception of Islam, which sees Islam as a reified entity that has been the primary, if not the only, factor in determining the conditions of women's lives.

In reality, however, not all women in Muslim societies feel compelled to identify themselves on the basis of their religious persuasion, Islamic or otherwise. This holds true also about Muslim communities that live as minorities within a non-Muslim majority in Western societies and are referred to simply as "the Muslims" in the popular press. Yet the self-perception of many members of these communities, such as Yemenis, Iranians, Pakistanis, Turks, Algerians, Egyptians, and Palestinians, is influenced by numerous factors, including pre-Islamic ethnic origin, modern national identity, language, socioeconomic status, and sectarian and political affiliation, as well as Islam.

Rather than a religiously determined fixed and reified identity, women's roles and status in Muslim communities are fluid and diverse. Islam, the Shari'a, and customary law have affected women's lives in a complex interaction with several other social institutions. The social construction of gender continues to be subject to an interplay between a host of factors, including urban versus rural parameters, class, education, age, and varying interpretations of Islamic normative sources.

Without minimizing the impact of Islam and Shari'a-based legislation on women's status, this book has tried to stay away from reductive accounts of women and Islam. For example, in her presentation of the situation of women in Niger, Barbara Cooper argues against the fallacy of "Islamic determinism." In line with scholars like Marina Lazreg, she refutes the assumption that holds religion at once to be the cause of and the solution to gender inequality. It can be inferred from Cooper's chapter that non-Islamic local practices are sometimes more oppressive and constraining than the Shari'a. In Chapter 12, Lucy Whalley shows the strength of local practices (*adat*) in the context of Sumatra, Indonesia. Another case in point is Noor Kassamali's chapter on the continuation of the practice of female circumcision among East African women, actually a pre-Islamic custom often assumed to be Islamic.

The contributors to this book have also aimed at dispelling the perception of Islam as an essentialist, monolithic, and static phenomenon. Each case study presented here provides us with insight into the complex ways in which religious belief and social reality accommodate one another, indicating that both gender and religion are ongoing social constructions. Like all religions, the interpretation and expression of Islam in society change with time, cross-cultural interplay, gender, ethnicity, and class. Islamic rules have been selectively applied, emphasized, ignored, or circumvented in accordance with the individual or group interests and current realities of each area. Islam has been widely used as a rationale to justify and strengthen patriarchy. But as Whalley shows in the case of Miningkabau women in Indonesia, it can be used as "an inspiration and rationale for women's personal and social development."

M. M. Charrad, moreover, discusses the multiple and at times contradictory meanings of the veil in the context of Tunisia. Originally a pre-Islamic, upper-class, and urban device of patriarchal control over women's bodies and spacial mobility, the veil has traditionally evoked images of seclusion, passivity, and subordination. Although this still holds true to a great extent, an overemphasis on denouncing the veil while disregarding the complex reasons behind it and the paradoxical functions of the recent "re-veiling" phenomenon has been problematic. Such a patronizing preoccupation with the veil, especially on the part of Western outsiders, has not been helpful in altering the obsession of the insecure male over covering the female body.

THE INTERPLAY OF COLONIALISM, NATIONALISM, STATE POLICY, AND GENDER

Colonial and semicolonial contacts, or even a minority status, have also affected women's status in many Muslim societies. Identity politics, interethnic conflicts, and nationalist reactions to an actual or perceived threat of colonial domination have usually resulted in an intensified community pressure on women to become the symbols of authenticity, the primary repositories of national or ethnic identity. This, in turn, has further strengthened traditional norms, *adat,* and Islamically inspired social mores and rituals, especially those associated with women and sexuality. This dynamism is presented here by Shahida Lateef in Chapter 13, on Muslim women in India, by Paula Michaels on Kazakstan (Chapter 10), Shahrbanou Tadjbakhsh on Tajikistan (Chapter 9), and me on Azerbaijan (Chapter 8). In such colonial or semicolonial contexts, women's movements for equal rights and feminism have inevitably been intertwined with nationalism. This linkage has further complicated and slowed the process of women's emancipation and individual rights.

It is cross-culturally and transnationally instructive to compare how and why gender, especially women's bodies and dress codes, become the symbolic focal point of conflict during interethnic and international tensions. This may relate to a goal of bringing about uniformity and de-ethnicization in the process of nation building and modernization, as in Turkey under Ataturk or in Iran under Reza Shah (in the latter case through a violent and forced unveiling). The emphasis on traditional dress codes, however, may relate to an assertion of ethnic distinction in defiance of a dominant majority or colonial assimilation, as in the cases of the formerly Soviet Central Asian republics. Glorification of the veil as the central identity marker of the "new Muslim woman" in present-day Iran, Tunisia, Egypt, and Algeria is, in part, related to a religio-nationalist reaction against a perceived Western anti-Islamic cultural imperialism and also results from the generalized or stereotypical notion of the West and particularly of Western women.

The gendered dynamic of ethnicity and nationalism becomes most sharply outlined when international conflicts enter a military stage. The systematic rape of Bosnian Muslim women, the most recent case in point, shows how women's bodies become a symbolic and indeed an actual stage upon which conflict is acted out. In Chapter 11, Dina Siddiqi demonstrates the same underlying ideology in the case of the Pakistan-Bangladesh conflict. As Siddiqi argues, the systematic rape of women during such wars is "simultaneously a violation of the enemy's territory/honor and a sign of its inability to protect its space/women."

The cases of the transitional Muslim societies of the former Soviet Union and Linda Boxberger's chapter on Yemen presented here are particularly illuminating with regard to the interplay between state policy, economic structure, Islam, and other cultural variables that shapes women's status and gender relations. Although the Soviet mixed legacy is difficult to evaluate, two sets of general conclusions can be made with respect to the dualistic nature of women's status, especially in Muslim communities: Under the Soviet system, women (Muslim and non-Muslim) made undeniable progress in the realms of education, gainful employment, primary health care, and equal legal rights (within the family and in society at large). On the basis of these achievements, one can argue that a supportive state with an egalitarian gender ideology is definitely needed for facilitating the process of change in favor of women as well as for protecting women's gains against any patriarchal backlash.

Nevertheless, the undeniable contradictions in Soviet women's lives, especially in Muslim republics, pertaining to the strain of the "double burden," the hazardous overwork for the rural majority, the durability of traditional sexual double standards, and the subordinate position of women within a male-dominated family structure all testify to the flaws within the Soviet model. One indication is that fundamental changes in women's lives in the public sphere found little or no parallel in the home even after more than seventy years.

Such a lack of progress seems to be due, in part, to both the state-centrist or top-down approach and the economic reductionism of the Soviet system concerning social change, including the "woman question." Statization of the woman question may take away women's initiative, confine their agency, and eliminate any genuine grassroots movement. It may eventually formalize women's issues into an artificially homogenized bureaucratic organ serving a sterile female elite.

Statization of women's emancipation, however, has not been peculiar to the Soviet experiment. A parallel may be found in several states of the Muslim world, like Iraq, Syria, and Iran (under the Shah). This strategy for women's emancipation has proved least effective when the acting state and its overall policies are seen as repressive, in complicity with an imperialist agenda. In the latter case, rather than accelerating the process of change in patriarchal norms, a defensive reaction may actually strengthen traditionalism, especially in family relations.

THE PARADOXICAL ROLE
OF THE TRADITIONAL FAMILY

Such defensive or reactive mechanisms may, in part, explain the persistence of the traditional family and the prevalence of such classic features of patriarchy as the interrelated cults of honor, shame, virginity, and *hijab* in the Muslim world. This, however, does not mean that a classic patriarchy is still in full force,[3] nor does it propose Islam as the main explanatory variable in this regard. One has to take into consideration structural as well as cultural and political factors, such as the persistence of precapitalist modes of production along with tribal structures and kin-ordered networks in some areas of the Muslim world.[4]

However, the painfully disorienting processes of modernization and globalization, as well as the disempowering consequences of "Western-style" rapid change, have in effect revived calls for patriarchal control over the family and female mobility. It is no puzzle then, why the family, the most intimate and private sphere of one's life, becomes the last to accept troubling changes. In an unsettling milieu, the family provides women as well as men—though differentially—the most important, if not the only, remaining source of stability, trust, and security. For the insecure and *mustaz'af* Muslim male, in particular, the patriarchal family provides, among other things, the last remaining bastion of authority and sense of honor.[5]

Thus, as discussed in this book, the tenacious hold on the traditional family by both Central Asian men and women, even in urban areas, cannot be attributed solely to patriarchy or to enslavement to religious dogmas. For many women, family and kin ties are seen as the primary network of socioeconomic protection, a way of gaining resources, power, recognition, and emotional gratification. Despite all the constraints and, at times, suffocating barriers that the traditional family and kin system render against individuation and self-actualization of the male and especially female persons, insulation within family and kin networks and other groups not incorporated into a repressive state may constitute a defense against state intrusion.[6]

Some Western-oriented feminists may find it difficult to accept the fact that in many "Third World" countries (Muslim and non-Muslim alike) women—and many men as well—value the interests of their families more than their own self-interests. In the rather atomized and individualistic context of many Western societies, this may be considered a product of low self-esteem.[7] Or it may be seen as tantamount to the "family values" stressed by the conservative right in the United States. Most women in developing countries, however, although wanting to ensure that their rights are respected and acknowledged, cannot afford or are unwilling to assert women's rights in a way that "estranges them not just from their family but also from their larger community."[8]

THE ISLAMIST REACTION
AND ITS GENDER PARADOXES

The gender dimension of the new Islamist politics or "fundamentalism" that began in the early 1970s has been particularly paradoxical.[9] The trend toward socioeconomic modernization in the Muslim world has included the emergence of an urban middle-class woman. Increasing access to education and small yet growing opportunities for gainful employment in the formal economy have provided such women with both a public presence and social mobility. This progressive trend has coincided with religious revival, politicization and ideologization of Islam, or the Islamization of protest movements.

At the center of these movements lies a nostalgia for the conservative patriarchal family and gender relations, an increasing pressure for control of women, enforcement of sex segregation, and hijab. More paradoxical yet is the active presence of many women among the supporters of these movements. This would appear incongruous were the divergent motivations behind the apparently similar behaviors of the female and male constituencies of these movements not understood.

The tendency to use religion as a platform to oppose delegitimized repressive regimes is related to the dialectic effects of a number of factors: the incoherent nature of capitalist development in many Muslim societies, the uneven socioeconomic consequences of globalization and structural adjustment programs,[10] the strains provoked by increasing internal and external migration, and the perceived failure of secular leaders to deliver an equitable government. It also relates to intensifying frustration with a sense of loss, disempowerment, identity crisis, alienation, anomie, moral decay, and fear of the future. The absence or weakness of democracy and civil society in the face of a growing state power seems to protect the privileged position of a small Western-oriented and nonrepresentative ruling elite and hence is a real or perceived threat as "Western cultural and economic imperialism."[11]

One factor specifically related to the family and intergender power dynamics is the growing sense of self-assertion among modern middle-class women aware of their more personal choices in marriage and motherhood. This trend in all societies has seriously altered the traditional definitions of gender roles, threatening patriarchy and male domination. Therefore, "reassertion of patriarchal power and of gender relations considered to be authorized by religion and tradition is central to virtually all fundamentalisms."[12]

It should be noted, however, that neither do the Islamists make up a homogeneously misogynistic force, nor have women responded to them in a uniform way. Although the conservative Islamic authorities in Saudi Arabia, for example, have forcefully forbidden women from taking part in public life (as reflected in the internationally publicized clash over women driving cars), many women in Egypt and Iran are using the hijab for the purpose of facilitating their public presence (including driving). In the territories under the control of the Taliban, one of the Islamist groups in Afghanistan, all women employees, even teachers and nurses, were fired in early 1996, because the Talibans banned women from any sort of public role. At the same time, in the neighboring Islamist regime of Iran, women's pressures have forced the Islamist clerics to make concessions in regard to women's rights, as Hisae Nakanishi demonstrates in Chapter 5.

Women in the Muslim world are fighting and strategizing against two sets of pressures, one stemming from the internal patriarchal system and the other emitted by those forces seen as external, threatening people's national and cultural boundaries. The latter, the global capitalist system, predominantly identified as "Western," has not been particularly friendly to the needs and concerns of the majority of women and men. While fighting against the internal patriarchy, women have to take care not to appear in complicity with the forces threatening their people's national interests. Close association or identification with Western images and discourses may jeopardize the effectiveness of women's internal struggles against male domination. Therefore, women in Muslim societies, like those in other Third World contexts, are trying to forge their very own images.

The multiplicity of differences between women's movements in Muslim and non-Muslim societies derives from their diverse societal heritages.

Women in their common struggle against different forms of male domination have to strategize in ways that may at times appear paradoxical. One such response of women is the recently growing phenomenon of "Islamic feminism."

ISLAMIC FEMINISM: DOES IT WORK?

As indicated throughout this book, in the Muslim world—as elsewhere—women's quest for equal rights and a just society have taken place within different persuasions and in various forms. Their fight for women's rights and feminism have usually been intertwined with nationalism and with anticolonial, anti-imperialist efforts.

Some women have joined male-oriented secular nationalist movements, benefiting from certain emancipatory policies in nation-states and from liberal male supporters of women's rights, as in Turkey, Tunisia, Iraq, and Syria. Others have pursued their liberation through socialism and more radical socioeconomic changes. When disappointed with the sexist treatment of the "woman question" by the nationalist, religious, and leftist parties, many women began articulating new feministic visions and organizing themselves into independent groups around specific gender issues.

At the same time, many women have maintained their religious beliefs while trying to promote egalitarian ethics of Islam by using the female-supportive verses of the Qur'an in their fight for women's rights, especially for women's access to education.[13] Still others have actively joined recent Islamist/fundamentalist movements despite the latter's patriarchal and sexist views and practices.

The most paradoxical and least understood aspect is the participation of so many women in recent Islamist movements and the subsequent emergence of "Islamic feminism" or "Islamic reformism." The studies of various countries presented here demonstrate that fundamentalists have further constrained and complicated women's lives and realities.

Many women, however, even among those initially standing by the Islamists in their protest movements, have not succumbed to all aspects of their leaders' patriarchal agenda. Even in Iran, where Islamists have seized state power and violently implemented a patriarchal mandate over women, they have not succeeded in subjugating all women or completely eliminating women's social agency. On the contrary, as described by Hisae Nakanishi, many women are asserting themselves, undermining the clerical agenda both within and outside the Islamist framework. They do this in various ways: by subtly circumventing the dictated rules (e.g., reappropriating the veil as a means to facilitate social presence rather than seclusion, or minimizing and diversifying the compulsory hijab and dress code into fashionable styles), engaging in a feministic *ijtihad*, emphasizing the egalitarian ethics of Islam, reinterpreting the Qur'an, and deconstructing Shari'a-related rules in a women-friendly egalitarian fashion (e.g., in terms of birth control, personal status law, and family code to the extent of legalizing a demand for "wages for housework").[14]

Ijtihad, that is, the use of individual reasoning by applying analogy (*qiyas*) to the Qur'an and the Sunna or exerting oneself to form an opinion in a case or as to a rule (*hukm*) of law, has been traditionally considered a male responsibility and prerogative in Shi'a Iran.[15] All but a few *mujtahids* (those conducting ijtihad) have been male clerics (mullahs). In present-day Iran, however, certain women's journals are offering feminist ijtihad by female and male scholars of Islam. A growing move toward nonclerical female as well as male ijtihad constitutes one of the significant characteristics of the new reform movement within Islam in Iran. As reflected in the writings of feminist scholars like Fatima Mernissi, Raffat Hassan, and Aziza Al-Hibri, this new trend is by no means limited to Iran.[16] Iran, however, despite its Shi'a distinction and many differences from other Muslim societies, has been widely assumed as an epitome of Islamism or fundamentalism.

Relative to the extent of sexist discrimination and repression in present-day Iran, women have shown a remarkable degree of resilience in maintaining their social presence and agency. The Islamic republic has ironically stimulated the growth of gender consciousness and feminism, including Islamic feminism. Thanks to women's massive participation in the 1979 revolution, the clerical rulers have found it almost impossible to redomesticate women completely. At least three sets of interactive factors continue to influence such gender dynamism in the Islamist regime of Iran: (1) the women's own resistance and agency; (2) the ongoing ambiguity, variation, and contradictions in the worldview and policies of the state and ruling fundamentalists; and (3) the socioeconomic imperatives of capitalist development and modernization in Iran.

Secular feminists, democrats, and liberals have not been alone in contesting the state's ideology and politics on gender issues. Many proponents of Islam are playing an important role in the reformation of women's rights in an Islamic context. These reformers originally represented the women of the traditional (bazaar-oriented) middle class who felt marginalized and endangered under the modernization process of the Shah's regime. It was during the Islamic revolution that this stratum of women, for the first time in their lives, could gain prominence and respect by engaging themselves in a protest movement sanctioned by religious and nationalist authorities.

The implications of their social praxis, however, have increasingly gone beyond the clergy's initial intention. The clergy, for the most part, meant to appeal to their frustration and to mobilize them into a controlled, veiled constituency against the Shah and subsequently against the antiveil, secular female and male opponents of Islamist rule. Following the victory of the fundamentalists in assuming state power, however, the extent of male bias in state policies and the restrictive measures imposed on women went beyond the tolerance of even their female constituency. Hisae Nakanishi details the manner in which one group of women articulated their protests in the media.

The Islamist government that had benefited from traditional women's support and trust could not ignore their demands for justice. Small yet significant gains have become possible because of an intensive campaign and lobbying efforts by secular and especially Islamist women who have greater access to the institutions of the government inside Iran. External pressures and the international outcry by both the Iranian diaspora and non-Iranian feminists and democrats against violation of women's rights under the Islamic Republic of Iran may also have played a role.

Women activists inside Iran believe that these small yet positive gains set important precedents for women's further maneuvering. They argue that such changes in the positions of Islamist governments indicate the reality that "many patriarchal interpretations, previously presented as written in stone, can be altered if the political constituency demanding change has enough power."[17]

It is encouraging to note that the size (but not yet the power) of the militant and extremist Islamist faction opposing women's rights in Iran is gradually shrinking. More important is the fact that—unlike a decade ago—fewer and fewer women continue to support the fundamentalists. Strong evidence for this lies in the significant gender dimension of the last parliamentary as well as the recent presidential elections (May 1997) in Iran. This was a highly polarized contest between two main ruling factions, the supporters of a more socially moderate platform and the cleric-based conservative Islamists. Women and the youth played a decisive role in the surprising victory of Hojjatul-Islam Khatami as president, who had been under attack by the conservatives for his liberal views and progressive programs.

Another irony within Islamist Iran is the growing tendency to adopt aspects of Western culture, especially the decadent aspects of it, among the younger generation. And this is related to a sort of reverse psychology, a reaction to the rigid and indiscriminate anti-West campaign of the Islamists. Before the revolution, with or without the Islamist reaction in Iran, there was widespread genuine dismay against aping Westerners or being preoccupied with consumerism and the "culture of display." After the revolution, however, regardless of the merit of such dismay, it lost its genuine moral value when the anti-imperialist (or actually anti-West) stance was imposed as a motto of a repressive and totalitarian Islamist regime. So ironically, one sees as much, if not more, obsession with Western pop culture, music, smoking and drinking, fashions, consumerism, and body ornaments (now undercover, of course) in the present Islamic

Republic of Iran as under the past Western-oriented regime of the Shah. This is suggestive of the fact that the impact of Islamism in *opposition* is very different from the impact of its *imposition* as a totalitarian state ideology.

THE INTERACTION BETWEEN
SECULAR AND ISLAMIC FEMINISTS

One overall conclusion is that, no matter how described, "Islamic gender activism," "Islamic gender reformism," or "Islamic feminism" is a growing and potent force that should be taken seriously. It should be welcomed as *one* of the various voices and discourses present within the multifaceted identity of the women's movement in the Muslim world. By promoting change and women-supportive reformation, this voice would help democratize and, ironically, secularize Muslim societies. Therefore, many secular feminist scholars from the Muslim world have welcomed Islamist feminists' contribution to women's rights movements. According to them, Islamic feminism presents a new addition to the already diversified and colorful spectrum of the international women's movement.

Some more radical feminists, however, tend to dismiss the positive efforts and contributions of Islamic feminists. They reject any collaboration with Islamic feminists because they see Islam to be essentially incompatible with feminist ideas. Such a view seems to be rooted in an essentialist perception of Islam, a misguided opinion that leads to a shortsighted policy and contradicts the feminist quest for pluralism, inclusiveness, and diversity in women's movements and in society at large. Moreover, an overwhelming majority of women in Muslim societies are concerned with workable formulas in their daily battles against oppressive rules. To them, the argument that "Islamic feminism is an oxymoron, hence useless," may sound like secular arrogance or an irrelevant academic concern.

As Madhu Kishvar, a leading advocate of women's rights in India, argues, some feminists in Third World societies whose ideology emanates from the West adopt a proselytizing role. "Their underlying assumption is that all those who refuse to be converted are steeped in ignorance or stupidity. . . . They are eager to save souls and tend to look down upon, be hostile to, or at least pity those not already converted" into their brand of feminism.[18]

The obstacles for dialogue and collaboration between secular and Islamic feminists are created by both sides. The Islamists have usually been exclusionary in their interaction with nonbelievers. Their insistence in imposing their version of Islam and its way of life on secularists has naturally created strong resentment against them and against Islam altogether. Secular feminists, however, should differentiate between those Islamic women who are genuinely promoting women's rights and hence inclusionary in their politics from those who insist on fanatic or totalitarian Islamism.

Despite the Qur'an's overall egalitarian messages, the Islamic tradition as it quite soon after evolved has encouraged certain discriminatory practices against women. As explained by Herbert Bodman in the Introduction to this book, historically it was virtually inevitable for Islamic societies to inherit patriarchy. But, religion, as Buchanan argues (in the context of North America), has not been for all women merely a social constraint or a set of passively accepted doctrines. "Taking a clergy-centered view of religion, scholars are likely to overlook the degree to which women reformers' relationship to religion was not defined and controlled by men or by male theological meanings."[19]

In conclusion, I concur with Iranian feminist lawyers like Shirin Ebadi and Mehranguiz Kar in emphasizing that Islamic feminism or a reformist women-centered interpretation of religious laws should be considered not as an alternative to secular and democratic demands but as a component of more holistic social change.[20]

WESTERN FEMINISTS VIS-À-VIS MUSLIM WOMEN

In recent decades, the corrective intellectual and theoretical exchange between white, Anglo, middle-class feminists, women of color, and immigrant and Third World women, including Muslims, has narrowed considerably the conceptual and information gaps between them. Yet the need remains for a purposive reeducation of students and the public in order to develop an informed international campaign supporting improvement in women's status and human rights in Muslim societies.

A well-publicized outcry against abusive customs such as female circumcision, domestic violence, dowry, and compulsory veiling and seclusion would naturally be a contributing factor to improvement of women's status. Past experience, however, indicates that given the hierarchical nature of the world system, external intervention, no matter how well intended, does not appear as a neutral and purely benevolent sisterly act. Noor Kassamali argues this point persuasively in Chapter 3, which discusses female circumcision.

The precious ideal of "global sisterhood" is no more than an illusion if the present divided and unequal world system is not taken into account. To prevent backlashes, such campaigns have to be free from the flaws of the Euro-centrist advocates of modernization "diffusion." One of these basic flaws could be defined in Gordon Alport's terms: "It is an axiom that people cannot be taught who feel that they are at the same time being attacked," exploited, or patronized.[21]

As a corrective to the widespread negative depiction of Muslim women in the Western media, however, some scholars in the West (a number of "postmodernist" anthropologists or advocates of "cultural relativism" in particular) tend to move far in the opposite direction, manifested in their treatment of such sensitive issues as female circumcision and the veil. For example, they overcompensate for the one-dimensional understanding and pejorative generalization of the veil in orientalist tradition by portraying the recent adoption of the veil as a "free choice" or symbol of "authentic identity" and a form of women's "empowerment."[22]

They tend to forget that, actually, many women resort to a more conservative hijab, particularly the restrictive veil, for lack of a better choice or on the basis of some conscious or subconscious calculations. Not wearing the hijab means much more restriction in their social space and mobility, since without the hijab they would be unable to engage in economic and social activities outside the home. As Bouthaina Shaaban argues in Chapter 6, by adopting the veil, some professional and working women in Syria try to reduce social and family pressures, secure a sense of dignity, and repulse male sexual harassment.

Instead of a free choice, then, the wearing of hijab and especially the veil under such circumstances would be a coping or defense mechanism, a protective device against more severe oppression, a means to bargain for more space and mobility. Many professional women may find themselves caught between two forms of obsession: covering the female body on the one hand or displaying it in a commoditizing or objectifying manner, especially in Western fashions, on the other. In such a context, a modest Islamic hijab would seem a more affordable and accommodating alternative. Even the all-covering veil may be perceived as a security blanket, a lesser evil, but certainly not a means for liberation or real empowerment.

This word of caution applies also to some diaspora feminist activists and scholars originally from Muslim societies and now living in the Western countries. In their contact with the widespread negative stereotypes and distorted images of Muslims perpetuated in the Western mainstream media, some have felt compelled to lose critical perspective. As a result they unwittingly retreat to either cultural relativism or a defensive, nationalistic stand about "Muslim cultures."

Some activists outside academic circles, however, seem to have joined the dominant imperial discourse. In a deliberate or unconscious attempt, they seek approval of an audience in their host country by becoming the token "exceptional," "modernized Muslim women" who hate and denounce anything Islamic more vocally and indiscriminately than any Westerner.

The diaspora feminists from Muslim societies have a critical and delicate role to play. They can best serve both "us" and "them" as a bridge to narrow the gap of ignorance, prejudice, and misconception by educating both communities about the problems of simplistic conceptions like Western versus Eastern, Muslims versus Judeo-Christians, secular versus fundamentalist, and modern versus traditional.

In short, we should remain unapologetic in criticizing and condemning any patriarchal, antidemocratic aspects of any culture, especially the ones we know firsthand. At the same time, by putting these criticisms in cross-cultural, comparative, and historical perspectives, we should avoid the perpetuation of ethnocentrism and essentialism among either "side." For concerned educators, communicating context and specificity to students and the public in talking about Muslim women as a category is indeed a pedagogical challenge.[23]

WOMEN'S/HUMAN RIGHTS, WOMEN'S ORGANIZATIONS, AND CIVIL SOCIETY

The Islamist reaction has, ironically, brought women's issues to the surface. As a result, the gender ideologies and women's status of many Muslim societies have been put under careful national and international scrutiny and are subjects of heated debates. Many women in these societies have been alarmed and increasingly mobilized around gender issues. In their daily confrontations with the new conservative backlash, many of them have become seasoned activists and sophisticated strategists. This was clearly evident during the Fourth World Conference on Women in Beijing in September 1995.[24]

The struggle for women's human rights gained a new momentum over the past two decades as a worldwide campaign for equality, development, and peace was orchestrated by the United Nations and tens of thousands of grassroots women's nongovernmental organizations (NGOs). Thanks, in part, to the national, regional, and international efforts and conferences supported by the United Nations, a vast amount of data and research reports is now available concerning the condition of women in various parts of the world, including Muslim societies.

Women of the Muslim world took active roles throughout the process leading up to and including the worldwide assembly of women's movements in Beijing. Although they expressed different views of Islam and feminism, their participation (some in their colorful ethnic or regional attires, some in various forms of veils, and some in Western dress) attested to their ethnic, class, and ideological diversities.

A major observation emerging from the Beijing conference, the UN reports, and current research is that women's movements and women's NGOs constitute a crucial component for the development of democracy in Muslim societies. The empowerment of women is seen as an inseparable part of civil society. At the same time, the emergence of such a society is contingent upon the existence of a state that enforces universal legal norms and guarantees protection of civil and human rights regardless of gender, race, ethnicity, class, and religious persuasion.[25]

The weakness, if not absence, of civil society and democracy in many Muslim societies; the authoritarian, state-centrist mode of modernization (underlining the political and cultural power of the Westernized elite); and the equation established between the "civilized" and the "Westernized" have contributed to a dualistic process of socioeconomic development. This in turn has resulted in complex and contradictory gender implications, including violations of women's/human rights.

Recent decades have witnessed some fundamental changes in women's social status toward an ever wider recognition of their equality with men. However, the actual achievement of gender equality is a slow, complicated, and controversial social process for all societies. The state of human development in different countries indicates that the decision to seek gender equality cuts across income levels, political ideology, cultures, and stages of development.

Although in some countries much investment in basic human capabilities is needed before women can catch up with men, in many others gender gaps have continued despite overall economic improvement. For example, a wide disparity between the indices of overall development and of "gender empowerment" are found in non-Muslim France, Japan, Greece, the United Kingdom, Ireland, and Spain. In Muslim societies of the United Arab Emirates, Bahrain, Saudi Arabia, Algeria, Yemen, Libya, and Egypt, such disparity has remained much wider.[26] However, based on UN reports, the Arab states have actually made significant advances in women's education, more than doubling female literacy rates in recent years. Among the developing countries, the United Arab Emirates shows the fastest closing of the gender gap in education: 68 percentage points between 1970 and 1990.

It should be noted, however, that although in many developing countries the overall state of human development has improved and gender gaps in health and education have narrowed rapidly, the doors to economic and political opportunities are still barely open for women.[27] On average, only 17 percent of Arab women (and 18.7 percent of women in the region of the Middle East and North Africa) participate in the formal labor force and only 4 percent of parliamentary seats are held by women, well below the 10 percent average in the developing world.[28]

Some countries in the wider Muslim world, however, depart from this pattern. For example, Azerbaijan, Indonesia, and Bangladesh, with respectively 13, 12.2, and 10.3 percent of parliamentary seats held by women, are in line with the percentage in the United States (10.3 percent). Moreover, the Central Asian Muslim republics, Morocco, Tunisia, and Turkey have high rates of female labor force participation in the formal economy.

Once again, these diversities indicate that cultural variables, including Islam, are not the only determining factors in regard to women's status. Valentine Moghadam draws our attention to a correlation between industrial strategy and female labor force participation, suggesting that oil-centered economies inhibit female employment, whereas export-led industrialization results in a higher demand for female labor.[29]

During the Beijing conference, the NGO Forum, and throughout about 300 workshops on topics concerning women in Islam and in Muslim societies (out of some 2,500 total), women engaged in lively discussions and debates about issues like compulsory hijab, gender segregation or sexual apartheid, polygyny, *sigheh* (temporary marriage), the role of Shari'a in family law, and the impact of Islamist movements. They discussed the ideal relationship between Islam and the state, what role states should play for women's empowerment, what kind of development strategy would reduce poverty and would enhance human capabilities, environmental sustainability, and gender equality.

In this historic worldwide gathering, women from Muslim societies played an active and critical role in the formulation of its Platform for Action. Many of the participants in the governmental conference were relatives of those in power. In the NGO Forum, however, participants represented mostly the elite and professional women as well as grassroots activists. Yet the depth of their devotion to and the degree of their success in implementing the Beijing platform in each Muslim society remains to be seen.

One post-Beijing trend that seems to be growing in most Muslim societies is the proliferation of women's NGOs. These may constitute old and established women's organizations or groups newly emerging in the preparatory process for the world conferences. Many of them seem to be determined to implement gender-sensitive development projects; to secure egalitarian legal reforms; to expand access to education, health care, gainful employment, and decisionmaking positions; to reconstruct gender-related cultural norms, including positive women's images in mass media; to reshape double standards in sexuality; and, in a word, to safeguard women's rights as human rights.

This is a most encouraging trend for the future of women in Muslim societies. As we have seen in so many of the chapters in this book, a strong, well-organized women's movement is a vital key for achieving the goals of equality, development, and peace.

NOTES

I am grateful to Nikki Keddie, Eliz Sanasarian, and Mary Hegland for their constructive suggestions on this chapter.
    1. See, for example, Nikki Keddie and Beth Baron, eds., *Women in Middle Eastern History* (New Haven: Yale University Press, 1991); Leila Ahmed, *Women and Gender in Islam: Historical Roots of a Modern Debate* (New Haven: Yale University Press, 1992); Judith Tucker, ed., *Arab Women: Old Boundaries and New Frontiers* (Bloomington: Indiana University Press, 1993); Deniz Kandiyoti, ed., *Women, Islam and State* (Philadelphia: Temple University Press, 1991); Valentine Moghadam, *Gender and National Identity: Women and Politics in Muslim Societies* (London: Zed Books, 1994); the introduction by Camillia Fawzi El-Solh and Judy

Mabro to their edited volume, *Muslim Women's Choices* (Providence: Berg Publishers, 1994); and the issue entitled "Gender and Citizenship in the Middle East," *Middle East Report* no. 198 (January–March 1996).

2. See Valentine Moghadam, "Development and Patriarchy: The Middle East and North Africa in Economic and Demographic Transition," WIDER Working Paper, July 1992, 4.

3. For a comparative analysis of patriarchy and criticism of its simplistic universalization, see Deniz Kandiyoti, "Islam and Patriarchy: A Comparative Perspective," in *Women in Middle Eastern History,* ed. Nikki Keddie and Beth Baron (New Haven: Yale University Press), 23–42.

4. See Nikki Keddie, "The Past and Present of Women in the Muslim World," *Journal of World History* 1, no. 1 (1990); Dale Eickelman, *The Middle East: An Anthropological Approach* (Englewood Cliffs, NJ: Prentice-Hall, 1989); Germaine Tillion, *The Republic of Cousins* (London: Al-Saqi, 1983); and Moghadam, *Development and Patriarchy,* 10–11.

5. For a political-psychology of the *mustaz'af,* literally "the disempowered," or "the belittled," the adjective that Iranian fundamentalists used in describing themselves, see Nayereh Tohidi, "Modernity, Islamization, and Women in Iran," in *Gender and National Identity: Women and Politics in Muslim Societies,* ed. Valentine Moghadam (London: Zed Books, 1994), 110–141.

6. For further elaboration on the impact of state on family, see Sue Ellen Charlton, Jana Everett, and Kathleen Staudt, eds., *Women, the State, and Development* (New York: State University of New York, 1989), 185.

7. See a powerful discussion of this issue by Madhu Kishvar, founder and editor of *Manushi,* a New Delhi women's journal, in "The Feminist Missionary," *Far Eastern Economic Review,* May 16, 1996, 30.

8. Ibid. See also Suad Joseph, "Gender and Family in the Arab World," a Special *MERIP* Publication (October 1994); Erika Friedl, "The Dynamics of Women's Spheres of Action in Rural Iran," in *Women in Middle Eastern History,* ed. Nikki Keddie and Beth Baron (New Haven: Yale University Press, 1991), 195–214; and Mary Hegland, "Shi'a Women of Northwest Pakistan and Agency Through Practice: Ritual, Resistance, Resilience," *Political and Legal Anthropology Review* 18, no. 2 (November 1995): 65–79.

9. It is only for the lack of a better term and for the sake of communication that I use the terms "fundamentalism" and "Islamism" despite my awareness of their problems. Other proposed terms like "the new religious politics" (Nikki Keddie, "The New Religious Politics: Where, When and Why Do 'Fundamentalisms' Appear?" forthcoming in the *Journal of Comparative Studies in Society and History*) and "Islamic resurgence" (John L. Esposito, "Introduction: Islam and Muslim Politics," in *Voices of Resurgent Islam,* ed. John L. Esposito [New York: Oxford University Press, 1983]) are also not free from shortcomings.

10. Moghadam, for example, refers to the wide social disparity, poverty, unemployment, and debt servicing that have led to popular protests and "IMF riots" in Algeria, Jordan, Tunisia, and Turkey. See *Gender and National Identity,* 2.

11. Some of the reasons listed here are in accord with reasoning and analysis presented in Nikki Keddie's articles on "Women, Gender, and Fundamentalism" (forthcoming in *Journal of Women's History*), and "The New Religious Politics: Where, When, and Why Do 'Fundamentalisms' Appear?" (forthcoming).

12. See Keddie, "Women, Gender, and Fundamentalism," 1.

13. See Eliz Sanasarian, "The Politics of Gender and Development in the Islamic Republic of Iran," *Journal of Developing Societies* 8 (January-April 1992): 56–68.

14. To be more precise, this legal provision known as *ojrat ol-mesl* (wages in kind) refers to the housework done by the wife during marriage. In case of divorce, "wages" can be demanded by the wife if the divorce is neither initiated by her nor caused by her.

15. See B. Lewis, V. L. Menage, Ch. Pellat, and J. Schacht, *The Encyclopedia of Islam* (London: Luzac, 1971), 1026–1027.

16. Regardless of whether these writers personally believe in Islam or not, their analyses of the Islamic texts would promote reform and Islamic feminism. See, for example, Fatima Mernissi, *The Veil and the Male Elite: A Feminist Interpretation of Women's Rights in Islam,* trans. Mary Jo Lakeland (Reading, MA: Addison-Wesley, 1991).

17. Cited in Mehranguiz Kar, a prominent feminist lawyer and writer in Iran, interviewed by Homa Hoodfar in *Middle East Report* (January-March 1996): 36.

18. Kishvar, "Feminist Missionary," 30.

19. See Constance H. Buchanan, *Choosing to Lead: Women and the Crisis of American Values* (Boston: Beacon Press, 1996), 138.

20. Kar, interview with Hoodfar, 38.

21. Cited in Gregory Massell, *The Surrogate Proletariat: Moslem Women and Revolutionary Strategies in Soviet Central Asia (1919–1929)* (Princeton, NJ: Princeton University Press, 1974), 397.

22. El Saadawi, for instance, discusses how the gender-related arguments of "fundamentalists" and some postmodernists whom she calls "cultural fundamentalists" at times parallel each other. See Nawal Al Sa'dawi, "Dissidence and Creativity," *Women: A Cultural Review* 6, no. 1 (summer 1995): 1–17.

23. See Eleanor Doumato's useful comments in this regard in her article "Am I 'Part of the Problem?'" *The Middle East Women's Studies Review* 11, no. 2 (June 1996): 11–13. Sondra Hale also makes helpful suggestions in her review of *Muslim Women's Choices: Religious Belief and Social Reality,* Camillia Fawzi El-Solh and Judy Mabro, eds. (Providence: Berg, 1994) in the same issue of *The Middle East Women's Studies Review,* 1–3.

24. For an analytical report on this, see Nayereh Tohidi, "'Fundamentalist' Backlash and Muslim Women in the Beijing Conference," *Canadian Woman Studies/Les Cahiers de la femme* 16, no. 3 (summer 1996).

25. For further discussion of the significance of civil society in Muslim contexts, see, for example, Jillian Schwedler, ed., *Toward Civil Society in the Middle East? A Primer* (Boulder, CO: Lynne Rienner, 1995).

26. See United Nations Development Programme, *Human Development Report, 1995* (New York: Oxford University Press, 1995), 78–86. It should be noted that, according to the UNDP's definition (p. 82), "gender empowerment" pertains to participation—economic, political, and professional. It differs from "gender development," which is concerned primarily with basic capabilities and living standards.

27. Ibid., 4.

28. Ibid., 24.

29. Moghadam, "Development and Patriarchy," 25–29.

About the Contributors

Herbert L. Bodman, after teaching courses in Islamic history at the University of North Carolina, Chapel Hill, and traveling throughout much of the Muslim world, instituted undergraduate seminars studying Muslim women. This book is the result of a continuing interest in emphasizing the unrecognized diversity among such women that rapidly became apparent in those courses.

Linda Boxberger enrolled in the doctoral history program at the University of Texas after spending the better part of a decade teaching English in Kuwait and North Yemen. Her dissertation deals with social change in the Hadramawt at the beginning of the twentieth century. She plans to return to the Hadramawt for further research.

M. M. Charrad, a sociologist and visiting scholar at the University of Pittsburgh, has published both in French and English on issues relating to state formation, women's rights, and family policy. Most recently she coedited *Femmes, Culture et Société au Maghreb* (2 vols., 1996) and wrote "Policy Shifts: State, Islam and Gender in Tunisia, 1930s–1990s," *Social Politics* 4, no. 2 (summer 1997). Currently she is completing a comparative-historical study of family law in the Maghreb. She has previously taught at Harvard University, Brown University, and the University of California, San Diego.

Barbara M. Cooper holds a doctorate in African history from Boston University and now teaches at the Gallatin School of Individualized Study at New York University. She has taught at the University of Florida and Bryn Mawr College. Her book, *Marriage in Maradi: Gender and Culture in a Hausa Society in Niger, 1900–1989,* was published in 1997.

Hisae Nakanishi received her doctorate from the University of California, Los Angeles, after a research trip to Iran and now teaches at Koryo International College in Japan.

Noor J. Kassamali, an East African physician trained in Great Britain, untangles the intricacies of female genital cutting. Now with the Harvard University Health Services, she brings a deeply concerned expertise to this seemingly intractable issue.

Shahida Lateef is an Indian Muslim scholar with a doctor of philosophy degree in development studies from the University of Sussex in England. She served on the Political Task Force of the National Committee on the Status of Women in India and is the author of *Muslim Women in India: Political and Private Realities* (1990).

Paula A. Michaels lived for two years in Russia and in various parts of Kazakstan while doing research for her doctorate in Russian and Soviet history from the University of North Carolina. She is now an assistant professor of history at the University of Iowa and is currently writing a book entitled *Shamans and Surgeons: The Politics of Health Care in Soviet Kazakstan, 1917–1956.*

Bouthaina Shaaban, associate professor of English literature at Damascus University in Syria, is an avowed feminist, as evidenced in her acclaimed book, *Both Right and Left Handed: Arab Women Talk About Their Lives* (1991), a series of frank and illuminating interviews with Syrian, Lebanese, Palestinian, and Algerian women. In 1990–1991, she was a Fulbright professor at Duke University.

Dina M. Siddiqi, born and raised in Bangladesh, is a graduate of Wellesley College and holds a doctorate in anthropology from the University of Michigan. She has taught at the University of Washington and the University of California, Santa Cruz. She is currently a visiting fellow in anthropology at the New School for Social Research in New York City. In addition to articles in Bangladeshi journals, she wrote "The Festival of Democracy: Media and the 1996 Elections in Bangladesh" for a special issue on the media and elections for the *Asian Journal of Communications.*

Shahrbanou Tadjbakhsh, a Tajik by heritage, received a doctorate in Central Asian Studies from Columbia University in 1994. After several consultancies with the United Nations, she returned to Central Asia in May 1997 as subregional project manager to the Commonwealth of Independent States for the Gender in Development Program of the United Nations.

Nayereh Tohidi, of Azerbaijani-Iranian origin, has written extensively on women and gender issues in Iran and post-Soviet Azerbaijan. With a doctorate from the University of Illinois, Urbana-Champaign, in sociology and educational psychology, she is currently assistant professor of women's studies at California State University, Northridge, and research associate at the Center for Near Eastern Studies at the University of California, Los Angeles. She has visited Azerbaijan a number of times as a consultant to UN agencies.

Lucy A. Whalley holds a doctorate in anthropology from the University of Illinois, Urbana-Champaign.

Index

299

About the Book

Study after study of women in the Muslim world has focused primarily on Middle Eastern societies, usually emphasizing the sexual ideology of a reified Islam. This book rounds out that view, exploring the status, roles, and contributions of Muslim women not only in the Middle East but also in Africa and Asia, including post-Soviet Central Asia.

The authors, many of them from the countries they examine, stress the importance of historical context, local customs, and policies in defining the status of Muslim women, the extent of their power, and the opportunities or constraints they may experience. Students will discover the immense diversity and change in these women's lives, enabling them to better understand and discuss "Muslim women" without relying on evidence from a single region or society.

Herbert L. Bodman is professor emeritus of Islamic history at the University of North Carolina, Chapel Hill. He is author of *Women in the Muslim World: A Bibliography of Books and Articles Primarily in the English Language*. *Nayereh Tohidi* teaches women's studies at California State University, Northridge.